INDEPENDENT ADOPTIONS

A Follow-up Study

By

HELEN L. WITMER

ELIZABETH HERZOG

EUGENE A. WEINSTEIN

MARY E. SULLIVAN

RUSSELL SAGE FOUNDATION

NEW YORK   1963

Contents

3

Tables and Figure

5

Acknowledgments

A CONSIDERABLE NUMBER of people participated, assisted, and advised during the planning, the data gathering, and the analysis of this study. To mention all would tax both reader and printer. However, to omit mention of some would be unthinkable.

This research endeavor was the joint undertaking of the Florida Department of Public Welfare, Russell Sage Foundation, and the United States Children's Bureau. The Florida Department was the source of the research idea and the impetus to put it into effect. The State and District Boards of the Department officially approved the study, provided most of the office space and equipment, and agreed to allow staff to assist in any way possible. Russell Sage Foundation supplied the funds for the field study and gave consultation on various phases of the study. The Children's Bureau provided the research direction, analyzed the data, and wrote the report. As authors of the report, we want first to acknowledge our indebtedness to the two organizations that were our colleagues in this effort.

In the Florida Department of Public Welfare, it was Margaret Ward, Supervisor of Adoption Services, who first urged the attack on some perennial questions about independent adoptions. She struggled against odds to maintain records and statistics that would make a follow-up study possible and drew up the first research plan, setting forth aims and objectives. Also she and Charlotte Jelks, Adoption Consultant, tested the feasibility of locating parents and enlisting their cooperation. In the planning phase of the study we profited greatly by documents Miss Ward had written concerning Florida adoption law and the experience of the Department in investigating and supervising independent

9

adoption placements. Frances Davis, Director of the Child Welfare Division of the Florida Department of Public Welfare, along with Miss Ward, gave many kinds of assistance to the project—in planning the study, in advising along the way, and in making administrative arrangements. They also made it possible for us to profit by the help of many of the Department's social work staff in locating the parents and children who were the subjects of the study and often in helping to arrange appointments for the psychologists. We regret that we cannot list separately the names of all the individuals who assisted so effectively in this arduous and indispensable part of the project.

The skills of the interviewers played a large part in securing the kind of information required as well as in keeping the refusal rate down. All of them were trained and experienced social workers. Those who participated from the very beginning until the interviewing was completed were Agnes Martin, Mary G. Wolff, and Patty Gregory. Two others were with the project for periods of several months: Beth Sumner and Joanne Harrison.

Members of seven child-placing agencies participated in the study by making ratings based on the records of the original social investigations that had been made by the Florida Department of Public Welfare in 1944 to 1947: Family and Child Services, Washington, D.C.; District of Columbia Department of Public Welfare, Washington; Children's Aid Society of Pennsylvania, Philadelphia; Department of Public Welfare, Baltimore, Maryland; Children's Bureau of Delaware, Wilmington, Delaware; The Spence-Chapin Adoption Service, New York; The Chicago Child Care Society, Chicago.

We appreciate the time they gave and also their willingness to work with records of a kind to which they were unaccustomed, written in a context unfamiliar to them.

In making judgments about the components of family functioning, the interviewers profited by the advice of George L. Perkins, M.D., Consultant to the Institute for Juvenile Research and other agencies. In strengthening the consistency of the home ratings, the authors were assisted by Anna Laura Kennedy, and for making a reliability test of the home ratings depended on the skill and painstaking care of Norman J. Booth and Marion Spasser.

The psychological testing in classrooms could not have been carried out without the cooperation of numerous members of the Florida school system. For help in the intricate arrangements involved we are indebted especially to Thomas D. Bailey, Superintendent of Public Instruction, J. K. Chapman, Deputy Superintendent, and Victor Johnson, Consultant on Guidance and Pupil Personnel Services. In benefiting by the help of these members of the school system, we were assisted at many points by the county superintendents in the 44 counties involved and the principals in the 295 schools where testing was done. Even more demanding, and greatly appreciated, was the contribution of the 412 teachers whose classes provided our study and control groups. Not only did they permit interruption of their classroom work by the testing, but they also filled out rating forms for each child who served as part of the sample or control group, and for a number of children not included in either group. In all, they filled out questionnaires and rating schedules concerning some 2,000 children.

We are greatly indebted to Paul H. Bowman for permission to use the Behavior Description Chart worked out by him and his colleagues in connection with their study of youth in Quincy, Illinois.

The testing of children in classrooms was originally organized and directed by Helen R. Marshall. Later, with the assistance of the field director, testing was conducted by Patricia Murphy, Jo Anne Smith, and Mimi Wanamaker, who together administered tests to some 12,000 children and scored the tests for our 448 sample children and their controls.

Because administrative arrangements were so complex, it became necessary to entrust the setting up of appointments of psychological testing in the classrooms to Mable Bittrich and Montine McDonald, staff members of the Department, and to Patricia Aiken, Addie F. Harper, Pauline Nichols, and Betty Pittman, former employees of the Department. The work of the psychologists was greatly facilitated by the energy, ingenuity, and tact of these people.

An advisory panel gave us advice about the sentence completion test that was devised and tried out. We are grateful for the time-consuming review as well as for the thoughtful and solidly based advice given to us by: Leonard Goodstein, State University of Iowa; Dale G. Harris, University of Minnesota; Helen Koch, University of Chicago; Maurice Lorr, Veterans Administration; Boyd McCandless, University of Iowa; Robert Winch, Northwestern University.

We are most grateful to T. Richard Witmer for contributing the section on the background of American adoption statutes, and to Max Rheinstein of the University of Chicago Law School and John S. Bradway of the Duke University Law School for helpful comments on adoption law and history.

Among those with whom we discussed our early plans, we would like especially to mention our appreciation of discussions with Harold M. Skeels and Nancy Bayley of the National Institute of Mental Health. Thanks are also due for assistance in our early planning to Walter M. Perkins, then with the Bureau of Public Assistance, and in later phases to Ralph K. White.

At various phases in the processing of data, research investigators rely on support that always requires more acumen, intuition, enterprise, and grasp of content than is commonly assumed. Our coding operations made unusually heavy demands that were fortunately met by Ruth Bloodgood, Lena Heyman, and Adele Richard. Mrs. Heyman also contributed content analyses of selected groups of records, and Mrs. Richard doubled as research clerk through many arduous hours. In the Washington office, Bertha T. Currie controlled the intricate flow of "traffic" between the Children's Bureau study staff, our Florida contingent, our helping agencies and consultants, as well as keeping the Washington files in order, doing and supervising endless amounts of typing, and helping with various stages of tabulation. In Florida, Evelyn Richardson served as secretary and office manager for the project, filling the strenuous and often competing needs of the far-flung staff. Thelma Byrd, Miss Ward's secretary, typed many of the revisions to the research plan and much of the transcription of interviews. The final phase of revising, collating, processing, and resisting the centrifugal force of the "almost situation" was greatly helped by the secretarial and editorial assistance of Mary Roark.

For a variety of obvious reasons we cannot name the respondents and subjects who made the study possible—both the parents and the children. We are none the less grateful to them for their contributions along the way, from the first group who made it evident that this kind of follow-up study was indeed possible to the last of those who, during the interview, offered response, interest, and invaluable information—demonstrating again the cheerful and perennial finding that most people are glad to have their own experience used in an effort to help others.

HELEN L. WITMER
ELIZABETH HERZOG
EUGENE A. WEINSTEIN
MARY E. SULLIVAN

Introduction

Among the hotly debated issues of public policy relating to children is that of adoption. In the United States about 50,000 children annually are adopted by people not related to them by blood or marriage.[1] This means that, at the present rate, such adopted children and youth will number about a million before the children adopted this year come of age. The question whether the present adoption process provides sufficient protection for these children is therefore quite properly a subject of public concern.

A little over half of these children have had their adoptive parents selected for them by the social agencies to whose legal custody they have been entrusted. The others are adopted "independently" or, as it is sometimes called, "privately." In this case, the would-be adoptive parents have secured the children either directly from their natural parents or relatives, or through intermediaries, such as physicians or lawyers, who know of the natural parents' interest in giving up their children.

The study reported in this book—a follow-up investigation made during 1956 and 1957—deals only with independent adoptions and is concerned with their outcome by the time the adopted children were about ten years old. About these adoptions it asks such questions as the following: How well satisfied were the adoptive parents with the children they received? How often did they encounter difficulties with the natural parents? How well did the children develop? How good were the homes in which they were placed? By what signs, if any, can good homes be identified before the adoption petition is granted?

Our purpose in studying independent adoptions was twofold. First, we wanted to find out how successful the independent

---

[1] Children's Bureau, Department of Health, Education, and Welfare, *Statistical Series 60, Child Welfare Statistics, 1959*, Washington, 1960, p. 28. See also Hornberger, Ralph C., and others, *Health Supervision of Young Children in California*, State of California, Department of Public Health, Sacramento, 1960, p. 8. Here it is stated that about 2 per cent of all children under six years of age in California are adopted.

adoption process is in achieving the purpose of American adoption law. Second, we wanted to see whether certain factors are predictive of adoption outcome, especially factors that are present and can be recognized at the time adoption decisions are being made.

The interest of the Florida Welfare Department in having these questions answered in regard to the independent adoption petitions it had investigated for the Court provided an opportunity for obtaining the needed information in one state. In that state, in the years 1944 to 1947, independent adoptions so far outnumbered agency adoptions that the findings of a study of independent adoptions would not be greatly influenced by selective factors that the presence of a vigorous social agency adoption program might bring into play. Florida, therefore, seemed an especially favorable location for the first of what we hoped would be a series of comparable adoption studies.

To achieve the purposes of the study, information on four main topics had to be secured: (1) The purpose of American adoption law had to be carefully examined so that we might know what the law seeks to achieve and thus have a standard by which to evaluate the findings of the follow-up investigation. (2) Information on the adopted children's home situation and the adoptive parents' experiences with adoption and opinions about it had to be obtained so that we would have material on which assessments of the homes could be based and the extent of the presumed risk to the adoptive parents be determined. (3) In order to be able to test whether the type of home was actually related to the child's chances of functioning well, we had to get information on the children's social and emotional adjustment. (4) In order to determine whether adoptive petitioners' potentiality for effective parenthood can be assessed at the outset, as well as whether certain traits of the children (such as age at placement and physical conditions at that time) are indicative of later good adjustment, information on a considerable number of possibly predictive factors had to be secured. How this information was obtained, what it showed, and what relations were found among the various items of information provide the subject matter of the succeeding chapters.

Part I

THE FOLLOW-UP STUDY

CHAPTER I

The Purpose of
American Adoption Laws[1]

THE PASSAGE, in the middle of the nineteenth century, of the first general adoption laws in the United States was not one of the great issues of the day. It left behind it little record save the bare words of the statutes and the dates they became effective. The whys and wherefores that led to the enactment of these laws are more matters of conjecture than of documentation. Perhaps a careful search of the daily press of the time and of manuscript sources would give us firmer clues than we now have, but, in the absence of such a search, we must rely almost wholly on surmise.

The chances are that the advent of these statutes, landmarks though they now seem to us, created little stir because they were then looked upon as little more than a normal and desirable next step in a development that was already taking place. It is true that the term "adoption" was not one the courts then generally recognized as meaningful, but it was in common use in other circles. The Oxford English Dictionary traces it and its cognates back to the fourteenth century with a meaning close to that assigned to it today, namely, the taking of another into a relationship with oneself that the other did not previously occupy. Its application to the creation of a parent-child relationship that nature had not supplied was, moreover, something the learned

---

[1] Pages 19–32 were prepared by T. Richard Witmer, Counsel for the House Committee on Interior and Insular Affairs.

ld readily have picked up either from Roman law[1] or from the Code Napoleon.[2] It was an idea that learned and unlearned alike could hardly have failed to absorb from Biblical texts that furnished the basis for thousands of sermons.[3] Legislators were

---

[1] For general discussions of the Roman law of adoption, see Sherman, Charles P., *Roman Law in the Modern World*, 3d ed., Baker, Voorhis and Co., New York, vol. 2, 1937, pp. 83 ff.; Hastings, James, editor, *Encyclopaedia of Religion and Ethics*, s.v. "Adoption."

[2] The Code Napoleon, 1804, articles 343 ff., provided only for adoption by a person who was at least fifty years old; who, at the time of the adoption had neither children nor legitimate descendants; who was at least fifteen years older than the person to be adopted; and who had (with certain exceptions) furnished assistance to, and taken care of, the person to be adopted during his minority and for at least six years. The person proposed to be adopted had to have reached his majority and he retained all his rights in his natural family.

The Louisiana Civil Code of 1808, article 35, permitted adoption by any person forty years of age or older and required the adoptive child to be at least fifteen years younger than the adopting parents. It provided that "The person adopted shall have all the rights of a legitimate child in the estate of the person adopting him" except that the "adoption shall not interfere with the rights of forced heirs [i.e., heirs who took by force of law]." Adoption was abolished by the Louisiana Civil Code of 1825, article 214.

Spanish law was influential in the early Texas legislation, particularly with respect to the method by which adoption was achieved. The Texas court outlined the method of adoption that was used in Texas' Mexican days in *Ortiz* v. *De Benavides*, 61 Tex. 60, 68 (1884): "A learned Spanish writer states that, in order to make a valid adoption, it is sufficient that the father of the child to be adopted, with the person adopting, present themselves before some judge and declare that the one desires to give, and the other to receive, the child in adoption, and that there shall be given an instrument bearing evidence of the act. 1 Alvarez, Derech Real, 82." See also *Eckford* v. *Knox*, 67 Tex. 200, 204, 2 S.W. 372, 374 (1886): "By the Spanish law the person adopted succeeded as heir to the one adopting him (4 Partides Lit., 16), but according to the law as it existed in Mexico while Texas was under the dominion of that government, no person having a legitimate child living could adopt a stranger as co-heir with his child. . . . Our statute imports the civil law as to adoption into our jurisdiction, but modifies it in some important respects. It gives to the adopted party the position of a child, only so far as to make him the heir of his adopter, but does not constitute him a member of the latter's family with such duties and privileges as that relation would imply. It allows him to inherit to a certain extent, though there be legitimate children born to the adopting party. But as to the inheritance in all other respects, it gives all the rights and privileges of a legitimate child." *Teal* v. *Sevier*, 26 Tex. 516 (1863): ". . . the law then in force [1832] did not permit anyone who had a legitimate child living, to adopt a stranger as co-heir with such child. Sideck [predecessor in interest of one of the parties to this suit] could at that time give away the one-fifth part of his estate, but he could not give away more than the fifth part, nor could he adopt a stranger to be co-heir with his legitimate child, one of the present plaintiffs."

[3] Romans 8: 14–17 and Galatians 4: 5–7. See also Exodus 2:10 and Esther 2:7. The term "adoption," with emphasis on heirship, occurs in the King James translation of the first two of these passages. The term is not used in the second two, but would seem to be applicable.

using it in private legislation[1] and courts were becoming familiar with the adoption of white men into Indian tribes and were using the very word to describe that process and its results.[2] And those who read the works of Shakespeare carefully would have noted both his use of the term and the problem posed by it.

When, in Shakespeare's words, Henry VI[3] argued his case for the crown with York,

> KING HENRY: Tell me, may not a king adopt an heir?
>
> YORK: What then?

----

[1] In addition to the examples cited in note 1 on p. 29, there are various instances of the use of the term in statutes providing for changes in name and/or for inheritance of property: Georgia Laws, 1852, p. 499 ("Whereas, the said John B. Chappel, and his wife, Margaret W. Chappel, are desirous of adopting as their child and heir at law, Margaret Jane Brooks . . ."); Pennsylvania Laws, 1844, p. 303 ("That Eliza Jane Jarvis . . . the daughter of Oliver J. Jarvis, and now the adopted child of James and Hannah Miles. . . ."); New York Session Laws, 1825, p. 11 ("Whereas, it has been represented by the petition, that Harriet Jane Perkins . . . , an infant child, has, by the consent of her parents, been adopted by Asa C. Winter and Abigail, his wife, as their child to be by them educated and brought up, and to bear their name . . ."); New York Session Laws, 1832, p. 280 ("The surname of Frederick Charles Bruce, William Henry Bruce, and Mary Elizabeth Bruce . . . is hereby changed to that of their adopted [sic] father, Frederick Gebhard. . . .").

[2] See *United States* v. *Rogers*, 4 How. 567, 572 (1846); *United States* v. *Ragsdale*, Fed. Cas. #16,113 (C.C.D. Ark., 1847): "The question here arises, whether a white man can become a member of the Cherokee tribe of Indians, and be adopted by them as an individual member of that tribe? [After quoting from *United States* v. *Rogers* that "He may by such adoption become entitled to certain privileges in the tribe, and make himself amenable to their laws and usages," the court continued:] The above language is too clear to be misunderstood; that in the opinion of the supreme court, a white man may incorporate himself with an Indian tribe, be adopted by it, and become a member of the tribe." "Adoption" in these cases was apparently something of a cross between naturalization and what we would regard as adoption.

[3] 3 Henry VI: I, i. See also Richard II: IV, i, in which York says to Bolingbroke:

> "Great Duke of Lancaster, I come to thee
> From plume-pluck'd Richard; who with willing soul
> Adopts thee heir, and his high sceptre yields
> To the possession of thy royal hand.
> Ascend his throne, descending now from him;
> And long live Henry, of that name the fourth!"

> KING HENRY: An if he may, then am I lawful king;
> For Richard, in the view of many lords,
> Resign'd the crown to Henry the Fourth
> Whose heir my father was, and I am his.

the answer was not only the accusation that Richard had been forced to abdicate in favor of Henry IV but Exeter's answer to Warwick's further question:

> WARWICK: Suppose, my lords, he did it unconstrain'd,
> Think you 'twere prejudicial to his crown?

> EXETER: No; for he could not so resign his crown
> But that the next heir should succeed and reign.

Shakespeare's use of the word "adopt" here is not quite ours, to be sure, but it is close enough so that Exeter's answer can well be taken as the answer of his time and of Shakespeare's to the question, Why do our courts not recognize adoption? If Exeter's rule may be restated, it amounts to saying that an outsider may not be brought into a family to the prejudice of the expected heirs.[1] This was an answer that appealed to every man whose father held an estate or a title which, under the usual rules of succession, he would probably inherit. In other words, the English rule against adoption can be taken as having been complementary to the laws governing the inheritance of real property.

Perhaps there was a time when, with a little further development in a direction it was then going, full-fledged adoption would have become a part of English law.[2] But this development, if such it was and not merely a few individual cases, was cut short and the law soon returned to Glanville's dictum of a century earlier:

---

[1] Cf. Pollock, Frederick, and Frederic W. Maitland, *History of English Law*, 2d ed., The University Press, Cambridge, England, vol. 2, 1898, p. 300: "In the thirteenth century no wide gulf could be fixed between the inheritance of a kingdom and other impartible inheritances."

[2] *Ibid.*, pp. 398–399: ". . . we may see a strong inclination to treat as legitimate any child whom the husband had down to his death accepted as his own and his wife's child, even though proof be forthcoming that it is neither the one nor the other. . . . Indeed, as Bracton sees, our law in such a case went far towards permitting something that was very like adoption. However, this really is no more than the result of a very strong presumption—a presumption which absolves the court from difficult inquiries—and from the time when it rejects the claims of the 'mantle-children' onwards to our own day, we have had no adoption in England."

"Only God can make a *heres*, not man."[1] Absence of a
we know it was, then, completely understandable in a
land could be conveyed by will and when, in fact, i
even be conveyed *inter vivos* except with the consent of the ...
apparent and perhaps not even then.[2] But after *inter vivos* con-
veyances of land, with or without the consent of the heirs, became accepted,[3] and particularly after freedom of testation of real
property was established,[4] it is less understandable. Yet even at
this time it was not the anomaly it might seem when we consider
that adoption would involve not only the adoptive parent's
estate, as a gift *inter vivos* or by will to an outsider also would,
but that, unless carefully controlled, it might also involve
the estates of all members of the adoptive parent's family and
even of his collaterals.[5] Add to this the treatment accorded by
the law to half-brothers and half-sisters, to mantle-children,
and to outright illegitimate children[6]—all of them with greater
claim to be considered members of a family, at least for purposes of inheritance, than an outsider—and it is not difficult
to appreciate the strength of a rule against adoption in the law
of the day.

Perhaps it will be thought that this lays too much stress on
inheritance which, for the purpose of this study, is not important.
Yet inheritance runs through the history of adoption and non-
adoption so much more prominently than any other factor—
from St. Paul to Glanville to the American developments of the
middle of the nineteenth century—that its importance can hardly
be overestimated. But another side of the picture—transfer of
custody, with its implications with respect to the child's mainte-

---

[1] Quoted in *ibid.*, p. 254; see also pp. 316 and 327.

[2] *Ibid.*, pp. 293, 308 ff.

[3] *Ibid.*

[4] Full freedom of testation came with enactment of the Statute of Wills in 1540,
but for a century or so before this time much the same result was achieved through
development of the use, a predecessor of the more modern trust.

[5] This is still a large and difficult problem with respect to which the statutes and
judicial decisions of our various jurisdictions arrive at differing solutions. For a
survey, see Note, "Legislation and Decisions on Inheritance Rights of Adopted
Children," *Iowa Law Review*, vol. 22, 1936, p. 145.

[6] Pollock and Maitland, *op. cit.*, vol. 2, p. 302 (children of the half-blood),
pp. 396 ff. (illegitimate and mantle children).

nance, welfare, education, discipline, and the like—also played a part, and it is to it that we now turn.

LEGAL BACKGROUND OF THE EARLY ADOPTION LAWS IN THE UNITED STATES

The most common method of transferring custody from the natural parent or parents to those who, for want of a better term, we may call the custodial parents—often members of the same family (grandparents, aunts, uncles, cousins) but sometimes others—has always been by simple informal agreement. In most instances such an arrangement would provoke no problems between the elders. In many it would be intended from the outset as an adoption. In others, given time, it might well ripen into a *de facto* adoption and be regarded as such in the public eye. Particularly would this be so if the arrangement were fortified and formalized by a writing—a contract or indenture, as the case might be—setting out the understanding of the parties. And it would be still more likely to be so regarded if it were further fortified by the expectation or knowledge, or even agreement, that the custodial parent would by will or otherwise see that the child eventually shared in his estate. That it was so regarded in the mid-nineteenth century in the United States is indicated by the report accompanying the draft of a civil code for New York State prepared by David Dudley Field and his associates in which enactment of a general adoption law was urged:[1]

> The total absence of any provision for the adoption of children is one of the most remarkable defects of our law. Thousands of children are actually, though not legally, adopted every year; yet there is no method by which the adopting parents can secure the children to themselves except by a fictitious apprenticeship, a form which, when applied to children in the cradle, becomes absurd and repulsive. It

---

[1] New York Commissioners of the Code, *The Civil Code of the State of New York*, 1865, p. 36. The passage quoted above goes on to explain that "There are very many childless parents who would gladly adopt children, but for their well-founded fears that they could never hold them securely." This arises from the probability that the more successful the adopted child turned out to be, the more likely that, as shown by "facts within the knowledge of almost everyone," the natural parents would "reclaim the child as soon as any money can be made out of it." The Civil Code failed of enactment in New York, but its adoption provisions were picked up in California legislation.

is, indeed, so inappropriate a form in every case that it is rarely resorted to.

Skipping over any discussion of the type of instrument used in such cases as these, a reading of contemporary judicial opinions clearly indicates that many American courts were inclined to countenance such arrangements when they could. During the lifetime of the natural parents any contest between them and the custodial parents would ordinarily be for the return of the child, and *habeas corpus* would be the usual form in which the question was presented to the courts. *Habeas corpus* has always been a rather flexible remedy, with a strong tinge of an action in equity to it. The American courts, whatever their views and the views of the English courts on the enforceability of the agreement as such,[1] took advantage of this flexibility to mold their judgments to fit the needs of the situations presented to them.

---

[1] The attitude of the English courts toward such an agreement can readily be surmised from the views expressed in *Vansittart* v. *Vansittart*, 2 DeG. and J. 249, 27 L. J. Ch. 290 (1858), involving a separation agreement which, among other things, called for relinquishment by a father of his paternal rights. The Lord Chancellor wrote:

"By one of its provisions the father agrees to divest himself of the authority which belongs to him by nature, and which law and public policy impose upon him as a duty. It has been said, that there is nothing contrary to public policy in this—that a father may, if he pleases, divest himself of the authority which he possessed over his children and transfer it to another. If this matter were *res integra*, I certainly should have a strong opinion the other way, and that this is opposed to a policy on which the best and dearest interests of society may depend. But this question, as it appears to me, has been decided more than once. . . ."

And Turner, *L. J.*, said:

"The father has not merely rights in respect of the children, but he has duties to discharge towards them, and the question which I mean to refer to in the few observations I shall make on this case is, whether it is competent to the father to fetter and abandon his parental power to the extent which by this agreement he has contracted to do?"

Shortly thereafter he answered his own question in the negative.

Cf. *Swift* v. *Swift*, 4 DeG., J. and S. 710, 46 Eng. Rep. 1095 (1865), a case in which the Master of the Rolls, concluding that the father's conduct had been so atrocious that he could be deprived of custody by order of the court and therefore ought to be permitted to divest himself of it by contract, remarked that the general "policy of the law is derived from what is most for the benefit of the child." On appeal, Turner, *L. J.*, referred to the earlier decisions thus:

"The cases which had been referred to on behalf of the Appellant went to this extent only, that the Court would not permit the right to the custody of the

Thus we find Mr. Justice Story, in 1824, saying in a *habeas corpus* action to recover a child from his maternal grandfather to whose care, it was alleged, his mother had committed him on her deathbed:[1]

> As to the question of the right of the father to have the custody of his infant child, in a general sense it is true. But this is not on account of any absolute right of the father, but for the benefit of the infant, the law presuming it to be for his interest to be under the nurture and care of his natural protector, both for maintenance and education. When, therefore, the Court is asked to lend its aid to put the infant in the custody of the father, and to withdraw him from other persons, it will look into all the circumstances and ascertain whether it will be for the real, permanent interests of the infant; and if the infant be of sufficient discretion, it will also consult its personal wishes. It will free it from all undue restraint, and endeavor, as far as possible, to administer a conscientious, parental duty with reference to its welfare. It is an entire mistake to suppose the Court is at all events bound to deliver over the infant to his father, or that the latter has an absolute vested right in the custody.

> children to be a mere matter of bargain and agreement between the husband and wife upon a separation between them. They fell far short of deciding that where the husband had misconducted himself towards the children, he could not by a separation deed or by any other deed covenant not to set up his paternal rights."

Among the American cases, *People ex rel. Barry* v. *Mercein*, 3 Hill (N.Y.) 399, 38 Am. Dec. 644 (1842), and *State ex rel. Mayne* v. *Baldwin*, 5 N.J. Eq. 454, 45 Am. Dec. 399 (1846) are representative of the stricter view of a father's right to custody and *State* v. *Smith*, 6 Greenleaf (Me.) 462, 20 Am. Dec. 324 (1830) and *Commonwealth* v. *Hammond*, 10 Pick. (Mass.) 274 (1830) of the more tolerant view. See also *Ex parte Schumpert* 6 Rich (S.C.) 344 (1853) and *Note*, 20 Am. Dec. 330 ff. for American critiques of the course of the English decisions.

For a summary of the present state of the law on this subject, consult 6 Williston, *Contracts* (rev. ed., 1938), 4938:

> "The sovereign has an interest in a minor child superior even to that of the parent; hence, there is a public policy against the custody of such a child becoming the subject of barter. It has been held, therefore, in many cases that a bargain by a parent or one entitled to the custody of a minor child to transfer the custody to a person other than its parent . . . is illegal, unless permitted by a statute providing for adoption, apprenticeship, or the like; but an increasing line of cases sustains the bargain when it is to the advantage of the child. As between the child's parents such a bargain may be valid. Yet, since the welfare of the child is the determining factor, the court in the exercise of its equitable powers may ignore the bargain, whether legal or illegal, and if the custody of the child has already been transferred may leave it with the transferee."

[1] *United States* v. *Green*, 3 Mason 482, 485, Fed. Cas. #15,256 (C.C.D. R.I., 1824).

So too by 1862, the New Hampshire court—while denying the writ in the case before it because the transfer had not been by indenture as prescribed by the statutes of the state—could summarize its understanding of the law thus:[1]

> Ordinarily, a father is entitled to the custody of his minor children, and upon habeas corpus both courts of law and equity have power to award it to him. The application, however, being addressed to the sound discretion of the court, such award will be withheld when it is made clearly to appear that by reason of unfitness in the father for the trust, or other causes, the permanent interests of the child would be sacrificed by such change of custody; and in deciding upon this question, the court will take into consideration the condition of the child with the persons from whose custody it is sought to be taken; its relation to them; the present and prospective provision for its support and welfare; the length of its residence there, and whether, with the consent of its father, and the understanding, tacit or otherwise, that it should be permanent; the strength of the ties that had been formed between them, and if the child has come to years of discretion, its wishes upon the subject.

Similarly, the Massachusetts court, speaking through Chief Justice Shaw, observed a few years earlier (in 1856) that "this is not a question of mere property" and that "the interest of the minor is the principal thing to be considered."[2] Saying that "the court are all of opinion that, so far as the rights of the mother are concerned, she has relinquished them by this instrument [an indenture]" which, however, would have to be looked at "with greater care" if the child objected to the arrangements made in it, the opinion went on:

> In all cases of this description, of the right to the custody and control of a female of an age to have a will, and a capacity to form some judgment for herself, it is the established custom of the court to ascertain the opinion or inclination of the minor. . . . We are satisfied, by an examination, that this girl is capable of judging what will best promote her own welfare; . . . that she is strongly inclined to remain with the society of Shakers [to whom the mother had transferred her]; and that they take sufficient care of her education. . . .

---

[1] *State ex rel Hodgdon* v. *Libbey*, 44 N.H. 321, 82 Am. Dec. 223 (1862).
[2] *Curtis* v. *Curtis*, 5 Gray (Mass.) 535, 537 (1856).

These cases[1] make it reasonably clear that the enactment of the first general adoption laws was not the completely novel step it might seem to have been. The standards embodied in many of the first laws were quite similar to standards set out in opinions such as those from which we have quoted. The practice of judicial control over transfers of custody, moreover, was already established when the first laws were put on the books. What most of the new laws did, in effect, was to move this control from a time after trouble had commenced to the beginning of the process. In so doing, of course, they (or many of them) overcame other problems as well. They put the adoptive process on a surer footing, and, in most cases, they solved the inheritance problem also. But, notwithstanding the inference to be drawn from a nearly contemporary statement that Massachusetts' first statute "was drawn with the avowed object of securing to adopted children a proper share in the estate of adopting parents who should die intestate,"[2] the achievement of this object can be regarded as merely incidental to the larger problem of securing permanent status for the child in his new family. In short, the chances are that a full-fledged law of adoption—at least on its custodial side—would sooner or later have been developed either judicially or legislatively as a response, to use Mr. Justice Holmes' language, to the "felt necessities of the times"[3] and as an outgrowth of current practice even if there had never been a Roman law to which the learned could refer for support and prestige.

---

[1] Although not so articulate, such cases as *Nickols* v. *Giles,* 2 Root (Conn.) 461 (1796), *Commonwealth* v. *Hamilton,* 6 Mass. 273 (1810), *Commonwealth* v. *Addicks,* 2 Binney (Pa.) 520 (1813), and *Ex parte Ralston,* Charlton (Ga. Super.) 119 (1821) can be regarded as their forerunners in the development of the welfare-of-the-child principle. Of these, the Pennsylvania case is the most interesting. In it the court refused to order the return of two children to a father even though the mother, according to the court, was not of overly good repute and had, after divorce, married her paramour contrary to the laws of the state. Remarking that the children "appear to have been well taken care of in all respects" by the mother, the court went on: "It is to them, that our anxiety is principally directed; and it appears to us, that considering their tender age, they stand in need of that kind of assistance, which can be afforded by none so well as a mother. It is on their account, therefore, that exercising the discretion with which the law has invested us, we think it best, at present, not to take them from her."

[2] Whitmore, William H., *The Law of Adoption in the United States.* J. Munsell, Albany, N. Y., 1876, p. iv.

[3] Holmes, Oliver Wendell, Jr., *The Common Law.* Little, Brown and Co., Boston, 1881, p. 1.

But there was at least one more factor in the background of the general adoption laws that needs to be borne in mind—the practice of the legislatures of passing special acts providing for the adoption of particular children by particular adults. Strange though this practice may seem to us today, such enactments were not unusual. They were part of a larger pattern that had developed and, as such, can be put side by side with other special enactments granting divorces, for instance, and providing for the legitimation of children. How far back this practice runs has never, to the best of our knowledge, been investigated, but a spot-check of a few states indicates that by the time with which we are concerned it was probably quite general.[1] In a very real sense the enactment of general adoption laws was but a generalization of this earlier practice—a generalization designed to open the doors to all comers, to relieve the legislatures of routine work, and to avoid the political and other hazards that frequently attend the legislative route.

THE EARLY AMERICAN ADOPTION STATUTES

This, then, was the background of the early American adoption statutes. Disregarding many of the details in which the statutes differed from each other—differences, for instance, with respect to parental consent to the child's adoption, the age at which the child himself had to consent, the possibility of the adoptive parent's inheriting from the child, requirements as to local residence on the part of the adopting parents, the effect of foreign adoptions, changing the child's name, and the like—the

---

[1] For examples, see: Illinois Laws, 1853, p. 485 (changing the name of Marshall Myrick "the adopted son of Jonathan E. Cooper," and declaring him "entitled to all the rights that would belong or pertain to him were he the natural son of the said Jonathan E. Cooper"); Kentucky Acts, 1841, p. 163 (". . . it shall be lawful for John Fonda to go before the County Court of Jefferson County, and to declare of record, that he does adopt John Edwin Blumenthal, his nephew, a minor, to be his son, and his lawful heir, as if said John Edwin had been his begotten son . . ."); Pennsylvania Laws, 1848, p. 201 ("That henceforth the name of David Richardson Bair, an adopted son of Thompson Richardson . . . shall be David Richardson . . . and he is hereby invested with all the legal rights of a legitimate son of said Thompson Richardson"); Wisconsin General Acts, 1855, p. 14 (changing the name of Anna Morley to Emma Carpenter and providing that "said Emma Carpenter shall be known as the adopted daughter and heir of Stephen D. Carpenter, and his wife, Mary B. Carpenter . . . and entitled to all the rights and privileges, and subject to all the duties of inheritance, support and maintenance, as fully and effectually, and in the same manner as . . . if she were the legitimate child of said Stephen D. Carpenter and Mary B. Carpenter").

statutes, in their first stages, can be classified in two broad groups, based on their provision or lack of provision for public inquiry into and control over proposed adoptions. The first and less important class comprises those legislative acts that may be regarded as being predominantly statutes to authenticate and make public record of private agreements of adoption. In this class are those of Texas[1] (1850), Vermont (1850), perhaps Tennessee (1851–1852), Missouri (1857), and Iowa (1858). None of these made express provision for public supervision of the adoption agreement, or for inquiry into its propriety or its effect on the welfare of the child.

Contrasted with these acts are the acts of Massachusetts (1851), Pennsylvania (1855),[2] Indiana (1855), Georgia (1855–1856), Wisconsin (1858), Ohio (1859), Michigan (1861), New Hampshire (1862), Oregon (1864), Connecticut (1864), Kansas (1868), California (1870), Maine (1871), Rhode Island (1872), North Carolina (1872–1873), and New York (1873).[3] All of these pro-

---

[1] In *Eckford* v. *Knox*, 67 Tex. 200, 204, 2 S.W. 372 (1886), the court described the effect of this first Texas statute thus: "Our statute imports the civil law as to adoption into our jurisprudence, but modifies it in some important respects. It gives to the adopted party the position of a child only so far as to make him the heir of his adopter, but does not constitute him a member of the latter's family with such duties and privileges as that relation would imply. . . ." See also *Taylor* v. *Deseve*, 81 Tex. 246, 249, 16 S.W. 1008 (1891), to the same effect.

[2] In 1872 this act was supplemented by another providing that "In all cases heretofore, as well as hereafter, when the common law form of adopting a child by deed has been practiced or done, it shall be lawful . . . to have the same recorded . . . ; and a duly certified copy thereof shall be received in evidence, with the same force and effect as the record of adoption would have in the mode provided in the act to which this is a supplement."

[3] In addition to providing for future adoptions, this act recognized that there had been adoptions in the past and attempted to ratify them: "Nothing herein contained shall prevent proof of the adoption of any child, heretofore made according to any method practiced in this State, from being received in evidence, nor such adoption from having the effect of an adoption hereunder." Dealing with this provision in *Matter of Thorne*, 155 N.Y. 140, 144, 49 N.E. 661 (1898), the court said:

> "While there has been some diversity of opinion in the lower courts as to the precise meaning of this clause, we think the only construction permissible is that it refers to those forms of adoption theretofore existing by virtue of special statutory enactments contained in the charters of charitable societies that received destitute and homeless children, and whose officers were permitted to execute agreements of adoption on their behalf with suitable persons willing to assume the obligations of parents. This is illustrated by the act to incorporate

vided, in greater or less degree, for judicial supervision over adoptions, although the lines along which the courts' inquiries were required to proceed varied considerably. In Massachusetts the requirement was that the court be "satisfied . . . that the petitioner, or . . . petitioners, are of sufficient ability to bring up the child, and furnish suitable nurture and education, having reference to the degree and condition of its parents, and that it is fit and proper that such adoption should take place. . . ."

This language, or language closely approximating it, was followed in the Wisconsin, Ohio, New Hampshire, Oregon, Maine, Rhode Island, Illinois, and Washington statutes.

In Pennsylvania, on the other hand, the test was more broadly stated. Adoption there was permitted if the court was "satisfied that the welfare of such child will be promoted by such adoption." A similar test was embodied in the early Connecticut act, with the additional requirement that the adoption be found to be "for the public interest." "When satisfied that it will be for the interest of such child" was the way the Indiana act read, and slight variants on this theme were written into the Georgia, California, and Idaho acts. In New York this was amplified to require the court to be "satisfied that the moral and temporal interests of the child will be promoted by the adoption. . . ." Michigan and North Carolina required no more than that, in the first case, the court be "satisfied of the good faith of [the] proceedings, and that the person or persons adopting such child is or are suitable to have charge thereof" and, in the second, that the court find the petitioner to be "a proper and suitable person."

Finally, in Kansas, all the jurisdictional requirements with consent and the like being satisfied, the adoption was to be allowed unless the court found "on investigation, that the person proposing to adopt such minor child is unfit to assume the relation of parent to such minor. . . ."

---

the American Female Guardian Society, a well-known charitable institution in the city of New York (Ch. 244, Laws of 1849.). . . .

"It is obvious that the legislature did not have in contemplation the legalizing of private agreements executed without authority of law and containing no safeguards or restrictions of any kind as to the transmission of property. . . ."

The welfare purpose of adoption laws[1] has been attested to by many court decisions; for instance, the following:

> The purpose of our adoption act is to promote the welfare of the child to be adopted.[2]

* * *

> The adoption statute is a humane provision that looks to the interest of children primarily. That is its controlling idea and policy. . . . That the statute was designed to enable those who are not blessed with the love and society of children in the family to acquire it by taking into the family fold and giving a home to those in need of such shelter, protection, and care, thus creating mutual obligations, promotive of mutual happiness and the moral well-being of society is most clear.[3]

* * *

> Under these statutes, orphaned or abandoned children are withdrawn from the charity of public institutions and taken into the homes of foster parents. Unfortunate children, whose parents . . . are unable to care and provide for them, are placed in wholesome surroundings under care of persons willing and able to provide for their protection and comfort. Under the beneficent provisions of these statutes, such children are accorded advantages and opportunities for better moral, intellectual and material advancement; a measure of happiness is secured to the adoptive parents and the children adopted . . . ; and inasmuch as the development of the child into a valuable member of society and an upright citizen depends upon healthy, moral home influences and parental solici-

---

[1] When England finally passed an adoption statute, in 1926, it too did so in order to protect children and parents and because, by reason of the low birth rate, the war, and the influenza epidemic, the practice of *de facto* adoption had become common. Children were in need of protection against both those who profited financially from placing them in foster homes and from those who profited from taking them into their homes. Natural parents needed protection against giving children up unwillingly and unnecessarily, while adopting parents needed protection against natural parents' later claims. All this was so forcefully argued in Parliament that a statute legalizing adoption was passed. See Great Britain, *Parliamentary Debates*, House of Commons, 192, Adoption of Children Bill, 2d Reading, 26, Feb. 26; House of Lords, LVI (5th Series, 18, March 24); also the Report of the Committee on Child Adoptions, 1921 and 1925.

[2] Cummin, J., in *Wolf's App.*, 10 Sad. 139, 13 Atl. 760, 764 (Pa. C. P., 1888).

[3] *Parsons* v. *Parsons*, 101 Wis., 76, 80, 77 NW 147, 148 (1898).

tude, to that all-important extent, then, under these laws, are the best interests of society and the state conserved.[1]

The social explanation of this welfare purpose is perhaps to be found in the long-standing public interest in homeless and destitute children, and in the commonly held belief that these children are best cared for by being attached to individual families. These attitudes go back to colonial days and represent a mixture of humanitarianism and concern for the community exchequer. A historian of poor relief in Massachusetts points out:

> It was the theory of the early community that every person should be attached to a family and that he should have some occupation. . . . When an abandoned child was found, the first quest was for a family home. . . . The sole objects of the first Plymouth authorities were to secure right family surroundings and to provide work for the growing child. . . . Cleaning off the account on the treasurer's book by a long-term indenture . . . was the constant effort of the early town authorities.[2]

For two hundred years and more, the homes secured for children were work homes, and the children were "bound out," on contract, to families that would feed, clothe, and house them, give them the rudiments of schooling, and train them to some occupation. Even when almshouses came into use as repositories of the poor, insane, and criminal, and children too were sent there, indenturing continued as a means of training when the children came of working age. Later, separate institutions for children took the place of almshouses but again, in Massachusetts at least, placement of children in foster homes was part of the institutions' business.

Early in the nineteenth century voluntary agencies for the care of mothers and children were established, and these too used foster homes for caring for the children. The American Female Guardian Society, for instance, was placing children for "adoption," as it called it, as early as 1834. The Children's Aid Society of New York, established in 1853, was the originator of a famous

---

[1] *McKeag's Estate*, 141 Cal. 403, 74 Pac. 1039, 1040, 99 A.S.R. 80 (1903.)

[2] Kelso, Robert, *History of Public Poor Relief in Massachusetts*. Houghton Mifflin Co., Boston, 1922, pp. 165–168.

plan of securing permanent homes for city children in the agricultural West.[1] With the enactment of adoption statutes, a considerable number of these children were formally adopted.[2]

LATER DEVELOPMENTS

Later developments in American adoption law inclined even more clearly in the welfare direction. In consequence, the adoption laws of most states now contain provisions aimed at protecting children from being adopted against their interest. Protection against being casually removed from their natural homes is afforded by such requirements as those that specify how the natural parents' willingness to have the child adopted is to be determined and that restrict the parents' right to transfer the custody of their children. Protection against being adopted by unsuitable persons is afforded by the provision that calls for a trial period before an adoption is made final. Most important, protection of the child is the aim of what Vernier calls "the most important development in the law of adoption during recent years": the requiring of a social investigation through which the suitability of home and child is determined before adoption is allowed.[3]

Recognition of the need for greater assurance that the home was a fit one was evidenced in the Michigan statute of 1891, which was one of the first to require that the judge "investigate" before entering a decree of adoption. How the judge was to do this was not specified; specific standards to guide him in the

---

[1] For the history of this development, see Kelso, Robert, *op. cit.;* Thurston, Henry, *The Dependent Child*, Columbia University Press, New York, 1930; Folks, Homer, "The Care of Destitute, Neglected, and Delinquent Children," *The Charities Review*, vol. 9, November and December, 1899, vol. 10, January, February, March, April, May, and July, 1900; Calhoun, Arthur, *A Social History of the American Family*, Clark Co., Cleveland, 1918.

[2] The numbers adopted are cited in reports of some public agencies; for example, the Michigan State Public School, 287 between 1874 and 1892. Randall, C. D., and Others, *History of Child Saving in the U. S.*, National Conference of Charities and Corrections, Chicago, 1893, p. 214.

[3] Vernier, Chester G., *American Family Laws*, Stanford University Press, Stanford, Calif., 1936, vol. 4, p. 279. For a historical account of these developments, see Heisterman, Carl A., "A Summary of Legislation on Adoption," *Social Service Review*, vol. 9, 1935, pp. 269–293; Colby, Ruth, "Progress in Adoption Legislation," *Social Service Review*, vol. 16, 1942, pp. 64–74.

conduct of the investigation were not set forth, and the judge was not expressly given power to have the investigation made for him. In practice, however, the requirement of an investigation was perhaps not so nullified by the omission of such provisions as this statement might suggest. For assistance, in certain cases at least, there were agents of the State Board of Corrections and Charities in each county, among whose duties (by a law of 1885)[1] was that of investigating "all proposals for adoption of children in state institutions."

The next step toward protecting children was taken in 1917, when Minnesota, following a recommendation of a Commission set up to revise and codify its child welfare laws, amended its adoption statute to provide, in substance, that the investigation should be made by the State Welfare Department, a licensed children's agency, a social worker of the court, or some other competent person.[2] In the 1920's and later, other states followed Minnesota's example.

The rationale of the social investigation is especially clearly stated in the report of the Wisconsin Children's Code Commission on this subject:

> Adoption proceedings are, for the adoptable child, next to birth itself, the most important single transaction in his life. It is imperative, therefore, that the child at this time have the benefit of the most thorough and careful work in the procedure that is to determine his whole future. Essential to this is the need that the court shall have for its guidance full and complete facts about the child and the adopting parents. This can be secured only through skillful investigation by completely trained persons.[3]

By 1954, provisions of this sort were part of the adoption law of 44 states. In 26 states, courts were required to have such investigations made, while in 18 the investigation was left to the

---

[1] Howell, Annotated Statutes, 1885–1889, secs. 9894, 9897.

[2] Heisterman, Carl, *op. cit.*, p. 271. See also Colby, Ruth, *op. cit.;* and Vernier, Chester, *op. cit.*, for variations in state laws regarding investigating parties, their responsibilities and power, and exceptions permitted.

[3] Cited by Sophonisba P. Breckinridge in *The Family and the State*, University of Chicago Press, Chicago, 1934, p. 402.

discretion of the court. The state public welfare agency was the most frequently specified source of investigation.[1]

The state laws vary somewhat with regard to the circumstances under which an investigation is to be made (adoptive placements arranged through licensed social agencies are usually excepted); with regard to what is to be investigated; in the specificity of their instructions to the investigators; and in the means by which the court is to be informed of the findings. On the last named point, nearly all states require written reports to the court, and many add that the investigator shall make a recommendation as to the desirability of the adoption.

Within recent years, other efforts have been made to devise legal protections. According to a review published in 1950, 11 jurisdictions forbade adoption placements not made by a natural parent, a guardian, a relative, or an authorized agency; 8 states prohibited all independent placements except when made with relatives; and 4 states required that "whenever a child is placed independently for adoptive purposes, either the person who places the child or the person who receives the child must notify the state welfare department."[2]

More recently two states, Delaware and Connecticut, have enacted stronger legislation, and now require that all placements of children for adoption by persons who are neither their stepparents nor their blood relatives shall be made by licensed social agencies or by the Department of Welfare.[3]

---

[1] Figures based on laws as abstracted by Mollie Margolis in *Summaries of State Laws Pertaining to Adoption of Children*, Council of State Governments, Albany, 1954.

[2] "Moppets on the Market: The Problem of Unregulated Adoptions," *Yale Law Journal*, vol. 59, March, 1950, pp. 715–736; see especially pp. 732–734. The author dismisses all these efforts as ineffectual, partly because of wide loopholes in the legislation, partly because in some instances deception is very easy, partly because little or no attempt is made to prosecute violations. In some instances, although a court order is required before placement, no investigation is required before the court order. A more serious problem, however, is disregard of existing statutes—often because officials are reluctant to prosecute when the agencies responsible for investigation are already overburdened far beyond their capacities. One state, for example, which makes an investigation mandatory after placement but before adoption "has a present caseload of 200 investigations per caseworker."

[3] Delaware Code of 1953, vol. 3, title 13, ch. O; Connecticut, Public Act 203, 1958.

THE LAW'S CONCEPTION OF A GOOD HOME

It is clear, then, that American adoption statutes have the welfare of children very much in mind and that they seek to assure through social investigations and other means that children who are to be adopted get into good homes. What, however, are the criteria the laws provide as guidance to the courts in approving or refusing adoption petitions? If, as is frequently the case, the laws have little to say on this point, what criteria are implied in the investigations and in the testimony on the basis of which changes in the adoption laws were made?

It has already been noted that many of the early laws required that the petitioners have the ability to bring up a child and to provide him with suitable nurture and education. Others said the adoption should be "in the interest" or "in the moral and temporal interests" of the child.

Some of the recent laws are more specific. Michigan's 1948 law (sec. 710–1 to 710–14), for instance, says that the purpose of the social investigation is to determine the integrity and health of the petitioners and the stability of their home, the physical and mental health of the child, the child's family background, and the suitability of the child and the adoptive parents on racial, religious, and cultural grounds.

Louisiana's revised statute of 1950 (sec. 9:427) calls for inquiry into "the moral and financial fitness of the petitioners and the conditions of the proposed adoptive home with respect to health, adjustment, and other advantages or disadvantages to the child."

Ohio's 1953 revised statute goes farther in specificity, saying that the investigation shall include "inquiries as to the physical and mental health, emotional stability, and personal integrity of the petitioner, and the ability of the petitioner to promote the welfare of the child." (Title 31:3107)

Further criteria for judging the quality of the homes that petitioners offer children are implied in the findings of early studies of adoptive homes that were made by official and voluntary bodies. Starting with Ohio in 1911, state after state set up a

.nmission to review and codify the laws relating to children, including, of course, those dealing with adoption.[1] Private organizations too (individual social agencies and councils of social agencies) looked into the adoption situation and issued reports. In connection with these activities, several large-scale studies of adoptions were carried on. These studies indicate the sorts of adoptive placements that were deemed undesirable and that would presumably be avoided if a social investigation were required by law.

The first field investigation of adoptions, so far as we could discover, was one made in Chicago in 1917 by the Juvenile Protective Association.[2] This study was directed at the practices of "baby farms," unscrupulous organizations that, for a fee, assumed charge of unwanted babies and "sold" them to would-be adopters. (The fact that such organizations existed probably testifies to a change in the adoption situation: the adoption of infants by persons other than their relatives was becoming popular, and the demand for babies was outrunning the supply.) Shocking abuses and a high incidence of deaths in infancy were found. Among the facts revealed were the following:

> It was found that there was a regular commercialized business of child placing being carried on in the city of Chicago; that there were many maternity hospitals which made regular charges . . . for disposing of unwelcome children; and that there were also doctors and other individuals who took advantage of the unmarried mother willing to pay any amount of money to dispose of her child. . . .
>
> No name, address, or reference was required to secure the custody of a child from these people. Many children placed in this manner were taken by people who could not have secured children through certified child-placing agencies because they were immoral, or wished to procure a child for a fraudulent purpose. . . .

This unfortunate situation could exist, said the investigators, because Illinois "has no law which requires a person who accepts the possession or permanent custody of a child to become legally responsible for its care. It has no law to prevent traffic in children.

---

[1] See Lundberg, Emma, *State Commissions for the Study and Revision of Child-Welfare Laws*, Children's Bureau, Publication No. 131, Washington, 1924.

[2] Quoted in Slingerland, William H., *Child-Placing in Families*. Russell Sage Foundation, New York, 1919, pp. 168–169.

Children may be adopted in any one of three courts, none of which makes adequate investigation."

In 1925 Pennsylvania, through its Children's Commission, conducted the first official investigation of the adequacy of the protection afforded by an adoption law and its administration.[1] In order to determine how children adopted under the existing law fared, information about the home background and present status of children adopted in Philadelphia County between 1919 and 1924 was sought. Such organizations as social agencies, the public schools, and the Philadelphia Housing Association provided relevant facts. The aim of the investigation was not to make a full accounting but to obtain "sufficient information to indicate the major problems from the standpoint of protecting the children involved in the present adoption practice."

It was found that many families who adopted children were "among the best in the city." Some adoptive families, however, were grossly inadequate, exhibiting all manner of social and psychological pathology: crime, immorality, alcoholism, extreme marital discord, mental disorders, severe poverty, cruelty to the children and neglect of their welfare. The investigators made no attempt to estimate what proportion of the children got into very unfavorable homes, saying that this could not be determined from the material at hand, but they cited many examples. They concluded that adoptions that "expose young children to neglect and hardship and an adverse and unsuitable home life do actually and will continue to take place if the adoption process continues to be unattended by the exercise of judgment and discretion on the part of those in authority to decree adoptions."[2]

A companion study, made by the Pennsylvania Department of Public Welfare in Allegheny County and twelve other counties,[3] came to the same conclusion. As examples of the kinds of poor adoptive homes discovered the following may be cited:

One family that had adopted three children lived in an extremely dirty, run-down farm-house and had been on relief. The husband

---

[1] Commission Appointed to Study and Revise the Statutes of Pennsylvania Relating to Children, *Report to the General Assembly Meeting in 1925*, Part I, Appendix I.

[2] *Ibid.*, p. 132; for case examples, see *ibid.*, pp. 92–103, 105–117.

[3] *Ibid.*, Appendix II.

had been arrested several times for bootlegging and was finally sent to jail. All three children showed severe lack of care and training, one was tubercular.

One child was indentured at two years of age and later adopted by a man who had a criminal record, had been discharged from the Army as a constitutional psychopath, and was a bigamist. At the time of this inquiry, he was said to be doing well as a bootlegger.

Another child was found to have been adopted by a prostitute. This adoptive mother was later charged with assault and battery and neglect of the child.

The home conditions of a thirteen-year-old child were discovered when she herself made application to a social agency, saying that her adoptive father had been having sexual relations with her during the last two years. This child had been sold to her adoptive parents by her mother for a quart of whiskey.[1]

The investigators concluded:

The outstanding fact of grave importance is the vast number of children who are adopted through our courts without adequate study of the home from which they come and to which they are going. . . . Laws designed to secure for the child sympathetic and intelligent service for his adequate protection seem to be gravely needed.[2]

On the basis of these and other findings, a draft of a new adoption statute was submitted to the legislature. This, among other points, provided that the judge "may make or cause to be made an investigation . . . to verify the statements in the petition and such other facts as will give the court full knowledge as to the desirability of the proposed adoption."

Two years later a somewhat comparable study was undertaken at the request of the Boston Council of Social Agencies.[3] In 1923 the Massachusetts adoption law had been changed to allow "the appointment by any probate judge of 'a guardian *ad litem* to investigate the facts in any proceeding . . . as to the care, custody, or maintenance of minor children.' " In 1924 a further amendment made it possible for "the probate judges of Suffolk

---

[1] Condensed from case material cited in *ibid.*, pp. 147–152.

[2] *Ibid.*, pp. 146, 157.

[3] Parker, Ida R., "*Fit and Proper*"? *A Study of Legal Adoption in Massachusetts*. The Church Home Society, Boston, 1927.

County [Boston] to appoint a permanent officer to perform the duties prescribed in the original act and 'such other duties as said judges may determine.' "[1] Nevertheless, a review of adoptions granted in Suffolk and Norfolk Counties at the time of the study still showed many poor placements.

Among the cases which this study cited as illustrative of unsuitable homes were the following: In one case the adoptive parents, both illiterate, were said to be well known in the neighborhood for drinking and immorality. In another, the adoptive mother, who had taken babies to board, had been refused more children because she had become partially paralyzed and was extremely nervous and irritable. She thereupon adopted a three-months-old baby. Another adoptive home's unsuitability for adoption was evidenced by the complaints neighbors made of the mother's abuse of the adopted infant. Another's was shown by the fact that the adopted child had been shifted back and forth between her own mother, who was mentally defective and of "loose moral standards," and the adoptive parents, who quarreled frequently and failed to provide properly for her. The author of the Massachusetts study concluded:

> The facts at hand warrant the statement that the foster parents varied greatly in their ability to carry the responsibilities inherent in adoption. . . . Some of the adoptive parents were people of sound character and intelligence who recognized the seriousness of voluntarily becoming . . . the parents of a child of other blood. . . . Others apparently did not reckon the cost of upbringing in terms of effort, patience, money or sacrifice and soon tired of their undertaking. Still others were totally unfit because of ignorance, lack of understanding of their duties, insufficient income, mental defect or instability, or vicious habits to be entrusted with a child's life.[2]

Thoroughly unsatisfactory homes were found (as was the case in the Pennsylvania studies also) among those provided by relatives and those provided by strangers, as well as among those in which social agencies arranged the placement and among those arranged without such help.

---

[1] *Ibid.*, p. 8.
[2] *Ibid.*, p. 60.

A second study of adoptions in Massachusetts, conducted by a special Commission in 1930, showed much the same situation.[1] Among the unsatisfactory adoptive parents found in this investigation, the report cites "a woman of questionable character with a long court record; a couple who neglected their own children; a family already broken by the vice of the father; people without financial ability or moral standards; feeble-minded mothers."

On the basis of these findings the Commission recommended that the Department of Welfare be notified of all petitions for the adoption of children under fourteen years of age and that it make appropriate inquiry and report to the court all essential facts regarding the child and the petitioners, so that the court may be fully informed as to whether the child is a proper subject for adoption and whether the proposed adoption is calculated to best serve the welfare of the child.[2]

These follow-up studies[3] make clear both what the legal requirement of a social investigation was designed to remedy and what manner of homes were deemed unsuitable. With regard to the latter point, not only were extreme poverty, immorality, and criminality to be avoided but the judges' attention was also to be called to low intelligence, physical and mental afflictions, "obviously unsuitable temperament," "serious personal and social problems," and (as one study put it) to inability to give children the affection and understanding they require. As the Massachusetts Commission said, "This proposed service to the court would not in any way restrict its freedom of judgment, but, by putting the court in possession of all pertinent facts, would help prevent such evils."[4]

In summary, this review of the origin and development of American adoption laws shows that, from the outset, most laws

---

[1] *Report of the Special Commission Established to Investigate the Laws Relative to Dependent, Neglected, and Delinquent Children and Children Otherwise Requiring Special Care,* January, 1931 (House No. 1200), quoted in Breckinridge, Sophonisba, *op. cit.,* pp. 403 ff.

[2] *Ibid.,* p. 403.

[3] English studies also showed children adopted into unsuitable homes because the court lacked facilities to investigate: *Report of the Departmental Committee on Adoption Societies and Agencies,* H.M. Stationery Office, London, 1937; *Report of the Care of Children Committee,* H.M. Stationery Office, London, 1946.

[4] Breckinridge, Sophonisba, *op. cit.,* p. 403.

(at least as interpreted judicially) have had the welfare of the children as their main purpose. As a means of promoting the children's well-being, the laws seek to assure that adoption is in the children's interest and that they are adopted by persons who are able and willing to provide adequately for their care. To aid the Court in making these determinations in individual cases, the social investigation procedure has been instituted.

The adoption law, then, sets a standard against which the accomplishments of the independent adoption process (or of any other adoption process) can be assessed. To evaluate this process we have to determine the extent to which it succeeds in securing homes of the sorts considered good for children and how well the children fare in these adoptive homes, as judged by their social-emotional adjustment.

By answering the second of these two questions and relating it to the first, the part of the standard that prescribes that adoptive parents shall have such-and-such characteristics can itself be evaluated. As our review has shown, the law's conception of what parental qualities are needed to make an adoptive home good has broadened over the years but is still far from precise. A major research task, then, is to discover which parental traits significantly enhance adopted children's chance of adjusting well.

CHAPTER II

Independent Adoptions in Florida[1]

As a step toward answering the question of how successful the independent adoption process is in achieving the purpose of adoption law, a ten-year follow-up study of independent adoptions granted in Florida during the years 1944 to 1947 was undertaken in 1956. Particularly at issue was whether social investigations provide a sufficient safeguard to children when their adoption is sought. Since the answer to that question depends in part on who conducts the investigations (and when and how and under what conditions) and on what the courts' attitudes are toward the findings, a review of the Florida situation in this respect is a necessary preface to the study.

FLORIDA'S 1943 ADOPTION ACT

Florida is a state that was rather late in revising its adoption law so as to make the welfare of children a primary concern. Such a law was enacted in Florida in 1943, supplanting the original act of 1885.

Movement toward such a change had begun in the early twenties. At that time Florida, following the example of other states, set up a Children's Code Commission to review its child welfare laws. After study, the Commission mapped out a ten-year program of legislation in the field of child welfare. Little was done, however, until 1941, when the Commission's leg-

---

[1] Based on a paper written by Margaret Ward, Supervisor of Adoption Services, Child Welfare Division, Florida Department of Public Welfare.

islative program was taken up by the state administration as the basis for action and was hastily added to and elaborated. Many proposals for child welfare legislation were considered; among them an adoption bill was given top priority. This bill, with certain compromises, was enacted in 1943.

The adoption bill was drawn along lines then suggested by the U.S. Children's Bureau, and the enacted law retained many of the recommended features. The law begins with the following "declaration of policy":

> SECTION 1. DECLARATION OF POLICY. The State Welfare Board for the purpose of adoption is hereby designated the official and proper guardian for all minor children of this State who have no natural parents, or who have been abandoned by their natural parents, or whose natural parents have voluntarily surrendered their rights as parents, and who have no legal guardian, and who have not been permanently committed to a licensed child placing agency. In the event of such permanent commitments, the licensed placing agency to which such children have been so committed is hereby designated the official and proper custodian and guardian of such children.

Subsequent sections of the law provide that as soon as a petition is filed, the Clerk of the Court shall mail a copy of it to the State Welfare Board[1], as well as to the licensed child-placing agency if the child is in its custody. Written consent of the child's own parents to the adoption is required if the child was born in wedlock; of its mother only, if born out of wedlock. The statement of consent must be signed before a notary public and in the presence of two witnesses. It can be dispensed with only if the child has already been legally committed to the care of a licensed child-placing agency, in which case the agency consents to the adoption.

The provision for social investigation is stated as follows:[2]

> SECTION 9. SOCIAL INVESTIGATION AND RECOMMENDATIONS. Upon or prior to the filing of a petition for the adoption of any minor child, a study shall be made of all pertinent details relating to such child

---

[1] The governing board of the Department of Public Welfare.

[2] The legal provisions referred to here and in the next few paragraphs were in effect when the adoptions included in this study took place. Some of the provisions were subsequently amended.

for the purpose of ascertaining whether he is a proper subject for adoption, and to the petitioner or petitioners, to determine whether they are suitable persons to adopt such child. If the child sought to be adopted has previously been permanently committed to a licensed child-placing agency, the social study shall be made by such agency, otherwise by the State Welfare Board. Written recommendations as to the desirability of the adoption shall be filed by such agency making such study or by the State Welfare Board, as the case may be, but such recommendations shall not contain any statement of fact or other evidence upon which recommendations are based. Thereupon such agency or the State Welfare Board, as the case may be, shall be deemed a party to the cause.

Other provisions in the 1943 Act allowed sixty days, following the filing of the petition, for the social investigation and required that the State Welfare Board or the licensed child-placing agency be notified of the time and place of the court hearing. After hearing the petition, the Court has the choice of dismissing the petition, continuing the hearing for further investigation, or entering an interlocutory order of adoption, granting temporary custody of the child to the petitioners. During this interlocutory period of not more than one year, the child resides in the home of the petitioners but is under the supervision of the Welfare Department or the licensed social agency that placed him in the home.

Within a month after the end of the interlocutory period, the supervising agency is required to file supplementary recommendations on the advisability of the adoption, notice of which is given to all parties in the case. These parties may file supplementary answers or objections within the same period of time. If, at this final hearing, it appears to the Court that the petitioners are "fit and proper persons" to adopt the child, that the "best interests of the child would be promoted by the adoption," and that the child is "suitable for adoption by the petitioners," a decree of adoption is entered. The Court may, however, continue the case from time to time or dismiss it.

The changes in adoption law brought about by the Act were highly controversial in the state at the time it was passed. Previously the statutes had permitted transfer of custody of children by gift and surrender, either by will or deed, or by indenture. The state's former adoption statute required of the petitioners only that, first, they announce their intention to adopt by inserting a notice for four weeks in the newspaper of the county where they resided; and, second, that they file a petition with the Court giving the child's age and their reasons for wanting to adopt. The judge would then appoint a guardian *pendente lite* to represent the child at the hearing. The judge had the authority to grant the adoption at his discretion after hearing the petition and evidence. In practice, the guardians were usually attorneys. In most cases they made no investigation of the situation or only a cursory one. Adoptions were usually granted within a day or so after the hearing.

The new adoption bill had the backing of the State Welfare Board, itself a rather recent innovation. This Board had among its chief duties studying welfare needs, particularly those of children. The bill was also supported by the Dade County Council of Social Agencies and the State Parent-Teachers Association. The Children's Code Advisory Committee was also largely in favor of the bill, though some members doubted the need for such a law. This commission, representative of educational, health, and welfare interests in the state, had recently been appointed by the Governor to counsel him on legislation affecting children. Aside from these supporters, the bill had few friends, and its passage was bitterly fought.

The opposition to the bill centered chiefly on the social investigation and supervision features, which were so different from the previous arrangements. The following excerpts from testimony taken at the legislative hearings on the bill show the nature of the opposition's argument:

> It is unadvisable to grant such broad powers to the State Welfare Board, subject as it necessarily is to political influence and changing administrations.
>
> The state should place as few impediments as reasonably possible in the way of those willing to provide a home for an unfortunate child. The proposed bill contains too many such impediments.
>
> The proposed bill disregards the fundamental principles that the very foundation of adoption is surrounding the child and the adopting parents with every protection afforded by the utmost secrecy.
>
> Why should adopting parents who deliberately and voluntarily assume the legal status of parents toward a particular child be sub-

jected, under the guise of serving the welfare of the child, to governmental supervision and inspection of their homes and personal lives?

It is easy to see that if onerous burdens are placed upon that great class of the good people of our state standing ready to open their homes to helpless and needy children with the idea of giving those children the names and legal status of natural children, this great class to which I have referred will shrink in size and fewer homes will be available to the children who are in great need of those homes and of the rights and privileges that would be theirs but for the burden of bureaucratic control.

The proponents of the bill, in contrast, expected great things from it. So-called "model" or "modern" adoption laws had already been enacted in many states, following upon the wide publicity that had been given to abuses under antiquated adoption statutes. Studies and surveys of the sort reported in Chapter I had provided some striking illustrations of abuses and of violations of the rights and interests of natural parents and adopted children. The State Welfare Board depended largely on information secured from such studies for its arguments regarding the need for the new law, but it had, as confirmatory evidence, the findings of a study of legal notices of pending adoptions appearing in Florida newspapers. This study supported the idea that social investigation preceding adoption decree was needed, for there seemed to be a considerable number of unsuitable petitions among those listed in the newspapers. It was particularly feared that some bright children were being adopted in order to exploit their talents; that others were being taken for their usefulness as farm laborers or as apprentices; that some were being used as companions for invalids or to satisfy the pathological needs of inadequate individuals.

The Florida Welfare Board[1], like welfare boards in other states, hoped that social investigation before legal adoption could serve as a substitute for the protection afforded the various parties by child-placement agencies. The Board's responsibility under the proposed law was conceived as that of investigating, applying

---

[1] The name was later changed to the Department of Public Welfare to distinguish it from the State Welfare Board, the Governing Board.

generally accepted criteria, and recommending denial if adoption seemed questionable. After the bill was passed, this expectation was modified to take account of the heated controversy over the bill and the Board's own limited staff resources. Even so, the Board for some time continued to expect that its work could be carried on in a more satisfactory way as soon as more favorable attitudes toward it had been established.

THE WELFARE BOARD'S POLICIES AND FINDINGS UNDER THE 1943 ACT

The policies that the Department of Public Welfare, with the approval of the Board, decided upon for carrying out its responsibilities under the 1943 Act were influenced both by the skeptical attitudes of many judges, attorneys, and private citizens and by the small size of its child welfare staff and its financial resources. The agency had been in existence for only fourteen years and had had a child welfare service program only since 1937. This program was a small one, supported largely by federal funds. Only eight counties had child welfare workers, the other 59 being served by public assistance workers, most of whom had not had professional social work training.

The Department's first policy decision was an unavoidable one. The social investigations for the Court would be conducted and the supervision of children during the interlocutory period would be carried on by public assistance workers in the counties. This work, however, was done under rather strict control from the state office. In that office the adoption studies made by the county workers were reviewed and recommendations to the courts formulated by the Consultant on Adoption in the Division of Child Welfare. This made possible a close, overall scrutiny of the program and more uniformity in administration than could have been achieved under local control.

To counter the opposition to the law and to try to secure a more favorable attitude toward its provisions and toward social workers' capacity to make valid recommendations, two other policies were decided upon. The first was to enlist the voluntary services of attorneys favorable to the Act, to serve as associate counsels for the Department. In this capacity, these attorneys could appear with the Department's representatives at adoption hearings on dubious cases and help to explain to the Court their findings and recommendations.

The other policy had to do with the kind of recommendations the Department would make. In view of the situation, internal and external, the Department decided not to make negative recommendations concerning adoptions except for reasons commonly recognized as detrimental to children. It might have gone farther and advised against adoption, for instance, if the petitioners seemed to have emotional disabilities that would probably affect children's development adversely. As it was, such recommendations were made especially difficult by the unavoidable use of untrained social workers for gathering the needed information and making the pertinent observations.

With these policies as guides, the Department embarked on its first year of work. Its chief discovery in that year was that the number of grossly unsuitable placements was small. Nothing like the expected number of shockingly inappropriate homes was found, and only a very few homes and children had the kinds of disabilities reported in the early studies of adoption. This finding was not taken to imply that these studies were wrong, but rather that the social and economic changes in the United States during the twenty years since the studies were made had altered the situation greatly. In all, the Board in that first year made negative recommendations in only 13 cases (2 per cent) out of the 636 it investigated. This was in addition to a few cases in which unsuitable petitioners were persuaded to withdraw.

The number of unfavorable recommendations that would have been made if the standards used by adoption agencies had been applied was considerably higher but, even so, not large. An experiment carried on by the Department in one section of the state gives some indication of what that proportion might have been. In that experiment the adoption investigations were made by a professionally trained social worker who had had recent experience in a private adoption agency. Her estimate was that from 80 to 90 per cent of the petitions she investigated were acceptable by social agency standards; in other words, that approximately 15 per cent would have entailed adverse recommendations to the Court. While this was far from a negligible proportion, the study indicated that the proportion of satisfactory placements was certainly higher than expected. On the other hand, it suggested a large discrepancy between what social investigation was accomplishing and what (in the Department's opinion at least) it should have accomplished.

Another early discovery was the usefulness of social investigations for detecting legal omissions or irregularities in the petitions. It was the attorneys acting as associate counsels who developed this aspect of the Department's work. During the first year of administration of the law, as was true to some extent in subsequent years, such defects were found in approximately one-third of the cases. These had to do with consent, notice, and jurisdiction; if uncorrected, they might have endangered the legality of the adoptions. For instance, the petitioners and their lawyer might say, correctly, that the whereabouts of the child's parents were unknown to them. In some such cases the Department, through its own resources or those of other social agencies, was able to locate the natural parents so that they could be notified of the pending adoption. Thus the natural parents' rights with respect to the child could be determined by the Court, safeguarding them and the child and protecting the petitioners against later litigation.

By the end of the year, too, the Department was beginning to realize the overall usefulness of the information the investigators provided about adoptions taking place throughout the state. Up to that time, information about adoptions was almost wholly lacking; not even was the annual number public information Now facts were at hand to indicate what sorts of people were adopting children, how and from whom they obtained them, why the children were being given up by their own parents, and so on. All of these facts were very pertinent to the Department's responsibility for guarding the welfare of children.

Besides these discoveries about the usefulness of social investigations, the Department soon found in the law two deficiencies that handicapped its services. The first was a provision that limited the Department's written recommendations to a flat "yes" or "no" and did not permit the giving of reasons in writing. Information about reasons could be presented orally at the hearings. This, however, required already overworked and inexperienced public assistance workers or representatives from the state office to appear at court hearings in scattered localities, often at inconvenient times, and therefore oral presentation of evidence was usually impossible. Moreover, this oral testimony had to be given in the presence of the petitioners, a requirement certain to produce many awkward situations, to say the least. This provision of the law was altered in 1947 to permit the Department to file with the Court a report of its findings, but it was not in effect throughout the period dealt with by the study reported in this book.

The second legal deficiency lay in the fact that circuit courts, which heard adoption petitions, did not have specific authority to remove children from the petitioners' homes when they disallowed adoptions. Some judges held that the courts did have this authority on the basis of their broad duties and responsibilities regarding children. Many, however, did not agree with this opinion. Adoption, therefore, could be denied but the child might still remain in an unsuitable home, without the benefits that legal adoption might afford. The only recourse the Department of Public Welfare had in such cases was to file a complaint of neglect in the juvenile court and possibly secure the removal of the child by this means.

This second deficiency in the law was also remedied in 1947, when specific authority was given to the circuit courts to remove children from the petitioners' homes if petitions were dismissed. In the meantime, and during the period this study covers, the Department's policy was to try to persuade some clearly unqualified petitioners to relinquish the children voluntarily and withdraw their petitions instead of coming before the Court. Voluntary withdrawal of a petition was often accomplished more easily than might be thought possible. Some petitioners were themselves dubious about wanting to adopt the child, particularly if it was the investigator's opinion that the child was not suitable for adoption by reason of serious physical or mental defect. Others after discussion were able to recognize their personal problems (for instance, excessive drinking or marital discord) and to realize either that they should not proceed with the adoption or that there was little chance that the Court would rule in their favor.

In addition to these legal deficiencies, two major limitations to the effectiveness of social investigation of independent adoption petitions became increasingly apparent as the Department's experience with the law grew.

One limitation is inherent in a social investigation that takes place after a child has been in the petitioners' home for some time. On this point the Supervisor of Adoption Services wrote in 1944:

> Some of the placements were not entirely satisfactory but in many of the cases the child had been in the family over a rather long period, the ties with "own" family and relatives were broken and, in some instances, no trace of the own family could be found, thus making a change of plan for the child much less plausible.

The other limitation was difficulty in substantiating recommendations of dismissal. On this the Adoption Consultant commented:

> It is apparent that many independent adoptions are made without sufficient inquiry and upon examination are found to be not actually desirable but merely passable. However, the difficulty in substantiating, to the satisfaction of the court, negative recommendations, especially those based on personality factors alone, is evident.

The experience of later years and a review by the Board of the nonrelative independent adoption petitions from 1943 to 1947 reinforced these early observations about the law's limitations. The Board's report concluded: "While only a very small percentage of independent adoptions is sufficiently unsuitable for the agency to recommend dismissal, it is evident that a number of criteria considered essential by placement agencies are not adhered to."

Despite the Department's doubts as to the adequacy of social-investigation procedure, many judges, attorneys, and others regarded it as a sufficient safeguard to the parties concerned. To provide facts by which either to counter this opinion or to quiet their own doubts, the Department administrators decided that a comprehensive, systematic study of the outcome of independent adoptions in their state should be undertaken. Such a study seemed especially needed because no adequate study of this sort, which might furnish a base for a realistic appraisal of policies and practices, had been made in any state. To ensure impartiality, a research team from outside the state and under unbiased sponsorship was sought. The result is the study reported in this book.

CHAPTER III

How the Study Was Made

This report, which is a follow-up study of independent adoptions granted in Florida from 1944 to 1947, seeks answers to three main questions:

1. How do the independent adoptions made under the Florida system about ten years ago seem to be working out?

2. What, if any, factors in the adoptive home, in the adopted child and his background, in the way the adoption was arranged distinguish placements that work out well from those that have an unsatisfactory outcome?

3. Which, if any, of these factors are determinable at the time of the social investigation, and on what sorts of evidence can a determination be made?

From the answers to these questions the Department hoped to be able to determine whether the social investigation provision of the Florida adoption law, as carried out, provides sufficient protection for children and adoptive parents; what changes, if any, should be made in the Department's mode of work in this area; whether adoption agencies should be urged to alter some of the criteria and procedures they use in selecting adoptive homes for children who are in their care.

The Children's Bureau had somewhat broader reasons for engaging in the study. It viewed this investigation as the first in a series that would eventually provide much-needed information on the effects and effectiveness of various kinds of adoption laws and procedures. In the present investigation a methodology would be worked out and tested, and, it was hoped, the ground laid for conducting such investigations more efficiently and more accurately in the future. It was hoped also that the research problems posed by the investigation would enlarge the interest of social scientists in practical studies, and that the findings of the study would incite other states and agencies to examine the results of their own adoption work.

Two questions about adoption, frequently asked and of great importance, will not be answered by this study. These concern (1) the success of independent adoptions as compared with those arranged by social agencies, and (2) the effects of adoption on children.

As to the first question, suitable material for such a comparison did not exist in Florida. To be meaningful, findings of adoption outcome should be based on placements made a number of years earlier. But at the time to which the present study applies there were few placement agencies in Florida, and those that did exist were not generally considered representative of approved social work practice. The very scarcity of agency placements, however, offered one advantage for this first large-scale study of independent adoptions. The absence of opportunity for agency adoptions meant that the independent placements in Florida during the study period probably covered nearly the full range of adoptive parents, instead of only those who would not or could not secure children through a social agency. That is, the effects of adoption practice would be less likely to be obscured by differences between the kinds of people who adopt a child through an agency and the kinds who adopt one independently.

The absence of this comparison was not a matter of choice. It needs to be made, and the sooner the better. However, the questions the present study attempts to answer are crucial in their own right; and inability to make the desired comparison for Florida does involve the one advantage noted.

The second question that cannot be answered by the present study concerns the effects of adoption on children. For such a study there would be needed a control group of nonadopted children and their families who were like the adopted children and their adoptive families in respects that bear significantly on children's adjustment. The present study does contain a matched control group of nonadopted children but the information that could be obtained about them referred only to their school adjustment and performance, not to their home situation. Such a comparison also needs to be made. To be fully useful, however, it should be made with agency as well as independent adoptions, so that it would be possible to determine whether differences, if found, relate to the adoptive status itself or to the way in which the adoption came about.

These limitations were inherent in the study as planned, and in its purposes. They are mentioned here so that the reader will not expect information beyond the limits originally set up.

TESTS OF FEASIBILITY

Before working out detailed plans or trying to get financial support for the study, the Department made a number of checks to determine the availability of the material called for and the feasibility of the general research conception. These preliminary checks showed: that although the records of the Department's social investigations lacked certain kinds of information usually found in records written by trained caseworkers, they did contain factual information sufficiently complete and consistent to permit tabulation and comparison; that probably at least half of the desired sample of adoptive parents were still living in Florida and that their home addresses could be found; that most adoptive parents would be willing to be interviewed, willing to have their children given psychological tests in school, and willing to have their doctors consulted about medical information.

It was found, too, that the Florida Department of Education was interested in the project and was ready to stimulate full cooperation by the schools—an essential ingredient of the study plan. The Welfare Department had previously secured an official opinion from the Attorney General of the state that the confidentiality section of the Florida adoption statute would not interfere with the contemplated research, also that the Florida statutes both authorized the Department to receive and accept aid for the study and offered no obstacles regarding its financial aspects and the employment status of the research staff.

THE SAMPLE

On the basis of preliminary calculations, a target sample of 500 was decided upon as the minimum that would allow for the necessary division into subgroups for statistical comparison and the maximum that our resources were likely to permit.

Defining the Sample

In theory, a sample for a study of this sort should be drawn from all nonrelative independent adoptions in the state during the time period under study. Practical considerations, however, made it necessary to define the population somewhat more sharply. Three limitations were set:

1. Age of the Child. In order to know how placements were working out it was desirable to have the child as old as possible at the time of the investigation. Nine years was set as the highest minimum that would give the numbers needed and at the same time provide a picture of outcome that offered a reasonable basis for assessment.

The sixteenth birthday was set as the upper age limit; no child in the sample was to be older than fifteen. The major reason for this upper limit was the decision to examine the children in school. After age sixteen some children leave school, a fact that introduces a number of complicating factors in addition to the difficulty of finding them.

With these limits in mind, it was determined that the sample would be drawn from placements made during the years 1944 to 1947. This meant that no child could be younger than nine years at the time the home interviewing was done in 1956 and 1957.

2. Race. In Florida, during the years under study, there were very few independent adoptions of children who did not belong to the white race. If children of other races had been included in the sample, there would not have been enough cases to hold constant the influence of racial factors when testing relations between variables, and the findings of the study might have been confused by this fact. We therefore decided to limit the sample to white children.

3. Locatability. The period selected for study meant that at least nine years had elapsed since the adoptive parents were known to be living in Florida. During this time a considerable number would have moved out of the state. To follow families all over the country, making necessary arrangements with widely scattered schools and moving a research team across great distances, would have involved time and expense beyond the resources of the study and probably out of proportion to the value of keeping the sample "pure." Accordingly, the sample was restricted to adoptive families still living in Florida.

These three limitations narrowed the definition of the population to be sampled from that of "independent adoptions in Florida" to "white independent adoptions in Florida that were completed in the years 1944 to 1947, in which the child was no older than fifteen when the follow-up data were gathered and the family still resided in the state." This definition satisfied the methodological and practical conditions of the study and at the same time accounted for the majority of all adoptions completed during the study period.

Setting Up the Sample

The first step for translating this definition into an actual sample was to compile a list of all adoption petitions granted during the years 1944 to 1947, identified by case number—a total of 1,628. Beginning with a randomly selected case, every tenth case number was selected until 500 were drawn. An additional 500 were drawn in the same manner, to be used as alternates for cases that had to be eliminated. To indicate their order of inclusion, these were numbered serially as drawn.

Forty names had to be eliminated from the list because the children were over fifteen, and 29 because the families were not white. The final list was then set up, using the following "tests" of locatability.

1. All cases were checked against the telephone book and city directory (if available) of the town or city in which the family

lived at the time the petition was granted. If the exact names of husband or wife appeared, the family was regarded as located.

2. The names of all remaining families were sent to each of the 79 District Offices of the Florida Department of Public Welfare, where they were checked against the telephone books and city directories in the district. Thus, the telephone book and city directory for each town and city in the state were examined. If the exact name of both husband and wife appeared, the case was regarded as located. If only one name was found, it was verified by telephone. In all, 432 families were located through telephone books and city directories.

3. All remaining unlocated cases were checked against the district files of the Florida Department of Welfare to determine if the families were currently receiving services or were personally known to the staff. Thirteen families were located in this way.

4. All remaining unlocated cases were checked against the driver's license register of the state (licenses are renewed yearly in Florida). Fifty-five additional cases were located by this means.

Of the 500 original sample cases, 404 children were located by the steps just described. It was necessary to check 134 alternate case numbers in order to locate the 96 children needed to bring the sample up to 500. Thirty-five additional alternates were also included to compensate for those thought to be located who might have moved recently or have been identified incorrectly. The field operations revealed 47 such children. In addition, they revealed four cases where the petition had been dismissed and the cases had been included in the sample by mistake. Thus, out of 665 children whom we tried to locate, 484 (73 per cent) were found still living in Florida.[1]

In view of the length of time between the granting of the petition and the gathering of data for the study, and the unusual mobility of many families during and after World War II, the proportion located would seem remarkably high and may be encouraging to others who plan to conduct follow-up studies.

---

[1] Since the sampling unit was adoptions rather than families, "cases" refers to children. Seven families had more than one adopted child in the sample, so that the number of *families* located was 477.

Was the Sample Representative?

The fact that 27 per cent of the families looked for were not found underlined the importance of checking for differences between the located and the unlocated. Accordingly a careful comparison was made between them, with respect to various kinds of information. This review, described below, led us to conclude that the differences between the located and unlocated were probably unimportant.

Very early in the planning it was agreed that data would be secured from several sources: (1) records of the social investigations conducted by the Welfare Department, to secure a picture of the placement process and the adoptive parents at the time the child first entered their home; (2) interviews with adoptive parents, to assess the present adoptive homes; (3) school records, present teachers' ratings, and psychological tests of children's adjustment, administered in the classrooms, to get some indication of how the children were getting along. The methods used in obtaining this information will be described in later chapters.

Records. The early adoption records were available for all the children in the selected group, the unlocated as well as the located. This was to be expected but it was also fortunate, since it permitted comparison of those who were located and those who were not, in order to discover any systematic differences that might distort our picture of adoption outcomes. The proportion of nonlocated cases is small enough that it would require a considerable difference to change materially the picture of outcome derived from the sample. Nevertheless, in order to generalize from our sample to the total population from which it was drawn it was necessary to determine whether and in what ways the nonlocated cases differed from the located. The only available basis for such a comparison lay in the records of the initial investigations.

The located and nonlocated cases were compared on relevant items that could be determined from these records. No statistically significant differences were found for the following: parents' socioeconomic characteristics, prior efforts to adopt through an agency, payment of natural mother's hospital expenses, marital history of adoptive parents, their expressed motivation for adopting, adoptive mother's participation in the labor force, children's age and sex distributions, age at placement, living arrangements before placement, and natural mother's education. Moreover, no significant differences were found in the evaluation of the adoptive families, either by the State Welfare Board or by staff members of adoption agencies who, in the course of the present study, rated a subsample of records drawn from located and unlocated cases.

Statistically significant differences[1] were found for six items. Perhaps the key difference was the disproportionate number of adoptive fathers in the nonlocated group who were in military service at the time of adoption: about one in four (27 per cent), as compared with about one in twenty of the located. The majority of the servicemen who adopted children in Florida at that time came from other states, and only one-third of them were living in Florida when our study was made.

Some characteristics of servicemen may account for other statistically significant differences between the located and the nonlocated families. For example, adoptive parents in the nonlocated group were younger on the average than those who were located. The average age of located fathers was 38.3 years; of nonlocated, 35.7 years. The average age of located mothers was 34.3 years; of nonlocated, 32.4 years. Some of this difference is probably accounted for by the younger average age of servicemen.

The younger average age of parents in the nonlocated group probably accounts for another difference. On the average, the nonlocated couples had been married for a shorter time before they took the child for adoption—6.3 years as compared with 7.3 years for the located.

The final significant difference between the located and nonlocated families has to do with the way in which the adoptions

---

[1] "Statistically significant," an expression which will be used repeatedly throughout the study, means that it is very unlikely that a difference of this size would have happened by chance. The chance of such a happening in the present instance was less than one in a hundred samples similarly drawn. In no case called statistically significant in this study was the chance over 5 in 100. It should be emphasized that the universe of significance is the locatable cases that conform to the specifications already given.

were arranged and whether there had been direct contact with the natural parents. Direct negotiation with the natural parents was relatively more frequent in the nonlocated group (33 per cent compared with 24 per cent), while those who were located were more likely to have arranged the placement through a professional person—usually, a doctor.

These differences in "arranger" account for the fact that a significantly larger proportion of the nonlocated (52 per cent) than of the located (38 per cent) had direct contact with the natural parents. When doctors or lawyers arranged the placements, the adoptive and natural parents usually did not meet. When natural parents or close relatives made the arrangements, direct contact with the adoptive parents was almost inevitable.

None of the available comparisons suggests that the distribution of outcomes would be substantially different if information had been obtained about the nonlocated families. Moreover, the heterogeneous nature of the items on which the two groups differ makes it appear unlikely that the overall findings for the unlocated families would differ significantly from those based on the ones who were located.

Parents' Willingness to Be Interviewed

Home interviews were held with the parents of 438 children.[1] The families lived in 78 different localities in Florida.

Most of the interviews were held with mothers. Our preference would have been to interview both parents, first separately and then together, but this procedure was beyond the resources of the study, so no systematic effort was made to interview fathers. It was hoped that through discussion with the adoptive mother an adequate picture would be obtained of the father, his role in the family, and his relations with both mother and child. Actually, in 152 cases (35 per cent of those interviewed) the father was present for all or part of the time. There was a slight

---

[1] Since the unit is adoptions, rather than families, and since relations between traits were analyzed in terms of home information as compared with outside information about each child, we shall refer to 438 home interviews—even though in several cases information about two children was obtained from one home. (See footnote, p. 60.) In these few cases one parent, in effect, gave two interviews—one concerning each child.

tendency for homes to be given higher ratings in these cases, the mean rating being 3.46 as compared with 3.08 for those in which the father was not present.[1]

It might be speculated that the fathers who made an effort to participate in the interview were more interested and active in the family life than those who did not; or that the wife spoke less frankly when the husband was there. The father's presence at the interview shows no significant correlations, however, with other variables describing him and his role in the family. Accordingly, a question remains about the meaning of the systematic difference observed. Perhaps the distribution of home ratings would have differed slightly if all fathers could have been interviewed. This question underlines the desirability of interviewing both parents whenever possible.

Forty-six families (10 per cent of the 477 families located) refused to be interviewed. In view of the intense feelings surrounding adoption, the low refusal rate bears testimony to the ability of the field staff in securing cooperation. Many other follow-up studies have shown that highly skilled staff and careful methods of approach usually result in a high response rate.

In ten of these 46 cases, the refusal was made on the worker's first call. Even those who delayed making a decision were doubtful from the beginning. Two made appointments but canceled them, either when the interviewer went to the home or when she found it necessary to call and change the date. A number put off saying "no" until the fourth, fifth, or sixth telephone call.

The manner of refusal varied. The majority of the refusals were courteous, but six mothers were abrupt and nine were angry, accusing, and belligerent, objecting to the invasion of privacy, to discussing "these things" and "stirring things up again" now that all was settled. No relation was found between the manner of refusal and such information as was available about the child and family.

Five mothers gave no reason for refusing the interview, but an equal number expressed fear that the child would discover

---

[1] Expressed as a correlation, $r = .13$, and thus would account for only about 2 per cent of the variance in the home rating distribution. The meaning of the home ratings and how they were made is described in detail in Chapter VI.

he was adopted, and several others seemed to imply a similar fear. Eight mothers merely reported that the adoptive father objected.

The refusal rate would probably have been lower had the study not entered the Miami area just at the time when an adoption case in the court there was receiving a great deal of local and nationwide publicity. Three parents explicitly linked their refusal to fear that someone might try to wrest their child from them, and others gave reasons that might stem from such a fear.

It seems possible that a larger proportion of children in the refusal group than of those whose parents granted an interview were unaware that they had been adopted. If so, this is the only material difference to which we have any clue. When the early placement records of the families refusing an interview were compared with those of the interviewed sample, no significant differences between the families were found. Nor, with one exception, did the children whose parents refused to be interviewed differ from the others with respect to their scores on the various psychological tests that were given by our staff.[1] In this one exception the difference between average scores was statistically significant but slight.

Information About Children's Adjustment

Psychological test data (described in Chapter X) were secured for 448 children in 412 classrooms of 295 schools scattered throughout the state. It was possible to obtain from school records Achievement Test data for 377 of these children and I.Q. information for 360. The tests used were not uniform, however, nor were they all administered at the same point in the child's school life. This information was unobtainable for the other children, either because school records were not available or because they did not include Achievement Test and I.Q. reports.

School information was lacking for 24 children because school officials were unwilling to cooperate with the study. That 19 of these 24 children attended parochial schools may have

---

[1] As a group, children whose parents refused an interview showed less than average "withdrawn maladjustment"—a difference small but statistically significant. Their overall adjustment ratings were like those of the other children. See Chapters X and XI for description of psychological tests of personality and overall adjustment ratings.

created a slight sampling bias, though the effects on our findings could not have been substantial. The other missing cases were accounted for by miscellaneous reasons, such as a child being absent from school, attending school out of the state, being too retarded to test, and so forth.

For some of the children whose parents were interviewed it was not possible to obtain psychological test and other school material; and for some whose parents could not be interviewed, school information was obtained. Both home interview and psychological test materials were obtained for 411 children, and comparisons between home and school information are limited to this number. Analysis of home information without reference to school information draws on home interviews concerning 438 children; and separate analysis of school information draws on the tests secured for 448 children.

On the whole, except for the children in parochial schools, the reasons for failure to obtain school information concerning all 438 of the children whose parents were interviewed seem heterogeneous enough to make unlikely any substantial distortion of findings based on comparison of home and school data, or on the results of school information concerning all those for whom it was available. Nor does it seem likely that the variation in base number introduces inconsistencies into our findings.

Although, as has been said, no attempt was made to secure control groups of parents, comparative data about the social and emotional adjustment of children were obtained. The control group was drawn from the adopted children's classmates and was selected at the time the psychological tests were administered. The process of selection is described in more detail in Chapter X, in which the findings are reported. Matching was done on the basis of sex, race, school grade (and thus roughly on age), and socioeconomic status as indicated by the father's occupation.

THE STUDY STAFF

The planning and research guidance of the study came from the Research Division of the Children's Bureau. The field staff consisted of:

Field director (psychiatric social worker)

Six interviewers (social caseworkers who had specialized in child welfare work)[1]

Chief psychologist (for initial phase only)

Three psychological research assistants (college graduates who had majored in psychology)

Two secretaries

One "arranger" (a person hired, on a temporary basis, to set up school appointments)

A staff of this size would not have sufficed if the Florida Department of Welfare had not contributed a great deal of assistance. Departmental staff helped in locating families for the sample, in finding what schools the children attended and what classes they were in, in checking for special information about children and parents, in arranging appointments, and in countless other ways. The Director of Child Welfare and the Adoption Consultant gave active consultation and assistance in all phases of the work.

The field director was responsible for two aspects of the work. One was giving supervision to the interviewers and participating in the joint ratings, described below. The other was carrying full administrative responsibility for the field operations, including the complicated plans for moving the research team about the state in order to secure home interviews in 78 localities and school information from 412 classrooms in 295 schools distributed among those localities—an undertaking that required close scheduling and great flexibility and ingenuity in changing plans to cope with unforeseen contingencies.

The interviewers were trained and experienced caseworkers, familiar with foster-home and adoption practice but not connected with the Florida Department of Public Welfare. The original plan was to have no interviewers who were at the time or ever had been connected with the Florida Department of Public Welfare, and to have no residents of Florida on the staff. This plan had to be modified somewhat, since qualified interviewers from out of state were not available and highly qualified ones

---

[1] Six interviewers took part in the study, but not more than five served at any one time, and, for most of the time, only four.

were found in Florida. Two of the six interviewers in the study had previously been associated with the Department, although they were not on its staff at the time of the study. Comparison of their interviews with those secured by the others revealed no indication that their findings were affected by previous affiliation with the Department. The initial plan also called for interviewers who had never been engaged in adoption work in social agencies. This too proved impracticable. Again, there was no evidence that the staff members who had done such work had a biased attitude toward independent adoptions.

The research assistants administered the tests and obtained information from school records, using previously prepared forms and following procedures in which they had been trained by a staff member of the U.S. Children's Bureau. They were also responsible for initial processing of test results, again following forms and procedures drawn up by the staff of the Children's Bureau. Final processing and analysis was done by the staff members supplied by the Children's Bureau, with assistance from the field director and one of the interviewers during the early parts of the analysis.

METHODS OF STUDY

Interviews

The interviews with parents were held in the adoptive homes and usually lasted two or three hours. As a rule it was the adoptive mother who was interviewed, although in about one-third of the cases the adoptive father was also present for all or part of the time. In a few instances, in which the mother was ill or out of the home, only the father was interviewed. Occasionally the adopted child in question would come into the room while the interview was in process, but no attempt to interview children was made.

In every phase of data gathering, first importance was given to guarding against singling out a child as adopted or revealing the adoptive status of a child to an outsider. Even though many children's adoptive status was known to teachers, there were instances in which to reveal it might have been damaging. Moreover, to let a child or teacher know that we regarded the adoptive status itself as "special" enough to merit study seemed undesirable, even though that status was well known to the child and his associates.

Accordingly, interview appointments were arranged with the adoptive mother by telephone, at an hour when the child would probably be in school. This approach, as reported above, was successful in 90 per cent of the cases. Some mothers said that they wished to consult their husbands before agreeing to make an appointment, and this wish was always respected. Some gave consent hesitantly, but their concern usually disappeared during the interview. The interviewer always suggested that the mother consult the Department of Public Welfare about the study if she wanted more information. Some mothers did consult the Department but the majority did not. The interviewers also carried credentials which they showed to the parents.

A small proportion of the families in the sample had no telephone. In such cases, the interviewer went to the house in person to make an appointment for the interview proper. In retrospect, the interviewers thought the proportion of refusals was lower when the initial contact was face to face, although they had expected the reverse to be true. This finding is in line with that of some other investigators: that to approach a respondent in person gives the best chance of obtaining an interview. There is still doubt, however, that the difference in results was large enough to have justified the considerable increase in time that would have been required by visits (sometimes more than one per family) for the purpose of setting up an interview.

In order to secure the benefits of caseworkers' skill in interviewing and at the same time ensure that comparable material was gathered, a topical outline of points to be covered was prepared. The interviewers were left free to follow their own methods of obtaining information and to use whatever sequence they (and their respondents) preferred, but they were required to cover certain points in every interview. The interview guide was based on a review of the relevant literature and discussion with the staff. (See Appendix B.)

When first proposed, the idea of so much structuring of the interview was not agreeable to the interviewers. Accordingly, they were asked to conduct some preliminary interviews with cases not in the sample, according to their own ideas of how to get the information desired. On analysis it was found that every point in the interview guide had been covered in most of the interviews. When it became evident that the guide was not a strait jacket but merely an aid to ensure full coverage and comparability, it was accepted. After the data had been gathered, all but one of the interviewers said the guide had been no hindrance but rather a help.

In addition to covering the required topics, each interviewer was asked to introduce, at an appropriate point, two or three questions which were to be asked always in the same words. This requirement also was found to impose no undue difficulties, although at the outset it caused some concern.

At the end of the interview, the parent was asked to fill out a brief questionnaire concerning child-rearing practices and experiences. (See Appendix B.) The parent often discussed the items with the interviewer while the questionnaire was being filled out, occasionally providing additional information relevant to the less formal interview. The interviewer waited until the questionnaire had been completed and took it with her, thus avoiding losses through mail returns. None of the parents refused to fill out the questionnaire, although some commented that it duplicated what had already been covered.

As is customary in this sort of study, the interviewers consistently avoided attempting to give direct advice or therapy. If the adoptive parents directly asked for help, they suggested consulting an appropriate agency. The supervision of the field director, and information obtained from the State Department of Public Welfare, equipped them to meet this familiar problem associated with intensive interviewing about family life.

As soon as possible after the interview, the interviewer dictated a report, using a tape recorder. She also filled out a checklist containing factual information, such as family composition and father's occupation, and some items concerning parental attitudes. (See Appendix B.) The information on this checklist was later supplemented by content analysis of the records and by special analyses of subgroups of cases with certain characteristics.

On the basis of the material obtained in the interviews, the homes were rated—at first independently by the interviewer and field director, and later in conference jointly. In this conference the final rating was agreed upon and recorded, with an indication of the degree of confidence with which it was made. The content of these ratings and the detailed procedures are described in Chapter VI, and rating forms are given in Appendix A.

School Information

In line with the determination to avoid revealing or emphasizing the adoptive status of the sample children, no attempt was made to examine or interview the children individually, much as this would have added to the study data. Instead, it was decided to rely on group tests administered in the classroom and supplemented by information from school records and from the child's teacher. For this reason also, at least in the classroom, the study was presented to the classroom teachers as a study of child development rather than as a study of adoption. The psychological tests used, how they were selected and how administered, are discussed in Chapter X. A word should be said here, however, about the arrangements and procedures by which the psychological tests were administered and information from school records was obtained.

For administrative reasons, the children and their classrooms were located independently of the home interview, and the research assistants who administered the tests traveled separately from the interviewers. Sometimes the one who reached a locality first was able to help the other in finding a parent or child. All traveled by automobile and the itinerary of each was carefully mapped out by the field director.

Although the interviewers arranged their own appointments with adoptive parents, obtaining information from the schools required so much preliminary exploration that it was expedient to make arrangements for school appointments before the research assistants arrived. In two areas of the state it proved necessary to employ temporary staff merely to complete arrangements for the school visit.

Before any of this work in schools was done, the cooperation of the State Superintendent of Education in the project was secured. After the purpose and nature of the study had been explained to him by a representative of the Department of Public Welfare, the State Superintendent gave his blanket permission and offered to communicate with the county school superintendents in the 44 counties involved. This notification was followed by conferences with the county superintendents—usually held by our field director. The county superintendent, in turn, either wrote or telephoned to the principals of the schools attended by the adopted children, to explain that someone would come to discuss the study with them, and to ask for their cooperation.

Discovering which schools the adoptive children were attending was in itself a considerable undertaking. In major cities the school system was likely to maintain a central index through which the schools could be identified. After this, a member of the study staff or a member of the Department of Public Welfare staff talked with the principal to find out which classroom a particular child was in, explain what was needed and why, and obtain permission to proceed. In smaller towns the staff of the local Welfare Department office found out where the adoptive children were and either made arrangements for the research assistant or reported to a member of the study staff who discussed arrangements with the principal.

In view of the demands made by the study it is a tribute to the cooperation of the school officials that only five principals in the schools decided not to cooperate in the study. Nineteen parochial schools, as already noted, also refused permission.

Without the constant help of the Department of Public Welfare it would have been impossible for the staff to set up the complex arrangements demanded by the situation and obtain the desired data. The perspective of hindsight suggests that administrative procedures could be simplified without detriment to findings by sampling different types of community rather than covering a whole state. In this way, proportionately less staff time would be required to pave the way for data-gathering.

CHAPTER IV

The Children, the Parents, and the Adoption Process

THE STUDY deals, then, with 484 adoptions that are representative (except for the omission of the few children who were over fifteen at the time of follow-up) of independent adoptions of white children in Florida during the period 1944 to 1947. From the study we would like to be able to say how adequately the social investigation procedure protects children who are adopted independently and by what signs the likelihood of poor outcome can be recognized.

At best, this aim can be accomplished only in a limited way, for there are local and temporal reasons why our findings may not apply to all independent adoptions. Some of these reasons have already been described. The study was carried on in a state and at a time when independent adoptions far outnumbered those arranged by social agencies, the requirement of a social investigation was a recent innovation and one not in high favor with the courts and the public, and the investigations were made by untrained social workers and recommendations against adoption were made only in extreme cases. If the situation in these respects is different in other states, it is possible that the outcome of their independent adoption procedure may be somewhat different from that reported here.

Other limitations on our ability to generalize from the findings of the study may lie in the characteristics of the individuals concerned—the adoptive parents, the adopted children, and the natural parents. If independent adoptions differ greatly in these respects from place to place and from time to time, studies comparable to ours might yield somewhat different findings. The extent of the difference would depend, to a considerable degree, on what factors are found to be related to the outcome of adoption, a matter that can be fruitfully discussed only after the findings of the study are reported. In the meantime, however, the reader will want to know (if only to compare with the situation he is familiar with) what manner of people our study deals with and how the adoptions under study came to be.

The source of this early information was the records of the investigation made by the Florida Department of Public Welfare at the time the petition was filed. These records, available for the total sample, will be drawn on throughout the report, as well as for this initial account of the bare facts about the parents and children involved in the adoptions under study.[1] We shall refer to them as the early or initial investigation records, to distinguish them from the later "home interviews" held with adoptive parents during the study.

One characteristic shared by all the parents and children was that they lived in Florida during the last year of World War II and the beginning of the postwar period. These years in Florida meant a great influx of men in military service, of their wives, and of some women who were not their wives. It also meant many departures from Florida of men in military service who left their wives behind. That the wartime situation probably affected the composition of the sample of cases studied is obvious. It does not necessarily follow, however, that the situation would affect the relations between traits or factors that are reported. Our estimate of the effects has been discussed in the preceding chapter.

THE CHILDREN

The "typical" child in our sample of adopted children was a healthy baby, born out of wedlock and placed directly from the

---

[1] As noted in the section on sampling, interviews were held in the homes of 438 children, and school information and psychological test material for 448 children. *Both* home interviews and testing were obtained for 411; and interviews, or testing, or both, were obtained for 484. Accordingly, there will be some variation in the base number, depending on the type of information that is being discussed.

hospital before he was one month old. Like most norms, however, this one was subject to a good deal of variation.

The child was a bit more likely to be a boy (261) than a girl (223).

The birth status of the children is given in Table 1.

TABLE 1. BIRTH STATUS OF CHILDREN

Birth status	Number	Per cent
Born in wedlock		
Parents living together	39	8
Parents separated or divorced	53	11
One parent dead	13	3
Both parents dead	0	0
Not sufficient information	3	0
Total born in wedlock	108	22
Born out of wedlock		
Mother unmarried	249	52
Mother married, marriage unbroken[a]	49	10
Mother married, marriage broken	73	15
Total born out of wedlock	371	77
Birth status not known	5	1
Total	484	100

[a] There may be some debate whether these children were born out of wedlock. In the statistical series of the Children's Bureau a child is so classified if it is quite clear that the natural father is not married to the natural mother. Legally, however, the husband of the natural mother is the child's father, and for legal purposes the child may be considered born in wedlock.

In contrast to the picture of days gone by, no child in the sample was a full orphan and, contrary to frequent assumptions about adopted children, almost a fourth of the children were born in wedlock. This figure, although probably out of line with popular expectation, is in line with the national picture. In 1960, according to the estimate of the Children's Bureau, one-fourth of the independent nonrelative adoptions in the United States involved children born in wedlock.[1]

About half of the children in the study were born to women who had never been married. Another 15 per cent were born out of wedlock to women who had once been married but who were now separated, divorced, or widowed. Ten per cent were born to married women who had become pregnant by other men, often while their husbands were in military service overseas.

---

[1] U.S. Children's Bureau, unpublished data.

Over half of the children born in wedlock came from homes broken by separation, divorce, or—much less often—by death. In these broken homes the remaining parent felt unable or unwilling to shoulder the dual role of breadwinner and homemaker.

On the other hand, 39 of the children had parents who were married and living together at the time of placement. Most of these parents mentioned money problems as the chief reason, or one of the chief reasons, for placing the child. The nature of the economic pressures varied considerably, however. Some of the couples were young and ambitious and felt that the responsibility of a baby would interfere with the father's education or his plans for getting a good start. Others were older, with little income and other children to support, and "just couldn't take care of one more." A few couples were on the verge of divorce. Also exceptional were several instances in which the child was born "too soon after the marriage" and was placed to avoid "talk." In a few others, the child was placed for adoption because the natural father suspected that the child was not his own.

The majority of the children born in unbroken homes (though not the majority born in wedlock) were placed directly from the hospital, according to a plan worked out by the expectant parents well in advance of the birth. Some of the parents deliberately avoided seeing the baby, in order "not to be so upset." A minority did give evidence of distress, and one or two said they later regretted their decision, although not enough to change it. One well-dressed mother, after keeping up a facade of indifference, broke down and wept when the baby had been given to his new mother. This same mother and her husband had four other children living in boarding homes, three of whom were subsequently placed for adoption.

On the whole, despite an occasional expression of grief, the married natural parents appear to have carried out their placement plans with equanimity. Rejection of the child was overt in several instances—for example, the mother who invariably referred to her child's birth as an unfortunate "operation," the one who insisted that the hospital had given her the wrong baby, mothers who referred to the baby only as a threat to the husband's career.

Age at Placement

Early placement is characteristic of independent adoptions, and our sample ran true to form. Nearly three-fourths of these children were placed in their adoptive homes before they were a month old, 10 per cent of them during the first day of life. The early investigation records hold some proud accounts by adoptive mothers of baby "firsts"—first bottle, first burp, first change of diaper, and so on. "Just as if he was really born to me," they sometimes exclaimed.

Of the children placed when they were older than one month, almost half were in their adoptive homes by the age of six months. As the following classification shows, fewer than 50 had passed the first year and only three were four years or older.

TABLE 2. AGE OF CHILDREN AT PLACEMENT

Age at placement	Number	Per cent
Under 1 day	51	11
1 to 6 days	137	28
1 to 4 weeks	168	35
1 to 2 months	31	6
3 to 5 months	27	6
6 to 12 months	24	5
13 to 18 months	13	3
19 to 24 months	12	2
25 to 30 months	6	1
31 to 36 months	6	1
37 to 48 months	6	1
48 months or more	3	1
Total	484	100

Children born out of wedlock were the ones most likely to be placed early. Four out of five were in their adoptive homes by the time they were a month old, and over half of these before they were a week old. About half of the children born in wedlock were placed by the time they were a month old.

The proportions given in the table are influenced slightly by the age limitations used in choosing the sample, children who had passed their sixteenth birthday having been excluded. By this rule, 41 children who would otherwise have been in the sample were taken out of it and a random selection of younger children substituted for them. The effect of this on the proportion of children placed at an early age was not great, however, as indicated by the fact that the proportion under one month in the sample (74 per cent) is much like that for all the children adopted in Florida during the years 1944 to 1947.

Age at Follow-up

The age of the child at the time of follow-up was related to, but not wholly determined by, his age at placement, since the sample was drawn from petitions granted during a three-year period. None of the children could be younger than nine or older than fifteen when the interviewing was done in 1956 and 1957. The majority were ten or eleven, a concentration due to the great increase in the number of adoptions during the last part of the study period. The total number of independent adoptions in Florida more than doubled between 1944 and 1947.

TABLE 3. CURRENT AGE OF CHILDREN

Age in years	Number	Per cent
9	53	11
10	152	32
11	151	31
12	69	14
13	28	6
14	16	3
15	15	3
Total	484	100

Only 11 per cent of the children were under ten years of age. The study dealt primarily, then, with children who were ten to twelve years old—with children, that is, who were in a period of emotional development that is usually fairly quiescent and yet one that is sufficiently advanced to justify an assessment of the outlook for mental health.

The proportion of children over twelve years of age was 12 per cent. This means a relatively small group in the "dangerous teens," which are widely regarded as a special hazard for adopted children, on the ground that problems of identity often become salient in adolescence. Moreover, since the study period is 1944 to 1947, any children in the sample who were over thirteen must have been placed after early infancy. Accordingly, in our sample it would be difficult if not impossible to separate unfavorable effects of late placement and possible pre-placement trauma from unfavorable effects of special adolescent adjustment problems for the adopted child. On the other hand, we are able to compare these children with a group of matched controls to see whether they seem to be at a disadvantage, according to any of the measures used.

Pre-placement History

The children placed by the age of a month or less went directly, or almost directly, from the hospital to their adoptive homes. Of the others, half lived only with the natural parents or relatives before placement in the adoptive home, most often with the mother. The other half lived in foster homes or institutions, or in combinations of these and their own homes.

TABLE 4. CHILDREN'S PRE-PLACEMENT LIVING ARRANGEMENTS

Pre-placement living arrangements	Number	Per cent
Placed within the first 31 days, usually from hospital	364	76
In hospital more than 31 days	9	2
Lived with natural parents	47	10
Lived with relatives	7	1
Lived in foster home	10	2
Lived in institution	7	1
Lived in other adoptive homes	5	1
Multiple arrangements	34	7
No information	1	..
Total	484	100

Table 4 shows that 34 of the children had had multiple living arrangements, frequently shuttling back and forth between the natural mother and some kind of informal foster care, and that five children had been in other adoptive homes before being placed in their present homes.

Some of the children showed evidence of serious physical neglect when they entered their adoptive homes. Many of these were children who had been moved repeatedly from one setting to another. Fifty-six records refer to such evidence as severe diaper rash, malnutrition, dirt, sores, and tell of children being left untended for long periods of time. Before the adoption was completed, 40 of these children appeared to be normal and in good health, with 37 having been examined by a physician and pronounced healthy.

Health Status

All but 20 of the social investigation records contained a report of a medical examination conducted at some time between placement and final adoption. Eighty-six per cent of the children were described by the examining physicians as normal and in good health. Another 3 per cent were said to be in good health but had apparently not been examined by a physician. Nineteen children (4 per cent) had a congenital malformation, and 31 either were ill or had sustained an injury.

The congenital anomalies reported for 19 children were chiefly minor defects, such as crossed eyes or slight clubfoot, and often were corrected before placement. A few were more serious. For example, one child required surgery for hernia and another for a stomach condition, while a third had a congenital heart defect.

The category "serious illness or injury" covers a variety of conditions. Several children had severe asthma or allergies, and several suffered from childhood diseases accompanied by high fever. One had severe jaundice as a newborn; two or three had poliomyelitis before or after placement; one developed toxic encephalitis; and one had contracted syphilis from his mother.

Of the 56 children who at placement showed the effects of abuse or neglect, 12 are included among those listed as having experienced serious illness or injury at some time before the adoption became final. One of these had rickets, another was malnourished to the danger point. For the most part, however, their ailments appeared less directly related to the effects of neglect.

It should also be mentioned that 19 children were known to have been born prematurely. The records do not give this information consistently; hence, this figure may be an understatement. The majority of the health problems noted in the early investigation records preceded placement and were known to the adoptive parents.

THE PARENTS

The Natural Parents

Rather little is known about the natural parents and it has to do chiefly with the mother. The State Welfare Department worker was often able to get in touch with her but rarely had contact with the natural father. Only in 39 cases was this possible, cases in which the parents were married and living together. An occasional bit of information about the father was gleaned through interviewing the mother, but such glimpses are few and so vague that efforts to include the father systematically had to be abandoned. The one consistently available item of information about the father was whether he was married to the mother; for the most part, as we have seen, he was not.

TABLE 5. AGE OF NATURAL MOTHERS AT THE TIME OF CHILDREN'S BIRTH

Age of natural mother	Number	Per cent
Under 15 years	1	..
15 to 20 years	139	29
21 to 24 years	136	28
25 to 29 years	78	16
30 to 34 years	20	4
35 to 39 years	9	2
40 and over	4	1
No information	97	20
Total	484	100

Age of Natural Mother. Information is far from complete even about the natural mothers. For example, the age of about one-fifth of them at the time the child was born is not known. Of the others, almost two-thirds were twenty-one or older when the child was born, and more than one in four were twenty-five or over.

The age level of these women may seem somewhat high. It must be remembered in this connection, however, that almost half of the natural mothers in our study were or had been married. In addition, use of the independent adoption method may be more characteristic of the older unmarried mothers. Vincent found that, in a sample drawn from a county in California, the majority of the unmarried mothers who placed their children for adoption independently were over twenty-one years of age, while the majority of those who placed their children through a social agency were twenty-one or younger.[1]

Natural Parents' Health Status. Whenever possible, the State Welfare Department worker tried to ascertain the medical histories of the natural parents. For the most part these efforts were fruitless, resulting in a perfunctory statement by the mother or someone who knew her, that she and her family had no known defect or disease. Information about the natural father's health status was even less often obtained.

In 20 cases the natural mother was reported as having a definite medical problem. Seven had a known history of mental disease, 11 had had either tuberculosis or syphilis, and 2 had had both syphilis and a mental disease.

TABLE 6. EDUCATION OF NATURAL MOTHERS

Education of natural mother	Number	Per cent
Did not finish eighth grade	34	7
Completed eight grades of elementary school	28	6
Some high school	91	19
Graduated from high school	110	23
Some college	28	6
Graduated from college	22	4
Some gradute or professional training	1	..
Advanced degree	..	..
No information	170	35
Total	484	100

Education of Natural Mother. We have data on the schooling of approximately two-thirds of the natural mothers. The great majority of them had had at least some high school training and at least half had completed high school. Some fifty had gone to college and about half of these had been graduated. Only a minority had left school during the eighth grade or had failed to finish elementary school. While the information summarized in Table 6 gives a basis for further analysis, it gives no ground for statements about the general educational level of the natural

[1] Vincent, Clark E., *Unmarried Mothers*. The Free Press of Glencoe, New York, 1961.

mothers, since information is lacking for one in three and there is always the possibility that these would pull down what appears to be a relatively favorable level of education.

The Adoptive Parents

Length of Marriage. The great majority of the children (80 per cent) had adoptive parents who had been married at least five years when placement occurred, and 39 per cent had been married ten or more years. Only 19 of the children were placed with couples who had been married less than two years; half of these had been married less than one year.

TABLE 7. ADOPTIVE PARENTS' LENGTH OF MAR-
RIAGE PRIOR TO PLACEMENT OF CHILD

Length of marriage	Number	Per cent
Less than 1 year	10	2
1 year	9	2
2 to 4 years	78	16
5 to 9 years	197	41
10 or more years	187	39
Adoptive parent unmarried	3	..
Total	484[a]	100

[a] In this table and comparable tabulations, the numbers refer to children rather than to parents or families. Accordingly, the total is 484 rather than 477. See footnote, Chapter III, p. 60.

Marital History. Considering the average duration of their marriages, a history of divorce was rather frequent among the adoptive parents. About a third of the children were placed in homes in which at least one of the marital partners had previously been divorced. A history of previous divorce was most frequent among couples who had been married less than five years. In all ten couples whose marriage had taken place less than one year before placement, either husband or wife or both had previously been divorced. In some instances the child was placed with the couple almost immediately after the second marriage.

Remarriage after the death of a spouse was rare, only 17 of the couples including a spouse who had been widowed. One of the adoptive mothers was a single woman, one was divorced, one was a widow.

TABLE 8. ADOPTIVE PARENTS' PRE-PLACEMENT
MARITAL HISTORY

Marital history	Number	Per cent
First marriage for both adoptive parents	322	67
One spouse widowed, first marriage for other	12	2
Both widowed	1	..
One widowed, one divorced	4	1
One divorced, first marriage for other	94	19
Both divorced	38	8
Both divorced, one or both more than once	10	2
No father in home	3	1
Total	484	100

Age of Adoptive Parents. The relatively long duration of a large proportion of the marriages is reflected in the average age of the adoptive parents at the time the child was placed in their home: 34.3 years for the mothers and 38.3 for the fathers. As Table 9 shows, 70 children had mothers who had reached or exceeded the forty-year age limit often recommended by child placement agencies. Sixty-nine had fathers who were at or beyond the forty-five usually set as the top age at which agencies consider adoption of an infant desirable. Even so, the majority of the adoptive parents were within the limits usually recommended by agencies. Sixty-four per cent of the adoptive mothers and 54 per cent of the adoptive fathers were in their thirties when the child was placed with them.

TABLE 9. AGE OF ADOPTIVE PARENTS
AT TIME OF PLACEMENT

Age in years	Adoptive mothers		Adoptive fathers	
	Number	Per cent	Number	Per cent
20 to 24	20	4	7	2
25 to 29	89	18	39	8
30 to 34	172	36	114	24
35 to 39	133	28	144	30
40 to 44	48	10	108	22
45 to 49	14	3	46	10
50 to 54	7	1	15	3
55 to 59	..	..	7	1
60 and over	1	..	1	..
Total	484	100	481[a]	100

[a] In three adoptive homes there were no fathers.

Since only 21 of the children in the sample were more than two years old at placement, it is clear that for the most part the older parents did not adopt older children during the years under study. Actually there was little relation between the age of adoptive parent and child at the time of placement.

Other Children of Adoptive Parents. A frequent question raised about adoption concerns the presence of other children in the home, especially natural children of the adoptive parents. A rather large proportion—30 per cent—of the children were adopted by parents who already had children. These children were more often adopted than "own," but 69 of the children in the sample were adopted by parents who had children of their own. Not all of these children were in the home when the child in question was placed there. A number of them were already adult and had set up households of their own. This was, of course, most likely to be the case in the homes of the older parents, some of whom turned to adoption because of the void left after their own children had struck out for themselves.

TABLE 10. STATUS OF OTHER CHILDREN IN ADOPTIVE FAMILY AT TIME OF PLACEMENT

Status of other children in the home	Number		Per cent	
"Own"	62		13	
Adopted	74		15	
Both "own" and adopted	7	143	2	30
No other children		341		70
Total		484		100

Occupation of Adoptive Father. It is often assumed that adoption is chiefly undertaken by people in the upper and upper-middle classes, as these are indicated by occupation, income, and education. However, the independent adoptions we studied give no support to this assumption. When the fathers' usual occupations were classified under the categories listed below, only one-fourth of the children were in families in the upper three occupational groups. Twenty-six fathers were in military service when the children were placed in their homes. In the following table, the three children placed in homes without fathers are represented by the occupational classification of their adoptive mothers.

TABLE 11. OCCUPATION OF HOUSEHOLD HEAD AT TIME OF PLACEMENT

Usual occupation of household head	Number	Per cent
Primary professional and top managerial—doctor, lawyer, professor, scientist, artist, newspaper editor, CPA, major executive in large company	35	7
Large proprietary and top sales—large farmer (owner), manager, bond or insurance agent or broker, real estate agent or broker	65	13
Secondary professional—school teacher, social worker, librarian, registered nurse; optometrist, newspaper reporter, podiatrist	23	5
Small business or salesman—proprietor of neighborhood business store, beauty parlor, and the like; small farmer, grocer, butcher, traveling salesman or bond salesman	124	26
Skilled labor, white collar—bookkeeper, secretary, foreman, electrician, carpenter, radio repair, watch repair	146	30
Semi-skilled labor, service and lower white collar work—factory worker, taxi or truck driver, waiter or waitress, gas station attendant, tenant farmer, sales lady, sales clerk, beauty parlor or telephone operator, bartender, policeman, garage mechanic	81	17
Unskilled labor—laborer, hired farm hand, domestic servant, janitor	5	1
Not in labor force	5	1
Total	484	100

The majority of the fathers were engaged in skilled labor, white collar and sales jobs, and small business. Almost a fifth had what are often referred to as working-class occupations.

Family Income. Data for income at time of placement reveal much the same pattern. Income alone is a deceptive figure, however, since 1944 to 1947 was a period of sharply rising income and living costs, wage and salary rates differed in rural and urban areas, and some fathers were in military service at the time.

The median income of the adoptive families was between $3,600 and $4,200. In 1947 the median national income for men with income who were family heads was $2,579; in Florida the median was $2,326.[1] Thus, the median in our sample was higher than for the state or the nation at large, although not as much higher as some might think.

Although these data are for family income, the breadwinner was almost exclusively the father. Only 28 of the adoptive

[1] Florida data from decennial census reports; U.S. data from *Current Population Reports*, Series P-60, No. 5.

mothers were in the labor force after the child was placed, although many more had worked previously. Very few of the incomes reported were strikingly high, even allowing for the value of the dollar in the period under study. Only six families reported $21,000 or more a year, and only 54 (11 per cent) had $9,000 or more. Since the figures reported were checked by the Welfare Department and since it is popularly assumed that economic substance increases the likelihood of a favorable judgment, it seems unlikely that there was much if any scaling downward in the reports.

TABLE 12. REPORTED FAMILY INCOME AT TIME OF PLACEMENT

Income at time of placement	Number	Per cent
$ 0 to $1,199	1	..
1,200 to 1,799	4	1
1,800 to 2,399	41	9
2,400 to 2,999	83	17
3,000 to 3,599	100	21
3,600 to 4,199	65	13
4,200 to 5,399	73	15
5,400 to 6,599	35	7
6,600 to 7,799	14	3
7,800 to 8,999	14	3
9,000 to 20,999	48	10
21,000 and over	6	1
Total	484	100

An important and never-neglected part of the investigation was directed toward establishing evidence of economic responsibility and an income sufficient to ensure that the child would not be deprived of basic physical essentials. None of the petitioning couples was found to be indigent, but some were in circumstances so modest that others in their place might have thought they "could not afford" to adopt a child.

Education of Adoptive Parents. Education, like income and occupation, shows the largest concentration below the upper levels. Almost half of the adoptive fathers whose education was noted in the record had attended high school but not college. The number who attended college was slightly larger than the number who did not go beyond the eighth grade. About one in eight graduated from college and over half of these had done some graduate work. Slightly more adoptive mothers than fathers graduated from high school and college, but fewer of them went on to graduate school.

TABLE 13. EDUCATION OF ADOPTIVE PARENTS

Education	Adoptive father		Adoptive mother	
	Number	Per cent	Number	Per cent
Did not finish eighth grade	38	8	24	5
Completed eight grades of elementary school	62	13	37	8
Some high school	83	17	107	22
Graduated from high school	126	26	166	34
Some college	75	16	51	11
Graduated from college	26	5	52	11
Some graduate or professional training	15	3	2	..
Advanced degree	16	3	6	1
No information	40	9	39	8
Total	481	100	484	100

Health of Adoptive Parents. A major concern of child placement agencies is the health of the adoptive parents. This is studied both to protect the health of the child and to take all reasonable and feasible precautions against risking the early death or disablement of an adoptive parent. The Florida procedures required that adoptive parents be given medical examinations and tests before their petitions could be granted. All the records contained statements signed by a physician— often their own— but the reports differed greatly in thoroughness and in coverage, some including and others omitting reference to health problems that had been cured.

According to the physicians' statements, most of the adoptive parents were in good health and free from contagious disease. A health problem was noted in 49 couples, and in five of these a past or present health defect was reported for both spouses.

With the help of a pediatrician, the known health problems were divided into four groups, according to the likelihood of the health handicap being a handicap to parenthood. This was a rough impressionistic grouping, based on scant medical information which often consisted merely of a diagnostic or descriptive label. Of the 49 adoptive couples for whom some health problem had been reported, almost half (20) were judged to have an ailment that probably would constitute no handicap to being a competent parent. Included in this group were ailments that had been relieved or brought under control by treatment: diabetes, nondisabling eye conditions, several slight disabilities incurred during military service, and several minor chronic problems such as sinus or mild digestive difficulties. The group also included three wives and two husbands (four couples) with positive Wassermann tests. All five, however, were pronounced cured, or at least not in a contagious stage of syphilis, by the time the petition was granted. Those not cured were continuing treatment.

Fifteen of the reported health problems were judged to raise some question as a possible future handicap to parenthood, partly because their severity could not be determined. This second group included such diagnostic labels as rheumatism, thyroid condition, chronic asthma in the adoptive mother; and malaria, chronic asthma, a kidney condition as the result of the removal of one kidney, unspecified service injury in the adoptive father.

Ten of the reported health problems suggested a probable handicap to successful parenthood. Among the adoptive parents whose diagnoses fell in this group were a mother who had experienced two "nervous collapses" and three others who had been treated for "nervousness" or "a nervous disorder." A few others reported general poor health or a "run-down condition" with no specific details, and one suffered from "a chronic back condition."

Four other petitioners had health problems that seemed very likely to prove a handicap to parenthood. One was subject to severe attacks of asthma, requiring hospitalization. Another had a history of institutionalization for feeble-mindedness, and a recorded I.Q. (at twelve years) of 75. A third, with a family history of tuberculosis, stated that she "just does not feel good at any time." One of the fathers had suffered a stroke two years earlier, at the age of forty.

According to our inadequate information, then, 14 of the adoptive couples (3 per cent) had health problems sufficient to raise a definite question about their medical suitability for parenthood, while 15 others had diagnoses that suggested the need for a thorough medical exploration—making a minimum of 6 per cent about whom health questions might be raised. Some of the parents realized the likelihood of concern on the part of the Welfare Department. Only one, however, strenuously objected to a medical examination—one who is included among the four most serious health questions. All the others complied without protest, although in some instances there may be doubt about the thoroughness of the checkup.

Religion. In religion, in the great majority of cases, both adoptive parents were Protestants. Thirty-six couples represented "mixed marriage," chiefly a Protestant-Catholic combination.

TABLE 14. RELIGION OF ADOPTIVE PARENTS

Religion	Adoptive parents	
	Number	Per cent
Protestant	410	85
Catholic	23	5
Jewish	15	3
One Protestant, one Catholic	27	5
One Jewish, one Protestant or Catholic	9	2
No religion	..	..
No information	..	..
Total	484	100

Enough information about the religion of the natural mother was not available to determine positively the extent to which children were placed in homes that corresponded with their own religious background. Probably a considerable amount of "natural matching" occurred. This seems the more likely, since the great majority of the adoptive parents were of the Protestant faith and, according to the figures of the Welfare Department, 65 per cent of all the unmarried mothers during the study period were known to belong to this denomination. The religion of another 20 per cent was unknown and probably a majority of these too were Protestant. It may be also that many of the doctors who placed children made a point of matching religious background, since many doctors say that they consider carefully the relation of the child's background to that of the prospective parents. It seems likely that they would put chief emphasis on socioeconomic status and education, but we have no evidence concerning the weight given to religion as a matching factor. In a few cases the record makes it clear that the natural mother's religion was different from that of the adoptive parents.

THE ADOPTION PROCESS

The Placement Agents

The most frequent source of adoptions was the medical profession and, in a few cases, other professional workers in hospitals. These constituted 40 per cent of the cases. The next most frequent adoption arrangers (24 per cent) were the natural parents themselves or their close relatives, such as the mother's parents. The third category of arrangers (14 per cent) consisted of people who were neither relatives nor professionals. These were likely to be friends or acquaintances of both natural and would-be adoptive parents. Some of them were very slight acquaintances indeed; some were fellow employees; and some were intimate friends.

TABLE 15. SOURCE OF ARRANGEMENTS FOR
PLACEMENT

Placement "arranger"	Number	Per cent
Physician, nurse, hospital personnel	195	40
Lawyer	11	2
Other professional person	52	11
Natural parent or close relative	115	24
Friend or acquaintance of parents	67	14
Juvenile Court	15	3
Other	29	6
Total	484	100

Few of the placements were arranged directly by lawyers— only 11 of them, in fact—but lawyers were usually involved at later stages of the adoption process. Eleven per cent of the children were placed by members of professions other than those associated with medicine, chiefly clergymen and, occasionally, social workers acting in a nonofficial capacity. Virtually all the rest of the children were placed by unlicensed social agencies or the juvenile court.

By definition, none of the adopted children was secured through a child-placement agency licensed in Florida. This, however, was not necessarily for lack of trying. Close to a third of the adoptive couples (29 per cent) had tried to obtain a child through some adoption agency in the state, and two adoptions through licensed agencies in other states got into our sample inadvertently. Most of the couples who had tried to use social agencies had given up in discouragement at the long waiting period, often two or more years. How many had been refused a child is not known.

The ways in which the children and the adoptive parents came together varied with the sort of person who arranged the placement. When the "arranger" was a physician, he was often the adoptive parents' family doctor and knew about their desire for a child. In some instances it was he who recommended adoption. Very often it was he who had delivered the baby and so he knew the natural mother's circumstances, her desire to place her child for adoption, and something about her education and social level.

Friends and relatives were also likely to be aware of both parties' interest in adoption. For instance, a friend of the adoptive mother might have a neighbor whose grandchild needed a home; or a fellow-employee of the adoptive father might know of a girl who wanted to make adoption plans for her unborn baby.

Among the 115 adoptions arranged directly between the adoptive and the natural parents or their relatives were 29 instances that resulted from newspaper advertisements, a practice now prohibited by law. Usually it was the adoptive couple who placed the advertisement, but occasionally the natural parents advertised that a child was available. In a number of instances, the advertisement was run and the arrangements completed before the child's birth. In such a case the child was taken to his adoptive home directly from the hospital.

A considerable proportion of the placements arranged directly by the adoptive parents were impromptu and somewhat haphazard. In some cases, the couple had previously considered adopting a child but had not followed up the idea; in others, adoption had not previously been considered.

Typical of such placements was the one worked out by a young mother who stopped for breakfast at a cafeteria. She told the owners that she was going to visit friends in another part of the state and asked whether they would take care of her infant until she returned. She did return and told them she was planning to place the child for adoption. Since they seemed to like taking care of him, she suggested that they keep him. After brief consideration, the couple agreed. The natural mother remained in town just long enough to sign the official "consent."

Contact with Natural Parents

Like the method of working out placements, the amount of contact between natural and adoptive parents also varied with the arranger. Some amount of contact was inevitable when the parents arranged the adoption directly. It occurred in fewer than 20 per cent of the other placements, and was least frequent in those arranged by doctors, lawyers, and unlicensed social agencies. In all, 186 (38 per cent) of the adoptive couples had direct contact with the natural parents before the adoption was completed. More than half of these contacts were brief—a short meeting when the new parents took the child or when the natural parents' legal consent to the adoption was obtained. Fifty-six adoptive couples had more extensive contact with the natural mother or someone close to her. The majority of these (46) had known the mother or her family before the question of adoption came up, sometimes as neighbors or friends, sometimes through baby-sitting or boarding arrangements.

Some of the parents regretted such a contact; a few welcomed it, feeling that knowledge about the natural parents contributed to their understanding of the child. Among all the parents interviewed, however, a majority (80 per cent) expressed a preference either to know nothing at all about the natural parents (26 per cent) or to know only some things (54 per cent), chiefly about the health of the natural family. Less than one in five expressed a wish to know as much as possible about the adopted child's natural parents.

Arrangement Patterns

Some interesting relationships appeared between the way in which the adoption was arranged and the socioeconomic characteristics of the parents involved. Very few natural mothers who had attended college made the adoption arrangements themselves or with the help of their relatives. They were much more likely to leave such arrangements to their physicians. In contrast, the mothers who had less than a high school education were more likely to make arrangements directly with the adoptive parents or to have them made by a close relative. Those with a high school education were between these two extremes. They relied on a professional person less often than the college-educated mothers, but more often than those not having a high school education. The differences among these groups are statistically significant.

The same relation appeared between the education of adoptive fathers and the person who arranged the adoption. The fathers with at least some college education were the most likely, and those with only elementary school were the least likely, to seek the help of a professional person in arranging for the adoption. Those with a high school education again fell in between. These differences also are statistically significant.

In the same way, the occupation of the adoptive father and the amount of family income were also related to the kind of person who arranged the placement.

Since there were rather similar relations between the education of the adoptive parents and the type of person who arranged the adoption, a certain amount of matching of socioeconomic backgrounds of the two sets of parents apparently took place. The extent of the matching is suggested by the correlation between the natural mother's and the adoptive father's education, which was .40—not a high degree of correlation but one that is well beyond what would be expected by chance. This matching may have come about both because many doctors and lawyers make a deliberate effort in this direction and because the better-educated couples were likely to secure babies for adoption through physicians.

Since presence or absence of contact between natural and adoptive parents was influenced by the identity of the arranger, and since the arranger's identity was related to the socioeconomic status of both sets of parents, a relation between contact and socioeconomic status of the adoptive parents was to be expected. This was found to be the case, contact with the natural parents being significantly more frequent at the lower socioeconomic level.

These relationships had further ramifications. The relation of the child's age at placement to type of arranger has already been mentioned. Almost all of the placements arranged by doctors were made directly from the hospital before the child was a month old. In contrast, almost half of the placements made by natural parents occurred at a later age.

Because of the socioeconomic pattern of arrangements, placements made later than a month of age were relatively less frequent in the upper than in the lower socioeconomic level. Moreover, age at placement was related to presence or absence of contact between natural and adoptive parents, contact being less likely to occur if the child was placed early. This follows from the fact that most doctors both placed the babies directly from the hospital and avoided contact between the two sets of parents, while natural parents or relatives usually had contact when they arranged the adoption directly; and they were more likely to place children who were over a month old.

The "Baby Market"

No solid estimate of the extent of "black market" practices in the adoptions under study could be made, especially since it is unlikely that the adoptive parents would readily disclose excessive payments. However, two-thirds of the adoptive couples reported that they had not paid the mother's medical expenses and that they had paid no fees other than routine legal costs. Though these people may have concealed facts, it seems rather unlikely, since paying the mother's expenses was not illegal and the Department investigators did not approach the subject in a way that would imply criticism of such a practice.

A third of the adoptive couples had no apparent hesitation in saying that they had paid the medical expenses of the natural mother, a contribution most frequent in placements arranged by physicians. Some others paid for more than medical expenses, in an effort to help the mother. Fifty-eight of the 145 couples who paid medical expenses reported giving money to the natural mother for living expenses also. Only 19 records reported expenses that appeared to be fees for the arrangement of the adoption.

Most of the physicians placed children with couples who were their patients. The records of these cases give no basis for assuming any motive on the doctor's part beyond a desire to help a patient—or, more often, to help two patients, since the natural mother was likely to be a patient also. There were a few physicians, however, whose names appeared rather frequently in the records and whose charges for "medical" expenses seemed high. About 30 children in the sample were placed by these doctors. In addition, among the few cases in which lawyers made the placement, there were several in which the fees seemed unusually high.

All in all, the proportion of "black market" babies in our sample seemed rather small. The only sure statement that can be made on the subject, however, is "insufficient information."

Reasons for Wanting to Adopt a Child

The records of the social investigations give some account of the parents' reasons for wanting to adopt a child but, for the most part, these statements were scanty and unrevealing. All but 26 of the couples either said or implied that the chief reason was inability to have a child of their own. Less than half of those who gave this reason said there was a physical basis for the inability.

Desire for companionship was a poor second among reasons, being mentioned by 70 couples. Most of these wanted a companion for a child or children already in the home. A few couples gave, as their reason, companionship for the adoptive mother after her own children had grown up and left the home.

The plight or appeal of a particular child was the reason given by 38 couples. This was especially likely to be a factor in the impromptu kind of arrangement in which the natural parents urged the adopting couple to accept their child. Sixteen couples chose adoption rather than pregnancy because they wanted to be sure to get a child of the "right" sex, and two because they feared pregnancy.

Filing of Petition for Adoption

The first legal step toward adoption was usually taken within one or two months after placement. For two-thirds of the children a petition was filed within six months after being placed in the adoptive home; and for about a fifth, filing occurred after they had been in their foster homes a year or more. In this latter group the first contact of the Department of Public Welfare with the family occurred when the child had been in the home for more than a year, so that the investigators for the Department of Public Welfare did not see the child as he was at the time of placement. This probably accounts for some instances in which their records described a healthy, normal child but the adoptive mother ten years later spoke of the "dreadful" condition of the baby at placement. In these cases, especially, any doubts the investigator might feel about the parents' suitability would have to be especially strong to justify an adverse recommendation.

Department Recommendations to the Court

As has been noted, during the period this study covers, the Department of Public Welfare had a policy of making adverse recommendations only when the unfavorable evidence was of the sort that a court would probably regard as substantial. Following this policy, the Department recommended dismissal of 2 per cent of all the petitions it studied in the period 1944 to 1947. The courts accepted the recommendation in half of these cases.

This action on the part of the courts meant that some cases that the Department regarded as unsuitable were included in our sample, a fact that permitted assessment, in a small way, of the Department's advice.

In addition to the cases in which the Department recommended dismissal of the petition, the records indicate that the investigator had doubts in some other cases about the suitability of the adoptive home. The misgivings noted had to do with such factors as the age or financial situation of the adoptive parents and the emotional climate of the home. These homes are discussed in Chapter XIII, where their relation to adoption outcome is explored.

Petitions Withdrawn or Refused

Information about adoption petitions withdrawn or refused will help to round out the picture of the independent adoption process. During our study period, 1,534 nonagency adoption petitions were filed in Florida by white applicants unrelated to the child they wished to adopt. Of these 48, or 3 per cent, failed to result in a completed adoption. No petition was dismissed against the advice of the Department of Welfare but some, as remarked above, were granted in spite of an adverse recommendation.

Of the 48 uncompleted adoptions, 9 represent legal technicalities rather than objections raised by the Department of Welfare or the courts. Eight of the adoptive couples moved to another state, and in each case the Welfare Department of the new state of residence was notified so that adoption proceedings could continue there. An error in the petition accounted for the ninth case.

The other 39 adoptions failed to be completed for one of three reasons: because the adoptive petitioners were judged unsuitable (23), or the child was judged unsuitable for adoption (4), or the natural parents withdrew consent (12).

Unsuitability of the adoptive parents was by far the leading reason for failure of the petition. In 8 of the 23 cases involving this reason, a member of the Department was able to persuade the applicants to withdraw the petition, thus avoiding the need for court action. One couple considered unsuitable disappeared and could not be found during a search that continued for five years. Court action was withheld on another petition because after ten years of unavailing persuasion the petitioners were not legally married, and while this was not sufficient basis for removing the child from their home it sufficed to prevent granting the petition. The petitions of the remaining 13 couples considered unsuitable were dismissed.

Of the 23 children whose would-be adoptive parents were judged unsuitable, one was returned to his natural mother, two remained with the petitioners, and six were in foster homes approved by the Department of Public Welfare or had been placed with relatives or friends by the time the petition had been dismissed. The remaining 14 children were placed in new adoptive homes through the licensed child-placing agencies to which they were referred by the Department.

Withdrawal of consent by the natural parents was the reason for 12 of the uncompleted adoptions. Nine of the petitioners returned the children voluntarily to the natural parents (or, more often, parent), and two did so upon the order of the court. The natural father of the twelfth child opposed the adoption but consented to leave the boy with the petitioners on a boarding-home basis.

Four petitions failed to lead to adoption because the child was judged unsuitable. Two children who were ill were released by the petitioners to the Department and later died. The third, a boy of eleven, presented problems that led the petitioners to release him to the Juvenile Court, which placed him in an industrial school. The fourth child was found to be mentally deficient. The petition was dismissed but the Court held the petitioners morally responsible for his support until the age of six, when he would become eligible to enter a public institution for the mentally retarded.

The figures just reviewed do not give information about placements that never reached the state of petition. Since an independent placement comes to the attention of the Welfare Department only when a petition is filed, we have no firm basis for forming a conclusion about how many people took children into their homes for the purpose of adoption but did not follow through by filing a petition. Speculation about the probable number should take into account the fact that the great majority of the petitions in our sample (91 per cent) were filed by the time the child was a year old, 75 per cent within the first month.

CHAPTER V

The Adoptive Parents' Experiences
With Independent Adoptions

IN THIS CHAPTER the outcome of these independent adoptions
will be considered from the point of view of the adoptive parents.
What these people (in many cases, the mothers only) had to say
about the degree of their satisfaction with the adoption will be
reported first. After that, the findings on two questions that are
often raised with particular reference to independent adoptions
will be reviewed: How often, and in what ways, and with what
consequences did adopting children independently involve contacts with the natural parents? How many of the children turned
out to be physically or intellectually "handicapped"?

THE PARENTS ASSESS THE ADOPTIONS

We tried both directly and indirectly to discover to what extent the adoptive parents were satisfied or disappointed with the
way the adoptions were working out. As often happens, the indirect ways seemed the more dependable, and the final estimate
took them fully into account.

Child's Resemblance to Adoptive Family

One way of exploring parental feelings about the children
was through a "projective question." During the interview each
parent was asked, "Is (the child) like anyone in your family?"

It was not assumed that seeing a resemblance would in itself imply satisfaction, but rather that the terms and the manner in which a feeling of similarity or difference was expressed would reveal a good deal about the parent's general attitude.

The question turned out to be more literally revealing than we had expected. As judged by other evidence, those who saw a resemblance of some sort were likely to be better pleased and more accepting of the child than those who saw none. This generalization held, whether the answers were made in terms of physical or psychological resemblances. "Everyone says he has my coloring," or "She sticks to her guns—just like her Daddy."

TABLE 16. ADOPTIVE PARENTS' CONCEPTION OF CHILD'S RESEMBLANCE TO ADOPTIVE FAMILY

Degree of similarity	Per cent
Very similar	52
Somewhat or in some ways similar	32
Little or no resemblance	14
Question not asked	2
Total	100

The great majority (84 per cent) of the adoptive parents said that the child resembled the adoptive family very much, or somewhat; that is, they perceived the child as "fitting in." Only 14 per cent reported little or no resemblance.

Special Problems of Adoptive Parenthood

Another indirect clue to parental satisfaction was gleaned by asking what were the special problems of being an adoptive parent.[1] Three-fourths of the parents who were asked this question (76 per cent) declared that there were no problems peculiar to adoptive parenthood, that it was no more difficult than rearing children of your own. It has been said at times that frank recognition of difference between adoptive and natural parenthood is favorable to the success of an adoption. Our own data do not support this hypothesis, for we found no significant relations between answers to this question and the home ratings described

---

[1] The question was answered directly in 318 of the 438 home interviews.

in later chapters. However, our analysis was directed primarily toward other questions, and lack of support for the hypothesis cannot be regarded as disproof of it.

About one-fourth of the 318 adoptive parents who were directly questioned mentioned one or more problems specific to adoptive parenthood. The table below suggests the main headings under which the problems fell. Some parents mentioned more than one problem so that the total number of problems is larger than the number of parents who mentioned them.

TABLE 17. PROBLEMS OF ADOPTIVE PARENTHOOD MENTIONED BY ADOPTIVE PARENTS

Type of problem	Number	Per cent
No special problems, same as any parents, just like "own" children, and so forth	243	76
Concern about special handling of child (discipline), special expectations for him, or "wanting to make it up to him" because he is adopted rather than "own" child	34	11
How, when, or whether to tell the child he is adopted	21	7
Concern with child's background; possibility of undesirable physical or personality traits	19	6
Mixing "own" and adopted children	18	6
What others may say, how they feel and act, about adoption	18	6
Worry about adoption process, legal or personal complications with natural parents, and the like	11	3
Other	31	10

Most of the problems noted by the adoptive parents did not imply reservations about their own experience in adoption. The only categories that seemed to suggest such reservations are those listed as "concern with child's background," and, possibly, "worry about the adoption process." The first is the only category that places the problem or risk directly on the child. Some parents who emphasized the danger of undesirable inherited traits seemed to think that their adopted children had brought an undesirable inheritance into their homes—more often psychological than physical. Only 19 parents (6 per cent) mentioned undesirable inheritance as a special problem, however, and even fewer (11) expressed concern about the adoption process.

The leading category of problems related to the parents' anxiety about their own reactions to the child's adoptive status—fear that, because he was adopted, they would expect either too much or too little from him. This anxiety was most evident in relation to discipline. Some of the parents said that they hesitated to discipline the adopted child as they would their own, either because they feared losing his love or because they felt a need to "make it up to him." Only 11 per cent of those who answered the direct question named such misgivings as a problem. Other comments and indications, however, suggest that the problem existed for a good many who were not articulate about it in answering the question.

Another problem was that of telling the child that he was adopted. Actually, most of the children (90 per cent) did know they were adopted and by far the majority had learned it directly from the adoptive parents. Telling children about their adoption appeared to be a serious problem, however, for more than the 21 parents who mentioned it in response to the direct question. One mother wept as she confessed her inability to tell the child, even though she thought she should. Six of the 46 who refused to be interviewed admitted being fearful that the child might learn through the interview of his adoptive status. Apparently the proportion of parents who thought children should be told of their adoption was even larger then the 90 per cent whose children had been told.

Advice to Persons Considering Adoption

An additional clue to parental satisfaction was gleaned by asking what advice these adoptive parents would give to people who were thinking about adopting a child. Often people will reveal indirectly, in answering such a question, reservations that they would not voice in talking about their own experience. The advice given by the parents in our sample is roughly classified below, with percentages based on the 401 interviews in which the question was answered. A few of the adoptive parents gave more than one suggestion.

The leading category merely advises people who are considering adopting a child to go ahead and do it because it is wonderful and rewarding. Thirty per cent of the parents questioned gave an answer that would fall under this expression of pleasure and satisfaction.

TABLE 18. ADOPTIVE PARENTS' ADVICE TO PROSPECTIVE
ADOPTIVE PARENTS

Advice given	Number	Per cent
Concerning the parents		
Just go ahead, it's wonderful, you'll be glad	122	30
Be sure you really want to adopt a child, be sure you both want to, really love children	94	23
Be sure you have a good marriage, don't adopt just to patch up marital difficulties	22	5
Couples with marital troubles should adopt, will help marriage	4	1
Don't wait until you are too old, do it while young enough, don't do it if you are not healthy	48	12
Don't do it too young, wait until you are in the thirties	3	1
Be sure you are economically stable, can support a child	7	2
Concerning the adoption process		
Don't know the natural parents personally, or too much about the child's background	39	10
Know all you can about the child's background, know the natural parents	27	7
Do it through a social agency or court, not independently	92	23
Do it through a professional person you can trust, such as doctor, lawyer, clergyman	75	19
Be sure it's all strictly legal, correct procedure, no "shady deal"	44	11
Do it independently, not through an agency, they are too slow and fussy	10	2
Concerning the child		
Adopt an infant	59	15
Adopt an older child, if you are older	2	..
Adopt more than one, don't rear him as an only child	25	6
Be sure the child is healthy, have examinations made, blood tests	3	1
Adopt a child whose background, nationality, religion resemble yours	3	1
Tell the child he is adopted	42	10
Rear the child as your own, love as your own, discipline as your own	10	2
Other	35	9

The other items advise about characteristics that are considered desirable or undesirable in adoptive parents, adoptive children, or the process of adoption. Once more the comments center on the parents and the adoption process rather than the child, which suggests that satisfaction with the child was the prevailing mood. Some of the parents interviewed gave conflicting advice. With one exception, however, there was clear consensus among those who mentioned a subject at all.

Couples who want to adopt a child, according to the prevailing view among those in our sample, should be sure that both members really love children and really want to adopt (23 per cent), that they are young and healthy enough to meet the demands of adoptive parenthood (12 per cent), and that their marriage is a good one (5 per cent).

A few characteristics are notable for infrequency of mention. For example, not quite 2 per cent of the parents interviewed mentioned income, although the majority of them were in modest circumstances. Apparently whatever economic sacrifices were imposed by parenthood were not considered important enough to mention. It is interesting too that a few (1 per cent) thought adoption would help a troubled marriage, and that a minority of three advised couples not to adopt a child when very young, but to wait until they and their marriage had matured.

Also noteworthy for rarity of mention are some characteristics of adoptive children that are often believed to plague nonagency adoptions. Less than 1 per cent of these adoptive parents warned against the danger of receiving an unhealthy child, and an equally small proportion urged that the adoptive parents find a child whose characteristics "match" those of his new family. The most frequent recommendation concerning the child was that he be adopted in infancy (as most of the study children were). This advice was given by 15 per cent of those answering, but by 46 per cent of those who had adopted older children, so that here some qualification to satisfaction is suggested. However, two of the adoptive parents suggested that older parents should adopt an older child.

Since these placements were made without agency help, it is interesting that one of the leading suggestions was to adopt a child through an agency (23 per cent). On the other hand, almost as many recommended arranging the placement through a trusted professional person (19 per cent), the procedure followed by a considerable proportion of the couples, and a few (2 per cent) advised evading a social agency. Apparently nearly one out of four couples, at the time of the follow-up interview, considered agency placement preferable to independent adoptions. Some of these, however, explicitly said that *they* had been lucky but others might be less so, so that, at least in some instances, this advice may not have implied reservations about the results of nonagency adoptions. Those who experienced difficulties with natural parents and those whose adopted children developed physical or intellectual handicaps were no more likely than the other adoptive parents to suggest arranging the placement through an agency.

In response to the general request for advice to others, 10 per cent of the parents advised against seeking information about the child's background or being personally acquainted with the natural parents. Seven per cent advised having such information or acquaintanceship. These proportions do not represent the actual distribution of opinion on the subject, however. Earlier in the interview, all the adoptive parents had been asked their preference about knowing the child's background. By far the majority (80 per cent) said they preferred either to know nothing about the natural family or to have only limited and impersonal information chiefly concerning health and hereditary disease. The minority (17 per cent) who preferred knowing as much as possible were apparently more likely to mention this point spontaneously in the context of giving advice to others.

Parents' Picture of the Adopted Child

Another indirect clue to the parents' view of the adoption was the picture they gave of the child—whether the child was presented as lovable, appealing, and easy to get on with; as unlovable or very difficult; or as somewhere in between. The interviewers rated the parents' projected picture of the children as indicated in Table 19.

TABLE 19. ADOPTIVE PARENTS' DESCRIPTION OF CHILD'S TEMPERAMENT

Parents' description	Number	Per cent
Predominantly positive	288	66
Mixed	140	32
Predominantly negative (moody, irritable, mean)	10	2
Total	438	100

Two-thirds of the parents presented a positive picture of the child, while only 2 per cent viewed him as unpleasant and difficult. About one-third painted a picture in between. The mixed view was not assumed to mean necessarily that the parents were disappointed with the adoption. Thirty-two per cent of the children were so described, but (as will be seen below) a rating of qualified satisfaction on the part of one or both parents was given for less than half that many. Whatever this kind of picture meant for the child's adjustment (to be discussed later), apparently it did not inevitably impair the parent's gratification.

Degree of Satisfaction with the Adoption as Judged by Interviewers

Answers to the questions just reported helped the interviewer assess the parents' general satisfaction with the way the adoption seemed to be working out so far. Sometimes the questions about satisfaction were put directly; sometimes they were answered in the course of conversation before the interviewer actually asked them. In addition, during the interview the interviewer picked up a number of clues, direct and indirect, to the parent's degree of satisfaction with the adoption. Toward the end of the interview the mother was asked directly how she thought the adoption was working out and, if the father was not present, how he felt about it.

In writing up their records of the interview, the interviewers made a rating, based on answers to this and the other questions relating to parental satisfaction, and also on clues that emerged in discussing other points. They noted on the checklist whether the parents evinced unqualified satisfaction with the adoption, mixed feelings, or negative feelings. The results are summarized in Table 20.

Regardless of others' judgment, in the view of the adoptive parents as perceived by the caseworkers who interviewed them, the great majority of these placements were highly satisfactory. Eighty-five per cent of the adoptive couples were classified as having unqualified satisfaction. In 37 additional couples, one parent evinced complete satisfaction while the other (more often the mother than the father) was said to have mixed or negative feelings. In only eight couples (2 per cent) did one parent evince

TABLE 20. PARENTAL SATISFACTION WITH ADOPTION OUTCOME

Degree of satisfaction	Number	Per cent
Unqualified satisfaction, both parents	371	85
One parent unqualified satisfaction, other mixed feelings	33	7
One parent positive, other negative	4	1
Both parents, mixed feelings	25	6
One mixed, one negative	4	1
Both parents, negative feelings	1	..
Total	438[a]	100

[a] Information derived from home interviews is based on the 438 adoptions regarding which such an interview was held. In this classification, when there was only one parent in the home (48 cases) the classification was recorded as both parents agreeing.

negative feelings about the adoption, and in only one of the 438 home interviews were negative feelings reported for both adoptive parents. Thus, in 408, or 93 per cent, of the couples at least one parent was reported to have unqualified satisfaction, and in 67, or 15 per cent, at least one was reported to have either mild reservations or more negative feelings about the adoption.

Parents were rated as having negative feelings on the basis of their own explicit statements. "Mixed feelings," however, were more likely to reflect indirect evidence. For example, a mother who was working full time to pay medical expenses for her handicapped child, declared roundly that she was quite satisfied with the adoption and would want to do it the same way again. The interviewer's rating of "mixed" feelings in such a case might be based on the mother's admission that the child's handicap had made it difficult for the family. In other cases, an interpretation of mixed feelings might be based on the statement of an older parent that perhaps it would be better for adoptive parents to be younger; or on acute difficulty and anxiety about telling the child he is adopted.

These examples are given to indicate that some of the parents classified as having mixed feelings about the adoption would not have described themselves as less than wholly satisfied. The proportion of couples in which at least one spouse actually admitted to dissatisfaction or reservations was less than the 15 per cent described by the interviewers as having mixed feelings.

If the apparent opinion of the adoptive parents is taken as the criterion, then, 85 per cent of the 438 adoptions were highly successful from the parents' standpoint. Later chapters discuss the outcome of adoptions from other points of view. How the parents feel is one important ingredient in outcome, however, and it is clear that the great majority of the parents in our sample felt well pleased with the way the adoptions were working out so far.

THE RISK OF DIFFICULTIES WITH NATURAL PARENTS

All adoptions (like all parenthood) involve risk. One of the most frequently cited risks of independent adoptions is that adoptive parents may have difficulties with the natural parents. Gellhorn[1] mentions "possible legal conflicts, and even the possibility of attempted extortion." An article in the *Yale Law Journal*[2] warns that adoptive parents may be "harassed by a mother who has changed her mind and wants her child back." Yet, although much is said about this sort of risk, there has been little systematic evidence about the actual frequency of problems with natural parents, the kinds of problems involved, and the circumstances under which they occur.

In our sample, the proportion of adoptive parents who were "harassed" by the natural parents was rather small. Thirty of the 484 adoptive couples had told the Welfare Department's investigators during the period 1944 to 1947 that they were having or had had difficulties with the natural parents, and six others told our interviewers at follow-up in 1956 and 1957 of having had such problems. Together, such cases constitute 7 per cent of all that were studied.

The post-adoption experience of the 46 couples who refused to be interviewed by our staff might increase that proportion, but this seems rather unlikely. Only three of these couples had had difficulties before adoption. (They were, of course, included in the above count.) Since none of the couples who were interviewed had problems with the natural parents that began after adoption, it is doubtful that many, if any, of the parents who refused to be interviewed had that experience.

---

[1] Gellhorn, Walter, *Children and Families in the Courts of New York City*. Dodd, Mead and Co., New York, 1954, p. 247.

[2] "Moppets on the Market: The Problem of Unregulated Adoptions," *Yale Law Journal*, vol. 59, March, 1950, pp. 715–736.

For a complete count of this sort of risk among independent adoptions in Florida, there should also be added the adoptions that were not completed because the natural parents revoked consent or because they raised other obstacles to adoption after the children were in the adoptive homes. Analysis of the uncompleted adoptions during the 1944 to 1947 period suggests that such cases would raise the total would-be adoptions that involved difficulties with the adoptive parents to about 8 per cent of the whole.[1]

In addition to these cases, there may, of course, have been some in which problems with the natural parents prevented even an initial petition from being filed. There are no figures on this point, but the accounts of placements reported in the State Welfare Board records suggest that the number was slight.

We conclude, then, that the risk of interference and "harassment" by natural parents is probably something less than a one in twelve chance. The seriousness of such a chance will, of course, be rated differently by different individuals.

Nature and Duration of the Difficulties

The problems raised by the natural parents took a variety of forms. The majority were such as to arouse fear that the child would be taken away, either by legal means or by abduction. In 16 cases, natural parents threatened to revoke consent and in nine they actually did. In ten cases they threatened to take the child and in four they actually took him away from the adoptive parents for a period of time. In a few of the cases the threat of legal and of physical measures was combined.

Since the threats were made before the adoption petition had been granted, they were very disturbing to the adoptive parents, whether or not they were followed up. For the most part it was the natural mother who made threats or moves toward reclaim-

---

[1] During 1944 to 1947, there were 1,534 independent petitions filed in Florida for the adoption of white children, unrelated to the petitioners. Forty-eight of these were not completed, 12 of them being withdrawn because the natural parents decided not to go through with the adoptions. Since the sample we studied represented something less than one-third of all the adoptions completed in Florida during the study period and since it was a random sample, it seems reasonable to add to the 36 cases already described an estimated four others (a third of the 12 mentioned above) for whom difficulties with the natural parents were known to have prevented adoption.

ing the child. Two natural fathers, however, joined their wives in threatening the removal of the child, and in six cases fathers were the sole source of difficulty. This latter happened chiefly when the natural mother placed the child without the father's knowledge. Two of these men threatened to contest the adoption but in the end did not appear at the adoption hearing.

A number of natural parents vacillated between wanting the child back and wanting the new parents to keep him. Perhaps the most extreme instance of such wavering is that of a natural mother who changed her mind about a month after her baby had been placed. She and her parents continued to vacillate, first offering objections and then consenting to have the adoption proceed. The problem was not resolved until shortly before the final hearing. After the adoption was completed there was no further trouble of this sort.

A different kind of problem, usually associated with threats of undoing the placement, was the insistence of a natural parent— usually the mother—on visiting the adoptive home and seeing the child. In some instances the visits were friendly and wistful. In some they were associated with weeping and pleas to have the child returned.

> One adoptive mother reported to the Department of Welfare worker that the natural mother constantly visited the child, wept over her, "spoiled her," said she wanted her back, and then declared that for her own good she must renounce her. The child, then twenty months old, wakened and saw the natural mother weeping. Later the mother asked to take the baby to town to buy her a doll, but this was refused for fear she really wanted to spirit her away. Finally, the adoptive mother called the Department of Welfare asking what to do and she was advised to put a stop to the visits. Summoning all her strength, she told the natural mother she must never come to the house again. The mother, weeping, promised to comply and never returned.

Some of the visits by natural parents began in a friendly spirit and then became tense and hostile. A few were belligerent throughout.

> One family was visited repeatedly by the natural mother, who once stayed for a week. The mother alternately asked to have the

child returned or to have the adoption delayed until her divorce was final, but finally decided to let the adoption proceed undisturbed. The adoptive parents gave her money and clothes, and tried to help her in various other ways. Later, however, when she and the natural father, both of whom had been drinking, tried to reclaim the child, the adoptive father drove them out with his shotgun. Still later, the natural mother came with friends, seized the child (then nearly four) and would have driven away with him, but the adoptive mother snatched him back. Even after the adoption became final, when the little boy was five, some visits were exchanged, although these were no longer regarded as a serious problem.

All the difficulties mentioned so far stemmed from the natural parent (usually the natural mother) changing her mind or at least clinging to the child. Five adoptive families experienced problems of a different order. Three of these involved attempts to get money. (These were the only reported instances of the "extortion" risk mentioned by Gellhorn.) A different kind of problem, reported only once, was the unsuccessful attempt of a natural mother to force the adoptive parents to assume custody of an older child as the price of keeping the one originally placed with them. The final sort of problem might more fairly be called a problem that the two mothers made for each other. In this case, the natural mother changed her mind and was awarded custody of the child at the preliminary hearing, but a year and a half later she succumbed to the constant pleading of the would-be adoptive mother and let her take the child.

For the most part, difficulties with natural parents persisted less than a year. In more than half of the cases (22), the difficulty was resolved by the end of ten months, usually within six. In a few cases the period of overt difficulty was very brief. In 11 cases, however, the problems lasted between twelve and eighteen months; in 6, they persisted for more than four years, and in one they were still continuing at the time of the study.

What the tension or bickering between adoptive and natural parents meant for the children is a matter of speculation. Four-fifths of the children were under three years old at the time the problems with their natural parents were resolved. Moreover, the majority of these problems were worked out without direct involvement of the child—in six of the 36 cases with no direct contact between natural and adoptive parents. On the other hand, in a few cases the child was directly involved at an age when he must have been aware of the tension and conflict centering on him. In several other instances, which did not involve the threat of his removal from the adoptive home, he was party to a strained and anxious situation caused by the visits of the natural parents. Actually, very few natural parents created problems after the adoption became final, but the adoptive parents could not be certain that this would be the case.

Circumstances Related to Problems with Natural Parents

The likelihood of the adoptive parents experiencing difficulties with the natural parents was increased by certain interrelated circumstances. Among them were: the amount of contact with the natural parents, the type of person making the adoption arrangements, the manner in which adoption came about, and the age of the child at placement.

Contact with the Natural Parents. Trouble between natural and adoptive parents is unlikely to occur if they do not know each other's identity. A pertinent question, then, is: In what proportion of these adoptions did the natural parents know who the adoptive parents were? Unfortunately, our data do not answer this question directly. If the placement was arranged by the natural parent or a close relative or friend, the identity of the adoptive parents was certainly known. If it was arranged by a doctor or some other less personal intermediary, it is difficult to be sure. The records indicate that in many cases the doctor did not divulge the identity of the two sets of parents. In other cases, the adoption procedure was such that in the process of signing the "consent" the natural parents might have access to the name and address of the adoptive parents.

It seems evident, then, that many adoptive parents did, and many did not, know who the natural parents were, but the records permit no reliable count of their number. We were, however, able to determine from the records the number of parents who had direct contact with each other. This number includes the 115 placements (24 per cent) arranged directly by the natural parents, as well as 71 of the others. In all, 186 (38 per cent) of the adoptive couples had direct contact with natural parents at some time before the adoption was completed. This establishes a minimal figure for known identity, although it may be assumed that some natural parents who knew the identity of the adoptive parents did not approach them.

For more than half of these couples the contact with the natural parents or parent was brief—a short meeting when they took the child or when natural parents' legal consent to the adoption was obtained. Fifty-six adoptive couples, however, had more extensive contact with the natural mother or someone close to her. The majority of these (46) had known the mother or her family before the question of adoption came up, sometimes as neighbors or friends, sometimes through baby-sitting services or boarding arrangements.

As would be expected, difficulties seldom occurred unless there had been direct, personal contact between natural and adoptive parents. Sixteen per cent of the 186 adoptive couples who had contact, as compared with 2 per cent of those who did not have contact, had severe difficulties with the natural parents. The total number who reported such difficulties was 36, 7 per cent of the 484 adoptive families. In these cases the natural parents either took steps to reclaim the child, threatened to do so, or caused trouble of some kind.

So far as we know, in all but six of these cases problems with the natural parents ceased once the adoption became final. In eight cases, however, the presence of difficulties delayed the adoption considerably.

Although difficulties with natural parents were unlikely to occur unless there was direct contact with the adoptive parents, the reverse of the coin is also worthy of notice. Eighty-four per cent of the adoptive families who had contact with the natural parents did not report it as a source of problems.

Adoption "Arranger." The importance of known identity probably accounts for the fact that difficulties with natural parents were most likely to occur when placement was arranged by the natural parent or some close relative or friend. They were much less likely to arise when placement was arranged by a doctor, a lawyer, a social worker, or some other professional person.

The less "personal" the arrangers were, of course, the more likely it was that the identities of the respective parents would not become known to each other. Again and again the adoptive parents informed the study interviewer that the physician who arranged the placement had told them only that the health history and educational status of the natural mother were favorable. A professional person arranged about half (53 per cent) of the placements in the total sample, but only four (11 per cent) of those followed by problems with the natural parents. On the other hand, natural parents or close relatives arranged not quite one-fourth of the adoptions, but over half of those in which problems developed. The difference between these proportions is statistically significant.

Mode of Arrangements. A third factor making for difficulties was the manner in which the adoption came about. The placements that were attended by problems with natural parents fell into three approximately equal groups with regard to decision to adopt:

a. Adoptive parents had no prior thought of adopting and just happened into it   13
b. Wanted to adopt but had not made any move to do so   10
c. Planned to adopt and had taken steps toward that end   13

Six of the 13 impromptu placements developed from babysitting or boarding arrangements, or from some sympathetic acquaintance having told the couple that a baby in a foster home was available for adoption.

> An adoptive mother said that one day when she was reading the newspaper, she heard that the neighbor's stepdaughter had run off and left her month-old baby behind. The step-grandmother then announced that she had a baby she was going to put into an orphans' home and asked if her neighbor would happen to want it. The baby was in a carriage "in awful condition—wet and nasty." But, as the adoptive mother told the story, he "held out his little hands so appealingly" that the visitor declared that she would "raise him up and educate him."

Of the ten placements in which the adoptive parents had thought about adoption but taken no steps toward it, nine grew out of hearing by chance that a child was available.

A couple had wanted a baby for years but had made no move toward getting one. By chance the husband overheard a telephone conversation between his uncle and the natural mother, in which the uncle kept begging the unseen speaker at the other end of the line not to dump her baby in a garbage pail. The nephew told his wife about it, and the next day they secured the baby from the natural mother.

A sales clerk jokingly suggested to a customer that she give him the baby she was carrying in her arms. He and his wife, who could not have one of her own, had talked "considerably" about adopting but had taken no steps toward doing so. The customer responded so readily to the suggestion that in a few days she brought him the child.

Decisions to adopt that were made on an impromptu basis were the most likely to be associated with problems with the natural parents. We do not have exact figures for the whole series of cases on this point but thorough acquaintance with the records leaves little doubt that most of the adoptive parents took a child after considerable thought. Thus, the proportion of impromptu arrangements among the parents who had difficulties was far out of line with what was usual.

Impromptu arrangements were also particularly likely to involve difficulties of long duration. Eight of the 13 impromptu placements entailed problems lasting over a year, as compared with only five of the 23 other cases.

Age of Child at Placement. The children in the 36 placements involving problems with natural parents tended to be placed at a somewhat later age than average. This may have followed from the fact that these adoptions were often spurred by the plight or availability of the child rather than by the planned action of the adoptive parents. While three-fourths of the children in the whole series were placed when they were less than a month old, three-fourths of those about whom problems with the natural parents developed were older at placement, a considerable proportion of them being a year or older.

Birth Status. In a striking number (12) of the 36 cases, the children were born in wedlock and some of the older ones had witnessed a good deal of marital conflict before they were finally placed. This proportion becomes less surprising when compared with the 22 per cent of the total sample born in wedlock. Nevertheless, it suggests that conditions likely to be associated with "parent problems" are also likely to exist when a married couple decides to place a child for adoption.

Effects of Problems with Natural Parents

It is impossible to assess the actual effects of these problems on the children or the parents.[1] One can merely speculate on the basis of what the adoptive parents said or revealed. Twelve adoptive mothers explicitly stated that although they suffered great worry and even anguish for a brief time, once the adoption was final the problem no longer existed. Yet some of these women, in their comments to the interviewer and in their advice to prospective adoptive parents, reflected the difficulties they had experienced. These implied anxieties were much like those openly stated by other parents, the most frequent being continued fear that the natural parents would reappear some day and take the child away. The degree of anxiety, very naturally, seemed to reflect the general nature and makeup of the adoptive parents. Several who seemed to be unusually secure emotionally apparently felt that by now the children were so much their own they had nothing to fear from the natural parents, except the disturbance their reappearance might cause for the children. Others were obviously still apprehensive that the natural mothers' reappearance might alienate the children from them.

The anxiety of the adoptive parents was not necessarily in direct proportion to the nature or duration of the difficulties with the natural parents. Some who experienced only a brief period of concern about possible legal steps to reclaim the children never ceased to fear that the natural parents might still come and take them, while some who went through protracted conflict seemed to dismiss the problem once it had been resolved. The differences in reactions appeared to relate more to the individual than to the problem itself. This impression is supported by the fact that some adoptive mothers who did not experience overt problems with the natural parents also harbored anxiety about their possible appearance or reappearance.

---

[1] Some differences in adoption outcome that were associated with the presence or absence of contact between the two sets of parents are reported in Chapter VII and Part II, Chapter XVII.

Some evidence concerning the impact of early problems with natural parents emerged in answer to a question asked of all who were interviewed: What advice would you give to others who want to adopt children? About one-third of the 36 parents who had had difficulties emphasized the need of protection against the kind of problems they had experienced. Nine advised using an adoption agency, although three of these hedged the recommendation—two remarking that this safer method was too slow for them, and another declaring that for her part she would be quite ready to take a child who had been left in a garbage pail. Two advised getting a child through a doctor in order to avoid problems, and four merely voiced warnings to be sure that everything was in order from the legal standpoint. Some of these, and one or two others, explicitly warned against knowing or having any contact with the natural parents.

Interestingly, however, the adoptive parents who had had problems with natural parents were no more likely to make such suggestions than those who had not experienced such problems. About the same proportion of the others recommended using an agency or making sure that legalities were well taken care of. And a somewhat larger proportion recommended arranging the placement through a professional person.

Apparently, then, the adoptive parents who had had problems with the natural parents were unlikely to regard these problems as an argument against independent adoptions. This suggests that most of them took the problems in stride and, at least on a conscious level, relegated them to the past once they ceased to be a present danger.

THE RISK OF RECEIVING A HANDICAPPED CHILD

The risk of adopting a handicapped child is thought to be especially great in independent adoptions because most of the children are taken in early infancy, before a dependable assessment of intellectual potential or even physical well-being can be made. In assessing the extent to which the parents in our sample were penalized by this risk, the key question is: How many couples adopted a child who turned out to be physically or intellectually handicapped?

The Number of Handicapped Children

An attempt to report the extent to which this particular risk materialized immediately runs into problems of definition. The usual conception of the word "handicapped," as used in connection with adoption, is probably the one stated by Gellhorn: that the adoptive parents "may accept responsibility for a child physically or mentally incapable of maturing into a healthy human being."[1] There are, however, less extreme defects (such as seriously impaired vision) that should probably be included as handicaps, since they may hamper a child and cause problems for his adoptive family. Then too a condition that is cured in infancy or early childhood, with little worry or expense, is obviously not to be equated with one that yields only after a great investment of anxiety and money on the part of the parents and after suffering for the child, with possible—and usually indeterminable—traumatic effects. Yet both kinds must be reviewed in reporting on the number of parents who received children with physical or intellectual handicaps.

Assessment of risk must also take into account whether an adoptive parent who received a handicapped child did so wittingly or unwittingly. This too poses difficult problems of classification. Some parents adopt a child they believe to be healthy and normal, often on the strength of a medical examination. Some adopt a child they know to be seriously ill or otherwise disabled and unlikely ever to be normal. In such cases it is relatively easy to say whether they received a handicapped child wittingly or unwittingly. Some, however, adopt a child who is obviously ailing or in bad shape generally, in the expectation that his condition will yield to tender, loving care. Such parents know the child is not well but may not realize that he will remain physically or mentally disadvantaged. Thus they are both witting and unwitting.

Since—for these and other reasons—opinions may differ about where to draw the line that separates seriously handicapped children from those less severely afflicted, the information about the children will be presented case by case under the following

[1] Gellhorn, Walter, *Children and Families in the Courts of New York City.* Dodd, Mead and Co., New York, 1954, p. 403.

two headings, so that the reader can make his own calculation. These classifications include only those children who had the disability at the time they came to their adoptive homes or in whom the likelihood of developing the disability was probably latent, and who were still handicapped when the follow-up study was made.

1. Disabilities and disorders that may greatly limit normal social functioning
2. Less serious disabilities and disorders that may somewhat handicap normal functioning

In Table 21, which covers both groups, information is given as to the nature and degree of the disability, age at placement, sex, time at which the adoptive parents became aware that "something was wrong," time at which the disability was diagnosed,[1] and source of adoption.

Serious Disabilities and Disorders

At the time of the follow-up interview, 13 children were reported to have physical or intellectual handicaps of the sort to which Gellhorn's definition apparently applies. As Table 21 shows, one of these children had a congenital heart defect, five had severe neurological disorders, three had brain injuries, and five (including some of the preceding) were mentally retarded.

Seven of these children were placed for adoption when they were less than a month old. In only one of these cases were the parents aware at that time that the child had the disability listed above. This child was a "blue baby," so ill at the time of placement that the adoptive parents were advised by their physician not to take him. He died during a tonsillectomy when he was six years old.

Five of the children who were placed very early had disabilities that showed up only considerably after adoption, although three of them were in bad physical condition at placement.

Three of the severely handicapped children were placed between three and six months of age. At placement the adoptive

---

[1] Omitted from the count were 16 children who had asthma at time of adoption that later cleared up. Also omitted were 13 children described as mentally retarded by their teachers but whose I.Q. and achievement tests were in the normal range.

TABLE 21. PERSISTENT HANDICAPS, PRESENT OR PROBABLY LATENT AT TIME OF PLACEMENT AND TIME OF RECOGNITION, TIME OF DIAGNOSIS, AND SOURCE OF PLACEMENT

Nature of disability	Age at placement	Sex	Time at which adoptive parents first recognized a health problem or disability [a]	Time at which disability was diagnosed	Source of adoption [b]
Severe handicap					
1. Congenital heart defect	15 days	M	Pl	Pl	1
2. Cerebral palsy	3 months	M	Pl	AP	5
3. Cerebral palsy	1 month	M	AA	AA	3
4. Brain damage from encephalitis	6 months	M	Pl	AP	5
5. Muscular dystrophy	1 week	M	AA	AA	3
6. Severe hand tremors and tic; learning difficulties	3 days	M	AA	AA	5
7. Severe glandular obesity; learning difficulties	3 days	M	AA	AA	5
8. Mental retardation attributed to brain injury	4 months	M	AA	AA	6
9. Mental retardation attributed to brain injury	12 days	M	AA	AA	3
10. Mental retardation attributed to brain injury	6 years	M	AP	AA	1
11. Mental retardation, cause unspecified	2 years	M	Pl	Pl	2
12. Severe visual and muscular impairment	1 day	M	Pl	AP	3
13. Mental retardation, cause unspecified	3 days	M	AA	AA	1
Less serious handicap					
14. Impaired vision	1 month	M	Pl	AA	5
15. Blindness in one eye	3 days	M	AA	AA	3
16. Short leg	10 days	F	Pl	AA	1
17. Partial hearing loss and emotional instability, attributed to brain abscess or tumor	2 weeks	F	AA	AA	1
18. Motor and speech disability, learning difficulties, strabismus	1 day	F	AP	AA	1
19. Severe asthma "from earliest infancy"	1 day	F	AP	AP	3

[a] Pl—At placement
AP—After placement, but before the adoption was completed
AA—After adoption petition had been granted

[b] Placement arranged by:
1. Natural parent directly
2. Close relative of natural parent
3. Doctor or other medical personnel
4. Lawyer
5. Friend of natural and/or adoptive parents (includes cousins, etc.)
6. Court

parents recognized that two of these children were ill, and the diagnosis of their condition (cerebral palsy and post-encephalitis) was made before adoption. The third child's disability, mental retardation, was neither recognized nor diagnosed until after adoption.

> One of these children (Case 2 on the list), presently badly crippled with cerebral palsy, weighed only three pounds at birth and was in an incubator for forty-two days before the natural mother took him home. When the adoptive mother received him two months later, he was "just skin and bones" and "was in such bad condition that he couldn't swallow or open his hands."
> Another child (Case 4), who suffers from the after-effects of toxic encephalitis, acquired the disease after placement, but it was said to have developed from his very poor condition and the severe throat infection he had when placed at the age of six months. Behavior problems, stemming from the effects of the disease, were evident before the adoption petition was granted.

Two other severely handicapped children were placed at two and six years, respectively. In both cases the disability, mental retardation, was evident at placement. Apparently, neither mother recognized its extent or permanence, one mother not realizing until after the adoption was final that the child was mentally retarded.

> One of these children (Case 11) was not only mentally retarded but, according to a psychiatric examination when he was eight years old, was probably psychopathic or psychotic as well. He was obviously physically retarded when he was placed at the age of two years. He could not walk or talk and was suffering from gross neglect. His natural mother was psychotic at that time but the adoptive parents were assured that the child could not have inherited her illness.
> The other (Case 10) was placed at the age of six but the adoptive mother thought he was about three because he did not talk and had "a baby gait." The doctor who examined him a few weeks after placement knew at once that he was retarded but assumed that the mother must realize this also, and therefore did not mention it to her until several years later. At the time of follow-up, the mother said she realized from the first that the boy was "backward," but she attributed this to his unfortunate history and thought she could help him "catch up."

Reviewing the 13 cases of severely handicapped children, we find that in only two was the nature of the child's disability known to the adoptive parents before or at the time he was placed for adoption. If one asks, then, how many couples unwittingly received a severely handicapped child, the answer is that 11 of the 13 thought either that they were adopting a healthy, normal baby or (sometimes against their doctor's warning) that they were adopting a baby who needed only loving care and medical attention to become healthy. Three of these couples, however, received diagnoses of the children's condition before the adoption became final and chose to keep them nevertheless. Therefore, if one thinks of adoption rather than placement, the number who unwittingly adopted a seriously handicapped child was eight out of 484 adoptive couples.

Less Handicapping Defects and Disorders

In addition to the children just described, six others had less severe disabilities of the sort usually classified as "handicaps." Two of these children had serious visual impairment, one being blind in one eye. One had partial loss of hearing and emotional instability, both of which were attributed to a brain tumor, which had been removed when he was four. Another had some sort of motor and speech impairment, as well as a low I.Q. The fifth child was handicapped by having one leg so much shorter than the other that walking and running were difficult. None of these conditions was clearly detectable at the time of placement.

The last on this list was a child, placed when she was a day old, who had severe asthma almost from the start and who still had it to a substantial degree at the time of follow-up. To include asthma in the list of handicapping conditions raises the question of whether 16 other children, who once had asthma but had improved greatly or were entirely relieved, should also be included,[1] since asthma is said by some authorities to be basically constitutional. We decided against including these cases, however, because they varied so widely in age at onset and in severity and duration of the disorder, and also because some authorities

---

[1] Three other asthmatic children had severe handicaps of various sorts and have already been included in the list of handicapped.

say that psychological factors at least trigger the disease. If the cases of mild or outgrown asthma had been included, they would have increased the proportion of couples who adopted handicapped children by 2.5 percentage points.

We have also omitted from the count 13 children who were described by their teachers as mentally retarded but whose I.Q. and achievement test scores cast doubt on the teachers' opinions. Eight other children so described have already been included in our count, two because of a diagnosis of mental retardation that was supported by psychological tests and other examinations, and six because of other disabilities.

By our way of reckoning, then, there were six children in the group who had less serious handicaps. All these children were placed when under a month of age, all but one of them when they were less than two weeks old. In only one case was the nature of disability diagnosed before adoption, but most of the children were either in poor physical condition at placement or were recognized before adoption as probably having "something wrong."

Our best answer to the question how many adoptive parents received a handicapped child is that at the time of the follow-up study 19 children (about 4 per cent of the total) were described as having some physical or intellectual problem (at least fairly serious in nature) that was not clearly acquired after placement.

Omitted from this figure are 16 children who had had asthma, as well as 13 who were described as "problem learners" or "slow learners" by their teachers and who did not have any of the other disabilities listed above. These children were omitted because the origin, severity, and outcome of such problems are in doubt, and because the parents did not appear to regard the children as handicapped.

To the count of handicapped children received for adoption should perhaps be added those who were received but not adopted. There were three such cases among the 1,534 petitions filed in 1944–1947 by white applicants unrelated to the child they wanted to adopt. Since our sample represents something less than a third of the total adoptions during the study period, the addition of such children would add only one child (about 0.07 per cent) to our count of handicapped.

As to the couples who received a handicapped child and never filed a petition for adoption, no count is possible. It seems unlikely that there were many, however, if only because serious handicaps were rarely discovered until after adoption.

Were the Handicaps Knowable at Adoption?

Could the parents have known that they were adopting a child who would grow up under a handicap? It has already been noted that two of the 19 couples were aware at the time of placement that they were taking a child with a serious disability, and four others knew the diagnosis before adoption. (See Table 21.)

Could the other parents have known they were adopting children who had overt or latent disabilities of the sorts we have considered handicaps? The question can be approached through several others. Were the children placed at an age when the disability could be detected? Who placed them? What was their physical condition at placement?

Most of the handicaps were of a kind that becomes detectable only after infancy. According to our medical advisers, who reviewed the evidence, two-thirds of the health problems probably could not have been recognized before the adoption was final, even with an unusually thorough examination; and most of them could not have been predicted by a full medical history of the natural parents.

Most of the children who developed these handicaps, however—like the other children in the sample—were placed at an early age: eight within the first week, six others within the first month, and three others within the first six months. One of the mentally retarded boys, however, was placed at two years, and one at six years. (Their retardation was evident at the time of placement.) For the most part, then, the age at which these children were placed made it unlikely that disabilities would be recognized before placement. Over half of the adoptive couples, however, did know that they were taking a child who was ill or in poor physical condition. And a few of the others recognized before the adoption was completed that the child had some health problem.

Table 22 shows the extent to which the handicaps could have been detected at the time of placement, and the relation of this point to the time when the parent realized that the child had a health problem. To recognize a health problem did not, of course, mean that the parent realized exactly what the problem was or that the child would not overcome it.

TABLE 22. EXISTING PHYSICAL OR INTELLECTUAL HANDICAPS, NOT CLEARLY ACQUIRED AFTER PLACEMENT: PARENTAL AWARENESS OF SOME HEALTH PROBLEM BY DETECTABILITY OF EXISTING HANDICAP

When current handicap was detectable	Adoptive parents aware of some health problem[a]			Total
	At placement	After placement	After adoption	
Detectable at placement	3	..	1	4
Pre-placement detectability uncertain	1	1	..	2
Probably not detectable before placement	3	2	8	13
Total	7	3	9	19

[a] Not necessarily the current handicap.

It is difficult to determine whether the source from which the child was received was a factor in the recognition of a present or latent defect. A somewhat larger proportion of children placed by close relatives than by physicians developed some handicapping condition. Moreover, there was no instance of a physician-arranger failing to point out a condition that could have been detected at placement. On the other hand, even among the children placed by close relatives there were very few whose future difficulty could have been predicted at placement.

Physical Condition at Placement

Were handicaps more likely to appear in children who were not in good health at the time of placement? To answer this question adequately requires a look at the health status of all the children when they were placed.

The records of the investigations conducted by the Department of Welfare reported that before the adoption was final (in many cases before placement), 31 children suffered some illness or injury, 19 others had some sort of congenital anomaly, and 56 children were in bad physical condition because of extreme neglect.

The illnesses varied in severity. Among them were asthma and other allergies, jaundice, poliomyelitis, toxic encephalitis, and syphilis. The congenital anomalies were chiefly rather minor or easily remediable defects, such as clubfoot and strabismus. Among the few severe defects were hernia and congenital heart disease.

Over two-thirds of the 31 children with a reported health problem recovered so well that no mention of its present existence was made by either mother or teacher at the time of follow-up. Much the same was true of the children with congenital anomalies. Of the 19 children reported to have such defects, 16 had had the defects corrected before our investigation took place. Two of the others developed apparently unrelated handicaps, and the third died from a congenital heart defect.

In summary, 36 (almost three-fourths) of the 50 children for whom health impairment was reported in the early investigation records had no reported difficulties at the time of our study. Eight had difficulties—mild or improved asthma (5), and learning problems at school (3)—that, for reasons already given, we decided not to include among the handicaps. With these cases added, then, no persistent handicap was reported for 88 per cent of the children classified as having had severe illness, injury, or a congenital anomaly before adoption. From this it seems clear that refusal to accept for placement or adoption a child who was ill or who had a congenital defect would have ruled out many potentially healthy children and avoided few of the handicapped—if avoidance was an objective.

In addition to illnesses and congenital defects, the children who at placement were seriously malnourished or who gave other evidence of having been neglected seem worthy of note, for these too are children who might be thought of as being more likely to become handicapped. There were 56 such children in the whole sample, a number that includes 12 of those who were ill and one who had a congenital defect.

Some of the children were thin and undernourished at placement. Some were dirty and covered with rash. One adoptive mother was urged by her physician to return the child because she was so malnourished he doubted that she could live two weeks more. One mother described how "pitiful" the baby was when she first saw her: "scarcely anything to her," her eyes rheumy, her sore little body wrapped in a diaper that had been used many times without washing.

Only one of these 56 children turned out to be handicapped, as we have used the word. This was the child whose mental retardation was recognized by the family physician (but not by the adoptive mother) shortly after he was placed at the age of six years. It is apparent, then, that the undernourished, abused, and neglected children were even less likely to have latent handicaps than were those who were ill or who had congenital defects.

Parents' Opinions About Having Adopted a Handicapped Child

In the whole group, only one mother expressed regret for having adopted the handicapped child, and this mother had always been opposed to adopting a boy. The others affirmed acceptance of the children as their own, with their handicaps. They tried to secure for the children whatever help was possible, often at great financial and psychological sacrifice. A number explicitly declared that the pleasure they received from having the children had been worth all the pain and heartache. As the mother of one severely handicapped child put it, "We've had a time but I wouldn't trade one minute of it. If everyone could be as lucky as we were in adoption, it would be wonderful."

Some mothers were actually moved to adopt by the physical plight of the children, although they probably looked forward to the gratification of complete rehabilitation. That such an expectation was not entirely unrealistic is suggested by some experiences they described to our interviewers.

> One mother, after unwittingly accepting a handicapped child for adoption, knowingly brought into her home three others (not included in our sample) with varying degrees of physical and emotional difficulties. One of these, for whom the doctors held out no hope at all, she said had "recovered completely" from a congenital heart defect. Another was improving constantly. For these children, the presence of siblings with various types of disabilities seemed to

have been helpful. According to the adoptive mother, the children have learned tolerance of each other's problems and of their own. The child she adopted unwittingly still labors under his physical handicap, but he nevertheless looks forward with zest to a professional career.

Several of the couples were urged by their doctors or lawyers to return the children before adoption was completed. They refused on the ground that the children were now theirs to love and to help. These parents knew there was some health problem before the adoption was final, if not before placement; therefore their choice was voluntary. Those whose children's handicaps were not apparent until some time after adoption did not have this choice, but the majority of them also appeared to have accepted the situation.

There was, of course, great variation in the response of the parents to the children's handicaps; some parents were not as wholly accepting and supporting as those just described. The striking finding, however, was the extent to which the adoptive parents appeared to feel warmly toward their handicapped children and to have made great efforts and sacrifices to give the children the best possible chance for development. Opinions might differ on how well advised some of the efforts were and on the degree of success with which some of the parents avoided the pitfalls of overprotection and overindulgence, but this is for another chapter.

A further reflection of the parents' feelings was the advice they offered others who want to adopt children. It seemed possible that those whose children had some sort of handicap or health problem would be more likely than others to advise getting a child through a social agency. The difference was negligible, however. Twenty-six per cent of the parents of handicapped children gave this advice as compared with 22 per cent of others interviewed, a difference that could be expected by chance.

All in all, then, we conclude that the chance of getting— especially of unwittingly getting—a handicapped child through the independent adoption process was small, and that even when such was the case, most parents rated the adoption as successful in spite of the handicap.

CHAPTER VI

Adoption Outcome
as Judged by Home Ratings

Having shown that the great majority of adoptive parents were apparently well satisfied with the children they adopted and that very few of the adoptive parents encountered serious difficulties with the natural parents or received children who were seriously handicapped, we continue our examination of the outcome of independent adoptions by asking next how good the adoptive home appeared to be from the standpoint of the children's welfare. To what extent were these homes the sort in which children would be expected to develop well? How many of them, if any, were "unsuitable"? How many lay between the two extremes?

These questions are central to this study as well as to the debate about independent adoptions. It is through exerting control over who adopts children (as well as whom it permits to be adopted) that adoption law seeks to achieve its purpose of promoting children's welfare. And it was the revelations in the 1920's about the seriously unsatisfactory character of some adoptive homes that led to the administrative and procedural reforms described in Chapter I, as well as to the increased interest of social agencies in helping to select adoptive homes for children.

There are two main ways by which the questions can be answered. They can be answered directly by summating judgments made case by case by competent observers—judgments that are

based on conceptions as to what parental and other characteristics promote or hinder children's development. The questions
can also be answered indirectly by determining (1) how well
the children's development appeared to be proceeding (how well
each child was "adjusting" at the time the study was made);
(2) what characteristics of the home were associated with good
adjustment; and (3) how many homes had such characteristics.
The first of these methods assumes (as do adoption law and
social work practice and the public generally) that we know
what kinds of homes are good and what are poor, and that dependable judgments about home quality can be made in individual cases. The second makes no such assumption but, instead,
seeks to discover what the desirable attributes are.

Both methods were used in this study. The procedures and
findings of the first method are reported in this and the succeeding four chapters. The search for estimates of the children's
adjustment and for home attributes that differentiated one grade
of adjustment from another is reported in Chapters XI to XIII.

Information on which to base a direct answer to the question
of home quality was procured by visiting the homes and obtaining facts and impressions through interviewing one or both
parents. The problem, then, was to set up standards and assess
the homes in such a way that reasonably solid statements could
be made about their quality, in terms of the extent to which
they seemed likely to favor or impede the social and emotional
development of children.

To make such assessments posed a tough problem. The standards should make sense to those who read this report. Criteria
should be clearly defined and recognizable, so that qualified
independent observers would be likely to agree in classifying a
given home. The assessment method should be capable of repe-
tition so that it could be used in future studies of adoption and the
findings compared. These are difficult requirements when something as complex and elusive as the quality of a child's home is
under study, and we make no claim to having met them entirely.

In our present state of knowledge, there is no assurance that
the criteria chosen for judging the homes were "right" in the
sense that they are precisely the characteristics that make homes

best (or worst) for children. What we have, in the conceptions that guided the evaluation of homes, are not wholly verified criteria but rather some present-day ideas, partially substantiated by research, as to what makes homes good or poor for children.[1]

WHAT IS A GOOD HOME?

Law provided one source of criteria by which the adoptive homes were judged. In some states the adoption laws specify attributes to be sought in adoptive parents. Georgia's law of 1927, for instance, listed "good character, moral fitness, and financial ability." South Dakota's law of 1929 required that petitioners "be able and morally fit to have the care, supervision and training" of the child they petition to adopt. The Wisconsin statute of 1933 said that those who adopt children should be of "good moral character," have "respectable standing in the community," be "able to maintain and educate the child." Recently some revised statutes have gone farther. Louisiana's Revised Act of 1950, for instance, adds "health and adjustment" of the parents to the usual list, and Ohio's 1953 revision says that inquiries shall be made as to "the physical and mental health, emotional stability, and personal integrity of the petitioner."[2]

Other laws indicate certain sorts of conduct on the part of parents that are so disapproved that court action may be taken. Laws relating to neglect, for instance, indicate a long-standing agreement that gross lack of care for a child's safety, sustenance, whereabouts, behavior, and moral and physical well-being are marks of poor parenthood. Physical abuse of a child, exploitation of him to his physical, emotional, or moral detriment, and contributing to a child's delinquency are other legally forbidden acts on a parent's part that would seem to make an adoptive home almost *ipso facto* undesirable.

In the laws having to do with desertion, nonsupport, and divorce, other unfavorable aspects of homes are pointed up. Laws relating to drunkenness, drug addiction, immorality, and other

---

[1] Criteria are discussed from a somewhat different viewpoint in Chapter XVI.

[2] Georgia Laws, 1927, p. 142; South Dakota, Comp. Laws, 1929, sec. 208; Wisconsin Statutes, 1933, sec. 322.05; Louisiana Revised Statutes, 1950, sec. 9:427; Ohio Revised Code, 1953, Title 31:3107.

delinquencies on the parents' part are further indications of the kinds of conduct that are generally regarded as incompatible with good parenthood.

Another source of criteria was found in the ideas that underlie the home assessments made by trained and experienced case-workers in family service and child welfare work and in child guidance clinics.[1] On the psychological side, these social work criteria derive in large part from dynamic psychiatry. On the social side, they reflect social workers' own observations as to how disastrous family disorganization can be to children. To a considerable extent, they are supported by experimental evidence from psychology and child development.[2]

Four aspects of the home were given special consideration in the overall rating: the relationship between husband and wife, the parent-child relations, mental health of the parents (especially the mother), and social-economic factors. Qualitative differences within these aspects served as the major criteria by which homes were judged.

1. The relationship between husband and wife was regarded as the major characteristic to be considered in judging the emotional climate of a home and its likelihood of favoring or impeding a child's development. Excessive conflict or coldness between husband and wife, reluctance or emotional inability of one or the other to assume marital and parental responsibilities, usurpation by one of the partners of both father and mother roles—these and other severe failures in role functioning were regarded as unfavorable for children, not only because of the feeling tone they give the home and the emotional turmoil they are likely to create in the children but also because of the example they set and the unfortunate basis for identification they provide.

---

[1] Information on this point was obtained through an analysis of the social work literature, through a review of prior evaluative studies of adoption outcome, and through discussions with the field director and her staff.

[2] See, for example: Baldwin, A. L., and others, "The Appraisal of Parent Behavior," *Psychological Monographs*, vol. 63 (entire issue, no. 299), 1949; Schaeffer, E. S., "Converging Conceptual Models for Maternal Behavior and for Child Behavior" in Glidewell, J. C., editor, *Parental Attitudes and Child Behavior*, Charles C Thomas, Springfield, Ill., 1961; Sears, Robert R., and others, *Patterns of Child Rearing*, Row, Peterson and Co., Evanston, Ill., 1961; White, Ralph K., and Ronald Lippitt, *Autocracy and Democracy*, Harper and Bros., New York, 1960.

In this connection divorce posed a special problem in rating. The presence of divorce did not automatically put a home in a low category, but divorce was seriously taken into consideration in rating a home. If the home situation improved after the divorce, it was assumed that a child's bad experiences during a period of severe marital disharmony were not likely to be wholly compensated by later favorable experiences with a stepparent. Accordingly, if sufficient information could be secured, a rough rating of the home before the break-up was attempted, and the final rating represented a kind of average between this and the current home situation.

2. The quality of the parent-child relations (which, in this study, was limited largely to mother-child relations) was another aspect of the home that was thought to be highly important for children's well-being. The degree of warmth, consistency, control, and regard for the child as an individual were the aspects of that relationship that were particularly stressed in assessing homes.

A warm person was conceived as one who is able to give and receive affection appropriately and without anxiety, and one whose need to receive affection—especially from a child—is not extreme. The amount and quality of the control parents exercised over the child were judged in part by the extent of the parents' expectation of conformity to their wishes, and in part by the measures they used in discipline, by the reasons they gave for applying punishment, and by evidences of consistency or inconsistency.

Particular attention was paid to the extent to which the parents regarded the child as an individual in his own right and encouraged him to develop in his own way. This was judged by such clues as parental delight in the child's uniqueness, encouragement of his interests, activities, and ambitions, respect for him as a person different from themselves, appropriate guidance in matters beyond his capacity to judge.

3. The third home aspect that was examined in the study of home quality was the personality and mental health of the parents, especially the mother. These broad and elusive categories could hardly be overlooked in assessing the extent to which a

home is likely to favor or to jeopardize a child's growth and development. Emphasis was put on the mother, partly because she was the one usually interviewed and partly because current theories tend to give special weight to her influence in the formation of a young child's personality. The father's influence was viewed as enhancing the mother's, detracting from it or, occasionally, as compensating for lacks or defects in it.

The theories and experience of psychiatrists, caseworkers, and family counselors provided ideas on what to look for at the lower end of the mental health scale: strikingly eccentric behavior, excessive rigidity, overwhelming anxiety, lack of feeling for other people were among the attributes that were deemed unhealthy. At the healthy end of the scale, criteria were somewhat harder to formulate. In an analysis prepared for the Joint Commission on Mental Health and Illness, Marie Jahoda[1] has shown how numerous and how divergent are the present-day conceptions of what constitutes mental health. She was talking about people generally, but to a large extent the criteria she developed apply specifically to parents' behavior and attitudes toward each other and toward their children.

Among the criteria proposed by Jahoda, the most significant for our purpose seemed to be: "independent behavior," "self-determination," "perception of other people and the environment in a way that is free from distortion by one's own personality needs," "empathy or social sensitivity" (the ability to perceive situations and behavior from another person's point of view), and "mastery of the environment." Under this last heading, Jahoda includes adequacy in love, play, and work, competence in interpersonal relations, and ability to meet reasonable requirements of situations and to approach problems with appropriate feelings and with directness. These criteria seemed applicable both to the parents themselves and to what they allowed or encouraged in their children.

4. The final aspect of homes considered in evaluation—social and economic factors and those relating to health care and moral training—was given weight only if conditions were clearly dis-

---

[1] Jahoda, Marie, *Current Concepts of Positive Mental Health*. Basic Books, New York, 1958. See particularly pp. 43–64.

advantageous. There is considerable evidence that living at subsistence level or below can be harmful to a child, but there is no reason to believe that income beyond that which is needed to supply basic living essentials necessarily increases a child's chances of developing to his full potential. Accordingly, importance was attached to family income, father's occupation, type of house and neighborhood only if poverty was extreme, the parent's occupation one that is socially condemned, the housing far below standards of health and decency, or the neighborhood a hazard to the child. Similarly, no attempt was made to distinguish degrees in the parents' physical and health care of children or in the moral training or example they provided, as long as these were adequate or above. It was only if there was evidence of obvious carelessness and inattention to health matters or gross disregard for "law and order" that these aspects of parental behavior were given weight in the home rating.

RATING METHOD

With these assumptions as background, points to be inquired about in the interviews were listed and forms were devised for summarizing and recording ratings.[1] The material on which the home assessments were based was secured in the course of the home interview, occasionally supplemented from official records. The type of interview has been described in Chapter III. Usually it was held with the mother alone, but in a third of the cases the father was present for all or part of the time, and in a few instances only the father was available for interviewing. Each interviewer was required to cover a standard list of points in each interview, although (with a few exceptions) the order and wording were not standardized, and usual social work methods of interviewing were used.

Before the overall home rating was decided upon, the interviewer (who was also one of the raters) went through a series of prescribed steps. A detailed record of the interview was dictated as soon as possible, and a checklist, which called for a good deal

---

[1] The forms, schedules, and instructions, given in Appendix B, represent a condensed reminder of decisions reached in joint discussions of the field director, the interviewers, and the research staff.

of factual information as well as ratings on some attitudes, was filled out. The interviewer then made notes for a "diagnostic summary" under the following headings, which include the various "aspects" of the home that were described above:

> Marital relations
> Mother's personality
> Mother-child relations
> Father's functioning as a family member
> Other significant facts about the home
> Summary description of child (as reported by mother)

The interviewer then indicated on a rating form the points at which she placed the mother with regard to marital relations and to four "components" of the mother-child relation:

> Manifest anxiety in the maternal role
> Emotional response to the child
> Control of the child's behavior
> Regard for the child as an individual

These ratings, obviously, drew on the information analyzed and condensed in the diagnostic summary. The overall home rating, in turn, drew upon both the diagnostic summary and the ratings. No numerical weighting of home "aspects" was made but the summary and review required by these post-interview steps helped to sort out and evaluate the many elements that enter into a home environment.

The overall home ratings, like the ratings of "components," were made on a five-point scale, running from high to low, A to E. They took into account both the number of areas in which conditions seemed favorable or unfavorable to a child's well-being and the degree of maladjustment, if any, that was present. The balance of favorable and unfavorable determined the rating on the scale from A to E:

A. Home seemed favorable in all aspects under consideration: personality and behavior of parents, marital relations, parent-child relations, social-economic conditions.
B. Home somewhat less than good in some ways but the balance was preponderantly favorable.
C. "Good" and "poor" were about in balance.

    D. Home was preponderantly unfavorable psychologically (and in some cases, socially and economically also).

    E. Home seemed unfavorable in all the above aspects except, in some cases, the social-economic.

Each category was conceived as representing a range, so that within each there was some variation from best to worst. The raters indicated this by attaching plus or minus, if needed, to the letter assigned. For the most part, these distinctions were disregarded in the final analysis, but they helped the raters in placing homes on a continuum from favorable to unfavorable.[1]

With the record, the summary notes, and the rating sheet in hand, the interviewer met with the field director, who meanwhile had studied and analyzed the record independently. The material on each case was reviewed jointly, in detail. Additional information and impressions were often elicited by the field director or recalled by the interviewer. This extended discussion led to joint decisions concerning the ratings of the "components" and the overall home rating, which were then entered on the rating form. After the conference the interviewer wrote a brief statement commenting on the chief reasons for the final ratings and incorporated the conference judgments in the diagnostic summary.

All ratings were marked as being made with first, second, or third degree of confidence. This was done to indicate how solidly based the raters thought their assessment was, and to counteract the raters' natural tendency to use the middle rating as an indication of uncertainty.

In making the home assessment, neither the field director nor the interviewers had any information about the results of the various tests given to the adopted children in school (see Chapter X). In addition, all raters made a careful attempt to avoid judging the quality of a home by the information the parents gave about the child's behavior and personality. They were instructed to base their ratings on the parental traits and behavior revealed in the interview, not on how well the child appeared to be adjusting.

---

[1] A detailed description of kinds of evidence on which the ratings were based is given in the succeeding three chapters.

Even for clinical ratings, our categories are far from precise. The nature of the classifications required, and the multiplicity of the possible indicators, appeared to us to preclude precise definition. Moreover, we used caseworkers as interviewers (because their professional training provided the qualities we thought were most needed in a study of this sort), and such workers are unaccustomed to the kind of categorizing such definitions would have involved. Accordingly, we settled for broad and "nonoperational" categories and attempted to "build in" as much consistency as possible.

After all the ratings were made, a final step was taken. The field director reread all the records, with two purposes in mind: (a) to test the consistency of the home ratings, and (b) to make more explicit the criteria that had been used in judging attitudes and interpersonal relations. Such refinement of criteria was thought to be necessary to provide a basis for replication of the study. The categories based upon it were used in the analysis of data in the present study. They are set forth, with much descriptive detail, in the following three chapters. As a result of this review, 28 of the 438 home ratings were revised upward or downward. In no instance was a change of more than one half step (for example, from C+ to B−) found to be needed.

THE FINDINGS

This assessment method led to rating 46 per cent of the homes as excellent or good (Category A or B). In these homes there was no evidence of social or emotional pathology. There was, on the contrary, much evidence of happy relations between parents and children and of social and psychological well-being on the part of the adults, including a capacity for parenthood.

At the other extreme, 29 per cent of the homes were classified as D or E. In one way or another—and often in several ways— these homes failed to meet minimum standards in the social and emotional support and guidance the parents provided the adopted children. The remaining homes (25 per cent) were judged to lie between these extremes (Category C).

Table 23 shows both the number of homes in each category and the number of adopted children in the sample who lived in such

TABLE 23. RATINGS GIVEN TO ADOPTIVE HOMES AT FOLLOW-UP

Home rating	Children		Homes	
	Number	Per cent	Number	Per cent
Excellent to good				
A	91	21	91	21
B	109	25	106	25
Fairly good to questionable				
C	108	25	107	25
Poor				
D	62	14	61	14
E	68	15	66	15
Total	438	100	431	100

homes. The difference in numbers is too small to affect the percentage distribution. Nevertheless, it needs to be recognized, since there were seven homes in which there were two sample children.[1]

The percentages can, of course, be combined in various ways. To us, the groupings above seem the most reasonable. This means that, in our judgment, nearly half of the children had adoptive homes that seemed "eminently satisfactory," while, at the other extreme, between a fourth and a third were in "unsuitable" homes. What we mean by "eminently satisfactory" and "unsuitable" (definitely unsatisfactory) homes is described and illustrated in the three chapters that follow.

The homes of 46 children could not be rated because the adoptive parents refused an interview. It has already been noted that these couples showed no systematic differences from the whole sample on any traits on which there was consistent information. Information about 37 of these children was secured from teachers and from tests given in school. On these tests and ratings the children scored much the same as those whose parents had been interviewed. It seems unlikely, then, that the percentage distribution of home ratings would be substantially changed if the information about those who refused an interview could have been included.

The confidence with which each rating was made was indicated on a three-point scale. Second-degree confidence was

---

[1] Throughout the report the total, 438, is used, often referred to as "438 homes." A more accurate, though less convenient, label would be "the homes in which the 438 adopted children lived."

recorded for the majority (301) of the overall home ratings. According to the explanatory notes in the evaluative summaries of the interview records, the uncertainty was likely to involve a half-step difference rather than doubt as to whether the home was favorable or unfavorable. There might be some question, for instance, whether additional information would change a D minus to an E plus, or a B plus to an A minus. There was no case in which it was thought that further observation would change an E to a C, or a C to an A. High confidence was noted for 118 ratings, and only 19 were recorded as made with low confidence.

It is well known that ratings are likely to be more stable and easier to make at the extremes than in the middle of a range, and the present study was no exception in this respect. As the following percentages show, the A and E ratings were much more likely to be made with high confidence than the B, C, and D ratings. It is interesting that the largest proportion of high-confidence ratings was at the favorable rather than the unfavorable extreme.

TABLE 24. PERCENTAGE DISTRIBUTION OF DE-
GREE OF CONFIDENCE IN RATING BY
LEVEL OF HOME RATING

Home rating	Degree of confidence		Total
	High confidence	Medium or low confidence	
A	69	31	100
B	13	87	100
C	4	96	100
D	4	96	100
E	53	47	100

Reliability of the Ratings[1]

In order to check whether our confidence in the consistency of these ratings was justified, two sets of data were obtained.[2] First a reliability test, based on a small number of records, was made

---

[1] See also Part II, Introductory Note.

[2] In the context of this research, the question of validity seems sufficiently covered by the discussion of "standards" on pages 131–132 of this chapter. The validity of our definitions is either a matter of opinion and values or a question to be answered by the use of criteria that have not yet been determined. It has been suggested that the children's adjustment might be used as a criterion. This, however, does not seem feasible until (a) adequate measures of adjustment are developed and (b) the usual relation between home and adjustment is much better established than at present.

by the interviewers themselves during the course of the study. The evaluative summaries were deleted from 27 case records, which were then rated independently by interviewers unfamiliar with the cases. A correlation of .42 was found between these ratings and the original conference judgments.

This figure is somewhat lower than the usual correlations reported for ratings of broad dimensions.[1]

Perhaps one explanation is that the raters (who felt their work was under fire) experienced a "re-rating anxiety" that inhibited them from giving either very high or very low ratings. As evidence of this, the standard deviation of the re-rating was less than half that of the original ratings. Then, too, in calculating the correlation, six cases were omitted. These were cases where the field director, a member of the Children's Bureau staff, and a member of the State Department of Welfare participated in the reliability test. Had they been added to the 27 on which the .42 was based, the coefficient would have been raised to about .52.

While the size of this coefficient did not inspire confidence in the ratings, the reliability-test situation did not inspire confidence in the coefficient. Accordingly, arrangements were made for a test that would involve more records, less psychological strain, and a conference judgment—even though it obviously could not reproduce the situation in which one rater has had a face-to-face interview and the other participates in rating all cases. The second check was made by two trained and experienced caseworkers who were living in Chicago and were wholly unconnected with the study. The field director explained the rating system to them and worked with them on making practice ratings of a few cases not included in the reliability sample. Following this, the two caseworkers independently rated a random sample of 50 interview records from which the evaluative summary and any other evidence of the original assessment had been removed. After making their independent judgments, the two raters conferred with each other, using the rating form of the study, and reached a conference judgment concerning the overall home rating.

---

[1] Sears, Robert R., Eleanor E. Maccoby, and Harry Levin, *Patterns of Child Rearing*. Row, Peterson and Co., Evanston, Ill., 1957.

The correlation between the ratings made by these outside experts and the home ratings used in the study was .74—a figure much like those found in other investigations based on somewhat analogous ratings made by caseworkers.[1] The percentage distribution on agreement between the two sets of raters, reflected in the correlation coefficient, was as follows:

Complete agreement	48
One-step disagreement	46
Two-step disagreement	6

As will be noted, almost half of the ratings made by the Chicago judges were exactly like those made in Florida, and 94 per cent were within one step of being alike. To be sure, a considerable amount of agreement would be expected on the basis of chance. However, it is clear that the extreme two-step disagreements were a good deal less frequent than chance alone could account for.

Judged by either the correlation coefficient or the percentages, then, the extent of agreement seemed sufficient to indicate that the home ratings were reliable. Nevertheless, we would emphasize the tentative character of some of them. Much of our information about a home was derived from a single, though fairly lengthy and well-conducted, interview usually with the adoptive mother. As a result, some of the ratings were rather speculative, being based on information that was suggestive but not always as detailed or comprehensive as might be desired. We feel confident, however, that few of them are seriously inaccurate, according to our definition of what constitutes a good home.

Generalization of the Ratings

In attempting to generalize about independent adoptions from these findings, at least two facts must be kept in mind. First, the study refers to a particular place and period of time and to all the

---

[1] Hunt, Joseph McV., Margaret Blenkner, and Leonard S. Kogan, *Testing Results in Social Casework: A Field Test of the Movement Scale*, Family Service Association of America, New York, 1950; Ripple, Lillian, "Motivation, Capacity, and Opportunity as Related to the Use of Casework Service: Theoretical Base and Plan of Study," *Social Service Review*, vol. 29, June, 1955, pp. 172–173.

conditions peculiar to that place and time. Among the latter are the nature of Florida's independent adoption system in the years 1944 to 1947 and the nature of the adoptive clientele in a state that had a few voluntary adoption agencies. Second, the study refers to a sample, a large sample to be sure but one that, like all samples, varies somewhat from the total population from which it is drawn.

The first of these facts puts an unavoidable limitation on the findings, even as applied to Florida and certainly as applied to independent adoptions in the United States in general. The extent of that limitation is unknown and cannot be known unless this study is repeated from time to time in Florida and elsewhere.

The limitations introduced by the second fact, however, can be estimated. According to this calculation, the chances were 95 out of 100 that the true proportion of adoptive homes ratable as D and E (that is, the proportion in the whole population from which the sample was drawn) lay somewhere between 25 and 35 per cent. For adoptive homes ratable as A and B the corresponding range was 41 to 50 per cent; for C homes, 19 to 29 per cent.

It appears, then, on the one hand, that in Florida between 1944 and 1947 the independent adoption process—which included a social investigation by the Department of Welfare—resulted in two-fifths to a half of the adopted children (who were white and under sixteen in 1956–1957) procuring homes of the kinds rated as good or excellent. On the other hand, the process permitted a fourth to a third of the children to be adopted into homes that ten years later seemed very poor. In addition, from 16 to 32 per cent of the children got into homes of the kinds we judged to be the lower edge of adequacy.

Whether this record is good or poor as compared with that of independent adoptions in other states is not known except for the findings of a rather small study in one state, Connecticut.[1] In that study proportions of good, fair, and poor adoptions almost identical with those of the present study were reported. As to adoptions arranged by social agencies, the proportions of adoption outcomes judged to be good or fairly good has ranged

[1] Amatruda, Catherine S., and Joseph V. Baldwin, "Current Adoption Practices," *Journal of Pediatrics*, vol. 38, February, 1951, pp. 208–212.

between 75 per cent and 90 per cent.[1] In such studies (which include the Connecticut one just mentioned) the samples were usually small, and neither the standards used in making ratings nor the methods of investigation employed were strictly comparable with ours. To know precisely how our results compare with those of other kinds of adoption placements we shall have to wait for studies that use similar standards and methods of investigation.

---

[1] See, for example: Brenner, Ruth, and others, *A Follow-Up Study of Adoptive Families*, Child Adoption Research Committee, New York, 1951; Davis, Ruth Medway, and Polly Bouck, "Crucial Importance of Adoption Home Study," *Child Welfare*, vol. 34, no. 3, 1955, pp. 20–21; Morrison, H. S., "Research Study in an Adoption Program," *Child Welfare*, vol. 29, July, 1950; Simon, Abraham Joseph, "Social Agency Adoption—A Psycho-Sociological Study in Prediction," unpublished doctoral dissertation, Washington University, St. Louis, Mo., 1953; Theis, S. Van S., *How Foster Children Turn Out*, State Charities Aid Association, New York, 1924.

CHAPTER VII

Homes Rated Good to Excellent

WHAT THE ADOPTIVE HOMES WERE LIKE and what sorts of evidence the ratings were based on are shown here and in Chapters VIII and IX through a few examples of interviews and through an analysis of the characteristics of the parents that were stressed in the study. In the present chapter, the homes rated A and B are described. These homes, constituting one-fifth and one-fourth of the total, respectively, were regarded as favorable to the development of children and, accordingly, as "suitable homes" within the meaning of the adoption law.

HOMES RATED A

When the A homes were reviewed as a group, the characteristic that stood out most prominently was the clarity and comfort with which these adoptive couples fulfilled their roles as parent and as spouse. In these homes, each parent had specific duties that he carried out appropriately and without evidence of "working at it," while in areas of shared responsibility they simply and harmoniously performed as a team. Each had status, both in his own eyes and in the eyes of his spouse. The naturalness and ease with which family life was carried on were most impressive.

The parents were proud of each other and sensitive to each other's needs. They indicated this quality in natural, unaffected ways, not by copy-book statements. It was evident in the security with which they discussed their individual points of view, in their freedom to differ, and in their mutual respect for each other's point of view. When the mothers were interviewed alone, they made clear their satisfaction with their husbands and their esteem for them, and they presented themselves as women whose husbands loved and esteemed them.

The family members enjoyed each other's companionship but they also had separate interests and activities. They did not use either their outside interests or their joint recreational activities as a substitute for close family life, nor did the parents' outside interests interfere with their essential mothering or fathering roles.

The parents' emotional needs were not such that they made excessive demands on the children or attempted to hold them too close. Each parent was pleased when a child identified himself with the other parent, and did not interfere in the relationship. Mothers frequently commented on how close a son had become to his father and how much like the father the son was.

The parents were proud of their children and warm in their feelings about them. They did not push them unduly for academic or other achievement but did help them over discouragements and shared with them in the joy of accomplishment. If the children had social or emotional difficulties, the parents described the problems without undue emotion and had taken appropriate steps (which included ignoring minor difficulties) to deal with them.

The following abridged record of an interview shows the kind of material drawn on in making the A ratings. No one case can be typical of A homes in every respect, for a variety of home situations fell within the limited, but perceptible, range represented by the A rating. The illustration represents the upper segment of that range. It shows that it was by no means necessary for a home to meet current ideals in every detail in order to be classified in the top category.

An A Home: The M Family

When I telephoned for an appointment, Mrs. M said that she would be happy to see me, that they love to talk about Dorothy, their adopted child. I called in the late afternoon and found a family composed of the parents, the adopted child, Dorothy, 11 years old, and Grace, the couple's own child, age 8. Mrs. M, age 41, was a nice-looking woman, short in stature. Her manner was friendly, relaxed, and direct. Her husband, age 46, was clearly very fond of his wife and children, as was evident by the way his face lighted up when he spoke of them. He took an active part in the interview.

Mr. M at first seemed a little skeptical of the study. I asked if he would like to see my identification card. He said he certainly would; then he inquired why I had not been given a letter of introduction. I said that we thought the identification card would usually be sufficient; I said, however, I would be glad to have him call the local Welfare Department to verify the authenticity of the study, adding that some other adoptive parents had done so. He said "no," he was satisfied; he just wanted to assure himself that this was a bona fide study.

Mrs. M then said that Dorothy had not yet returned home from her Scout meeting. Mr. M added that they had not told her about my visit, since he himself was not too sure of its purpose. To this I replied that, while they could tell Dorothy about the interview after I left, it would be best that she not be in the room while we were talking about adoption.

We had been talking only a short time when Dorothy came in. She is a large child for her age, well-proportioned and wholesome-looking. She politely acknowledged being introduced to me. Then she turned to her father and told him she'd have to have a quarter a week from today for something the Scouts were doing. Mrs. M told Dorothy she'd like her to go play with her friend, Dianne, a-while. Dorothy replied that if she didn't mind she would like to get her homework out of the way first. Mrs. M said that would be fine; she should go to her room and close the door. Dorothy left without further question and could be heard singing and whistling while she worked.

Mrs. M then commented that, except for arithmetic, Dorothy never had any difficulty now with her school work, although last year she did. Mr. M added that this was partly due to the fact that she had a man teacher last year with whom she did not get along very well. None of the children did, and he felt that the school year was one that did the child more harm than if she had stayed out. He spoke kindly of the teacher, however, saying it was not that the teacher was inadequate but that he should have been assigned to a high school rather than to an elementary grade.

Mrs. M added that they know that Dorothy has ability. Even last year she got mostly A's and B's. Arithmetic was the only subject she got C in. An IQ test, given when she was four years old, showed her two years in advance of her age. Mrs. M said she and her husband were very happy to know that but they have never pushed

Dorothy "as far as keeping her pinned down to school work." Mr. M added that they both believe she needs other activities.

Dorothy gets along very well with other children. In fact, Mr. M said, she gets along "almost too well" with some of them, for they keep calling her all the time on the phone. The parents have had to "draw a line" on these calls because they have a party phone. Parents often have to "draw lines," he added, in order to teach children to respect other people's privacy and property, as well as their own; they are not doing their children a favor if they do not make some rules.

I asked about what forms of discipline they use. Mrs. M said that Dorothy balks once in a while, but it is seldom that they find it necessary to discipline her. Mr. M commented that they might just as well tell me that they are "stern" parents. "Oh, I don't believe I'd say that!" Mrs. M rejoined. "Well, that's the way I feel about it," said Mr. M. "It's no disgrace to let a child know where he stands with you; it's really a help. For example," he went on to say, "we don't let the children stand up and sass us or other adults." Later on in the interview, when the parents were discussing how to check our questionnaire on discipline, Mrs. M said she thought they should check each item in the first section as "supervise closely." At this, Mr. M winked at me and said that his wife was backing him up in everything he had told me. Mother replied that she just thought the word he had used ("stern") did not exactly describe the way they help their children live up to their standards.

One incident that occurred during the interview gave further light on how these parents feel about their children's behavior. Soon after Dorothy left the room, Grace came bounding in. She acknowledged her introduction to me politely but when her father told her either to play with her friend or go to Dorothy's room, she cried. During the marking of the discipline questionnaire, Mrs. M alluded to the "scene" Grace caused, and Mr. M good-naturedly said, "Now, honey, Grace isn't in on it, this time."

In addition to her Scout work, in which she is quite interested at present, Dorothy is also very active in Sunday School and church activities. Mrs. M said that neither of the children will miss a Sunday. Occasionally she and her husband would like to "backslide" but they are "kept in line" by their children. She then told about the square dances which the church sponsors once a month and which the whole family attends. The children look forward with great pleasure to these dances. Mrs. M said the dances are a source of good family fun; the price for the entire family is only 70 cents.

Last summer Dorothy went to the camp run by the church and also participated in its summer recreation program. Mrs. M was proud of Dorothy for her choice of activities: swimming, baseball, drawing, etc., all of which would benefit her later. She added that Dorothy loves to sing.

I asked whether the family had any plans for Dorothy's future. Mr. M said that he definitely wants both girls to finish high school; they may go to college if they want to and it is financially possible. As to what they do later, they may make their own choice of jobs within reason. He said that's his feeling; his wife could express hers.

Mrs. M said she agreed with her husband about the high school education. As to further education, she feels they should not be pushed into something which will make them unhappy. If they have some definite choice, they should be encouraged in it. As yet, Dorothy has no particular choice. Right now, she loves to sing and says she wants to be a singer and a movie star, but that's an ambition of the present. Regardless of the type of work one is in, Mrs. M feels that if you're happy you can do a good job. For example, she would rather that Dorothy be a happy dime-store clerk who does her job well than a person who is highly educated but is miserable in her choice of occupation. She said she aspired to something better for Dorothy than being a dime-store clerk, of course; she was just giving that as an example.

On this point, Mr. M said that all his life he wanted to learn to fly—wanted it more than anything else in the world. His parents would never give their consent. He took other courses, but they did not prepare him for what he wanted to do. In consequence, he has never been outstanding in any particular field. His wife disagreed with this estimate and pointed out that on his job he has gone from laborer, to mechanic, to clerk, and finally to supervisor, and that he has worked for the same company for twenty-one years. She said she was proud of his record, and I agreed that he seemed to have made steady advance.

Mrs. M then told of her present, temporary job as clerk with her husband's company. For years she worked in a department store. At the time they adopted Dorothy she was employed there. She gave up her job to be with Dorothy, but when Dorothy was about five she went back to work on a seasonal basis. At present they have a very efficient maid. She and her husband both finish work at 4:00 p.m., and the children get home from school only a short time before the parents arrive. Mrs. M commented that they all get home early enough to enjoy themselves in the evenings as a family.

How they came to adopt a child was discussed earlier in the interview. Mrs. M said that they had been married ten years without a pregnancy. They spent a great deal of money on trying to have children but without success. They had a happy life together but it was as if they were seeking something which they had not found until Dorothy came into their home.

It was through a friend that they found her. Mrs. M said that she went to the hospital and talked with Dorothy's mother the day the baby was born. Some other couple had promised to take the child and changed their minds, and the mother was "desperate." I wondered why Mrs. M went to see the mother instead of just getting the baby direct from the hospital. She replied that the mother insisted. She would not relinquish her rights to the child unless she was very sure her child would be loved and would have a Christian home. She thought the mother felt better about her decision after having talked with her.

Mr. and Mrs. M have never had any contact with the natural mother since that time. "No problems as yet," said Mr. M. I wondered whether he still feared problems from the natural parents. He said he did not; he is a "pretty stubborn old duck"; he knows that he and his wife had an excellent lawyer and that everything is legally sound with the adoption.

I asked how much they know about Dorothy's background. Mrs. M replied, "Only what the Welfare Board got." She felt that the natural parents' mental and physical health was important but that if you really love and want a child it makes little difference whether you have information on this or not. Mr. M said he thought any background information you can get would be of value, but both he and Mrs. M are satisfied with the little they know about Dorothy.

Dorothy knew about her adoption. Both parents felt it important to let a child know very early that he is adopted. They began at about three, as that was what the Welfare Board suggested. They told her a story about a boy and girl who grew up and loved each other. They were married and were happy, but they felt something was missing in their home; they had no children. They visited a hospital and were told that there was a certain baby there that they could have. When they saw her they could not resist her. They took her home with them and named her Dorothy, and they've all been happy ever since.

They added more details to the story about the boy and girl as Dorothy grew older. She often used to ask them to repeat it. Occasionally even now, she asked questions about her adoption. As yet she has shown no curiosity about her natural parents. Mrs. M said she has thought a lot about that recently: just how much she should tell Dorothy. She had been trying to "prepare herself" so that she would be ready for questions when they arise.

I asked Mrs. M whether she could remember how she felt when she first saw Dorothy. She replied that it was a "glorious feeling";

the only way to explain it was that there was just an "overflowing of love." She said that often people asked her if there is not a great difference between the way one feels toward one's own and an adopted child; but she could honestly say there is none. She got both of her children on their fifth day: that is, she came home from the hospital with her "own" child, Grace, on the fifth day. She felt that Dorothy was just as much her own as Grace. "You can't care for a child who is so dependent on you without having a feeling of love," she added. "For this reason, babies should be taken for adoption as early as possible."

When I asked whether they ever felt Dorothy was like them, Mrs. M said that since infancy Dorothy has been "just like her Daddy." She pointed to pictures on the wall. She said Dorothy idolized him, that she nearly always spoke of him as "my Daddy," not just "Daddy." Mr. M said, "Oh, yes, it's always 'my Daddy.' " Mrs. M said, too, that they thought the two children looked alike. They even thought alike in many ways. They got along wonderfully well together, although they had the usual little conflicts that sisters normally have. Both parents said the children loved each other dearly and were very loyal to each other. Grace had been told of Dorothy's adoption in much the same way Dorothy was told of it, and there had never been problems of any kind related to the difference in status of the two children.

Dorothy had had a very normal development physically, the parents reported. She walked young and talked young; by the time she was a year old she could "hold a conversation," said Mrs. M. Mr. M laughed and said when their own came along it took her such a long time to learn to talk that they almost gave up. He added, however, that when she did learn she made up for lost time and hadn't hushed since.

Dorothy had had no serious illnesses—only measles and chicken pox. Her tonsils were removed because she had frequent tonsillitis. When I asked about the "roughest spots" in rearing Dorothy, Mrs. M said that one time she fell and split her forehead open. Mr. M said he would also consider her tonsillectomy a "pretty rough spot." Mrs. M said that perhaps they were a little overanxious but that they felt the operation was taking much longer than it should. Dorothy did not suffer any serious after-effects but the operation was "very hard on her parents."

I said at this point that we had already talked about many of Dorothy's good points and wondered whether there were other strengths the parents could mention. To this, Mrs. M responded that one of Dorothy's greatest strengths was that she could adjust herself to any situation; that even if the situation was not just to her liking, she was willing to adjust to it if necessary. Mr. M added he thought Dorothy was more adaptable than Grace, and his wife agreed.

As to her weaknesses, both parents felt that the only real weakness they could point to was a "little streak of jealousy" in relation to her closest friends. If one little girl is playing with Dorothy and another comes to join them, they notice that Dorothy objects to the first one showing any attention to the newcomer. Mother said she only recently noticed this developing. This made her think it was probably related to her age, and she hoped that maturity would take care of it. Mr. M said that they had tried to help Dorothy understand the importance of sharing her close friends but that neither he nor Mrs. M thought of this jealousy as being a real problem.

Mrs. M then said that Dorothy had never shown any qualities of real leadership but that she is a "wonderful follower." She added that she did not mean that Dorothy had no convictions and would just follow along with any plan but that, once convinced a thing is right, she was always most cooperative with others. Both parents felt that Dorothy had developed a good set of standards and that they could trust her to do the thing she thinks is right.

When I inquired about the family's recreational activities, the dances sponsored by a community agency and their church work were mentioned. They both enjoyed the latter especially. Mr. M seemed quite proud of the confidence the congregation had placed in electing him vestryman.

As to their advice to others concerning adoption (another question I asked), Mrs. M said that they would thoroughly recommend adoption to couples who do not have children of their own. "These people may think that they know happiness, but if they adopted a child they would find an 'overabundance' of happiness and love resulting." Mr. M added that the couple should "definitely secure the services of a competent lawyer to ensure the complete legality of the adoption." Mrs. M agreed that this was of utmost importance. She said it would have "killed both of us" if the baby had been taken away after they had taken her into their home. "The 'waiting period' between the time you file your original petition and the time that the adoption becomes final is an anxious time," she said. "In your heart you know there is nothing wrong but you can't help feeling a great sense of relief when the whole thing becomes final and you know no one can ever take the child away from you."

As I was about to leave, Mr. M said he had another question he wanted to ask me: "How will this information be used?" I said I could not tell him definitely but that the Children's Bureau published booklets, pamphlets such as *Infant Care*, and that perhaps

ething helpful to adoptive parents would be written. By getting
opinions and attitudes of 500 adoptive parents chosen at random
we felt that some conclusions could be reached that would be helpful
to people who work in the field of adoption. I again assured them
that no names would be used.[1]

In the preceding chapter it was noted that the final step taken
in rating the homes was a review by the field director of all the
records of home interviews. In addition to checking on the consistency and accuracy of the home ratings, the field director
made a descriptive analysis of the chief characteristics of the
homes in each group. From this she derived a new set of categories and made ratings of the four parental characteristics (the
four home "aspects," as they were called) on which the home
assessments had been chiefly based: marital relations, mother's
personality, mother-child relations, father's functioning as a
family member.[2]

The ratings of each of these parental characteristics were made
on a rough, five-point scale, running from high to low (1 to 5).
The subcategories were designated as Group 1 (most favorable),
Group 2, and so forth, to differentiate them from others used in
the study. For each parental characteristic, the five subcategories
represented different levels of likelihood that a child's adjustment and development would be favored. Thus, Group 1 in
marital relations represented the kind of marriage regarded as
most favorable to a child's well-being; Group 5, the kind considered least favorable.

It was not expected, nor was it found, that all the parents in
homes rated A could be similarly classified under each of the

---

[1] In each of the personality and interpersonal-relations classifications described
below, both parents were classified as Group 1.

The scores and ratings of the children, obtained through the schools (and explained in Chapter X), were not known to those who rated the homes.

Dorothy was described by her teacher as "quite helpful in class. She is always one
of the first girls to be chosen when the class is divided in teams. She is a very able
student." Her scores in the Behavior Description Chart were: leadership, 32; withdrawn behavior, 8; aggressive behavior, 22. Sociometric score was 23. California
Test scores were: personal, 30 percentile; social, 70 percentile; total, 50 percentile.
IQ not known; achievement at grade level. Rating on Combination V, 1; Combination VI, 1.

[2] "Marital relations" had previously been rated as one of the "components" on
the evaluative summary sheet. The new ratings corresponded closely to those made
earlier.

characteristics rated. It turned out, however, that most of the mothers in A homes received a Group 1 rating on marital relations, mother-child relations, and so on, while most of those in E homes received a Group 5 rating for these characteristics.

If most cases had not shown this agreement, the home ratings themselves would have been judged erratic. In some cases, however, a rather low rating on one trait might be balanced by high ratings on others; for instance, some personality difficulty on the part of one parent might be balanced by evidence of greater than usual interpersonal adequacy in the other. Thus, as has been pointed out, each overall home rating, A through E, in itself represents a range and also a variety of combinations of traits.

Marital Relations in A Homes

Eighty-eight per cent of the couples in A homes were rated in the top category (Group 1) with regard to marital relations, the others being in Group 2.

All the mothers in Group 1 were positive in their feelings about their husbands, frank about how much emotional support they received from them, and appreciative of the part they played in the children's lives. These women were able to give their husbands love and affection and to accept emotional support without emotional conflict. Two illustrations merely suggest the many ways in which this was displayed:

> One mother, who had talked considerably about her husband in a way that recognized the value of his affection and support, commented with pleasure on the close relation existing between him and their adopted son. She felt that their son was lucky to have such a good father. She was proud of father's activities in the community and expressed pleasure in their quiet evenings at home together.

> Another, who was equally positive about her husband, stated at one point that she wanted the children to feel that "he is the head of the family." When she and her husband had differences about discipline they were always able to work them out, she said. She had recently told a young niece, who was considering marriage and asked for her advice, "Be sure you feel you can't live without him and then go ahead."

These examples do not convey quite adequately how indicative of their capacity to give to and receive from their husbands were the feelings these mothers expressed. This capacity was evident in their pleasure as they talked about them, in the sense of fulfillment they conveyed, in their tolerance for differences of opinion, in their willingness to share burdens and responsibilities. Quite naturally, and without questioning on the part of the interviewer, they talked about their common interests, about their vacations and other recreation with their husbands, and about their mutual participation in family life. Their comments left no doubt that husband and wife were happy with each other, provided mutual support, took pleasure in each other and in their children. Each had respect for his own role as well as for the other's.

Mothers in A Homes: Personality and Mother-Child Relations

Eighty-five per cent of the mothers in A homes were rated 1 (the top category) in personality makeup, and 90 per cent (for the most part the same mothers) were rated 1 in mother-child relations. The others were rated 2 in these respects. In the following descriptions of the traits characteristic of Group 1, no distinction between personality makeup and attitudes toward and relations with the children is made. (The criteria for the two sets of traits separately are listed in Appendix A.)

Nearly all the mothers who were rated 1 had in common: warmth, security, the capacity for giving and receiving affection, and the ability to accept maternal responsibilities with ease. As far as could be judged, they were basically happy women whose emotional needs were gratified to an extent that made them able to provide a secure, warm, mothering experience for their children and to participate in mature, mutually satisfying relations with their husbands. A small number of women in Group 1 did not have all these traits to a marked degree but, even so, in the judgment of our raters, their mental health was excellent.

The interviewers usually described these mothers as follows: first, they were easy and friendly in the interviewing situation and seemed both spontaneous and honest in their remarks. It was not that none of them was reserved initially or that none of them inquired about the nature and purpose of the study. It was rather that none of them seemed guarded or artificial in relation to the interviewer or in regard to the topics discussed.

Second, as was said above, these women seemed happy and contented in their roles as wife and mother, and secure in their place in the family. This was evidenced in the enjoyment with which they discussed their children and their husbands, in the way they described themselves, and in their interest in their homes.

The evidence of these mothers' easy acceptance of themselves as adult women, wives, and mothers was exemplified by the pleasure they took in homemaking and in their personal appearance. In almost every instance the interviewer commented that the dwelling-place had an air of warmth and comfort about it—a lived-in feeling. Possessions of the children and others were much in evidence. Some of the homes or apartments were very modest; nevertheless, they showed the mothers' "touch" and interest.

The third outstanding characteristic of these mothers was their sensitivity to the feelings of others and their great capacity for empathy. This was indicated by what they had to say about people and by their ways of handling their children. Their sensitivity came out most graphically in the manner in which they described their children. They were able to tell sympathetically and yet with some objectivity what the children were like as individuals. They described the children not only as to appearance and the ways in which they pleased or did not please them and their husbands, but also as to personality and feelings and problems. These mothers were sensitive to the children's reactions to their adoptive status and their feelings about their own parents, as well as to their disappointments and troubled feelings generally. This awareness enabled them to anticipate and handle crises in the children's lives in a supportive and understanding way. They did not have to rely on intellectualized prescriptions; instead, they had a facility for understanding a child's feelings and needs and reacting in a positive, natural manner.

A mother who had two adopted children had taken several other children into her home for temporary care. Although she enjoyed doing this work for the local welfare department, she gave it up because she sensed that the coming and going of the other children was making her adopted children somewhat anxious about their own status. She did not wait for this to become a problem but sensed the feelings of her children by the questions they asked.

These qualities of understanding and acceptance were shown too in the adoptive mothers' attitudes toward the natural mothers, which enabled them to handle the adopted children's feelings about their own parents with sensitivity and without destructiveness. For instance, one mother who had told her child about adoption in a warm way, told the interviewer that she had a pair of booties which were knitted for the child by her natural mother. She was saving these to give the child some day as evidence of her mother's love. Another mother, who had much the same attitudes, was keeping for the adopted child a picture of her natural mother.

All these mothers were free in telling the adopted children about the favorable qualities of their natural parents. The adoptive mothers' lack of anxiety on the subject and their tolerant feelings for the natural mothers were such that the adopted children apparently were satisfied and accepted adoption easily. This was in contrast to some of the situations in other groups. There the adoptive mothers tended to be less accepting of the natural mothers and were likely to tell the interviewers that their children never asked questions about their parents.

Understanding and acceptance were apparent also in the feelings and attitudes of these mothers toward relatives, friends, neighbors, and others in their environment. For the most part, their relations with others were friendly and enjoyable; when negative attitudes were expressed, they were within the context of reality and did not cause these women undue concern. The women maintained contact both with their own and with their husbands' relatives, and were accepted by and accepting of the grandparents on both sides of the family.

The majority of these mothers had apparently made good social and emotional adjustments prior to their marriage. While we did not have time to secure full familial histories about all the adoptive parents who were interviewed, many of the mothers in this group spontaneously told about their own parents and their brothers and sisters. When information on this subject was given by mothers rated 3 or 4 in personal adjustment, it was likely to suggest very poor family relations, frequently complicated by poor first marriages and other problems in adjustment prior to the current marriage. In contrast, the mothers in Group 1 had been able to establish their identity apart from the larger family group without any break in communication and good relations.

With respect to other aspects of these mothers' lives, all had friends whom they enjoyed, and all took part in some group activity, such as church work, Parent-Teacher Associations, or social clubs. They enjoyed their relations with their colleagues and had a sense of contributing to the common effort. They frequently told the interviewers about certain teachers, ministers, neighbors who had been unusually helpful or particularly talented. In other words, they were generous in their appraisal of other people's abilities and deeds.

A particularly important indication of the mental health of these mothers was their freedom from the need to make excessive demands on their children. While they were pleased by their children's affection and interested in their development, they did not become overinvolved in the children's activities. This attitude was revealed in many ways, such as by their appreciation of the children's need for friends and of their right to have an appropriate degree of freedom, and by their acceptance of the necessary separation that would come when the children were older. They looked forward to the children's growth and maturation. It was as though they were "tuned in" on their children's needs and interests without having to play the central role in every aspect in their lives. The following are a few examples of this in the reports of the interviews:

Mother wants Freddy to be independent and able to stand on his own feet when he is grown. She said she was "so happy" that when he started to school it was not a difficult experience for him.

The mother has seen to it that Jimmie has certain privileges but, at the same time, has worked out other activities that Joe, the younger child, can enjoy so that he will not feel neglected. She would like Jimmie to go into his father's business when he is grown up. She is not at all sure, however, that he will be interested, for he has scientific talents. In the long run, she wants him to follow the line of work he desires and is the best fitted for.

Mrs. W said that she has prepared Joan for sexual development and that the child is looking forward to adolescence with enthusiasm.

The mothers were pleased that their children had friends, encouraged them in their interests, and permitted them, when appropriate, to engage in activities with their friends that took them away from home. In short, they supported the children in their growing independence by their delight in and encouragement of their progress. In other groups, in contrast, some mothers had to deny that their children were getting older and were worried by the thought of their approaching adolescence.

This recognition of the need for individual identity within the family was further illustrated by the fact that the mothers could enjoy lives of their own apart from their children. They had their own friends and activities and enjoyed having time with their husbands apart from the children.

The mothers in this group handled problems, such as illnesses, financial reverses, and other stresses, exceedingly well, indicating that they were able to face reality even when such reality involved painful or unhappy experiences. This evidence of "ego strength" was apparent in their lack of need to deny reality or to give an idealized version of their situations.

One woman's husband was seriously injured, and she had the responsibility of nursing him for a year as a bed-ridden invalid, as well as having two young adopted children to look after. This mother was able to weather the situation in such a way that neither she nor the children suffered unduly. While she described this as a difficult period, it was not one that adversely affected family relations or the adjustment of the family members.

All in all, then, these mothers possessed the quality of personal security. This is implicit in all that has been said about them. Security is a relative term, of course, and does not mean that they were without anxiety or were always secure. Such security is rarely achieved in life. These women's security in themselves was such, however, that they were not fearful of others' opinions and did not feel unduly dependent on others. They were able to express their feelings directly (perhaps one should say that they were aware of their feelings and not afraid or ashamed of them) and were able to discuss them without undue anxiety. This self-tolerance meant that they recognized both their capacities and their limitations and were comfortable with the demands imposed by marriage and motherhood.

Personal security enabled these mothers to criticize themselves without feeling wholly inadequate; they could, therefore, usually move ahead to do something about what they felt was wrong. It meant that they did not have to have the children and others think they were always "good mothers." It meant that they could discipline their children without self-recrimination and that they could, easily and comfortably, set appropriate limits to the children's behavior. They neither overcontrolled nor inappropriately indulged the children; at least they rarely did so. In general, personal security enabled them to devote their energies to developing constructive relations within the family and saved them from having to waste energy in dealing with conflicting emotions within themselves.

Fathers in A Homes

Less is known about the fathers than about the mothers, since most of the interviews were held with the mothers. Nevertheless, a good deal was revealed by what the mothers said—or did not say—about their husbands. What could be learned about the fathers in the A homes indicated that, in the qualities discussed above, they much resembled their wives and were equally well "related" to their children.

Eighty-five per cent of the fathers in the A homes were classified in the top category on family functioning (Group 1), the remainder in the second category. The common characteristics of these fathers include the capacity to assume adult responsibility in family and in work life and to give and receive love and affection. That these traits were evident in their functioning as husbands, fathers, workers, friends, and community members came out clearly in the interviews with their wives.

In these interviews there was abundant evidence that the father enjoyed status in the family and was looked upon with love and respect by his wife and children. The wives pictured these men as kind, considerate, and as taking an important part in family activities. Although income and social level varied widely, all these fathers were considered "good providers" by their families. There was also evidence that the fathers enjoyed their work and received satisfaction from it—whether employed as farmer, laborer, or professional. Their wives were proud of them and commented about how highly they were esteemed and how well they got on.

Although there were differences related to economic and cultural factors, these fathers had friends outside the immediate family and most of them were involved in some aspects of community life. Those in the lower economic bracket were less likely to participate in Scout groups or Rotary clubs but were usually active in church circles or in some other local group.

> One of these men was a machinist who had been with the same company for thirty years and was especially contented with his work. He learned his trade from his own father who was with the same company. His father lived next door, loved the children and was regarded with affection and esteem by his son and daughter-in-law. The adoptive mother was proud of her husband's record and considered him a very good provider as well as a "wonderful man."

HOMES RATED B

The B homes, like the A's, seemed to provide a good emotional environment for the children. They were not quite up to the A's, however, in that some relatively slight problems in one or the other parent's personality or interpersonal relations interfered somewhat with family functioning. In the B homes, the qualities of personal security, clarity of role, satisfaction and affection, ease and naturalness in family life did not stand out quite as clearly and positively or in such an even way as in the A homes.

In six of these B homes one of the original adoptive parents was deceased. In two the adoptive father and in four the adoptive mother had died. In all of these homes the original marriage had apparently been happy and stable. Two of the adoptive parents died when the child was five, and the others when the child was somewhat older. Two of the surviving fathers had remarried; in each case the stepmother appeared to be working out an excellent relationship with the child. Although the other widowed parents had not remarried, they seemed to be handling the situation fairly well, despite the overinvolvement of one mother with her child. All of them seemed to be warm parents, devoted to the children and remarkably successful in their effort to meet the demands of a one-parent home situation.

Marital Relations in B Homes

The marital relations of most of the parents in the B homes were rated as Group 2. These were good marriages, according to our criteria, but not as strikingly so as the marriages that were rated Group 1 and that predominated in the A homes.

Some women complained a bit about their husbands not sharing sufficiently in bringing up the children. The husband's unwillingness to help with discipline was mentioned rather often. Some apparently thought their husbands a bit too "bossy." (Some husbands may have had the same opinion of their wives.)

Wives rather often said that their husbands did not talk with them enough and implied that communication between them was not free and easy. Others talked of not seeing enough of their husbands or of not having enough "good times" together.

A few women seemed a bit resentful of the husband's good relations with the adopted child. In a few cases, husband and wife were apparently a bit competitive about the child or tried, in a mild way, to isolate the child from the other. Some women seemed not quite sure that they were sufficiently good wives.

As is indicated by the rating, Group 2, all these difficulties between husband and wife were of a mild order, and the predominant feeling indicated in the interviews was one of pleasure and satisfaction. Not all couples in homes rated B were rated 2 in marital adjustment, however. A rating of 1 was given in 17 per cent of the cases; and in 6 per cent, the couples' marital relation was rated 3.

Mothers in B Homes: Personality and Mother-Child Relations

About three-fourths of the mothers in the B homes were classified as Group 2 in personal adjustment. The same proportion

h not necessarily the same mothers) were rated 2 in their
es toward the adopted children and their relations with
.... The following account of their characteristics in these respects serves both to describe most of the B-home mothers and to
define the Group 2 ratings.

These mothers had many of the qualities of those rated Group
1. Like most of the mothers in A homes, they did not feel weighed
down by the responsibilities of homemaking and mothering.
Whatever mild dissatisfactions they had with their marriage or
small problems they had in coping with certain aspects of their roles
as wives and mothers were far outweighed by their satisfactions.

These mothers differed from the majority of A-home mothers,
however, in not being as able to utilize their potentials and energies in achieving a full life for themselves and in contributing to
others in their environment. In addition, they were not uniformly
competent in all areas of their lives. There was an unevenness
about their adjustment that was not perceptible in the mothers
rated 1.

As compared with Group 3 mothers, however (the type that
predominated in C homes), these women's personality problems
seemed minor. For instance, while many mothers rated 2 had a
slight tendency to overprotect their children, they were not as
overprotective as the mothers rated 3. If they were anxious, the
anxiety did not seem to be so pervasive or to interfere so much
with their functioning. All of them were warm and mothering
with their children, and there were many more positives than
negatives in the mother-child relationship.

To be more specific in describing the mothers rated 2 in adjustment, we can say that most of them differed chiefly from the
Group 1 mothers in having less security in accepting their maternal responsibilities. Like these other women, they were affectionate and outgoing, "related" easily in the interview, seemed
to have happy, satisfying relations with their husbands and others
in the immediate family. It was with their children that their
insecurity, if any, usually showed up.

The insecurity of some was expressed in a tendency to be somewhat overprotective and indulgent. These women expressed concern about discipline and said they had trouble in setting limits

to what they allowed their children to do. For example, one of these mothers, who otherwise seemed a secure, friendly person, said she felt "sick" when she had to discipline her child and that she knew she protected him too much and permitted him to do too much as he pleased.

For others, insecurity in being a mother resulted in keeping the children somewhat too close and not allowing them enough freedom to develop independence. These mothers' fears and personal needs were not so extensive as to restrict the children greatly, but the tendency toward restriction was suggestive of problems in their own personal adjustment.

> A woman who evidenced affection and pride in her husband and family and had good relations generally, was overconcerned about doing the "right thing" as a mother. She kept her daughter very close to her and waited on her excessively. Although sensitive and intuitive in most ways, she did not seem to realize that the child, about thirteen years old, was having trouble separating herself from home.

Other mothers' insecurity was evidenced by their difficulty in handling a specific problem, although they usually felt quite adequate as mothers. It might be rivalry or jealousy between the children that was particularly upsetting to these mothers or they may have had excessive anxiety about telling their children about adoption or about sexual matters. While these are questions that bothered most of the adoptive mothers somewhat, the mothers who were rated 2 overreacted in a way that somewhat limited their ability to handle these issues helpfully.

> A mother described as being a very adequate person and particularly warm and sensitive in handling her child, said she had been "thrown" by her little girl's curiosity about sex and had been unable to discuss her questions with her. She also expressed some fear about the child's approaching adolescence.

A few who were rated 2 apparently needed to be assured that they were adequate mothers by requiring the children to be overconforming and unusually "good." One of them, for example, put so much stress on consideration and politeness that she overlooked her child's inability to be relaxed with her own friends.

A small proportion of the mothers were inclined to be over-controlling and to push their children too hard for achievement, particularly in school. Yet these somewhat rigid mothers were flexible in some respects.

> Mrs. X had very rigid ideas about conduct, religious observance, and choice of friends. She was the dominant member of the family and had a number of very definite rules that the children had to observe. However, she was warm in her relations with the children and very proud of them, and was able to be consistently fair.

> Another mother, who was somewhat overrestrictive, was not satisfied unless her son got the best grades in the class. This pushing was somewhat compensated by her ability to allow the boy a very close relation with the adoptive father, who was much more permissive than she was.

Most of these mothers rated 2 expressed satisfaction with their marriage and seemed able to give affection to their husbands and to receive it from them. Some of them, however, expressed a little dissatisfaction, feeling that they did not get quite enough emotional support from their husbands, particularly in disciplining the children. While this may have been a commentary on the husbands, it also suggested some unresolved feelings on the part of the mothers.

> A mother who was generally very well satisfied with her marriage, expressed some impatience with her husband's overconcern and permissiveness with the child. As she said, "Everything is an emergency where Joe is concerned."

> Another mother, although saying much that was favorable, said that she had to bear the onus of spoiling the fun because her husband wouldn't discipline the child.

A few mothers showed less interest in homemaking than in careers and other activities, and were inclined to be slightly aggressive and dominant in the marriage. They were not greatly uncomfortable, however, in their adjustment as women, and they were happy in their marriages. For example, one who usually made decisions in the home, and seemed to belittle her husband in certain ways, nevertheless seemed very fond of him and was appreciative of what he did for her and the children.

About a fourth of the mothers in B homes were not rated 2 in personal adjustment. Six per cent were rated 1, and 17 per cent were rated 3. The tally for degree of adequacy in mother-child relations (which has here been described concurrently with personal adjustment) was much the same. Divergencies between ratings on these two traits and combinations other than the usual one of 2—2 occurred in one-third of the B homes. Some of these out-of-line combinations, in conjunction with others referring to other aspects of the home, provided the basis for distinguishing "high B" and "low B" homes from the rest—a point discussed below.

Fathers in B Homes

Most of the fathers in the B homes (85 per cent) were rated 2 in personal adjustment and in relations with their children. The evidence suggested that these men were emotionally healthy individuals. From what little we learned about them, however, it seemed that they were not as secure and did not function as well in all areas as did the fathers rated 1.

A composite picture of the fathers rated 2 was this: On the positive side, they fully accepted parental responsibility. Almost all of them earned enough money to provide adequately for their families. They were kind individuals and affectionate toward their children. Most of them participated with their wives in planning and carrying on family life, although not to the same degree as men rated 1.

The following are examples of fathers who manifested these traits but had some minor problems:

Mr. R, described as especially kind and affectionate, took pride in being a husband and a father but was inclined to be a little overpossessive of his adopted daughter. This latter trait interfered with the child's relations with other children and suggested that the father was a bit immature.

Another father, a successful lawyer, was reluctant to let his wife know about their financial affairs and was unable to be relaxed in his relations with his adopted child. In this latter respect, however, his wife said that he had "unbent" considerably since the adoption.

Not all fathers in B homes were rated 2, of course, but the number not so rated was small. Thirteen of the 113 fathers were given a rating of 1 and four of them a 3 rating. Whether this somewhat more favorable standing of fathers as compared with mothers in these homes means anything more than that many fathers were not interviewed could not be determined.

Subgroups Within B Homes

Within the B group, about a third of the homes were rated "high B," since they had ratings of Group 1 on one or more of the home aspects that were classified. These 1 ratings were most frequently given either to the couples' marital adjustment or to personality makeup of one or the other of them. Ratings of 1 on mother-child relations were infrequent, but seven couples were rated 1 on all four aspects.

The following family illustrates the high-B group. It will be noted that, though this home was a bit superior to the majority of B homes, it did not come up to the specifications for the homes rated A.

> The father and mother were warm, accepting people, greatly interested in their adopted child. Both spoke positively of their daughter, were sensitive to her needs, and proud of her achievements. The mother, however, was inclined to be very rigid about manners, social activity, and social graces. The father denied the child nothing and was not able to participate in disciplining. The mother, too, was somewhat overindulgent.
>
> The mother was supportive of her husband and, to all appearances, the marriage met the needs of both of them. The parents seemed to have a good time together, had many interests in common, and appeared to be in agreement on all important matters.

The average B home did not overlap either the A homes or the C homes in any of the areas we evaluated. The parents described below exemplify this group, in that both their personalities and interpersonal relations involved difficulties which were reflected in the composite functioning of the family.

> One mother was proud of her adopted child and affectionate toward both child and husband. In personality makeup, however, she seemed a rather anxious type. Neither she nor her husband was able

to discuss adoption with their daughter, and the mother worried about this. She tended to push the child for school achievement.

The adoptive parents did not have a close relationship with their own families or with others in their environment.

The mother was the dominant member of the family. Although she expressed no explicit dissatisfaction with their marriage, she indicated that there were certain things that her husband did not share with her, such as information about insurance and income, and this bothered her. While the interviewer felt that this home was essentially a good one for a child, she also noted that there was evidence of less maturity and satisfaction in the parents than was wholly desirable, as well as certain other lacks in family relationships.

Another mother apparently needed to live by the rules; she tried hard not to be too rigid but was somewhat insecure. She said she had had a difficult early life but notwithstanding this had been able to develop and maintain good relations with her husband's family and others. She was warm and accepting of her adopted daughter but somewhat anxious in regard to her.

The father was a "good provider" but the mother said she was also employed in order to maintain the standard of living they wanted. The father showed great interest in the child and was affectionate and sensitive in his dealings with her, but was rather overprotective. Although both parents seemed satisfied with the marriage, they gave little information that would indicate a plus value in it for them.

A third group were more like C homes than B in certain respects. In each case one of the parents had a personal adjustment rated 3, a rating most frequent among the C homes. The overall functioning of these families, however, was sufficiently strong that the home was thought to provide a rather favorable emotional climate for its members.

The mother in one of these "low-B" homes was a rather tense woman who appeared to "relate" rather slowly to people, as judged by her response to the interviewer. She did not get along with her own mother, whom she always thought of as a "driver." She had practically no friends outside her immediate family. She was fairly happy in her marriage, however, proud of her husband and affectionate toward him, but she spoke of being lonely at times and complained that she has to "draw things out of 'Father.'"

The husband got along well in his profession and participated in the life of the family, but without free and easy relationships. He appeared to be the dominant member of the family. He seemed accepting of the children but was a bit overcontrolling.

The mother found it difficult to accept or handle jealousy between her two adopted children or to let them have responsibility. At times she, too, was overcontrolling. She was able to relax more with the younger child and was less fond of the older one, whom she identified with the child's natural mother. She described her as inheriting a "mean streak."

These brief summaries of cases may serve to indicate some ways in which the subgroups within the B range differed from one another. To show the kind of material in which judgments of these intangible matters were based, an account of the T family is presented in almost the full detail given in the social worker's record of the interview.

The T Family

When I arrived for my appointment, Mrs. T greeted me cheerfully, keeping up a steady flow of conversation about the weather and her Siamese cat until we sat down in the living room. An effervescent woman, she spoke so freely and spontaneously that I rarely had to ask questions. She was obviously pleased to talk about Ruth. As she said at the close of the interview, she would probably have gone on for two more hours if Mr. T had not arrived for lunch. Although I offered to show her my identification card, she said it was not necessary; she trusted me.

The T family consisted of Mr. T, age 60, Mrs. T, age 55, and the adopted child, Ruth, age 10. Mr. T was a draughtsman for an engineering firm. The family lived in a large, well-furnished apartment in the suburbs. The living room, in which we had our talk, was neat but Mrs. T apologized for not having had time to "ready up" after having had guests the night before.

I began by asking Mrs. T if she had any questions about the study, but she said no, she understood it was an investigation to see how the adoptions had turned out. I replied that we saw it as an opportunity to learn about parents' experiences with adoption and that the study had no legal implications. Mrs. T said that she rather thought so, and that the study should be very helpful.

She went on to tell me how very much Ruth had meant to them, saying that she had never been sick, had never caused them any worry, and that she was a beautiful child, as indeed her picture showed her to be. By that she didn't mean that Ruth was a perfect child, for she had her ups and downs, as do most children, but she and her husband were very proud of Ruth and had had a wonderful time with her.

Mrs. T then interrupted herself and asked me just what kinds of things I would be interested in knowing, and I suggested that perhaps she would tell me how they had happened to adopt Ruth. This question led to a long complicated explanation that began with Mr. and Mrs. T's inability to have children, although both had sought medical help on this problem. After seventeen years of trying, they gave up and inquired at two social agencies about getting a baby. This seemed hopeless because of the long waiting list. Then, in what seemed to Mrs. T a fate-determined way, they obtained a baby without agency help. Friends of friends told them about a baby a doctor had offered them; they had not accepted because they had changed their minds about adoption. Mr. and Mrs. T went to talk with the doctor and he decided they were satisfactory.

The natural mother was a dental technician and the father a young dental student. Mrs. T did not meet the mother, but she said with much warmth and feeling that she must have been a "gorgeous woman" in personality, a good woman and a good mother, and that it must have been very hard for her to give up the baby.

When told by the physician of the baby's birth, Mrs. T and her husband rushed down that very night to the hospital to see her and visited her every evening the rest of the week. The doctor and the T's lawyer suggested that the natural mother be given five days in order to be sure of her decision, so that she would not be making it under duress. The T's were quite willing to allow her this time, but Mrs. T said they were "on pins and needles" during those five days, praying that the mother would not change her mind.

Recently, the couple who had decided not to adopt Ruth came to see her. Mrs. T, without embarrassment or sham modesty, said they told her she had done a wonderful job with Ruth. Mrs. T's response was that it was Ruth herself who had the wonderful things in her, and that they were just fortunate in having gotten her. Ruth is a lovely child, Mrs. T went on to say; she is unspoiled. From a very early age, Ruth had known she was adopted. Mrs. T "kind of made up a little story" to tell her about this. It had to do with their being unable to have children of their own; so they went to a hospital and picked Ruth out because she was the most beautiful and seemed to be their very own child. She told Ruth this story when she was very young, but old enough to have stories told to her and to understand them. Recently Ruth asked what her mother was like and why she had to "give me up." Mrs. T said she replied without thinking, telling Ruth that both her parents were in the service at the time because of the war and so weren't able to care for her or to give her the things they wanted her to have. Ruth seemed to accept this explanation and asked no more questions.

Mrs. T went on to say that they had had several letters from Ruth's real mother before the adoption became final. They were lovely letters but she decided not to answer them. When the decree was final, however, she asked the Welfare Department to let Ruth's mother know and to tell her her how well she was getting along. They had heard nothing from her since; they hope she is happily married. She and her husband had some discussion over whether they should save these letters, her husband saying that they should be destroyed. She finally persuaded him to keep them so that Ruth could read them if, when she was older, she asked again about her mother.

Ruth, Mrs. T went on to say without being questioned, is an athletic child, interested in all sorts of outdoor sports. Her father usually took her horseback riding on Saturdays. Mrs. T explained at this point that Mr. T had always been a somewhat nervous man, but with Ruth he was never nervous or irritable. He loved to take her places and was very proud of her. Sometimes they all went to the beach for an afternoon, and occasionally to a movie. Ruth liked to watch certain children's programs but for the most part she would rather be outdoors roller skating or riding her bicycle.

Ruth played with the other children in the neighborhood and once a week attended a Girl Scout meeting. She had never been particularly interested in books, though once in a while she read. Mrs. T wished she did like books; maybe she would develop a liking for them later on.

When I asked what plans they had for Ruth's future, Mrs. T said they were going to leave this up to her. Since Ruth's mother was a dental technician, however, Mrs. T said that at one time she thought Ruth might be interested in being one. She didn't really know, however, what Ruth would decide to do. With her athletic ability, it might be that she would eventually become interested in working in that field. They would be able to send her to college if she wanted to go. Ruth was something of a leader, and occasionally became annoyed if another child wanted to lead. Last year she had one especially good friend whose parents the T's knew. The friendship became too close, however, with Ruth staying overnight frequently and wanting to play with no one else. So the T's and the girl's parents discussed the matter, and the girl was sent to camp for the summer. By the time school began, the friendship had quieted down.

Mrs. T then said she realized she had perhaps kept Ruth too close to her. Recently she had been trying to help her to be more independent, for instance, by encouraging her to go shopping in the center of the city with friends. She gave other examples of the sort and said she found Ruth very dependable and sensible.

"Ruth is an affectionate child—maybe sometimes too affectionate," Mrs. T said. She hoped this would not get her into trouble of the sort her own mother had gotten into. She thought, however, that Ruth would be wise enough to avoid this. "If Ruth came in now," said Mrs. T, "and met and chatted with you as she does so easily with grownups and children alike, she would probably kiss you goodbye when leaving."

Ruth had always gotten A's and B's at school. She liked school very much and usually got along easily with the other children. For a while she took music lessons but asked to stop because she preferred to be outside playing, as well as wanting to have time to do her homework. Mrs. T agreed but still felt that playing a piano could be a great pleasure. When Ruth was ready for high school, they would send her to a private school, for they both thought there were too many tough boys in the public high schools.

When I asked Mrs. T whether Ruth was like either of them, she said that she had some of her ways and some of her husband's. She was tall, however, in contrast to them. Aside from some resemblances in mannerisms, Ruth is an individual in her own right.

Mrs. T told me that her husband had ulcers two years ago and was unable to work because of nervousness. At that time he decided to have a bedroom of his own. Since then, Ruth had shared a room with Mrs. T. She had often, as a child, held out her little arms and said she wanted to sleep with one or the other of them. Mrs. T said she had never been the kind of mother that could say to a child, "No, you go and sleep in your own bed." Recently Mrs. T had begun to feel that Ruth would probably like to have a room of her own, although she would probably deny it if asked. Shortly, however, Mrs. T was going to see that Ruth had her own bedroom, for the present room was really crowded.

When I asked Mrs. T whether she felt there were any special problems in being an adoptive parent, she said that she did not. The only thing she could say is that she wished they had been a little younger when they adopted Ruth. However, she herself had always been "disgustingly healthy" and had had very little difficulty with the menopause, so perhaps her age had not mattered much. She knew herself well enough to handle any little irritability she had by going off by herself and doing something quietly. Actually, she said with much warmth and feeling that she and her husband did not know what they would ever have done without Ruth; she had meant so much to them.

As for advice to would-be adoptive parents, she would tell them not to stop and ponder over it. If they both want a child, they should go right ahead. Age should not be a limiting factor in adoptions, as it is when an agency is used, for age is a thing that depends on the individual parents. Some people are old at thirty-five and others are still young at sixty. With pride, Mrs. T told me that her husband was taken for at least eight years younger than his actual age, and that she maybe felt younger than her own fifty-four years.

To my question about discipline, Mrs. T said that they seldom had to discipline Ruth. The best way of doing this, if needed, she found was just to talk with her. For the most part she had handled the discipline, since she was with Ruth more. Occasionally, when Ruth was a child, she had to spank her "bottom" but her husband never spanked her. She guessed the only thing that could be a "problem" was that Ruth loved to go barefoot, which Mr. T did not approve of. Once in a while Ruth was untidy about hanging up her clothes but was pretty good in this respect most of the time. Usually she helped Mrs. T with the dishes. They never had any difficulty getting her to go to bed on time. In fact, Mrs. T really could think of nothing serious for which she and her husband had to discipline Ruth; she supposed Ruth learned early, as a little girl, the things that were expected of her.

As we were talking in this vein, Mr. T came in with the groceries. He greeted me and walked on through into the kitchen. Mrs. T suddenly appeared to be in a rush to terminate the interview, saying he had to return to his work. In closing, Mrs. T laughed as she said she hadn't really given me much of an opportunity to ask her questions. I told her how valuable her experience had been and how much pleasure it was to talk with her. In telling me goodbye, she said that she knew our study would be helpful to other adoptive parents, and that she just hoped their experience would be as good as hers and her husband's had been.

CHAPTER VIII

The Middle Group of Homes

ONE-FOURTH OF THE HOMES in which the adoptive parents were interviewed were rated C. In a fivefold classification of qualitative data, the middle category often represents "average" in the quality or qualities under consideration. This could mean that the C category is the most usual category, the one that predominates in the population. Or it could mean that, being the middle category in a range of good-fair-poor, the C group is the one in which cases display the designated quality or qualities to a moderate degree rather than to one that is extreme.

The C homes were not "average" in the first of these two meanings of the word. (It was perhaps a tribute to the judges' discriminatory power that they did not rate most homes as belonging to the middle category.) Nor does the concept "moderate" (moderately good mental health on the part of the parents, moderately good parent-child relations, moderately good marital adjustment) describe the C homes adequately. Some of them might be so characterized but most C homes were more of a mixture than that description would imply.

"Average," then, is not an appropriate term to use in describing the C homes. Although C was the midpoint on the scale, that fact in itself says little about its meaning, other than that the C homes were "worse" than the A's and B's and "better" than those below them.

One explicit meaning of C is that it denotes the lower limit of acceptability as an adoptive home. Even so, like the other home categories, C contained a range of cases. Some of the C homes were just barely acceptable, and a few were almost as "good" as the low B's. Most C homes lay between these extremes.

The following extracts from the records of interviews with two mothers are illustrative of homes rated C. The R family is regarded as a typical C home, while the O family is one classified as low C.

The R Family

This family consisted of the father, age 55; the mother, age 53; the adopted child, Betty, nearly 11; and an "own" child, Patty, a year and a half younger than Betty; and another own child, Joe, 3 years younger. The family lived in a comfortable, rather small house in a good neighborhood in a small town.

Mrs. R was friendly in her manner. She talked in such a soft tone that at times I could hardly hear her. Mr. R was present when I entered the house but he said if he was not actually needed he would go out and mow the lawn.

After describing our study, I asked Mrs. R how they became interested in adoption. Mrs. R replied that she herself came from a family of 15 children, having been brought up in Ireland, where large families are common. She had wanted children but had one miscarriage after another. She does not know the medical reason. After years of this, she "got desperate." Many people told her that if she and her husband adopted a child they probably would have one of their own, and so it worked out. They got Betty through a maternity hospital from which a friend of theirs had secured three children. They have never had any contact with the natural mother, and Mrs. R has pretty much forgotten what little she was told about her. . . .

When I asked whether she had told Betty that she was adopted, Mrs. R said she had done so long ago. She told Betty she and Daddy had wanted a baby very much but that she had been too sick to have one. Then she heard of a doctor through whom she might get one. She said that the mamma of this baby had died, and the baby was going to be sent to a home. So she and Daddy went over to the hospital and took a look at the baby and they wanted her immediately.

Mrs. R added that it certainly didn't take them long to learn to love Betty. As an infant, Betty was not pretty, but Mrs. R "just loves babies whatever they look like. They're so helpless, and they respond so well to care." She went on to say that recently her husband had asked whether she had said anything to Betty lately about being adopted. He thinks it's a good thing to remind her from time to time, so it will not be a shock to her if someone says something about it. So last night, when they were washing dishes together, she told Betty about my telephone call and asked whether Betty could guess what it was about. Betty guessed everyone she could think of. Then Mrs. R told her I was a lady from the Welfare Board making a survey. That didn't mean much to Betty, so Mrs. R reminded her that she had told her about the Welfare Board study of their home when she was adopted. Perhaps I was coming to see if she was "in the right family." Betty replied, "Well, I *am* in the right family." Mrs. R then told Betty that if she didn't like this family she could find herself another one. She said this, she added, just to see what Betty would say. She is sure Betty understands adoption and that it does not seem to bother her at all. . . .

I asked Mrs. R if she ever felt that Betty is like any of them. She replied that Betty is just like her sister: she has a big mouth and talks all the time. Their own children are more like her husband and herself, both in being quiet and in physical appearance. . . .

I then asked her to tell me something about Betty as an individual. To this she replied that not long ago she was telling her husband that she thinks Betty has great possibilities of leadership, if her ability is channeled properly. She is not the least "backward," and she is very energetic. She wants to be a teacher when she grows up. Mrs. R thinks that this would at least "let out her energy." Then, too, Betty's not being afraid to speak up is a quality a teacher should possess. She can also reason pretty well, she seems to be a rather good mixer, and she gets along well with children.

Betty is a rather affectionate child. She often tells them how much she loves them. Mrs. R wishes she would not say it so often but would really mean it. As it is, it's hard to tell whether she really does love them or not, because she says it so frequently.

I asked Mrs. R what she considered Betty's greatest strength. She replied that all the family call her "Gabble-Gabble" but, for herself, she really admires her for that trait. Her other two children are really too quiet, she feels. Having Betty the way she is gives the family some balance.

As to Betty's greatest weakness, it is table manners. The other day her husband told Betty that he was absolutely ashamed to let her go to other people's homes because of the way she eats. Mrs. R has recently learned to her amazement that some of her friends' children are just as bad as Betty when they are at home. When they are away from home, they are very polite, as she has seen. She can only hope Betty is like them in this respect.

Another difficulty Mrs. R has with both Betty and her sister is to get them moving in the morning in order to be ready for school. The other day she took a ruler to them and hit Patty with it. Betty jerked out of the way and Mrs. R was not even sure that she touched her. Betty, however, was very dramatic about this and walked around until schooltime dragging her leg as if she had been severely injured. "That is like Betty," she said. "She likes to do things for effect." Later on something caught her interest and she walked on both legs just as if nothing had ever happened, so Mrs. R felt sure that she was not hurt. . . .

I asked about Betty's special interests. "Music is one of the chief," Mrs. R replied. "She wants the family to get her a saxophone." Betty does have some ability in this line, Mrs. R thinks, but wind instruments are too noisy to have in a home. Betty also dearly loves sailing and riding. She is very athletic, and she likes to brag about how good she is. Actually, she does have a great deal of endurance. The whole family enjoy swimming, boating, and picnicking and often do these things together. . . .

Betty is in the fifth grade in the local public school and has always received good marks. She claims she doesn't like school but Mrs. R thinks that is "just a lot of talk." Recently, she has been trying to talk Betty into going to a boarding school for a year. She herself and her brothers and sisters went to boarding school—not because they needed to be "straightened out" but because boarding school helps one not to take things too much for granted. Betty has not wanted to go but recently she has said she might like it. . . .

Concerning discipline, Mrs. R said that she had to keep after all the children about cleaning their rooms. For a long time they wouldn't make their beds in the morning, but now all of them have become pretty good about that. She and her husband share in disciplining the children. Mrs. R tries to keep quiet when her husband is in charge. If parents don't stick together, the children are apt to side with one against the other, she said. Another important thing, she thinks, is that when a parent promises something, he must be sure to carry out his promise. She and her husband have been very careful in this respect. . . .

I asked whether Mrs. R felt there were any special problems related to adoption. She replied that rearing an adopted child might be more difficult if he were an older child. However, if a child is given affection and knows that he is loved, that is three-fourths of the battle. She said there is no difference at all in her feeling for the three children. Betty is just like her own. Mrs. R has no stronger feelings, she thinks, for the other two children than she has for Betty. In fact, she and her husband have an especially strong feeling for Betty because she was their first.

Mrs. R then recalled an experience she had with a neighbor's little children. There had been some difficulty in the neighbor's home, so Mrs. R offered to take the children for a time. It was no trouble because the neighbor sent her maid along, and she did all the work. The one child who could talk started calling Mrs. R "Mamma" almost immediately. Mrs. R thinks that shows how quickly a little one will respond to loving attention. She said she thoroughly enjoyed this experience. . . .

When I asked Mrs. R what advice she would give to prospective adoptive parents, she said that they should have no preference for a girl or boy. "In fact, it's a nice surprise not to know what sex you're going to get. Then, too, unless they have children of their own, they should adopt more than one child." She feels strongly that is is not fair to rear one child alone. She would also advise adoptive parents not to pay an exorbitant sum for the child. I asked her how she felt about the home study the Department of Public Welfare makes. She said this is a protection; she approves of it highly.

The O Family

Mrs. O was an intelligent, good-looking woman in the middle forties. Her first husband had died and she had shortly afterward married a well-to-do engineer. She and her husband lived in a large town-house and led an active social life.

Mrs. O had studied child psychology in a finishing school and prided herself on her wide reading about and knowledge of mental health. She was active in the work of an organization in the child-service field and had recently been the "lay leader" of a child-study group. The following are some quotations from the record of our social worker's interview with her.

Mrs. O had a ready flow of speech and never hesitated for a word. She had a slight nervous twitching of her lips when she talked. I asked whether she objected to my taking some notes and she said she certainly did not; that such a thing would be necessary in a research study. . . .

When I asked her how she happened to be interested in adoption, she said she had three daughters, one of whom had died at birth. Then she had a son. He was the largest and healthiest of her children but in a few days he became ill and died. Mrs. O said she was in a very disturbed emotional state after the loss of her little boy, so they got Kim through their doctor in order to help her get over her trouble. They kept Kim in a nursing home until everything could be worked out, because she could not risk losing a second baby. He is now eleven years old.

I asked Mrs. O whether she remembered how she felt when she first saw Kim. She replied, "Well, I first saw him in the hospital. Well, now, how did I feel?" She supposed she had mixed emotions.

She remembers she wanted him very much if she could get him; that he was such a cute, precious little thing. She added that she loves children and always wants to have them around. . . .

To assure that Kim was physically healthy, they had four doctors examine him. One doctor praised her for being willing to provide a home for an unfortunate infant. . . .

I asked whether Kim knows of his adoption. Mrs. O said he does. When he was about two, she told him about the hot day on which she brought him home from the hospital (she didn't mention the nursing home and her visits to him there, she said) and about how she kept fanning him all the way home so that he would be comfortable. She had repeated this story to him from time to time. Just recently he has again asked about his adoption. . . .

They have had many problems with Kim, she went on to say, and she doesn't know why. He has an awful temper. If he has not become "less rambunctious" by the time he comes back from camp this summer, she may take him to a psychiatrist whom she has known in her work in the mental health field. Perhaps he can find out what "troubles our little boy." It may be because he's adopted, but she does not know why that should trouble him.

Kim has had temper tantrums since infancy. Adolescence is going to be harder on him, she is afraid, than it was with her daughters, and it will also be harder on the people that will have to be around him. . . . Kim seems to have very definite feelings of rejection. Recently he said that his own mother could not have loved him much, since she gave him away. Even when he was only four years old he talked about his own mother having been mean, so much so that she had been struck by lightning. Actually, Mrs. O realizes Kim has not had too easy a time in life. Her first husband did not really want to adopt a child. He accepted the baby only because she was so upset about losing her little boy. She can see now that this was not a good basis for adoption. Later her husband took to drinking very hard. No, Kim has not had a really stable life.

Her new husband "is as good as he can be to Kim," even though he often gets "put out" when Kim kicks and storms and screams to get attention. She herself is perhaps somewhat to blame. She has been too permissive, she thinks, and has felt more responsible for Kim than for her daughters. The result is that when she acts normal and doesn't let him do everything he wants to, he feels rejected. . . .

I asked how her daughters feel about Kim. They accept him very well, she said; just the same as if he were their real brother. Of course, at their present age they can't stand to have him around but that is normal, she thinks. The other day, Pauline, her teenager, said that she wished she would never see Kim again. After this happened, Kim went out on his bike and stayed away for several hours and had the whole household terrified and upset—which, of course, was just exactly what he wanted to accomplish.

Mrs. O spoke briefly about her present husband, describing him as a loving person who shows affection for all the children. Kim hangs around him and likes him very much, but Kim's idea of love is a rather distorted one because he seems to feel that "if you love me I can do exactly as I want to." All children, she is sure, want to know at times that "beyond this point I cannot go."

Kim has difficulties everywhere: at home, at school, at camp. Mrs. O has sent him to several different schools but the teachers either handled him badly or wouldn't work with her on understanding and dealing with Kim's problems. Even at camp last summer, he did poorly, nearly driving the counselors to distraction. Still, the counselors later told her what a nice boy he was. Actually, Kim is as cute as he can be and extremely bright, she thinks. In fact, he is almost too bright because he can figure out "too many angles". . . .

Mrs. O is not exactly sure what her next plans for Kim's schooling will develop into but right now she is thinking she may send him to a military school in the Southwest. It would do him a world of good to be in such a school and to be more on his own. She will take him on a trip to look at various schools and let him decide for himself. She thinks, however, he should go to a small school, not to a great big one. "You have to know what your own individual child needs," she said. . . .

To my question of whether Mrs. O ever feels that Kim is like someone in the family, she replied "What do you mean—that he looks like Grandma or Grandpa or something like that?" I said either that or perhaps he might remind her of relatives in his mannerisms and actions. She was thoughtful for a moment and then said it is strange but she had never even thought about that, even with her own children. She remembers that with her first husband, it was a family joke that Kim had such large brown eyes. Her husband had eyes like that, and everybody used to say that finally they had a "brown-eyed O——." She used to joke with the relatives and say that she supposed she had "tainted the strain," as she and the girls have light eyes. . . .

To my question of what she considered Kim's greatest strength, Mrs. O said she supposed it could be his determination, but to be a strength such a trait must get into "the proper channel." She said that she hopes some day it is properly channeled but that so far she has found no way to channel it.

As to his greatest weakness, she noted his ungovernable temper— that, and his destructiveness. Kim respects only his own property. Just a few weeks ago he used the wall of the newly painted breakfast room as a target for his water pistol, into which he had put ink. In spite of all this, she added, Kim is a very affectionate, lovable child. He is always seeking affection. If he can't get his share, he uses all sorts of tricks to secure it. . . .

To my question about plans for Kim's future, she said that she hopes he will want to go to college, but she is not going to be "the insistent mother" about this. Unless he shows some "particular bent" she will not insist on a college education, though it will be too bad if he doesn't go to college in view of his intellectual capacity. However, if he doesn't want to go, it might be better for him to go to work right after high school. She mentioned selling as a job he would probably be good at, just as she and her brother have been in the past.

As to health, Kim had polio when he was four but there was almost no paralysis. There is one thing about his health, however, that bothers her greatly. When he gets a high fever (which happens infrequently) he sees things that aren't there. Her doctor is sure this is not an incipient psychosis, so they have had no tests made. Otherwise, Kim's health has been pretty good. . . .

We talked about discipline and I asked who usually takes care of it in their family. She said she supposes it is she. There have been so many problems in their family she seems to be the logical one to take care of discipline. At times her first husband tried to discipline the children to some extent, and now her present husband tries, particularly with Kim, but he is "not too successful." As to herself, she is not the kind who wants to "wait 'till Daddy comes home" for discipline to be taken care of.

The guiltiest she ever felt—she went on to say—was about spanking Kim. He used to insist on running out into the street to play, and she simply could not permit that from the standpoint of his physical safety. She spanked him pretty hard and it worked, but her conscience hurt her for a long time. Usually, when he is too annoying, she makes him stay by himself or stay home when the rest of the family goes away. This works well, and he is cooperative for a considerable length of time. . . .

To my question of what she would advise prospective adoptive parents if she had the opportunity, Mrs. O said she would tell them that she strongly believes in adoption. She doesn't take any stock in this "business of saying you cannot tell what kind you'll get. You can't tell too much about your own either."

She certainly does not believe in the black market and in buying babies. The fact that she took a child without going to a social agency might make it seem that she would concur in this type of thing. In their particular instance, however, the doctor knew that Kim needed a home and that she needed to have a child.

Of course, you can't tell someone else what to do, because circumstances vary so, but as a general rule she would advise people to go to a licensed child-placing agency because social workers know what they are doing and they have "at their finger-tips the means for placing the right child with the right people." Both the adoptive parents and the child are more protected that way. However, she would not say that adoption couldn't work out well getting a child the way they did. It is too bad that there is so long a waiting period when one goes through an agency. When you get into big operations, however, things take longer.

When I asked her whether she felt there were any specific problems related to adoption, she said that, of course, she had probably had more than the usual number of problems with Kim, but they might have happened with her own little boy if he had lived. Anyway, this is her own personal experience and is not related to adoption as such. Her family lawyer has an adopted child, and he has had more difficulty with her than she has had. On the other hand, she has seen many instances where adoption worked out beautifully and where parents have been terribly pleased and happy with the outcome.

This led Mrs. O to talk about her attempts at getting psychiatric treatment for Kim for his personality problem. This supersedes everything else, in her opinion. She so much wants Kim to be well adjusted. Unless he can change to a certain extent, she is sure he will not be a happy adult.

Her husband had gone to a psychiatrist for help in trying to overcome alcoholism. She had great difficulty in getting him to go because he disliked the psychiatrist so much just as a person, saying he was crude, harsh, and cold. Nevertheless, he went to see him, but he got no help. Mrs. O has also tried psychiatric treatment for herself, but this was not helpful either, for they never got around to talking about her own problems, only those of the family. Actually, she suspects her need for help was due to her husband's drinking and his personality difficulties. As to Kim, she tried to make an appointment with her husband's psychiatrist for him (since he was said to be good with children) but he has never called her back, as he said he would.

As the interview came to a close, Mrs. O asked the maid to bring us some "cokes." In the course of the subsequent conversation, she asked what form the report on our research would take. I said I could not be specific about the report but there would undoubtedly be a publication of some kind. She thanked me for coming and said that she would be interested in knowing the outcome of the study. She hoped her experiences would be of value to other adoptive parents.

GENERAL CHARACTERISTICS OF C HOMES

Homes rated C were chiefly characterized by inadequacies in the functioning capacity of one or both parents, by a certain lack of satisfaction in the marital relationship, by clearly evidenced but not extreme problems in the parents' relations with the adopted children. In addition, evidence of positive functioning (of "pluses" in family life), which so much characterized the A and, to some extent, the B homes, was lacking. It was these two considerations that provided the basis for rating homes C: the presence of problems that, though not extreme, interfered with family functioning and the absence of an atmosphere of affection and good will that would compensate in part for such lacks.

With respect to marital relations, the marriages were, for the most part, of long enough duration to suggest that they were stable and that they were not wholly dissatisfying to the two parties. The marriages, however, did not afford husband and wife the degree of satisfaction and the kind of status within the family that were so apparent in the A and B homes.

As to attitudes toward, and feelings about, the adopted children, all these parents evidenced some affection for the children and interest in them, and overtly negative or rejecting attitudes were minimal. The parents did, however, create considerable stress for the children through overprotection, excessive emotional demands, push for academic and other sorts of achievement, overcontrol, and so forth. More serious problems in parent-child relations were suspected in some cases but the evidence was not sufficiently clear for evaluation. The following examples are typical of C homes.

> Joe, age 10, had been with the adoptive couple since he was three days old and was their only child. The mother expressed some satisfaction in regard to her home, husband, and child but indicated that she was not too happy with herself or her life as it was. She had few friends, felt inferior, and was always tired because she had to have everything perfect. She felt that her husband was not sufficiently affectionate, that he did not participate enough in activities with her and the child, and never accepted any responsibility for disciplining. She had always had disappointments. For instance, when her parents went on vacation, she had had to supervise the younger children—a situation that she resented greatly. Then, too,

she had wanted to go to college but had been unable to do so because of the younger children.

The father was quiet and easy-going but had few real interests. He had been quite undecided about wanting to adopt a child. While providing adequately for the family, he seemed to play rather little part in it.

The mother described the marriage as "agreeable" but gave very little information of a positive nature. She complained that although she and Joe liked to "eat out," her husband refused to accompany them. She and Joe did many things together; her husband rarely shared in these activities. Apparently, although there was no overt conflict between the parents, there was considerable distance between them.

The mother had warm feelings for Joe, whom she identified with her own family. She recognized that she placed considerable pressure on him but was clearly pleased by his conformity, neatness, obedience, and the fact that he was a quiet child who was respectful to older people. She said Joe was fussy about his clothes, but she regarded this as a virtue, even though Joe was criticized for it by other boys.

Another couple had one adopted child, Irene, age 11. The mother was an attractive, rather spontaneous young woman who evidenced warmth and pride in discussing her adopted child. She was, however, very insecure and anxious about her adequacy as a mother. This came out in many ways. She was unable to tell the child she was adopted; she felt overwhelmed when the child had minor physical illnesses; she tended to keep the child too close to her for the child's own good. (For example, when Irene spent a week at a church camp, the mother insisted on staying with her there.) She lacked sensitivity to the child's extreme shyness and fear of strangers, and actually seemed to foster these traits.

She described her husband as a very anxious person, one who "worked and worried" all the time. He had to give up his own business because, under the pressure of it, he had developed ulcers.

She gave the interviewer little spontaneous information about family relationships. She hardly mentioned her husband unless directly questioned. She described what she and her daughter did together and implied that her husband rarely participated in family activities.

MARITAL RELATIONS IN C HOMES

Three-fourths of the couples whose homes were rated C were classified as belonging to Group 3 in quality of marital relations.

One-third of the rest were classified as belonging to Group 2, and the others to Group 4.

There was only one broken family in the C group of homes. This relative absence of divorce or separation was one reason for rating some homes C rather than D. This is not because the raters prized marital stability above all. Rather, it is because the continuance of the marriages suggested that there was perhaps more satisfaction in them for the adoptive parents than met the eye, and that, therefore, the homes were not outright bad for the children.

The Group 3 marriages appeared to be stable but, so far as could be judged by the limited information forthcoming, not deeply satisfying to the wife or, perhaps, to the husband. For instance, some of the adoptive mothers mentioned lack of emotional support from their husbands. Then, too, there was seldom any evidence that the parents enjoyed each other's companionship greatly, appreciated each other's contribution to family life, or had a close relationship with each other, apart from that with the children.

Many of the women said little about their husbands in the course of the interviews, a fact that seemed significant in contrast with the very different behavior of the mothers in the A and B homes. The average length of the interviews was the same as in the A and B cases, the mothers participated in the interviews just as willingly, and, for the most part, they talked just as freely about themselves and their adopted children. What they did say about their husbands implied that the men took little part in family life and child rearing. If this is not a correct interpretation of their relative silence, it was at least clear that these women did not spontaneously think of their husbands when talking about the adopted children.

Other mothers, less silent about their husbands, were inclined to complain about them. They made such remarks as that their husbands were rather unsociable, or that they did not help enough in disciplining the children, or that they and their husbands did not agree about how children should be brought up.

It seemed that these couples did little mutual planning and had little respect for each other's ideas and desires. They apparently had points of conflict that involved some discussion, but genuine "communication" between them seemed to be minimal. In general, a certain lack of mutuality seemed to characterize these marriages, and often this was particularly evident in relation to the children.

These couples, however, were far from being outright incompatible. A considerable number of mothers mentioned having some interests in common with their husbands or sharing some pleasures with them, and none of them complained about their husbands as inadequate "providers." A few implied that they and their husbands at least had mutual pleasure in the children. No evidence of widespread, overt dissatisfaction with the marriage appeared in any of the interviews. In fact, many of these women, if asked, would probably have described their marriages as fairly happy, even though, to an outsider, it seemed that both husbands and wives were going their own rather separate ways and, perhaps, passively accepting a less than wholly satisfactory family situation.

MOTHERS IN C HOMES: PERSONALITY AND MOTHER-CHILD RELATIONS

Over 90 per cent of the mothers in the C homes were rated as Group 3 in personality makeup and a similar proportion as 3 in parent-child relations. Three mothers were rated 2 and several were rated 4 in each of these categories. The personality characteristics of these mothers are more difficult to describe than those of the women rated 1 or 2, in part because of their heterogeneity and in part because these women were neither well adjusted nor seriously disabled emotionally.

Group 1 mothers, as described under the A homes, were women whose mental health was apparently very good. Group 2 mothers, although not quite as well adjusted, were able to function successfully in their life situations. Such problems as they may have had seemed rather insignificant from the standpoint of the family's functioning as a whole. Groups 4 and 5 (to be described later) had clear symptoms of emotional disorder.

In contrast, the functioning capacity of Group 3 mothers was limited by their emotional problems but their mental health was not extremely poor. Since our information was restricted to the material obtained in the interviews and within the purpose of the study, diagnostic statements about the character structure and underlying conflicts of these Group 3 mothers cannot be attempted. It is possible only to describe how their underlying problems were manifested in attitudes and significant relationships with their husbands and children. Even here, only broad differences and similarities among the mothers can be noted.

Since Group 3 mothers stood, as it were, between those who were able to function well in all or most areas of family life and those whose capacity for adequate interpersonal relations was seriously impaired, the first comment to be made about them is that they shared some characteristics of both groups, the difference being one of degree. For instance, Group 3 mothers who were warm and positive about their children were not as clearly so as were the Group 2 mothers. The mother's warmth was usually interfered with by some of her personality problems, such as her great need to keep the child close to her or her anxiety in handling him. On the other hand, such demands on the child were not as extensive or all-enveloping as those of comparable mothers in Group 4.

A second characteristic of these mothers was that they had some capacity for positive relations with their children and, with a few exceptions, their husbands also. This was evidenced in the feeling-tone with which they talked about them (especially about the children), even though their attitudes might appear to be rather hostile, overcontrolling, or undesirable in some other respect. In subtle ways these women apparently communicated to their children some warmth of feeling and were not the cold or remote or insensitive persons that their words, taken literally, implied.

Although these women, in their rather peculiar way, were fond of their husbands and children, many of them were apparently not at all close to their own parents and other relatives or to their husband's families. If they talked of their own childhood, they often described it as deprived and unhappy, regardless of their parents' income.

A third characteristic of all the Group 3 mothers was their lack of personal security and sense of adequacy. Their feelings in this respect showed up in many different ways, such as in exces sive overt anxiety, dependency, self-depreciation, lack of satisfaction in being a woman, rigidity, and dominance. In spite of such different "defenses" and such different concerns about coping with their responsibilities, it may be that basically these women had fairly similar personality problems.

A fourth common characteristic appeared in their lack of sources of satisfaction beyond the confines of their immediate families. For the most part, these mothers did not participate actively in social or community affairs but found in their homes their chief source of satisfaction. The few who were exceptions to this rule participated so extensively and with so much anxiety and compulsiveness that they probably got little real satisfaction out of their activities.

Within the Group 3 category there were two subgroups. The first consisted of those mothers who were anxious and somewhat overly dependent and who felt incompetent with respect to some of their responsibilities as wives and mothers. The other subgroup consisted of mothers whose anxiety and insecurity was not so apparent, in part because they were rather rigid and "controlling" individuals.

The first subgroup had particular difficulty in dealing with their children at crucial points or about crucial issues. For instance, they found it hard to discuss adoption or sexual matters, and they were uncertain and worried about how and when to discipline. Their insecurity and dependency also showed up clearly in the way they related to our interviewers. After telling of their feelings of helplessness, they were likely to ask for advice about how to do better or to seek assurance that what they had done was good.

Many of these mothers, although usually warm and positive in their feelings toward and about their children, were insensitive or blind to their problems. For instance, one mother was somewhat pleased by her daughter's extreme shyness. Another seemed unconcerned about her child's migraine headaches, nervousness, and compulsion to do everything perfectly. Instead, she thought this latter trait very desirable. A third mother easily accounted for her child's lying and his rather severe "sibling rivalry" and emphasized his goodness and his eagerness to help her. The insecurity of these women about their responsibilities as mothers is illustrated by the following cases, which are fairly typical.

> One mother related to the interviewer in an anxious, dependent way, frequently seeking advice and assurance from her. She was warm in her feeling toward her child and apparently fairly capable of conveying that feeling to him. She had great difficulty, however, in dealing with her child's expressions of anger or hostility. She felt incapable of setting firm limits to what she allowed him to do, and she worried excessively about what might happen to him. To prove that she was a "good mother," as she put it, she took an active part in community affairs.

> Another mother looked to her husband to make all decisions and was frankly self-deprecatory. She was a poor housekeeper, had little interest in her appearance, and dressed very poorly. She was pleased that her husband was willing to take most of the responsibility for the family. She was able (perhaps in consequence) to be warm and accepting of their child.

> A third mother, a tense, anxious woman, said she had great doubt about her ability to do anything well. Her husband was better with the baby, could cook better, and was more capable than she was in all household tasks. This woman had very poor relations with her mother and with her brother, who thought she was "dumb," but she got along fairly well with her father. She had great fondness for her adopted child, of whom she was proud.

Many of the mothers in this subgroup revealed similar doubts about themselves as persons. This was evident in their way of relating to the interviewer, in their lack of interest in their physical appearance or unconcern about it, and in their lack of trust of persons outside the family. In the interview, they either made no mention of people with whom they were close or they were openly critical and suspicious of most people. It was not that they were essentially paranoid but rather that their own feelings of inadequacy were involved. They were likely to be less critical of people they knew well, such as their doctors and the children's teachers, than of others. After they had blamed others for some of their difficulties, they were likely to seek assurance that they themselves were not to blame.

Many of these women told of having had a very unhappy childhood. One of them, for instance, had been greatly deprived emotionally and financially, her parents having been harsh and demanding. Another said she had always felt herself to be a "misfit" in her family and had married to escape. Another said that her sisters had been much prettier than she was, and that this had made her feel inferior in most ways.

In spite of these childhood feelings and experiences (some might say perhaps because of them), the women in this subgroup usually derived considerable satisfaction out of their marriage, their children, or both, even though in their anxiety and insecurity they were far from ideal mothers.

The second subgroup of mothers consisted of women who were rather rigid in personality and who tried to control events and people in their lives, including, of course, their children. They apparently felt quite self-sufficient and seldom looked to others for advice or emotional support; they tended to have little doubt about the correctness of their attitudes toward their children and their ways of handling them. While these women had rather warm feelings about their children, they were likely to be insensitive and were often unaware of how their words and deeds might appear to the children. They exercised more than the usual amount of control over their children and husbands. This control, however, was not of such proportions as to encompass the children completely or to exclude the fathers from close relations with them, as was the case with the women in Group 4 who had similar characteristics.

One of these mothers related easily to the interviewer, seemed quite self-confident, and showed little anxiety about any aspect of being a mother. Although she loved the adopted child, she seemed insensitive to his feelings and needs. With no apology, she described herself as being rigid and hard at times, demanding from him a high degree of conformity to her wishes.

Another mother in this subgroup seemed very "driving" in relation to all members of the family. She put much emphasis on school achievement, was overprotective of her child, and kept him in close control. Nevertheless, she had kindly feelings toward him and put no obstacles in the way of his having a close relation with his father, who was a warmer person than she.

A third mother was a serious-minded, rigid woman who had a strict religious background. She was very set in her ways and had high standards for her children and not much sensitivity to their feelings. She was consistent, however, in handling them and did not interfere with their attachment to their father. In spite of being rather dominating, she was supportive of her husband in his interests.

FATHERS IN C HOMES

About 70 per cent of the fathers in C homes were rated as in Group 3 in personal adjustment and parent-child relations. As has been said, this rating was based usually on what the mother said or implied about her husband's status and role in the family, his emotional support of her, his participation in family life, and his relations with the adopted child. Twenty per cent were rated as belonging to Group 2 and 10 per cent to Group 4. In some cases these ratings were made with minimum confidence because the mothers had said so little about their husbands.

One subgroup of fathers rated 3 appeared to be rather passive, ineffectual men who apparently had a good deal of warmth for the adopted children. Many of them were rather belittled by their wives, who tended to be domineering. In spite of their affection for the children, these men were apparently not effective in protecting the children from their wives' overcontrol. The rest of the fathers in this subgroup were more adequate in the family role but they seemed to lack some of the key ingredients of mental health.

The mothers' descriptions of these fathers usually showed them either as participating to some extent in family life but with little real enjoyment, or as having considerable difficulty in functioning at all adequately as family members. They apparently were able, however, to give their wives and children some emotional support. Almost all of them were "good providers" financially, in their wives' opinion.

The majority of the fathers were described as liking their adopted children, although only a few of them did "much of anything" with them. The mothers frequently complained that their husbands did not take part in disciplining the children or did not back them up sufficiently in their own efforts. They also said that they were not sufficiently active in helping the children.

Apparently these fathers rarely discussed their work with their wives. In fact, only a few of them had much in common with their wives, and few engaged in recreational or other activities with them.

Illustrative of the mothers' comments was the complaint of a mother who barely mentioned her husband of her own accord. When asked about him, she said he was too strict with both her and the child and expected too much of them. Another typical remark was that the father was very busy, worked day and night, and had little time for his family. Several fathers, described as being nervous, were said to be irritated when demands were made on them. One was said to be very solitary and not able to express his feelings.

HIGH-C HOMES

About a fourth (24) of the C homes were like the majority of the B homes in some of the aspects under consideration. Sixteen fathers, but only 3 mothers, were rated 2 in personal adjustment. Eighteen couples were rated 2 in marital relationship. The major reason for classifying these homes as high C rather than B lay in the mother-child relationship. Most of the mothers either over-protected their children or overcontrolled them; in only three cases was the mother-child relation such as to be rated 2. In these three cases the mother was rated 2 in personality also. The following illustrations of homes classified as high C show that in some important respects they are much alike.

> A couple had one adopted child, a girl, age 12. The mother seemed insecure and timid. She said that most people were critical of her, and so she did not like to tell how she was handling her little girl. She did say that she had never been able to discipline her or refuse to let her do as she pleased, and that she relied on her husband to discuss adoption and on her doctor to give sex information. She was sincerely trying to cope with what problems she was aware of, however, and was clearly very fond of the child.
>
> Her husband, in addition to being a good provider, was greatly interested in the child. He supported his wife emotionally and took the responsibility for much of the planning in the home. In other words, he was able to take over in areas where his wife felt unable to function and, at the same time, to give her support and affection.
>
> In spite of (or perhaps because of) the wife's great dependency and insecurity, the marital relationship was good. Mrs. D was positive in speaking of her husband and said she felt happier since her marriage than ever before.

In relation to the child, the wife was overprotective and waited on her to an excessive degree. Her husband was also somewhat overprotective and overpermissive. However, neither parent was very insensitive to the feelings and needs of the child, and both gave her their affectionate attention.

In another case both spouses had had previous, unsuccessful marriages. The present marriage had lasted fifteen years and seemed to be a good one. The husband appeared to have real status in the family. His wife said he was a rock of strength. She was proud of his work, and they planned many things together.

The wife tended to handle her adopted child as strictly and rigidly as her own parents handled her. This behavior on her parents' part had led her into an unhappy marriage in order to get away from home. She was trying hard to rear her child well but was fearful that she might make mistakes.

Both parents were affectionate with the child but had much trouble in letting him grow up. They were so protective that, for instance, they could not allow him, a 10-year-old boy, to be even five minutes late in coming home from school. The mother had some awareness that this attitude was related to her own early experiences and expressed a desire to change.

LOW-C HOMES

Twenty families were at the low end of the C range, and were much like the D's in one or several respects. Six fathers and ten mothers were classified as 4 in personality. Eight families had such an extremely poor marital relationship that they were rated 4 in that trait. However, even these low-C families seemed to function somewhat better than those rated D, and, with a few exceptions, the parents' attitudes toward their children were somewhat more positive. In a few cases the fact that the parents lived together and that the home (in this respect at least) was stable for the adopted child, was the chief differentiating factor between the low-C and the D homes. The following summary is illustrative of these low-C homes.

The couple had two adopted children, age 11 and 12. By the way in which the mother stated her views and controlled the family functioning, she impressed the interviewer as being a rather dominating, aggressive woman. She had had very poor relations with her own family, and with her husband also, especially in the early years of marriage. She and her husband disagreed greatly about religion, about money, and about how to rear children. She said that she could never feel close to him.

To the interviewer, the husband seemed a kindly but passive man. He was described by his wife as "too tired" to be with the children. He had not much wanted to adopt children and he apparently had willingly accepted his wife's refusal to let him have anything to do with disciplining them.

She overcontrolled the children and was reluctant to let them grow up. Nevertheless, she was affectionate and kind with them. The father apparently was not close to either of them. He spoke of them with affection, however, and gave no hint that he had once been rather opposed to adoption.

The most marginal families in this group were the four in which both parents' relations with the children were rated 4, a rating that predominated in the D homes. In each instance, however, even these homes seemed a bit better than the D's, though it may be that additional contact with the parents might have revised our opinion.

One of these families consisted of two quite elderly parents and an emotionally disturbed adopted child. This couple, seemingly affectionate and fairly well-adjusted, had undertaken adoption only in order to befriend an unmarried mother who was very neglectful of her infant. They took the child for adoption out of pity and a sense of duty. Later they rather regretted having done so, for the child was a burden on them financially and otherwise. They "did well by him" but were overstrict and wanted him to conform to their wishes completely. They were frank to say that they thought the adoption was not good for the child or for themselves.

In another of these low-C families, the mother was an emotionally disturbed woman who was extremely dependent on her own mother. She had much anxiety and was so childlike that she was almost unable to function, let alone be a parent to an adopted child. Her husband seemed much more adequate, was fond of his family, and compensated somewhat for the mother's lack of stability. The mother complained about her eleven-year-old adopted daughter's behavior, could not discipline her, expected great love from her, and put her in charge of the younger children. In no way was she a real mother to the child, but she could not tell her she was adopted.

The other two families had somewhat the same pattern. Both mothers were nervous, tense, and rather isolated. One of them was so remote from reality that she was not aware of her child's serious neurotic symptoms, such as her need to take five baths a day and her isolation from other children. The fathers in these homes, however, were fairly adequate individuals and were interested in the children. Both marriages had lasted more than fifteen years.

CHAPTER IX

Homes Rated Poor

OVER A FOURTH OF THE ADOPTIVE HOMES (29 per cent) were rated
D or E. These homes had characteristics that were thought likely
to jeopardize the social and emotional development of the adopted children, and therefore were regarded as clearly unsuitable.
As with the A, B, and C homes, evidence for this judgment was
found in the marital relations of the parents, in the personality
makeup of the mother, in the mother's relations with the adopted
child, in the father's functioning as a family member, and, occasionally, in the presence of factors classified as social-path-
ological.

Nearly all the homes rated E were seriously unfavorable with
respect to the first three of these points, somewhat less frequently
with respect to the fourth, and occasionally with respect to the
fifth. The homes rated D were somewhat less unfavorable, qualitatively or quantitatively. For instance, in most of them the
mother was less seriously disturbed emotionally and was able to
give the child a modicum of emotional security. In some, the
mother was no less handicapped than in the E homes but the
marital relationship was somewhat better. Even so, the characteristics of these D homes seemed to justify classifying them
with the E group as seriously unfavorable to the emotional development of children.

These homes were not, however, the worst imaginable. In
only a few were the children abused or grossly neglected. Few
homes were near the bottom of the economic scale. Crime and
immorality were very rarely in evidence, nor was there any in-

dication that parents deliberately incited children to delinquency or exploited them economically. This is different from earlier days, to judge by the studies cited in Chapter I—perhaps because the law that requires study by the Welfare Department pending adoption has improved the situation or, more likely, because social and economic conditions have changed.

Without going into detail in each case it is difficult to document adequately the reasons for rating homes D or E. It did not seem feasible, as with the A, B, and C groups, to choose one or two homes as illustrations, for the D and E homes seemed even less homogeneous than the others. Accordingly, we decided to describe the D and E homes rather fully under the categorical headings used in the previous chapters (marital relations, mother's personality, and so forth), and to cite under those headings the various types encountered. This detailed accounting seemed especially appropriate because the statement that 29 per cent of the homes were unsatisfactory calls for strong documentation.

MARITAL RELATIONS

All the homes rated E and all but three of those rated D were so classified partly because they failed to provide the experience of a childhood spent with parents whose marriage was at least fairly sound and stable.

In the A, B, and C homes the marriages of the adoptive parents ranged from those that were highly satisfactory (Group 1) to those that were stable but rather lacking in "togetherness" and mutuality (Group 3). Continuing this scale, the field director rated most of the marriages in D homes as belonging to Group 4 and most of those in E homes as Group 5, but there was some overlapping. Within Groups 4 and 5, several different sorts of unharmonious or otherwise unsatisfactory marital situations were distinguished, as is shown below.

Marriage Probably Fairly Good (Group 3)

At the top of the list were three D homes in which the marriage was fairly adequate as far as the parents were concerned. Two of these couples were rather elderly people who were preoccupied with financial worries and illness. Their marriage was probably fairly satisfactory to them, for they were fond of each other. Their infirmities and their emotional rigidity, however, made the home an undesirable place for a child. In the third case the mother expressed some satisfaction with her marriage, and there was other evidence of a fairly good relationship between her and her husband.

Marriage Probably Not a Good One but Evidence Meager (Group 4)

For 19 families (16 D and 3 E homes) the quality of the marital relationship could not be determined adequately enough for classification. Nevertheless, if only by omission of detail, there was no evidence that the marriage was one that would be helpful to a child. These marriages were rated as belonging to Group 4.

In seven of these homes the mother was so emotionally involved with the adopted child that she gave the interviewer practically no information about her husband or her marriage. These women did not specifically disparage their husbands and, if questioned directly, made some conventional remark about them, such as "he's a good man." But it seemed clear that their husbands meant little to them.

> One of these mothers said she spent all available time, day and night, with her ten-year-old daughter. She was glad she had adopted a girl, she said, although her husband had wanted a boy. This latter remark was the only spontaneous comment she made about her husband, but she told of many vacations she had spent with the child and added that as a family they did little together.

In the other 12 cases the mothers also said little, but some hinted that the marriage was not satisfactory. When asked directly about their husbands, these women said only that they saw little of them or that their husbands agreed with them in their handling of the children. Otherwise, they gave no indication of what their husbands were like.

The interviews that elicited so little information about the husbands and the marriages were not briefer than the others, nor did the mothers seem suspicious or stand-offish. It was rather that these women either seemed completely absorbed in themselves and, in some cases, in their children, or appeared to be cold, reserved individuals who had little to give to either husband or child. Whether the husbands were dissatisfied with this state of affairs could not be determined.

Chronic and Usually Severe Marital Discord or Dissatisfaction (Groups 4 and 5)

In 6 D and in 17 E homes there was either open conflict between the parents or such belittling and exclusion of the husband by the wife that the marriage was essentially a broken one.

> One couple had been divorced several years before our study, after many quarrels and violent accusations about each other's behavior. At the time of the interview they were again living together but the wife, who seemed highly unstable, was preoccupied with her own feelings and most intolerant of her husband's wishes. The quarreling and the accusations that characterized their first marriage were continuing.

> One wife bitterly expressed her dissatisfaction with her marriage, saying that her husband thought only of his business; that she had no real relation with him; and that, from time to time, she threatened to leave. She added, however, that she knew which side her bread was buttered on and would probably never get a divorce, in spite of their numerous quarrels.

The sort of home in which the father was relegated to an inferior position and was much disparaged is illustrated by the remark of one adoptive mother who, when asked whether her husband liked the child, said abruptly that, of course, he had no interest in the child—his only duty in the family was to hand over his pay check.

Except for two D homes that were rated 4 because the marital discord was chronic but not overtly severe, the homes in this category were put in Group 5.

Marriage Distorted to Meet Parents' Emotional Needs (Groups 4 and 5)

Dr. Theodore Lidz and his associates describe in detail two kinds of marital relations, which they designate marital schism and marital skew.[1] "Marital schism" refers to the state of severe or chronic discord and dissatisfaction of the sort we have been describing, that in which the stability of the marriage is constantly threatened or the marriage has been dissolved. "Marital skew," in contrast, provides some satisfaction to one or both spouses. This satisfaction is achieved, however, in ways that create an unhealthy or unnatural environment for a child.

The marital schisms that had not led to a complete break have already been noted. Under the present heading are grouped the 32 families (33 children) in which the marriage appeared to be skewed. Thirteen of these were D homes, 19 were E.

One type of skewed marriage (18 homes) was that in which a husband apparently accepted his wife's abnormal behavior as natural or in which an emotionally disturbed husband was permitted by his wife to have the kind of marriage he wanted. Marriages of this sort were rated as belonging to Group 5.

> The kind of skew in which the husband seemed to accept his wife's bizarre behavior as normal appeared in the marriage of a couple who had adopted a child on their doctor's advice because the mother was too intensely concerned about her own child and his illnesses. This woman acted toward the adopted child and toward other people in a very odd way, but her husband seemed to go along with her ideas and not think her behavior unusual.

> A marriage skewed to fit the emotional needs of a disturbed husband was seen in a family in which a patently eccentric woman, once divorced, was married to a very passive man, many years her junior. This husband spent most of his spare time sleeping and took no responsibility in the family except to give the wife his pay check. This arrangement, as far as the interviewer could discover, was satisfactory to both marital partners.

In all these families the wife had a severe personality disorder. Four mothers had symptoms that could only be described as psychotic. Others had had a nervous breakdown and were still erratic in their attitudes and relations with people. Some were very eccentric, and the rest highly "nervous" or hysterical.

---

[1] Lidz, Theodore, Alice Cornelison, Stephen Fleck, and Dorothy Terry, "The Intrafamilial Environment of Schizophrenic Patients—II, Marital Schism and Marital Skew," *American Journal of Psychiatry*, vol. 114, September, 1957, pp. 241–248.

Most of the husbands were less obviously disturbed than the wives, and a few of them seemed to be fairly adequate individuals. They apparently had made a personal adjustment to their wives' peculiarities and showed some affection for the children, but the children's position was insecure and unhappy nevertheless.

A second type of skewed marriage (five homes) was put in Group 4. This was a type in which both members of the couple were emotionally maladjusted but not to such a degree as the mothers in the preceding group.

Two of these couples were immature, dependent people who expressed their interest in each other through the child. In both cases the marital relationship seemed like a "threesome," since the child slept with the parents and was allowed to make most of the family decisions. Both mothers said they would have had little satisfaction in the marriage if they had not adopted a child.

Two other couples had, in part at least, exchanged roles, in that the father assumed many of a mother's duties. One of these men had slept with his daughter, now nearly an adolescent, since infancy, and the child's primary relationship was with him.

In the fifth family the father was a domineering, erratic man who controlled every facet of the family's life. The mother, who had married very early to escape a bad home situation, was fearful and withdrawn but completely subject to her husband and apparently accepted his domination.

The third type of skewed marriage (nine homes) was one in which both parents seemed to be affectless, insensitive people. This type, too, was put in Group 4. These people said nothing that would indicate dissatisfaction with each other, and they were apparently in agreement in their handling of the children and in other matters. Yet when parents of this sort were seen together, one sensed an emotional sterility in their marriage and in their capacity for human relations. It was our impression that the reason these marriages were reasonably satisfactory to the couples was that neither husband nor wife could have involved himself or herself in a more demanding relationship. It was not clear why these couples adopted children. It seemed likely that they did so, not because they really wanted them, but because children are a conventional part of marriage. All these families had a rather high income and the fathers were regarded as successful men in business or a profession.

This sort of marriage was seen in a family that had adopted two children. Both parents were highly critical of the child we were inquiring about but were very vague as to what was wrong with him. Both were preoccupied with their own feelings and were unable to understand or sympathize with other people. They seemed to have some general resentment against the world but they were not expressly dissatisfied with each other.

Divorce or Separation Following Severe Discord (Group 5)

In 35 families (36 children) there had been divorce or separation following severe marital discord. Fifteen of these were homes rated D; 20 were homes rated E. Not only was there considerable disorganization in these families just prior to the divorce but most of the marriages had been quarrelsome, unsatisfactory ones, even at the time of adoption. Alcoholism was a factor in a number of the divorces, in conjunction with other personality problems. Marital infidelity and family neglect were other reasons given for divorce.

One mother said she divorced her first husband after seven years and married the adoptive father in retaliation. She said she did not love this man and thought it might make matters better to adopt a child. She left the second husband after a year and a half, returned to her first husband for two years, and then separated again.

Another woman described her husband as alcoholic and irresponsible. This couple had been separated before they adopted their first child. They separated again when the child was two years old, at which time the mother started adoption proceedings for a second child. Before that adoption became final, the couple remarried but within a few years were again divorced.

Eight of the 36 children were living with their adoptive fathers at the time of our study. Most of these men obtained custody because of the mother's drinking, but this did not happen until the mothers had had the children in their care from one to five years. In the one case in which the separation was due to the father's drinking, the mother left the child with her husband nevertheless. One father secured custody because the mother was psychotic. (She was under the care of a psychiatrist at the time of adoption.) But here, too, the mother had charge of the child for over five years, during which time she was neglectful and abusive.

Seven of the eight divorced fathers who retained custody of the adopted children remarried, but later two of them were again divorced. In neither of these cases were good arrangements made for the care of the children.

> One of these men had divorced his second wife because she was promiscuous and drank too much. At the time of the interview, he and the children were living with the wife's mother, an elderly, incompetent person who found the children a burden. The father told our interviewer he planned to set up a home of his own and let his adopted fourteen-year-old child do the housekeeping.

In three of the five other remarriages there was clear evidence that the stepmothers disliked the children and made home life difficult for them. One of the stepmothers who did not seem to reject the child was an emotionally immature woman who had married the adoptive father when she was only fourteen. Neither she nor the husband, a very dominating man, could provide emotional support for the child. The other stepmother had only recently married the adoptive father. In this case, the adopted child had spent some years with her psychotic adoptive mother and had had many subsequent foster home placements. As a result perhaps, she had behavior problems that the stepmother found objectionable.

Twenty of these 36 children were living with their adoptive mothers at the time of our study. Only four of these mothers had remarried. All these adoptive mothers, remarried or not, were emotionally disturbed women, whose treatment of the children ranged from neglect to extreme overprotection and emotional dependence on the child.

In two of the four instances of remarriage, the marriage had taken place so recently that it was too early to determine how the new stepfathers' relations with the adopted children would work out. One of these two mothers, however, was so rejecting of the child that it seemed unlikely that the stepfather would be able to improve the situation greatly. In the third case, the stepfather had been in the home since the child was about a year old. He seemed to be a warm but ineffectual person. In the fourth instance, the mother had separated from the stepfather and taken the child with her.

Three of the remaining four children in the total group of 36 did not live with either of their adoptive parents. Two of them had been removed from the home by the court. The third had married at fifteen, partly to escape home difficulties. The fourth child had been sent away from home after his adoptive parents' separation. Recently the parents had reestablished their home and brought the boy back to live with them, but they were still frankly dissatisfied with each other and with the child.

Adoptive Father or Mother Died (Groups 4 and 5)

Nine homes rated D and three rated E (containing 13 adoptive children) had been broken by the death of the mother (five cases) or father (seven cases). Four of the mothers and five of the fathers died when the children were less than six years old. In only one case was the child fourteen or older when the death occurred. If the marriage had been an especially unhappy one before the death of the parent and/or the subsequent situation was especially hard on the children, the marital situation was rated as belonging to Group 5. Otherwise, it was rated 4.

Little is known concerning the home situations before the five mothers died, but in each case the death of the mother brought the adopted children very unhappy experiences with caretakers. For instance, one child was sent to live with her elderly, ill grandmother. For another, there was a series of housekeepers interspersed with attempts by the father, a neurotic, difficult person, to do the housework and look after the child himself.

Three of the five widowed fathers remarried, but one did not remarry until five years after his first wife's death. In no case did the home situation improve markedly with the second marriage. Two of the stepmothers appeared to be emotionally unstable and to reject the adoptive children. The third may have been more adequate but the father was a very dominating man who insisted on having his way with the child.

The seven homes in which the father died had never been ve satisfactory for the children, though several of the mothers said they had been happy with their husbands. Six of these seven fathers were twenty or more years older than their wives. In several of these homes the wife had apparently had a rather childlike relationship with her husband. The one mother who was near her husband's age complained of his unfaithfulness in marriage and said that the adopted child was probably his own. Only one of these seven mothers married a second time, a rather odd marriage of the "skewed" type.

With one exception, the mothers who did not remarry seemed to be excessively dependent on the adopted children and made great demands on them. They had apparently always been individuals who looked to their husbands for support and guidance, even if the men were old and ill. In the absence of their husbands they had great difficulty managing the children and their own affairs.

The one exception was a competent woman who was doing well financially. She, however, had adopted a child only at her husband's insistence and she had left the care of the child largely to him. After her husband's death, she went into business and saw even less of her adopted son, who soon got into trouble at school and with his companions.

No Adoptive Father (Group 5)

Three children in homes rated E had never had an adoptive father. One of them had been adopted by a single woman, one by a woman who was divorced, and the third child had been adopted as an infant by a widow over sixty years old whose children were grown.

These three adoptive mothers were lonely, unhappy people who said they adopted children because they badly needed companionship. The elderly widow was described in the report of the social investigation for the court as "emotionally high-strung and given to frequent outbursts of temper." The other two women were also recognized at that time as being unsuitable adoption applicants. Our interviews showed that all three were overly concerned about their own problems and made excessive demands on the children. Because of the severity of the mothers' personality problems, the absence of a father from these homes seemed to justify classifying the marital situation as Group 5.

MOTHER'S PERSONALITY

As has been indicated in previous chapters, our attempt at classifying the adoptive mothers on the basis of personality or personal adjustment gave particular attention to their capacity in interpersonal relations. Five degrees were recognized, ranging from "emotionally healthy" to "seriously impaired capacity for interpersonal relations," a category that included the psychotic and the very eccentric.

All the original adoptive mothers in homes rated D or E were judged to belong to one or the other of the two lowest categories, 41 of the 53 in D homes being classified as belonging to Group 4, and all 61 in E homes as belonging to Group 5. Not included in the count were the 13 homes from which the original adoptive mother was absent.

Group 4 was described by the field director as being composed of women who had little capacity for adult functioning but who had at times some ability to give and receive affection, and to be aware of the feelings and desires of others. Group 5 consisted of those whose capacity for interpersonal relations was seriously impaired. The following are descriptions of subtypes within Groups 4 and 5.

Self-centered and Insensitive; Some Ability to Relate to People (Group 4)

In the first subtype of Group 4 were placed three women (four adopted children) who were extroverted, talkative individuals with little anxiety in the parental role. They regarded themselves as perfect, all-giving mothers and were controlling and dominating. Nevertheless, they had some warmth for people and some slight understanding of their feelings.

> One mother, who had had many foster children in her care, spent most of the time telling the interviewer that many people turned to her for advice and guidance, and that she had been very

successful in helping them. She felt that she could make any child perfectly healthy and happy. She said she thought of the adopted child as "my baby" and refused to let him play with rough boys or have much time alone with her husband because he was too easy with the child. She was apparently a benign despot, controlling every aspect of the lives of her husband, her own daughter, and the adopted child but she was probably fairly warm, though insensitive, in her relation with the child.

In this subgroup was also a type of woman (six cases) that was in some ways the opposite of the first. These six women were individuals who apparently had a great need for perfection, which was expressed in rigid standards for themselves and others. In spite of this, they too showed some capacity for feeling affection, sorrow, anger. In contrast with their counterparts in Group 5 (described below), these women seemed to have conscious and rigid control over their feelings, whereas those in Group 5 had probably learned this control so early in life that they were barely conscious of it.

A mother who had a facade of great confidence and rigid control of all her own actions carried over to others what she expected of herself. She was greatly pleased with her child, she said, adding that he had never asked any questions about adoption—in fact, never asked questions of any sort that might be disturbing to her and her husband. The child never questioned anything she told him to do. He always came straight home from school and, before he went out to play, asked if he could help her in any way.

Neurotic Behavior (Group 4)

A second subtype in Group 4 consisted of eight women who combined physical and psychological symptoms with a great deal of neurotic behavior. Some of these mothers had had a nervous breakdown, either before adoption or shortly after. Nevertheless, they were able to carry out some of their responsibilities fairly adequately and to be moderately effective in their personal relationships.

One of these mothers was extremely tense and anxious and had many physical complaints, among them migraine headaches. She was quite dependent on her own mother, who lived with her and her husband. Because she was so nervous, she found it impossible to stay at home, she said. She had taken a job and left to her mother all responsibility of homemaking and care of the child.

Another woman, very anxious and excitable, handled her children in an erratic manner. She had high blood pressure and had had psychiatric treatment. According to her statement, her marriage was poor, as were her relations with her parents. Her children had behavior problems, she said, and she had always had a great deal of difficulty with them.

Included in this subtype were several women who seemed to have an overwhelming desire for babies, whether or not they were physically or economically able to provide for them. Their tendency was either to turn away from the children when they became older or to try to keep them babies as long as possible. Their focus on infants seemed evidence of some neurotic problem rather than a real love for children.

Immature, Dependent, Anxious (Group 4)

The third subtype contained the largest number of women— 24 in all. These were very dependent, anxious individuals whose chief difficulty lay in their incapacity for assuming adult responsibilities. They were childlike people, both in appearance and in the way they conducted themselves during the interview. They had great difficulty in expressing themselves and were very uncertain about the ideas they did express.

These women showed great anxiety in relation to most aspects of their functioning as adults and parents. They disliked responsibility and had no idea how to deal with problems. Their inability to make mature judgments often led to impulsive and unrealistic decisions. They were exceptionally dependent on others in their environment, even on their young children. They tended to be self-centered and preoccupied with their own needs, being especially concerned about their "nervousness," which they described as long-standing. Nevertheless, they had some capacity for affection, especially for their children.

A woman who impressed the interviewer as unusually dependent said her first two marriages were unhappy, and that her third husband, whom she liked better and had called "Daddy," had recently died. This man was fifteen years older than she. Since his death she had leaned heavily on her pre-adolescent adopted daughter, to the point where there was almost a reversal of roles. She participated with her daughter in the activities of her group of friends and looked to the child for advice. In spite of this behavior, the mother had some resourcefulness, desired good things for her daughter, and allowed her some freedom.

Another mother in the group was much less accepting of her child. Because she could not endure staying at home, this mother had been employed ever since the adoption, even though the family had a comfortable income. She said she felt repelled by the child's demands and expressions of affection and "threw up" if any problem arose. This mother was confused and inconsistent in her handling of her child and felt inadequate in all aspects of homemaking.

Although the interview did not regularly cover the mothers' childhood experiences, many of these mothers spontaneously described gross deprivation in their early years. Some had married very young to escape an intolerable home situation; others assumed responsibility for younger siblings from the age of five or six; two had been abandoned by their parents and reared in institutions. These early experiences may well have had much to do with these women's inability to be mature, adequate parents.

Markedly Self-centered, Insensitive, Incapable of Affection (Group 5)

In spite of many differences in personality makeup, the 63 women (64 children) whose emotional adjustment was classified as of the first subtype of Group 5 had several traits in common. All of them were markedly narcissistic and self-centered. They did not express normal affection, and they seemed unusually insensitive to the needs and feelings of other people.

The majority of these women were superficially friendly and outgoing and talked freely with the interviewers. Their outstanding traits were their apparent lack of anxiety and their narcissism. Even when describing serious problems they did not seem to be worried. Serious illness on the children's part did not upset them greatly. Bad behavior and poor performance in school they took with equanimity, being concerned neither with what it meant to the children nor with what it implied for themselves.

These women appeared to have very shallow relations with people and little capacity to understand or feel close even to their own spouses and children. The statements they made about their husbands or their children, although expressed in the words others would use, did not carry the feeling one would normally expect. There were great discrepancies between what they said and what they did.

> One mother, a divorced woman, seemed to the interviewer to behave more like an adolescent than a grown-up. This mother seemed wholly unconcerned about her children, even though one was in a correctional school. On her own initiative and with little feeling, she described intimate details of her marriage and her problems in sexual relations. She cut the interview short because she had "a date with Daddy."

> Another, who had had many foster children in her care, was completely confident about her methods of child rearing, although she described ways of handling them that would ordinarily be regarded as very destructive. Her lack of feeling for children was extreme. For example, she said she had told the adopted child of his adoptive status by showing him a newspaper picture of a man who had killed himself and saying that this man was his real father.

In contrast, a few of the women in this subcategory, instead of being open and seemingly unconcerned, were guarded and suspicious in their talk with the interviewers and presumably in their relations with other people. These women had many of the characteristics of the mothers just described, but differed in that they presented a perfect picture of the children and could not admit that they had any problems. They tried to keep their children very close to them and to control every facet of their lives. Apparently they did this, not out of deep affection but because they felt that they and their children were one unit against the world. As to their husbands, if they were not divorced from them, they disregarded them. By these relations with husband and child they indicated the narcissism noted above.

Psychotic or Very Eccentric (Group 5)

The second subtype in Group 5 consisted of four mothers (five children) in homes rated E who displayed such peculiar behavior, made such confused statements, or were so unable to communicate with the interviewers that it seemed likely they were psychotic.

One of these mothers spoke in a cautious, restrained manner about people and forces that were hostile to her. She was especially paranoid in describing her husband, alluding mysteriously to the terrible things he had done to her and the children. From time to time her statements were more lucid, and she would say that families like hers should not be allowed to adopt children.

Another of these mothers was so withdrawn that she was almost unable to speak. She responded to all questions in monosyllables and seemed unaware of the presence of the interviewer or of the reason for the interview.

Another varied from being highly suspicious of the interviewer and threatening to kill her to being very calm and giving pertinent information about herself and the child.

The seven other women in this subcategory (one in an E home and six in D) had less extreme symptoms but by their descriptions of their past or by their eccentric behavior they, too, displayed a mental state that seemed to border on the psychotic.

One of these mothers kept up a constant stream of remarks, jumping nervously from one topic to another. Much of what she had to say concerned her own illnesses. About them and other matters she made many unconnected, irrelevant comments. She told, for instance, about having been irrational for several weeks when the adopted child was an infant. This and later mental states she vaguely attributed to medication.

Another was a very erratic, elderly woman who had adopted the child after her own children had grown up. In her discussion with the interviewer she was preoccupied with her religious experiences and talked of having had "visions."

MOTHER–CHILD RELATIONS

In no D or E home did the mother feel about the child and behave toward him in a way that could be regarded as healthy and helpful. On the contrary, the mother-child relation in every case seemed to be one that would seriously handicap the adopted child in his personality development sooner or later.

When the field director analyzed what the adoptive mothers said about the children and about their own actions toward the children, and their feelings concerning them, a division into the following two broad types of mother-child relationship seemed warranted:

Group 4 Mother overpermissive and ineffectual or insensitive and inconsistent

Group 5 Mother greatly involved with child or very rejecting or highly ambivalent

Within these groups the following subtypes were noted.

Overpermissive and Ineffectual; Child in Control (Group 4)

The 29 mothers in this subtype, all of whom were in homes rated D, were insecure or immature, ineffectual, overwhelmed women who looked to their children for affection and security and felt unimportant in the role of mother. Many of them, especially those who were separated from their husbands, put heavy responsibility on the children, both in making decisions and in sharing in their own problems. One mother, for example, told how her child had comforted her about her husband's desertion and helped her decide what to do next. Others mentioned how concerned the children were about them—about their health, their hard work, or the precarious state of their finances.

Most of these mothers were satisfied with their children. They expected a great deal of maturity of them and many obtained it, at least in the form they desired. They gave practically no evidence of punitiveness or rejection in the way they handled the children.

One of these mothers said she felt helpless and unable to make decisions. She knew she did not give adequate care to the adopted child or to her own children. Their illnesses and other problems worried her but she never knew what to do. She loved them very much, she said (and her affection for them was clear to the interviewer), but sometimes she felt they were too much for her.

Another mother expressed great concern about her inability to set limits to her child's behavior and said she knew she was indulgent and inconsistent. She felt that her ten-year-old daughter's judgment was better than her own, so she hesitated to deny her anything for fear she would be wrong. This woman lived with her own mother and seemed more like a sister than a mother to her adopted child.

Another mother, a clearly insecure, nervous woman, said she was having great difficulty with her child. Because of his physical handicap, she said, she was unable to be firm with him. She apparently gave in to his every demand and was never able to punish him. As a result, she was completely controlled by the child.

Mother Affectionate but Seriously Limited Intellectually and Culturally (Group 4)

Four mothers, in homes rated E, had a rather poor relationship with their children because of intellectual and cultural deficiencies and associated emotional deprivations. These women were fond of the children but insensitive to their needs, and were inconsistent and baffled by the children. Old age, illness, and/or financial worries, in addition to their inherent limitations, made it impossible for these mothers to give the children adequate guidance and understanding.

The adopted child of one such mother had married at fourteen to escape from her dismal, disorganized home. Her marriage was not working out well, and the adoptive mother felt bewildered and incapable of helping. In another home an eleven-year-old husky, active boy was proving too much for his sixty-five-year-old mother to handle, preoccupied as she was with financial problems and her husband's long illness. In the other two homes, the situation was equally unpropitious. The most that can be said favorably is that these mothers had good intentions. They had neither the personal competence nor the environmental support to maintain a helpful relation with their children.

Highly Involved; Demanding, Controlling; Overidentified with Child (Group 5)

Eleven mothers in this group were in homes rated E and seven in homes rated D. These women had an engulfing, incorporating attitude toward their children, apparently feeling that they were extensions of themselves. At the extreme, they tried to isolate the children entirely and did not permit them more than minimum contact with other people, including the adoptive fathers. As some of these mothers said, they just could not let the children out of their sight.

In addition, they controlled the children rigidly and made great demands for conformity to their wishes. If they permitted the children any activities apart from themselves, they decided what the activities should be and when the children should engage in them. It was the same with friends; if they allowed the children to have any, they chose them carefully or scrutinized closely those the children chose. Some of these women slept with their children and bathed them and waited on them long after the usual age. Many of them were very indulgent, giving the children more clothes, toys, spending money, and the like than they could afford.

There was variation, of course, within the group, not all mothers being quite so extreme in their possessiveness and exclusion of the children from contacts with others. All of them, however, were very controlling and very much overidentified with the children, in a narcissistic, self-centered way.

In binding the children to them and securing their affection, these mothers were apparently very successful, at least as far as they were aware. They spoke proudly of how good the children were, how affectionate, considerate, thoughtful of their wishes. They told with pleasure that the children preferred their company to that of others. In all, they had nothing but good to report about the children and the adoption.

One mother stated that her eleven-year-old boy had never been out of her sight for more than five minutes except when he was in school. Her descriptions of bathing him and otherwise caring for him sounded as though she was talking about an infant. The boy slept with her and, as far as the interviewer could learn, the father was never allowed any part in rearing the child.

A second mother said that her child, a twelve-year-old boy, preferred her company to anyone else's. She always walked part of the way to school with him and kissed him on parting. She commented that some people thought it funny to see such a big boy kissing his mother but she was proud that he loved her so much.

A third mother, who said she had greatly wanted a girl, was pleased that her adopted son, age twelve, was more like a girl than a boy and was such a companion to her. All his playmates were girls, she said, for boys were too rough. Actually, the boy spent most of his time with the mother. He greatly liked to play at being a girl by dressing in girls' clothing.

Largely Rejecting (Group 5)

In contrast to this subgroup, 6 mothers in D homes and 17 in E homes had little good to say about their adopted children. Instead, they were very critical of them and punitive in attitude and behavior. Some of them encouraged their children's dependency and seemed at times to be affectionate, but they repulsed the children when their behavior was even slightly demanding or unacceptable. The most forthright statement of this rejecting attitude was made by a mother who opened the interview by saying, "You'll hear a different story from me. I just don't like this child at all."

If these women made positive comments about the children, the remarks almost always referred to something a child had done that reflected favorably on the mother's competence or status, or met some of her need for affection. For example, after telling about the many difficulties she had had with her child and the ways in which his behavior was unsatisfactory, a mother might say that the child was very loving toward her but disliked her husband or that he did well in school after she had tutored him. By such statements the mothers showed that they were not wholly disparaging and detached. Even the most critical and most antagonistic of them gave evidence of some emotional involvement with her child.

One mother complained that her child had been nothing but trouble to her from the beginning. As an infant he frequently vomited, and she felt that he had done this to spite her. She cured him of the habit, she said by, holding his head under a cold-water faucet. Toilet training was also a battle, which was finally resolved, when the child was two, by a severe, prolonged switching. At seven the child was sent to military school because he was such a "mamma's boy." Whatever "mothering" the child received as an infant came from his father, who gave him his night bottles and rocked him to sleep.

Some of these mothers encouraged the very behavior of which they complained. One, who was highly rejecting of her adolescent daughter and spoke most critically of her lying, stealing, and sexual interests, gave the interviewer several examples of how she herself had succeeded in having someone else blamed for something she had done. She also told of encouraging her daughter to tell her of erotic incidents, particularly the "terrible things" her girl friends did with boys.

Somewhat less extreme was a mother who was greatly disappointed in her child because he was not a companion to her and did not help her around the house. She said she had adopted this child because she was lonely; she now wished she had taken a girl. This mother was critical of all the child's activities, did not want his friends around, and had no interest in what he was doing. Since he would not do what she wanted, she had, in effect, washed her hands of him.

Ambivalent in Attitude and Inconsistent in Behavior (Group 5)

To the 41 mothers in this group (12 from D homes and 29 from E) certain of their children's qualities, sometimes even their behavioral and personality difficulties, were pleasing. These mothers, however, were inherently lacking in the capacity to give affection and were extremely insensitive to other people's emotional needs. Consequently, they tended to be harsh and inconsistent in handling the children and could afford them little security or sense of continuity in a personal relationship.

Characteristically, these mothers were certain that their ways of dealing with their children were right, even though they might give convincing evidence that their methods did not work. Some of them were particularly pleased with their success in dealing with physical illnesses, telling, for instance, how they brought the children through "in spite of the doctor," or saying that it was they alone who were successful in finding the "correct formula" for feeding an infant.

These mothers had certain other traits in common. For one, most of them, in spite of their complaints, minimized the seriousness of the physical and behavioral difficulties they described. For another, only one mother gave any indication that she thought she might have had a part in producing her child's problems. All the others put the responsibility elsewhere: on the school, the husband, heredity, and the like. This denying of responsibility and putting the blame on others is, of course, not unusual, especially when parents feel threatened by their children's problems. What was different from usual was these mothers' apparent absence of anxiety, their bland acceptance of the fact that difficulties existed and their lack of worry about it.

These mothers' ambivalence toward their children was heavily weighted on the rejecting side, but many of them were also overprotective and overcontrolling. Some, for instance, described themselves as nervous and were overconcerned about their children's health or about dangers to which they might be exposed. One insisted her adopted son had a heart condition, in spite of her doctor's opinion to the contrary, and greatly limited his physical activities.

With regard to rules and discipline, these mothers were characteristically inconsistent, being permissive at one time or in one respect and rigidly controlling otherwise. There was little logic in what they did, and the effect on the children must have been one of confusion, to say the least.

In a number of cases in this group, it was learned that the mother had had difficulty with the child since infancy. This was true of some mothers in the preceding group also, that in which the mother overtly rejected the child. In all these cases there seemed to be a close relation between physical and emotional problems. Perhaps the children's early problems (some of which suggested organic damage) created the mothers' negative attitudes through causing anxiety, which in turn made for greater problems in the infant. Perhaps the mothers' inherent lack of tenderness was communicated to the infants and made for lack of good adjustment in the children from the outset. Both explanations seemed possible but, given these mothers' personality makeup, it seemed likely that they at least aggravated whatever constitutional weaknesses or defects the children might have had.

FATHER AS A FAMILY MEMBER

In none of the D and E homes was the father the sort of person who could adequately compensate the child for the shortcomings of the mother.

As has already been said, there were three homes in which the child never had an adoptive father. Seven adoptive fathers had died, five of them before the child was of school age. Separation or divorce had deprived the child of his adoptive father in 21 other homes. In short, at the time of the follow-up interview there was no father in a fourth of the homes in the D and E groups.

Because of the nature of the interview situation, the information about the adoptive fathers was sketchy in most cases and usually reflected the mother's estimate of what the father was like as a husband and parent. It seemed sufficient, however, to justify the following crude assessments of the fathers who were living with their wives or, if out of the home, were in contact with them.

> *Group 4* a. Father ineffectual as parent and husband but apparently had some affection for, and interest in, the child—22 E, 17 D homes
>
> b. Father a withdrawn, solitary individual or one who, for other reasons, took little part in family life—16 E, 19 D homes
>
> c. Father overinvolved with the child; somewhat like the corresponding group of mothers described above— 5 D homes
>
> *Group 5* a. Father resentful of the child or highly critical of him or actually abusive—6 E, 3 D homes
>
> b. Father highly irresponsible; unable or unwilling to provide at all adequately for the children—5 E, 3 D homes

Of the first subcategory in Group 4, there is little concrete to be reported. A few of these men were interviewed, either with the wife or in the course of securing an appointment to talk with her. In commenting on these men and the others in the subcategory, the interviewers made such remarks as that they occasionally took the children on outings, that they seemed less maladjusted than their wives and rather affectionate toward the children, or that they were passive, incompetent individuals but kindly disposed toward the children.

One mother, who disparaged her husband greatly, complained that he was too indulgent toward their son and did not punish him sufficiently. She added that he was planning to give the child a bicycle for Christmas and that he was always sympathetic with him.

Another mother, an erratic sort of person, said in a derogatory way that her house was all cluttered with "Boy Scout junk." Her husband was a Scout leader, she added, and participated with the child in some of the Scout activities. While the interviewer did not see the father, she thought he was at least fairly companionable with the child.

The second group has been commented upon above in connection with the marital situation. Typical of these men were the following: a husband described by the interviewer as a man who passively sat by and made no attempt to intervene in the morbidly close mother-child relationship; one who stayed home while his wife and daughter spent long holidays together; one whose wife complained that he thought only of himself and never took any interest in either her or the child, preferring to take his recreation alone.

The third subcategory of fathers in Group 4 had overinvolved attitudes toward, and relations with, the adopted children. Two of them had separated from their wives and were maintaining homes for the children by themselves.

One was described by his wife as being so completely wrapped up in the child that he gave in to her every whim. This father had slept with his daughter, now eleven years old, ever since infancy. He attended to her needs in ways more typical of mothers and generally played a feminine role in the house.

In the two other homes both father and mother were excessively attached to the adopted children and apparently had no separate life of their own. In these families, everything—even sleeping—was done as a threesome, with the child being the dominant member and making decisions for the parents.

The first subcategory in Group 5 was composed of nine fathers who openly resented the adopted children and were very critical of them. Some of them actually abused the children physically.

One father was said to have always disliked the child and to be abusive to him at times. The mother said her husband never noticed the child other than to be critical and that he blamed her for all the problems the child had in school and elsewhere.

Another father, during the interview, expressed great dissatisfaction with his adopted son, stating that from infancy on he had been untrustworthy, that he thought only of himself, and had no good traits. The father made these comments in a cold, hostile manner and was most critical of even minor misbehavior on the part of the child.

The final subgroup consisted of irresponsible fathers who did not provide at all adequate financial or other support for their wives and children. Three of these men had sole responsibility for the children; three had left home but maintained some contact with the family. The other two lived at home with wife and child.

One of these fathers was described by the interviewer as a boastful, insecure man who bragged of the many people in high places who were his friends. He had been jobless frequently and had no regular source of income at the time of the interview. His wife had left him, he said, and he was taking care of their two adopted daughters, about eleven years old. All three slept in one bed. He said he knew this was not a good arrangement but he did not want to hurt the girls' feelings. In personality, he seemed an immature, dependent individual, irresponsible and self-centered.

Another father, mentioned earlier, had never been able to provide even a semblance of a home for the adopted child, who was now in foster care. He was alcoholic and unstable. His present wife was the fourth woman he had married.

Another father was divorced from the adoptive mother and from a subsequent wife. He said the adopted children were his own by a common-law marriage. The house in which he and the children lived was in the worst slum section of the city, a notorious red-light district. As he told the story of his life with the children, it was clear that he was quite incompetent to provide emotional security or even proper protection for them, and it seemed likely that the children had been exposed to highly questionable conditions.

GROSS SOCIAL PATHOLOGY

When listing the criteria used in rating homes, we mentioned that social-economic factors were taken into account only when they were extreme. Even when extreme, these factors were not given disproportionate weight as compared with those so far described, though they might reduce the home rating somewhat. There were, for instance, a few B and C homes in which the housing and neighborhood conditions were poor and/or the family's social status clearly "lower-lower" class but in which the parents' personality and family relations were fairly adequate. For the most part, however, when gross social-economic conditions appeared it was in D and E homes, where they were combined with other factors disadvantageous to children.

Poor Living Conditions

Among the homes rated D or E there were 15 (4 D and 11 E) in which low income was combined with other sorts of handicaps to make the home an unsuitable place in which to rear a child.

One of these families lived in a shanty-like house that the mother and son had built in an unimproved, isolated area on the outskirts of the city. The house was dirty and dilapidated, its character being suggested by the fact that old pieces of cloth had been hung over the windows for shades. There was no provision for privacy of any sort. In addition, the father was chronically ill, and the mother seemed to be intellectually far below par.

Another family lived in a filthy, broken-down house in a deteriorated section of the city. In addition to the adopted child, the mother had four foster children and several of her own to provide for.

A third family, consisting of the parents and the adopted child, lived in squalid rooms adjoining a disreputable-looking tavern they operated. These people apparently spent much of their time in the tavern, which had as part of its accommodations a dance hall and rooms for "guests."

A fourth family, consisting of an emotionally unstable mother and her ten-year-old adopted daughter, lived in two small, cheerless rooms in a run-down boarding house. The mother complained that the living quarters and the house itself were so dilapidated that she could not let her daughter bring her friends home. Nevertheless, she had apparently made no attempt to find more suitable housing.

A few of these families had the attitudes, values, and ways of life of the "lower-lower" class. This was shown by the methods the mothers used in training and disciplining their children and by their attitudes toward school attendance.

> One mother, in describing how she toilet-trained her child, said she thought it wrong for parents to be so lazy as to let children who slept with them wet the bed. She said that when her children were young she always made them get out of bed and "wet on the floor," for that was easier to clean up.

> Another mother, who lived in a very small, run-down house, kept her child out of school frequently in order to do the shopping and housework.

> Another said she pitied her child because he had to go to school, was surprised that he liked it, and did not mind at all that he was recently expelled for misbehavior.

Most of the families' disadvantageous ways of life were attributable, however, to psychological rather than cultural factors. All the mothers were emotionally maladjusted women. In most cases their financial difficulties and makeshift living arrangements resulted from their inability to manage after divorce or death had deprived them of a husband.

> One of these mothers, who was divorced from her third husband, had sold her house and invested in a trailer. In it she and the adopted child had lived a nomad life until their resources were exhausted. At the time of the interview they were living in a dingy house in a very poor neighborhood. The mother was ill, and the child was left largely to his own resources.

Neglect and Abuse; Excessive Drinking

Twenty children in 7 D and 12 E homes were seriously neglected or mistreated. One child, for instance, was so abused by his alcoholic and mentally-ill adoptive parents that a court had adjudged neglect and removed him from the home. Three others had been sent away from home by their adoptive parents. Two of these had had a series of foster-home placements and at the time of our study were in correctional schools. The third had been in and out of institutions from the time she was four years old. At age fifteen, when our study was made, she was on temporary discharge from a mental hospital, and the adoptive mother was trying to find a foster home for her. While this girl undoubtedly had a serious personality disorder, it was clear from the information secured that she had never been given proper care by the adoptive parents.

In most of these cases the mistreatment or neglect resulted from excessive drinking or from serious personality disturbance on the part of one or both parents.

> One mother, who impressed the interviewer as being possibly psychotic, herself told of being abusive and neglectful. The child's teacher reported that the child frequently said his parents did not want him, and she added that the mother once offered to give the child to her.

> An adoptive father who was mentally ill could function fairly well at times. When he was in one of his upset periods, however, he was abusive both to his wife and to his child.

In all, there were 17 homes in which one or both parents drank to excess. Four mothers were such heavy drinkers that, according to the fathers, they were completely unable to care for the children.

As would be expected, the excessive drinking was related not only to neglect and abuse of children but also to divorce. Ten of the 19 D and E homes in which the adoptive parents were classified as neglectful or abusive were also homes in which parents drank excessively. In 11 of the 17 cases of excessive drinking, this behavior, among other things, led to the break-up of the home.

Summary

The findings reported for the homes rated D or E are summarized in Table 25.

As has been evident throughout this chapter, the D homes were somewhat less unfavorable than those rated E, as shown by the higher proportion of Group 4 ratings and a lower proportion of Group 5 than in the E homes. The differences between the homes in this respect was more marked in some traits than in

TABLE 25. CHARACTERISTICS OF HOMES RATED POOR

Characteristics	D homes (61)	E homes (66)
1. Low income and/or poor living conditions	4	11
2. Serious neglect and/or abuse of children	7	12
3. Adoptive father or mother drank excessively	8	9
4. Adverse marital situation:		
No adoptive father ever (Group 5)	..	3
One adoptive parent dead:		
Group 4	5	1
Group 5	4	2
Divorce or separation (Group 5)	15	20
Marital discord:		
Group 4	2	..
Group 5	4	17
Skewed marriage:		
Group 4	8	7
Group 5	4	13
Poor marriage; type not known (Group 4)	16	3
5. Mother in home; personal adjustment poor		
Group 4	41	..
Group 5	12	61
6. Mother-child relations poor		
Group 4	29	4
Group 5	25	57
7. Father in home or in contact; poor functioning as family member		
Group 4	17	22
Group 5	30	27

others. The greatest difference occurred in the ratings given to the mother's personality and to mother-child relations, the E homes having a much larger proportion of mothers rated as belonging to Group 5. The fathers, in contrast, were rated about similarly in the two sets of homes, the apparent excess of Group 5 ratings in D homes being too small for statistical significance.

As to combinations of factors in Table 25, only 8 E homes had as few as two of the listed disadvantages. Forty-two of the 66 E homes and 54 of the 61 D homes had three or four of the adverse traits, and 16 E and 7 D had from five to seven of them. Although the D's and E's differed in degree, the characteristics reported seem to justify the statement that all of these homes were far from favorable to a child's development.

CHAPTER X

Present Adjustment
of the Adopted Children

So far, this analysis of the outcome of independent adoptions has led to two main conclusions. On the one hand, the adoptive parents did not find independent adoption very risky and most of them were greatly pleased with the adoption outcome. Even when adoption had entailed difficulties with the natural parents or receiving a child who was severely handicapped, very few considered the adoption unsatisfactory. On the other hand, the risk that independent adoption entailed for the adopted children was considerable. Nearly 30 per cent of the children were in adoptive homes that were rated by our interviewers as definitely poor, and an additional 25 per cent were in homes considered fair. Only about half of the children were in homes that seemed fully up to standard.

The first finding is gratifying but the second is much less so. Since the chief aim of adoption law is to promote the welfare of the children concerned (largely through court scrutiny of the suitability of the adoption petitioners), it seemed that the question of how well the children in the sample under study were faring should be pursued further. This was done by attempting to determine the adequacy of the children's social-emotional adjustment.

Information on how well the adoptive children are turning out has disadvantages and advantages as a measurement of the outcome of adoptions. It is disadvantageous because many factors other than adoption and its concomitants (indeed, factors other than parental influences) determine how well a child develops.

The approach is advantageous, however, for at least three reasons. First, it provides information that is interesting in and of itself. Even though the causal factors may be unclear, everybody wants to know how well adopted children develop and adjust. Second, through comparison with the home ratings, it enables us to assess how important it is that children get into the kinds of homes we called satisfactory. Third, through comparison with other home and parental characteristics, it enables us to explore whether better criteria than those we used in judging homes were to be found among the data collected in this study.

In this and the next chapter, then, we shall present information bearing on the adequacy of the adopted children's functioning at the time the study was made. This information was secured from official records; from parents, teachers, and classmates; and from the children themselves. It is a partial picture at best and, as with the home ratings and the judgments about various aspects of the homes, the accuracy of any particular score or rating can be challenged. Yet we think that the sum of the information about adjustment is fairly dependable and that it is bolstered by enough evidence to make the conclusions drawn from it at least reasonable.

HOW THE INFORMATION ABOUT ADJUSTMENT WAS SECURED

In planning the study, much thought was given to how and from whom dependable information about the children's current adjustment could be secured. The adoptive parents were one obvious source of information about the children's adjustment, and the interviews with them (mostly mothers) were a means of obtaining it. Much of the home interview centered on the mother's description of the child; her account of his doings and attitudes at home, school, and play; and her pleasures and problems with him. From such comments and others, as well as from the accompanying gestures and emotional tone, the interviewer obtained clues to the children's behavior and personality, as well as to the nature of the parent-child relations.

As objective reports of the children's present functioning, it seemed likely that some parents' descriptions would be undependable. Some parents would be accurate but others probably would be biased. One mother might describe as heinous certain behavior that a presumably more neutral interviewer might regard as normal adolescent high spirits, while another might regard with pride behavior that seemed to the interviewer indicative of serious emotional difficulties. Although it was recognized that these descriptions would not have to be taken at face value, nevertheless, the interviewers' interpretations would themselves have limitations. All in all, then, the home interviews could be regarded as only a partial source of information about the children's well-being.

The children themselves were another obvious source of information as were their peers, their teachers, and the school records. Through the cooperation of the schools, access to these sources was easily obtained.

We had next to decide by what means the information should be obtained at school. Individual interviews with the children and comparable "controls" were considered but ruled out by time and staff limitations. Brief interviews that would yield worthwhile information could be carried on only by well-trained persons with considerable clinical experience. Such persons were not available to the study in the numbers that would have been needed for this large-scale operation. Group interviews were suggested as an alternative possibility but this too seemed unfeasible.

Paper-and-pencil tests were finally decided upon as the method of choice. These had several advantages in this study. It was much easier to give tests than to interview, and tests were less time-consuming both for the children and their teachers and for the staff. Moreover, some research workers report that ratings based on psychiatric interviews are less reliable than those based on tests. While this is a debatable point, it had some influence on our decision.

Two ways of giving tests in school were suggested. One was to test all the children in the classrooms that contained the adopted children. The other was to take from each classroom the adopted ren and, say, four of their classmates and give tests to this group in another room. In either case, certain minimum facts about each child in the classroom could be obtained, on the basis of which "controls" could be chosen.

Actually, both methods were used—the first with the least time-consuming tests, and the second with the one that was longer. The longer test was given to each adopted child and to four of his classmates. Included in the group of four was a "control" child—of the same sex and race as the adopted child and from a home of comparable social economic status as judged by the father's occupation. The facts needed to select the child who was to be the control were secured by the staff psychologist from all the children in the classroom, just before the first test was given to them. The matching was done while the children were taking the test.

The tests and schedules chosen for use in the schools were of four kinds. Each presumably tapped a different and important area of a child's adjustment. First, there was a sociometric test, through which an indication of the standing or popularity of the adopted children and their controls was to be secured. The second test was of the sentence-completion type and was directed at ascertaining parent-child relations.[1] Third, the California Test of Personality was used to evaluate social and emotional adjustment from the children's own viewpoint. Fourth, the Behavior Description Chart, devised by Bowman and his associates in conjunction with the Quincy Youth Development Study, was used to secure teachers' opinions about the children's attitudes and behavior at school. In addition, "cumulative records" kept by the schools furnished information on intelligence and school achievement for some children.

The testing program reached all but 36 of the sample of adopted children under study. Most of the children who were not tested were either absent from school on the day the tests were given or were attending schools that did not cooperate in the study. A few were in schools outside the state. Three children

---

[1] This test proved not to be fruitful because most of the children completed the sentences in what seemed to be conventional, stereotyped ways. The decision not to score or otherwise use this material followed a review of a representative sample of completed tests by a panel of distinguished psychologists.

who were severely incapacitated physically or intellectually were not in school at all, and one child in a "special class" was not testable. In spite of these losses, 448 adopted children were tested—93 per cent of the 484 children in the study.

Table 33, on page 253, contains the only information at hand for testing how much bias was introduced into the study by the omission of the 36 nontested children. This table shows the distributions of tested and nontested children according to the social workers' ratings of the children's adjustment, these ratings being based on information secured through the home interviews. Ten of the 36 children could not be rated. Of the remaining 26, the proportion classified as maladjusted was considerably higher than among the children who were tested, being 35 per cent as compared with 9 per cent, a statistically significant difference. Nevertheless, because all but a few children were tested, the overall proportions in the various adjustment categories were practically the same as if all the children had been included.

INTELLIGENCE AND SCHOOL ACHIEVEMENT

The only available measure of the intelligence of the adopted children was that which the schools had secured through group tests and reported in the pupils' "cumulative records." The various schools used different tests, the California Mental Maturity and the Otis Beta being the most frequent. The schools also differed in the grades at which they gave the tests. Some school systems apparently did no testing of intelligence, for the school records of a number of children contained no intelligence estimates of any sort.

In view of these limitations, the intelligence scores, based on group tests, are chiefly useful for comparing the adopted children with their matched controls.

Table 26 shows the percentage distribution of the I.Q. ratings of the adopted children and of their controls who were in the cooperating schools. It will be seen that the two distributions are very similar. The average I.Q. is 109 for the adopted children and 109.2 for the controls, an insignificant difference both statistically and practically.

This finding of similarity between adopted and control children in intelligence is important, for, while not conclusive evidence, it makes it unlikely that differences subsequently found between the adopted and the control children can be explained on constitutional or genetic grounds alone.

TABLE 26. PERCENTAGE DISTRIBUTION OF I.Q. SCORES OF ADOPTED AND CONTROL CHILDREN[a]

Score	Adopted	Control
59 or below	..	..
60 to 69	..	..
70 to 79	2	1
80 to 89	8	7
90 to 99	14	17
100 to 109	30	29
110 to 119	25	23
120 to 129	14	16
130 to 139	5	5
140 and over	2	2
Total	100	100

[a] These scores, being obtained from school records, do not include the few mentally retarded and otherwise severely handicapped children who did not attend school or were in a "special class."

Achievement-test scores were included in the school records of nearly all the children who were in schools that cooperated in the study. These scores referred to the children's performance in various school grades and on various types of achievement tests. For instance, a child in the eighth grade at the time of our study might have been given a California AA achievement test in the sixth grade, while a child now in the sixth grade might have been given a Stanford L test in the fifth grade, and so on.

For many purposes, comparisons based on different tests given at different times would be useless. In the present situation, the comparison seemed justifiable, since in most cases study and control pairs had been given the same test in the same grade. In making the comparison, the test scores were recorded in terms of the extent to which the child's achievement was above or below grade level at the time he took the test. The distribution of the adopted and the control children on the achievement tests so recorded is shown in Table 27.

As with the intelligence test scores, the findings on the achievement tests indicate that, on the average, the children—both the adopted and the natural children—were functioning a bit above normal. The average for the adopted children was an achievement of 0.56 grades above placement level; for the controls, 0.67 grades. In other words, both groups were performing, on the average, about a half-grade above the one they were actually in at school when the test was given. The difference between these average scores was not statistically significant.

TABLE 27. PERCENTAGE DISTRIBUTION OF ACHIEVEMENT-TEST SCORES IN RELATION TO GRADE LEVEL OF ADOPTED AND CONTROL CHILDREN

Years above or below grade level		Adopted	Control
Below grade	3.1 or more	..	1
	2.1 to 3.0	2	2
	1.1 to 2.0	7	6
	0.1 to 1.0	22	23
At grade	0.9 above	36	29
Above grade	1.0 to 1.9	23	26
	2.0 to 2.9	7	10
	3.0 or more	3	3
Total		100	100

Concealed within the tables on I.Q. and achievement, however, is the fact that certain children's achievement test scores were not in line with their I.Q. scores. This was true of both the control children and the adopted children, the correlation between I.Q. and achievement being .51 in each group.

The adopted children's performance in this respect is of particular interest, for this is information pertinent to the question of how many adopted children were functioning poorly. Unfortunately, this information is not very dependable, because the intelligence ratings were based on group tests and because the I.Q. and achievement ratings listed in the school records for a given child may have been secured in different years of his school life. For what they are worth, however, the facts about the adopted children's scores on I.Q. and achievement were as follows: At least 20 adopted children were achieving at a level much below the average of the others in their I.Q. range. Two of these had I.Q.'s in the 80 to 89 range; two were between 90 and 99; five, 100 to 109; five, 110 to 119; six, 130 and up. About ten other children were overachieving as judged by this standard. Together these 30 children constituted about 10 per cent of all the adopted children whose I.Q. scores and achievement scores were known.

THE SOCIOMETRIC TEST

Sociometric tests aim to measure the extent to which the individuals examined are accepted, rejected, or ignored by their peers in a social group to which they belong. Typical tests ask the individuals in a group to name the group members with whom they prefer to associate, those they prefer to avoid, and those to whom they are indifferent. The circumstances under which they would make such choices are also usually specified.

Some studies indicate that tests of this sort are fairly reliable, at least over short periods of time, in the sense that repeating a test with the same subjects has produced much the same scores. The validity of the tests, however—their ability to measure accurately what they aim to measure—has not been satisfactorily assessed.[1]

The sociometric test used in this study was one devised especially for it by the chief psychologist. The aim in giving such a test was to secure an index to that segment of a child's social adjustment that consists of his acceptability and standing among his age-mates. Put crudely, this was to be determined by how popular he was with the children in his classroom in work and play, at school and away from school.

The test dealt only with the positive side of children's relations with their classmates. It asked which children they preferred but not which they disliked or avoided. A copy of the questionnaire appears in Appendix B, page 452.

Findings from sociometric tests are usually presented in the form of numerical scores. For the present test this scoring was done by assigning values to the various degrees of choice under

---

[1] For a review and critique of sociometry, see Loomis, Charles P., "Sociometry: 1937–1947: Theory and Method," *Sociometry*, vol. 11, 1948, pp. 262–286. In regard to the reliability and validity of sociometric tests, see, for instance, Mouton, J. S., R. R. Blake, and B. Fruchter, *Sociometry*, vol. 18, 1955, pp. 181–206.

each question. First choices carried a value of 3; second choices, 2; third choices, 1. These values were summated to yield a total score for each individual mentioned in the questionnaire. Although it would seem that such a scoring system would favor the children who had many classmates, an inspection of the data suggested no relation between class size and scores.

This scoring system, it will be noted, is one that disregards the possible distinction between popularity at play and popularity as a work companion, a distinction that some studies have shown to exist among children. On this point we can say only that the measure was regarded as a crude one at best, and that the scanty information the test produced did not seem to justify refined handling. Important independent conclusions were not expected to result from the findings of this test, but it was thought that the test might yield information supportive or illuminative of other conclusions.

In the schools that participated in the study, the sociometric test was given to all the children in the classrooms that contained adopted children who were in the sample. For analysis, however, only the scores of the adopted children and of those selected as their controls were used.

The distribution of the scores of these two groups is shown in Table 28. It will be noted that, again, the number of children having given scores was much the same in the adopted group as in the control group. The average score for the control children was a bit higher than for the adopted children, being 20.7 as compared with 18.7. This difference, though small, was statistically significant.

TABLE 28. PERCENTAGE DISTRIBUTION OF SCORES OF ADOPTED AND CONTROL CHILDREN ON THE SOCIOMETRIC TEST

Score	Adopted	Control
Under 5	15	13
5 to 14	31	28
15 to 24	27	26
25 to 34	14	14
35 to 44	6	10
45 and up	7	9
Total	100	100

The chief use of the figures for the control children is to provide a standard for comparison with the distribution of the adopted children's scores. Looked at in this way, Table 28 indicates that the adopted children's performance on this test was only slightly out of line with that of the controls. In other words, the fact that, for instance, nearly half of the adopted children had scores under 15 is not to be regarded as in some way indicative of the adverse effects of adoption.

It is one thing to say that the adopted children were not very different from their peers on this test. It is quite another to say what the scores mean for the well-being of individual adopted children, and what they indicate as to how many of them were maladjusted.

Taken at face value, the scores suggest that some adopted children were much less popular than others. Thirty-three of these children (those with scores of 45 and up) may have been picked as at least third choice on all three points by 15 or more of their classmates, a number which usually constituted about half the class. In contrast, 17 adopted children (out of the 69 who received scores under 5) were not selected as even third choice on any of the three points by any child. The scores, however, give little indication of what combination of choices entered into them, and no indication of how unpopular any child was. Not to be a third choice is not necessarily to be disliked or avoided. Even among the 17 children not selected by any other child, there may have been some who were well liked (who would have been, say, fourth choice), as well as some who were disliked by all classmates. Indeed, the very fact that only 17 adopted children were not chosen by anybody seems worthy of comment.

Viewed as indicators of social adjustment, segmentally or globally considered, the meaning of the scores for individuals is even more equivocal. The scores, obviously, cannot reveal what it was about a child that caused him to be chosen. It is sometimes assumed that the children chosen through such a test have the characteristics that other children prize and so are, *ipso facto*, socially adjusted to the environment in which the choices are made. Such reasoning, however, ignores the fact that children may occasionally be chosen out of pity or out of guilt or even out of fear, or that the very fact of deviant character may be a basis for choice. These probably are not the usual reasons children are selected, but as possibilities in individual cases they should not be overlooked in our eagerness to find a so-called objective measure of social adjustment.

Along the same line, the scores can give no indication of what motivated the chosen children to the kind of behavior that others found attractive. It may be that most of the popular children displayed the admired behavior and personality traits because their mental health was good, but this is far from the only possibility. As is well known, some insecure children strive hard to be popular and do become so; some children are pushed into socially attractive behavior by their parents; and so on. In addition, it is not at all certain that the more popular a child is, the better adjusted he is. After all, among other reasons, there is such a thing as being popular among maladjusted children.

Altogether, then, neither high scores nor low scores on the sociometric test were sure signs of the social or emotional well-being of particular adopted children. The scores are useful, nevertheless, as crude indices. Combined with other scores and ratings, they help to identify the adopted children who were probably adjusting unusually well or unusually poorly.

THE CALIFORNIA TEST OF PERSONALITY

The California Test of Personality is a well-known test that was devised to measure a number of aspects of personal and social adjustment. There are five forms of the test, each for a different age level. In the present study, the forms used were the 1953 revision of the elementary (grades 4 to 8) and the intermediate (grades 7 to 10) AA versions.

The forms of the test are divided into two main parts, one having questions bearing on "personal adjustment," the other on "social adjustment." Each part is further subdivided to tap the following areas: (1) personal adjustment: the areas of self-reliance, sense of personal worth, sense of personal freedom, feeling of belonging, withdrawing tendencies, and nervous symptoms; (2) social adjustment: social standards, social skills, anti-social tendencies, family relations, school relations, and community relations. In each of these areas, eight to fifteen questions are asked, depending on the age level to which the test is directed. They are framed in ways that are expected to reveal significant feelings or actions of the individual who is being tested. For instance, instead of asking a child whether he thinks teachers are "down" on him, the test phrases the question in this way: "Does it seem to you that some of the teachers 'have it in' for pupils?"

To what extent children answer the test questions in terms of their real feelings and actions is largely unknown. Nor is it definitely known how well the test scores correspond with the tested individuals' social and emotional adjustment as observed clinically or in "real life."[1] The authors of the test maintain that this problem is almost nonexistent "on the levels where personality tests are of greatest assistance to teachers."[2] They add, however, that the problem probably increases with the age of the individual being tested. Some other research workers suggest that children who get low scores on the test probably give truthful answers, while among those who get high scores there are probably some children who are not saying what they actually think or feel. In our own factor analysis of test scores and other measurements secured through the study (Chapter XVII), the California test was found to be a separate factor, associated only with I.Q. and achievement-test scores. This finding may possibly indicate that bright children know the "proper" responses to questions on the test and that, for such children, the test does not reveal true thoughts and feelings.

This question of the test's validity is of chief importance when the test scores are used to judge individual adjustment. It is perhaps less important when groups are being compared, for in this situation the question of the relative performance of the groups perhaps outranks the question of what the performance means.

---

[1] A review of studies bearing on the questions is contained in *Summary of Investigations Number One, Enlarged Edition, California Test of Personality Manual*, published by the California Test Bureau, 5916 Hollywood Blvd., Los Angeles, 1953. The test is also evaluated in *Mental Measurements Yearbook*, edited by Oscar K. Buros, Rutgers University Press, New Brunswick, N. J., and in many articles in psychological journals.

[2] *California Test of Personality Manual*, 1953, p. 9.

Scores for the test are computed by counting the number of "right" answers given to the questions ("right" being the answer regarded as indicative of good adjustment) and then converting the sum into a standard score, as directed in the *Manual*. Norms for the test have been computed on the basis of tests given to several thousand pupils in various parts of the United States. These norms show the percentage of pupils who achieve given standard scores. By thus enabling the translation of standard scores into percentile ranks, they provide an easy means of determining where any particular child stands in relation to those on whose performance the norms were based.

In the schools participating in our study, the California Test of Personality was given to each adopted child who was in the sample and to four of his classmates, including the one selected as his control. The test was administered by staff psychologists, who took the children out of the classrooms for this purpose. For the following analysis of findings, only the test scores of the adopted children and their controls were used.

Table 29 gives the distribution of the standard scores on this test for the adopted children and the controls. The test, as has been said, yields three measures: personal adjustment, social adjustment, and a combination of the two that is called total adjustment. All three are shown in Table 29.

For all three measures, the proportion of adopted children who received low scores was larger than that of the controls. On per-

TABLE 29. PERCENTAGE DISTRIBUTION OF SCORES OF ADOPTED AND CONTROL CHILDREN ON THE CALIFORNIA TEST OF PERSONALITY

Standard scores	Personal adjustment		Social adjustment		Total adjustment	
	Adopted	Control	Adopted	Control	Adopted	Control
36 and under	5	2	6	4	4	2
37 to 39	4	3	6	5	6	3
40 to 42	11	6	9	7	9	7
43 to 45	13	15	12	9	14	14
46 to 48	15	17	18	16	13	15
49 to 51	13	14	11	18	16	14
52 to 54	13	11	9	8	13	13
55 to 57	9	12	9	13	9	14
58 to 60	8	9	10	8	7	7
61 and over	9	11	10	12	9	11
Total	100	100	100	100	100	100

sonal adjustment, scores under 43, for instance, accounted for 20 per cent of the adopted children and 11 per cent of the controls. For social adjustment, the comparable percentages were 21 and 16; for total adjustment, 19 and 12. At the favorable end of the scale, the differences were somewhat less marked. Twenty-six per cent of the adopted children and 32 per cent of the controls had a personal adjustment score of 55 or better. For social adjustment, the comparable percentages were 29 and 33; for total adjustment, 25 and 32.

Average scores also showed consistent though small differences between the two groups. The average for personal adjustment was 49.31 for the adopted children and 50.54 for the controls. For social adjustment, the comparable figures were 49.25 and 50.39; for total adjustment, 49.37 and 50.60. All these differences are of statistical significance.

The California test findings thus agree with those of the sociometric test in indicating a tendency for the adopted children to rate a bit lower than their classmates of the same sex and comparable socioeconomic level. These findings suggest a possible, though slight, relation between adjustment and the status of being adopted. The comparison also serves to indicate that the adopted children's showing on the test was not far out of line with expectations.

Such a conclusion, however, does not answer the question of how many, and which, adopted children are to be regarded—for the purpose of comparison with factors later to be examined—as seriously maladjusted or as having any stated degree of adjustment or maladjustment. This question, which poses problems of interpretation for all the tests, is partly one of "cutting points": below what point on the scale shall children be regarded as maladjusted? It is also partly one of how much variation in actual adjustment exists among individuals who get similar scores.

TEACHERS' RATINGS

For securing ratings of the children by their teachers, the Behavior Description Chart (BDC) was used.[1] This chart con-

---

[1] Bowman, Paul H., Robert F. DeHaan, John K. Kough, and Gordon P. Liddle, *Mobilizing Community Resources for Youth.* Supplementary Educational Monographs, No. 85, University of Chicago Press, Chicago, 1956.

sists of ten groups of statements about a child's personality or behavior as observed by his teacher, each group consisting of five descriptive statements. Each group of five contains one statement that is regarded by the author of the test as indicative of leadership, one indicative of "aggressive maladjustment," one indicative of "withdrawn maladjustment," and two that are neutral, in the sense that they are so broadly phrased that the average child might be so described. The following are examples of the groups:

> A. Others come to him for help
> B. Causes disturbance
> C. Lacks confidence in himself
> D. Reports those who break rules
> E. Shows emotion in a restrained way

> A. Frequently gets into fights
> B. Helps to make and enforce rules
> C. Seems anxious and fearful
> D. Criticizes other people
> E. Is generous when in the mood

In rating a child the teacher is asked to mark in each group of statements the one that the child is most like and the one he is least like. As can be seen above, the statements are put in varied order with respect to their significance. In all groups, however, statements D and E are neutral and are given no weight in scoring. From this information the child's score on "leadership," "aggressive maladjustment," and "withdrawn maladjustment" are calculated.

Behavior Description Charts were filled out by the teacher for almost every child who took the California Test of Personality. As noted before, the testing had been described to the teachers as part of a study of child development and no reference to its relation to adoption was made. This was to protect the adopted children and their parents and to avoid highlighting the adopted children's status. Because of these precautions, we do not know for certain how many teachers knew that one of the five children they were rating was adopted, but apparently a considerable number had this information.

As with the other tests, the scores children obtained on the BDC are probably more useful for group comparisons than for individual evaluation. Teachers, like all informants, vary in their standards of what is, for instance, "sensitive" or "boastful" or "self-confident" behavior. Moreover, similar scores can refer to different and perhaps unequal evidence of adjustment or maladjustment.

The BDC yielded three scores for each child. The distribution of these scores, in adopted and control groups, is shown in Table 30.

TABLE 30. PERCENTAGE DISTRIBUTION OF SCORES OF ADOPTED AND CONTROL CHILDREN ON THE BEHAVIOR DE-SCRIPTION CHART

Scores	Leadership		Withdrawn maladjustment		Aggressive maladjustment	
	Adopted	Control	Adopted	Control	Adopted	Control
0 to 3	..	..	..	..	2	2
4 to 7	4	2	2	3	10	17
8 to 11	6	5	7	6	19	25
12 to 15	10	8	13	13	21	16
16 to 19	10	11	20	19	14	14
20 to 23	16	12	21	21	13	13
24 to 27	11	14	17	16	11	6
28 to 31	14	14	12	14	7	6
32 to 35	18	18	6	6	3	1
36 and over	11	16	2	2	..	..
Total	100	100	100	100	100	100

Again, the distribution of scores shows considerable similarity between the two groups of children, although the control-group children were a bit superior on two of the three traits. Thirty-four per cent of the controls, as compared with 29 per cent of the adopted children, had scores above 31 on leadership, while 20 per cent of the latter and 15 per cent of the former scored 15 or less on this trait. On aggressive maladjustment, 21 per cent of the adopted—as compared with 13 per cent of the controls—received scores of 24 or above, which indicated aggressive behavior considerably in excess of average. On withdrawn maladjustment, however, the two groups of children had very similar scores.

The averages point to the same conclusion. They are:

	Adopted	Control
Leadership	24.34	25.86
Withdrawn maladjustment	21.14	21.30
Aggressive maladjustment	16.34	14.50

With the exception of withdrawn maladjustment, the differences between the groups are too large to be attributed to chance, but they are probably not large enough to be of practical value in adoption work.

In attempting to determine the usefulness of these scores for the identification of maladjusted children, difficulties presented by the other tests were somewhat increased owing to the fact that there were three scores instead of one to deal with. It seemed that evaluation of individual children should take all of these into account, and yet no tested method for combining scores was at hand. The following combination of scores was therefore devised. In subsequent tables, it is referred to as "average BDC."

The first step taken toward combining the scores was to divide the categories shown in the preceding table into approximate quintile groups on the basis of the distribution of control-group scores; that is, to reduce the categories to five, ranging from A (highest) to E. Next, these quintile ratings were combined in a way that took into account how the child ranked on leadership and on either aggressive or withdrawn behavior, depending on which of these latter traits most characterized him. For instance, a child who had a high score in aggression and who rated low in withdrawn behavior had only his aggression score counted. This score was combined with his rating on leadership, chief consideration being given, however, to the leadership score. If the letter ratings were E for aggression and C for leadership, the average score was said to be D. If, however, the leadership score was E and the aggression score D, the average of the two was also said to be E.

This scoring method yielded unduly high proportions of both adopted and controls in the lowest (E) category. The scores in the lowest quintiles were therefore further subdivided and two new categories of "average" BDC scores, E and F, were set up.

The percentages of adopted and control children who received the various scores were:

	Adopted	Control
A	6.8	10.1
B	16.2	19.1
C	27.1	25.5
D	20.5	25.5
E	16.2	12.4
F	13.2	7.4

By this way of scoring adjustment, 23 per cent of the adopted children as contrasted with 29 per cent of the controls were rated A or B; 29 per cent of the former and 19 per cent of the latter were rated E or F. The average score (calling A, 6; B, 5; and so on) was 3.29 for the adopted children and 3.77 for the controls, a difference that could not be accounted for on the basis of chance.

In terms of percentages (for instance, the 13 per cent rated F) this seemed a reasonable distribution, but what did the scores mean in individual cases: Were the children in the F group really seriously maladjusted? What about those in E? Was the adjustment of those rated A or B as good as this designation implies? These are questions that cannot be answered wholly satisfactorily, but the informal comments that many teachers wrote on the BDC forms provided some useful information.

TEACHERS' COMMENTS ON CHILDREN'S ADJUSTMENT

At the end of the Behavior Description Chart, two questions of our own devising were inserted. These inquired as to whether "there is anything unusual about this child, such as special assets, problems, or unusual circumstances" and whether the child had any of the following traits: mental retardation, juvenile court or police record, truancy, physical handicap (specify), or frequent absences due to illness.

Most teachers responded by writing brief comments. These statements varied greatly in subject matter and explicitness. Some dealt with the parents and the home situations rather than with the children themselves. Some referred only to the academic side of the children's behavior and attitudes and afforded little insight into other characteristics. Some were very brief and uninformative from the angle of our study. In about two-thirds of the cases, however, teachers made comments that were helpful in showing what they thought about the children's social and emotional adjustment or about their academic work as it related to such traits.

The teachers' comments about the children were classified according to the following categories, which are followed by examples.

1. *Children were described in terms that ranged from outstanding in behavior and personality to well adjusted but not exceptional*

Well adjusted, good disposition, happy. Excellent student. Good sport. Best adjusted kid in class.

An excellent student and boy. Can go far and should be urged forward at all times. Safety patrol member. Can be a "cut-up" until checked. Good athlete.

Children like her very much. I have never seen a display of temper from her. She is apparently in a happy mood and good spirits always at school. A joy to work with. Always polite and courteous.

A good all-round child. Qualities of a good leader but not a "pushy" type.

Adopted by parents who accept his limitations [low intelligence]. A happy boy: he was pleased with himself for learning to write his name in cursive script and enjoys making things for various projects.

Confined to wheel chair—poliomyelitis. Has excellent grades. Is well adjusted, as physically active as possible, and well liked by both students and teachers.

A very nice pupil.

2. *Children were described in terms somewhat suggestive of slight maladjustment, usually in only one area*

Moody, careless with work. She is sassy and nervous at home, generous and popular with other children at school. Likable, has good sense of humor, is easily influenced.

Immature, does poor work, is a show-off.

Constant tattle-tale and very critical of others. Very good student. Above average in personal and social assets.

Very impulsive due to nervousness.

3. *A somewhat more serious difficulty and one that was more widely manifested was described*

Feels inferior to a much brighter sister and is easily discouraged. Does not have much self-confidence and at first had fights continuously.

Seems to crave affection. Wants to kiss teacher each day on leaving.

Blames everyone else for all trouble. Feels persecuted. Cheats. Restless and uneasy; quarrelsome, resentful if corrected in private. Accepts no responsibility. Disliked in general by class.

Below average in school work; mentally retarded. Tendency to cheat. (I.Q. on group test—108.)

4. *Children were described in such a way as to suggest that they were probably seriously maladjusted*

Very nervous: very short attention span. Immature. Capable of good work but extremely nervous.

Emotional conflict; discipline problem; socially maladjusted. A frustrated, maladjusted boy. Attended Youth Hall and a school for delinquents.

Has been referred to Child Guidance. Is closed to contact with me; I cannot reach her at all. Does very little work and does not seem to care about it. Very immature.

Is capable but his extreme nervous condition will not permit his participating in activities.

His past history is only a series of problems. Teachers say they are happy when he is absent and glad to promote him to get rid of him . . . . Lies daily about insignificant things or makes up tales . . . . Constantly annoys others . . . . Has stolen a violin . . . .

These categories were devised by two members of the research staff and the classification of comments was made by them. Each rater classified all the relevant comments; then the two conferred and agreed upon the rating to be used in each case. The judgments they arrived at, shown in the following tables, were "conference judgments."

The reliability of these two judges' original ratings is indicated by the correlation coefficient of .80. There was complete agreement between the two raters in 78 per cent of the adopted cases and 82 per cent of the controls. A two-step disagreement was found in only two cases, one in each group.

The proportion of children, adopted and controls, who were classified as belonging to the various categories listed above is shown in Table 31. The teachers were a bit more likely to comment about the adopted children's adjustment than about the controls. Since, however, the difference between the proportions amounted to only six percentage points (which was within the range of chance), it seems likely that in their selection of children on whom to comment, the teachers were not biased by knowledge of adoption.

Table 31 is of particular interest because, more than any previous table, it shows a considerable difference between adopted and control children in level of adjustment. The proportion of adopted children classified as seriously maladjusted was higher than that of the controls, as was the proportion classified as somewhat maladjusted, the total in these two categories being 31 per cent for the adopted children and 19 per cent

TABLE 31. PERCENTAGE DISTRIBUTION OF RATINGS OF ADOPTED AND CONTROL CHILDREN'S ADJUSTMENT AS JUDGED BY TEACHERS' COMMENTS

Teachers' comments	Adopted	Control
Well adjusted	33	53
Slight problems	36	28
Somewhat maladjusted	21	15
Seriously maladjusted	10	4
Total	100	100

for the controls. The relative proportions were even more in the control children's favor in the well-adjusted category, over half of these children as compared with one-third of the adopted children being classified as well adjusted. Both of these differences between percentages were statistically significant.

In considering possible reasons for the difference between the two groups of children, it occurred to us (on the basis of other evidence) that the children's age at adoption might be a factor that should be taken into consideration. This, indeed, proved to be the case. Taking only children placed at less than a month of age (who constituted three-fourths of the sample), we found that 60 per cent of these children were described by their teachers as well adjusted, 25 per cent as having slight problems, 13 per cent as being somewhat maladjusted, and 2 per cent as seriously maladjusted. These percentages are practically the same as those for the control children shown in Table 31.[1]

When the same comparison was made with respect to the other test scores, all but one of the differences between adopted and control children that were reported above disappeared. The one difference that remained was in "aggressive maladjustment," the adopted children having a slightly higher average score than their controls. These findings suggest that it was not adoption *per se* that accounted for the less favorable scores or ratings of the adopted children as a whole. The explanation apparently lay in some factors that were associated with the adopted children's age at placement, such as the socioeconomic standing of their natural and adoptive parents, the adoptive parents' attitudes toward the children, pre-placement history, and the like.

To turn to another aspect of the teacher-comment ratings, it should be noted that while the figures in Table 31 are adequate for comparative purposes, the large number of "no comment" cases (163 adopted and 189 controls out of a total of 448 in each group) throws doubt on the accuracy of the proportions. It raises the question of what sorts of children the teachers were likely to choose to comment about. A check on these points is afforded in Table 32, in which the "BDC average" scores for the adopted children are cross-classified with the teachers' comment ratings. The table indicates that, with the exception of cases classified as A in "BDC average" scores, the likelihood of comments by the teachers increased as the children's BDC scores decreased, rising from 48 per cent of the B cases to 78 per cent of the F. The question, then, is whether the teachers' bias was so large that it destroys the usefulness of their comments as a measure of the children's adjustment.

This question can be at least partly answered by noting the extent to which the proportion of children in the various adjustment groups changed when the figures were prorated to obtain the best estimate of what the figures would have been if the

---

[1] The differences between the adopted and controls also disappeared when the comparison was limited to cases (172 in each group) in which teachers had commented both about the adopted child and his control. The percentages were: well adjusted or slight problems: adopted—74, control—77; somewhat maladjusted: adopted—18, control—18; seriously maladjusted: adopted—8, control—5.

teachers had made relevant comments on all the children. When this was done it was found that the proportions of adopted children in the various teacher-comment categories became 35, 36, 20, and 8 instead of the 33, 36, 21, and 10 shown there. Apparently, then, the teachers' bias in selection of children for comment was not large enough to affect the figures greatly and so does not disqualify the further use of the teacher-comment ratings.

Table 32 also serves to show the extent to which the BDC scores and the teachers' ratings jibed. It indicates that the correspondence was not exact, the correlation between the two sets of ratings being .63. This, however, is not a very poor result in view of the crudity of the measures.

TABLE 32. AVERAGE BDC SCORES BY TEACHER-COMMENT RATINGS: ADOPTED CHILDREN ONLY

Average BDC scores	Teachers' comments					Total	Per cent with comment
	Well adjusted	Slight problems	Somewhat mal-adjusted	Seriously mal-adjusted	No relevant comments		
A	23	3	..	..	4	30	87
B	24	9	1	..	37	71	48
C	39	24	5	2	49	119	58
D	6	30	15	5	34	90	62
E	3	21	21	5	21	71	70
F	1	13	16	15	13	58	78
Tests incomplete	..	2	2	..	5	9	45
Total	96	102	60	27	163	448	64

Table 32 shows too that the correspondence between the two sets of ratings was greatest at the top level and declined thereafter. Seventy-eight per cent of the children rated A or B on the "BDC average" scale were classified as well adjusted on the basis of the teachers' comments. A bit more than half of the D's were in the slight-problem category and the rest were widely dispersed. About 40 per cent of the E's were in the "somewhat maladjusted" group, while only a third of the F's were described by the teachers in such a way as to be classified seriously maladjusted. Apparently, teachers are more likely to agree with the BDC about well-adjusted children than about those who are maladjusted. In view of the makeup of the BDC, this is not a surprising finding. Cooperative, conforming children can be readily identified by the descriptive statements in the table, but its provision for discriminating among degrees and kinds of maladjustment seems minimal.

SOCIAL WORKERS' RATINGS OF CHILDREN'S ADJUSTMENT

In the course of the home interviews, the social workers learned much about the adopted children's personalities, attitudes, interests, and activities as they were perceived by the adoptive mothers and, in some cases, the fathers. On the basis of this material, ratings of the adopted children's adjustment were made by the field director and one of the interviewers. The categories used represented the raters' inferences about the children's adjustment as based on the evidence presented in the records of the home interviews.

In assigning children to categories, attention was paid to the evidence the parents gave about their children's behavior and attitudes rather than to their stated opinions about their children's adjustment. The raters were instructed to base their judgment of a child's adjustment on the parents' descriptions of his behavior and not on inferences drawn from their attitudes toward him. Parents' personality and motives were not disregarded, however, for they often provided clues to the probable accuracy of their descriptions of the children, as the following example shows.

> A mother in a home rated B described her adopted ten-year-old son as having a wonderful disposition and as being well liked by his teachers and classmates. He loves school, she said, makes average grades but should study harder. He has many friends and much interest in outdoor and mechanical pursuits.
>
> The interviewer had some doubt about the accuracy of this report because the mother seemed so determined to see everything about her way of life as perfect and regarded "peace and harmony" as being of predominant importance. She seemed to have her children unusually closely attached to her or under very firm control, for she said that her adopted son would leave a movie in the middle rather than disappoint her by being out late.[1]

---

[1] This boy's scores were average on the BDC, very low on the sociometric, high on the personality segment of the California and rather low on the social segment. Teachers described him as "not well; very nervous"; as "having a hard time finishing his work, and as perhaps having suffered a brain injury at birth."

The following categories were devised for rating the children's adjustment. They refer both to the child's apparent degree of social-emotional adjustment and to the sufficiency of the evidence in the rater's opinion.

1. Evidence given by parent seemed clearly to indicate satisfactory adjustment.

2. Parent described child's adjustment as good but either gave little supporting evidence or conflicting evidence or seemed untrustworthy as a reporter.

3. Evidence given by parent was suggestive of emotional or behavioral difficulties; seriousness of the disturbance could not be estimated.

4. Evidence given by parent clearly indicated problems in adjustment; seriousness could not be estimated.

5. Evidence given by parent clearly indicated serious problems.

6. Parent's description was insufficient as a basis for judgment.

Examples of these categories follow. The descriptions were prepared by the field director and one of the social workers. They were based on material in the records of interviews with parents and other material that came out in the conferences.

1. *Clear evidence of satisfactory adjustment*

Mary, age 9, was described by her mother as an affectionate, lovable child. She makes friends easily, the mother said, and has a number of boy and girl friends. She likes school, does well in it, and gets along well with her teachers. Her chief interest is music. She is not a very active child but does enjoy swimming and skating. Her health has always been good.

Al, age 12, a tall, heavy boy, was said by his father to be the all-round type, with a happy nature, much liked by everybody. He enjoys all outdoor activities—hunting, fishing, all sports. He has never been hard to discipline, even as an adolescent. He belongs to several organizations, including the Scouts, and is active in church affairs. School work has always been satisfactory. He has many friends, largely boys. There have been no health problems.

Gladys, age 11, was described as a "homebody," who likes to cook and iron and help with other household work. Her disposition is very even, her mother said. She added that she is a little on the quiet side but can hold her own easily when with her friends. Her school work has always been excellent and she has never had to study hard. She has many friends among girls and has recently shown interest in a thirteen-year-old boy.

2. *Mother said child's adjustment was good but gave little supporting evidence, made somewhat contradictory statements, or seemed an untrustworthy reporter*[1]

Jim, age 10, was described by his mother at one moment in terms of high praise and in the next as a child who worried and rather annoyed her. Jim, she said, is a willing child but one with a mind of his own, which is difficult to influence. The mother always tried to avoid arguments with him, she said, because he always gets his own way. He is often complaining and sulky, yet he is a very lovable child. He has many friends and plays well with all of them. She wishes he made better grades in school and worked harder at it; nevertheless, he likes school and gets along well with his teachers and classmates. Jim is spoiled by his father (the mother said) and is given too many presents, yet he "minds well" and really is a good boy. He is slightly crippled from polio but not seriously handicapped.

The mother's description of Nancy, age 11, was a rather restrained and guarded one. The interviewer was not sure that what she had to say was fully accurate. She described Nancy as very healthy and very mature, and said she was a lovable, kind, affectionate child with a wonderful sense of humor. She added, however, that she has a "big mouth" which she cannot keep quiet in school, that she lacks interest in her personal appearance, and that she is a "good apple polisher." Talking of her square dancing, she said that the child is "graceful as an ox." She said Nancy was "intelligent enough" but not one who applied herself well in school. Until recently, she had been "a good leader and joiner," but now she has given up some activities. Nevertheless, the mother said she had many friends and was "definitely the extrovert type."

3. *Evidence given by mother suggested emotional or behavioral difficulties; seriousness of the disturbance could not be estimated*

Max, age 10, was said by his mother to be "an extrovert" but also a "sensitive, affectionate boy." The father said that Max is just like his wife: on top of the world at one moment and way down the next. When he was little, the parents had quite a bit of trouble with him: feeding and toilet training were difficult; he had a "depression" when his adopted sister was sent away for a time; he once or twice tried to set fires. In the last couple of years he had done better, however, especially in school, where his work had

[1] An example of an untrustworthy report is the case cited on p. 248.

improved greatly. He has friends, goes to camp regularly in the summer, and has after-school employment at which he works conscientiously.

Jack, age 11, is a handsome, healthy boy, his mother reported, but one who could do much better in school if he tried. His only interest is in playing, she said. In this, he stays close to home and plays only with boys whom he chooses. Recently he had developed some interest in reading his Bible and likes to go to church with an elderly neighbor. He is accustomed to being waited on hand and foot and very much expects service, the mother added. She finds him very hard to discipline because he cries easily and then buys her presents to make up for his misdeeds.

4. *Evidence given by mother clearly indicated problems in adjustment; seriousness could not be estimated*

The parents said this boy is lonely, so they often invite girl cousins to the house. The boy likes girls better than boys, has almost always played with them, seldom has had a boy friend. He doesn't like rough and tumble games; has no interest in sports. He is very serious-minded, being unlike themselves, the parents added. He is greatly attached to animals; he was "hysterical" and upset for weeks after the death of a pet dog.

This boy was described by his adoptive mother as being like herself—emotional, tense, and highstrung. He is upset by loud voices and says his mother screams at him, which she does at times. She said he becomes tense if he remains too long with too many activities or too many people. His school work has gone down a great deal in the last two years. He is now under treatment in a child guidance clinic.

This intelligent and precocious eleven-year-old girl is much brighter than her sister. She gets into trouble because of her interest in boys and her talk of sexual matters. Teachers have complained to the mother about her.

The mother said that this girl is a follower and lets her friends boss her. She described her as full of energy and very aggressive. She has difficulty getting along with people and goes around with a chip on her shoulder. She has only one real friend, the mother reported, and the mother disapproves of that one.

5. *Evidence given by mother clearly indicated serious problems*

This boy has had a long history of school and behavioral difficulties. He has been in a correctional school and on probation several times.

This child has had extreme behavior problems since the age of two; he may be an autistic child. He has been in many private schools and treatment centers; was just recently released from a mental hospital.

A very compulsive, perfectionistic boy; cries, for instance, if he cannot play the piano perfectly. He is greatly concerned about cleanliness. He had a nervous breakdown at three, during which he lost his ability to talk.

This boy was described by his mother as extremely nervous. He bites his nails constantly and sometimes soils himself, she said. He does poor work in school, and has been a problem to the mother since infancy.

The mother said this child is like his real father, a blow-hard and a braggart. He has had constant difficulty in school, both in academic work and in behavior, and was expelled from a military school. He has never been able to make friends with either boys or girls.

To test the reliability of the ratings, the field director and the social worker each chose at random 30 of the cases they had rated and exchanged them for rerating. The correlation between the two sets of ratings was .89, indicating a high degree of reliability in the raters' judgments.

The number of children in the various categories is shown in Table 33. Since this table contains ratings for the children who were not tested in school as well as for those who were tested there, it gives information about a larger number of children than was shown in previous tables. The distinction between the two groups was made because the social workers' ratings provided the only material we had for judging the adjustment of the 36 children who were not given tests by our psychologists.

Proportionately, the children who were not tested in school were more likely than the others to be maladjusted,[1] one-third of them as compared with 9 per cent of the others. The nine children in the nontested group that were in Category 5 included three of the four who were so intellectually retarded that they could not attend school or were in "special classes." The fourth child was classified as belonging to Category 3.

---

[1] The biasing effect of this fact is discussed on p. 229 of this chapter.

As to the total group of children, Table 33 shows that 11 per cent of those about whom the parents gave information were classified as seriously maladjusted, and another 11 per cent as having behavior or personality problems of an unknown degree of seriousness. The former figure is much the same as the proportion judged definitely maladjusted on the basis of the teachers' comments (10 per cent) and much like the proportion (13 per cent) rated F on "BDC average."

TABLE 33. SOCIAL WORKERS' RATINGS OF CHILDREN'S ADJUST-
MENT

Adjustment ratings	Psychological tests given		Not tested		Total	
	Num-ber	Per cent	Num-ber	Per cent	Num-ber	Per cent
1. Clear evidence of satisfactory adjustment	174	44	9	35	183	43
2. Parent said adjustment satisfactory; little supporting evidence	42	11	..	..	42	10
3. Difficulties suggested; seriousness not known	100	25	6	22	106	25
4. Difficulties clearly indicated; seriousness not known	42	11	2	8	44	11
5. Clear evidence of serious problems	37	9	9	35	46	11
6. Insufficient evidence to rate	16	..	1	..	17	..
No home interview	37	..	9	..	46	..
Total	448	100	36	100	484	100

At the other extreme were 44 per cent of the children, those who appeared, from their parents' reports, to be adjusting well. The teachers who wrote comments agreed or nearly agreed with this rating in 88 per cent of the cases.

Between the extremes, in the third category, lay a fourth of the children, classified as having been described by their parents in ways suggestive of difficulties.

For the remaining children, those in the second and sixth categories, the evidence given by the parents was inconclusive. No judgment about the adjustment of 17 of these children was made, and the remaining 42 (10 per cent) were put in the second category. Since about two-thirds of them were described by their teachers as at least somewhat maladjusted, it seems likely that the adjustment of many in this second group was less good than their parents' descriptions implied.

SUMMARY

This analysis of the adopted children's adjustment leads, then, to two main conclusions. First, according to the tests and rating methods used, the majority of adopted children were making what appeared to be an adequate social-emotional adjustment. This was clearly indicated by the teacher-comment ratings, which were classified in a way that produced categories bearing directly on this point.

The proportion of adopted children who had low scores on the tests ranged from 9 per cent on the California Test of Personality to 15 per cent on the sociometric test. Eight per cent of the children were described by their teachers in words that appeared to connote serious maladjustment. These percentages are remarkably similar but, to a considerable extent, they refer to different children. For an adequate assessment of individual children's adjustment, single ratings that take into account the findings of the various measuring devices are needed. Such ratings are presented in the following chapter.

Second, in I.Q. and school achievement, and in withdrawn adjustment, the adopted children and the controls were much alike, but the adopted children were slightly more likely than the controls to have poor ratings on the other tests. Specifically, the adopted children were, on the average, a bit less popular with their classmates. Their teachers were a bit less likely to rate them as leaders, and a bit more likely to describe them as aggressive. As measured by the California Test of Personality, their average social and personal adjustment scores were slightly less favorable than those of the controls. The teachers' informal descriptions also pictured a few more of the adopted children as maladjusted.

All but one of these slight differences between the adopted and the control children disappeared, however, when the comparison was confined to children who were less than a month old when they were adopted.

Does this mean that, in spite of our findings about the quality of the adoptive homes, the outcome of the independent adoptions was satisfactory? For answer we refer to the purpose of adoption law—the well-being of adopted children.

The adoption law presumably expects to achieve this aim by securing adoptive homes for children that are of average or better quality. In contrast, the homes of the children in the control group probably represented the full range of quality (good, bad, and indifferent) within the socioeconomic groups to which the parents belonged. The question of what the adopted children's adjustment implies for the evaluation of independent adoptions cannot be answered, therefore, by reference to the control group alone. Instead, it must be answered primarily in terms of the results to be expected if children are in the kinds of homes the law seeks to secure for them—a question to which the analysis in the following chapter is directed.

CHAPTER XI

Home Ratings and
Children's Adjustment[1]

THE FIGURES PRESENTED IN CHAPTER X suggest that if adoption outcome is judged by the adopted children's scores on the various tests, most of the adoptions were working out well. The proportion of poor outcomes, however, was not inconsiderable, and the comparison with the control children was a bit in favor of non-adopted children. Since, on the one hand, adoption law presumably seeks a more favorable situation for its charges than a random selection of adoptive homes would supply, while, on the other hand, adoption and the conditions out of which it arises may handicap the children's adjustment, these findings are equivocal, to say the least.

Another way of answering the question of adoption outcome lies in combining the findings about children's adjustment with those about the quality of the adoptive homes. Such an approach not only produces joint home and adjustment ratings; it also enables us to estimate how dependent the children's adjustment was on their getting into the sorts of homes we regarded as good. If the study had included comparable home ratings of a control group of children living with their natural parents, we would have a partial means of estimating what proportion of the less than satisfactory adjustment outcomes was due to adoptive status rather than to home environment.

---

[1] For an alternative approach to this subject see Part II, Chapters XV and XVII.

EXTENT OF AGREEMENT AMONG ADJUSTMENT RATINGS

For making a comparison between home rating and adjustment, a single adjustment measure seemed needed. A high degree of correspondence between the various measures and ratings was not to be expected, of course. This follows from two facts. First, the reliability of at least some of them was probably not high. Second, they referred to different aspects of the children's behavior and personality. They gave such probably divergent information as: how bright the children were and how well they were achieving in school; how they behaved in the classroom and how popular they were among their classmates; what the children had to say about themselves; how well adjusted the interviewers thought the children were as judged by what the parents said about them. Not only were the judges and the tests different; what was being judged and tested was also different for the most part. All of these factors reduced the likelihood of high correlation.

The correlations between each test's scores and those of each other test or part of a test are listed in Table 34. For the Behavior Description Chart there were five scores to be correlated—the three the test itself yielded, the combined scores on the test

TABLE 34. INTERCORRELATIONS AMONG ADOPTED CHILDREN'S SCORES ON ADJUSTMENT MEASURES

Tests and measures	Behavior Description Chart					California Test of Personality			Socio-metric	Social worker rating	I.Q.
	With-drawn	Aggres-sive	Leader-ship	Aver-age	Teacher com-ment	Social	Per-sonal	Total			
BDC											
Withdrawn											
Aggressive	−.27										
Leadership	−.47	−.67									
"Average"	−.37	−.56	.81								
Teacher-comment	−.21	−.51	.65	.63							
CTP											
Social	.00	−.29	.27	.22	.38						
Personal	−.06	−.22	.22	.21	.36	.73					
Total	−.03	−.27	.27	.24	.39	.92	.90				
Sociometric	−.30	−.20	.36	.31	.44	.15	.23	.20			
Social worker ratings	−.13	−.18	.27	.26	.50	.17	.22	.24	.20		
I.Q.	−.16	−.17	.27	.26	.30	.12	.22	.21	.16	.20	
Achievement	−.17	−.20	.28	.25	.25	.20	.24	.23	.23	.17	.51

(calculated as described above and here designated as "average") and the ratings that were used on the teachers' comments. For the California Test of Personality there were three scores, while the other tests and measures yielded only one score each. In Table 34 the coefficients that refer to the relation between different parts of the same test are italicized.

The correlation between the various parts of the same test was high, as was to be expected, and I.Q. and achievement also correlated fairly well. Other than this, the highest correlation coefficients were those that involved teacher-comment ratings, the highest being the correlation (.50) between the two most "subjective" measures, teacher-comment and social worker ratings. The other inter-test correlations were low, more than half of them being under .25. Those that were .25 or higher were the following:

Aggressive behavior and:	
California total	−.27
California social	−.29
Withdrawn behavior and:	
sociometric	−.30
Leadership and:	
California social	.27
California total	.27
social worker ratings	.27
I.Q.	.27
achievement	.28
sociometric	.36
BDC average and:	
achievement	.25
I.Q.	.26
social worker ratings	.26
sociometric	.31
Teacher-comment ratings and:	
achievement	.25
I.Q.	.30
California personal	.36
California social	.38
California total	.39
sociometric	.44
social worker ratings	.50
I.Q. and achievement	.51

This low level of correlation among tests is a rather common finding in studies of adjustment.[1] It emphasizes the point made earlier; that in judging a child's adjustment, reliance can seldom be put on single tests, if only because tests usually measure only one aspect of behavior and interpersonal relations.

Since teachers' and social workers' ratings correlated more highly than any others, further examination of this relation seemed called for, as well as further analysis of the relation of these two measures to the formal test scores. Figures on the first point are given in Table 35.

TABLE 35. SOCIAL WORKER RATINGS OF CHILDREN'S ADJUSTMENT BY TEACHER-COMMENT RATINGS

Social worker ratings	Ratings of teacher-comments				Total with comments	No relevant comments	Total tested
	Well adjusted	Fairly well adjusted	Somewhat maladjusted	Seriously maladjusted			
Well adjusted; clear evidence	53	49	11	2	115	59	174
Well adjusted; little evidence presented	9	7	8	1	25	17	42
Evidence suggestive of problems	14	28	12	4	58	42	100
Problems clearly indicated; seriousness not known	7	5	12	2	26	16	42
Clear evidence of serious problems	1	5	6	15	27	10	37
Insufficient evidence for rating	1	3	4	..	8	8	16
No home interview	11	6	7	3	27	10	37
Total	96	103	60	27	286	162	448

In considering the figures in this table, it should be remembered that the two sets of ratings differed in several ways. First, they were based on information given by persons who stood in different relations to the children and who saw the children's behavior in different types of situations. The teachers described the children on the basis of observations of their behavior and attitudes in school; the mothers or fathers described them on the basis of what they observed in home and elsewhere. Second, the

[1] See Scott, W. A., "Research Definitions of Mental Health and Mental Illness," *Psychological Bulletin*, vol. 55, 1958, pp. 29–45.

ratings of teachers' comments were made by the research staff, and those of parents by two members of the field staff; and somewhat different categories were used in rating.[1] Third, the categories referred to different sorts of data. The teacher-comment categories were classifications of the teachers' own words, while the social worker categories represented clinical judgment of the children's adjustment, based not on what the mothers literally said but on what degree of maladjustment the classifiers thought the mothers' interviews indicated.

The agreement between teacher and social worker ratings was greatest at the extremes, as Table 35 indicates. Of the 115 children whom the social workers rated as clearly well adjusted and on whom the teachers commented, 53 (46 per cent) were described by the teachers in terms that also indicated good adjustment, and 49 others had teacher-comment ratings indicating fairly good adjustment. Added together, these two categories comprise 88 per cent of the children in the top group of social worker ratings. As to serious maladjustment, social worker and teacher-comment ratings agreed completely in 55 per cent of the cases, and were in one-step disagreement in another 23 per cent.[2]

The ratings made by social workers agreed much less well with the scores the children received on the formal tests, the correlation coefficients being .26, .24, and .20, respectively. (Table 34).

There was closer agreement between the social workers' ratings and the test scores when children were classified as well adjusted than when they were classified as having personality difficulties. The ratings agreed with the test scores in from 60 to 76 per cent of the cases when the children were classified as well adjusted, while at the other extreme there was agreement in only about 30 per cent of the cases.

The ratings based on the teachers' comments correlated fairly well with the formal BDC ratings, as would be expected. With the scores on the other tests, the teacher-comment ratings corre-

---

[1] The social worker ratings took into account not only the rater's impression of the degree of the child's adjustment but also the amount or quality of the information on which the judgment was based.

[2] This amount of agreement is much like that reported by Gildea, Glidewell, and Kantor in *Parental Attitudes and Child Behavior*, edited by John C. Glidewell, Charles C Thomas, Springfield, Ill., 1961, p. 50.

lated better in every instance than did the social worker ratings. In fact, the ratings based on teachers' descriptions almost always correlated more highly with the formal tests than did any other measure. Although this may be partially due to the slight bias in the teachers' selection of children for comment, it probably is not the whole explanation.

In general, then, (1) the two sets of ratings based on descriptive statements correlated closer with each other than with the formal test scores; (2) except for a few intra-test coefficients, their correlation with the formal tests was higher than the correlation among the formal tests themselves; (3) the teacher-comment ratings were more strongly correlated with the formal test scores than were the social worker ratings. These findings seemed to justify putting special reliance on the teachers' comments when devising ways of measuring the children's overall adjustment.

VARIOUS WAYS OF COMBINING ADJUSTMENT RATINGS

Before proceeding with a description of how the scores were combined, note should be taken of the assumption underlying this procedure. The assumption is that, though adjustment is many faceted and has no single underlying dimension, nevertheless it is reasonable to describe some individuals as being better adjusted than others. To enter into a detailed discussion of the meaning of the term adjustment and the various ways, degrees, situations, and areas in which maladjustment can be displayed would take us far afield. Suffice to say, perhaps, that we are using the term in a loose way and are particularly interested in distinguishing the children who seemed to be rather seriously "emotionally disturbed" from those whose behavior and personality deviations were within "normal" limits.

On the assumption, then, that the rather low correlations among the tests indicate that the tests measured different facets of adjustment, the next question was how the scores or ratings on these and other measures could be combined to produce a single adjustment rating for each child. This involved both the problem of combining the scores and the problem of determining where the cutting points (between good and poor adjustment or between various degrees of adjustment) should be placed along the continuum of scores on each test.

Several ways of combining scores were tried, ranging from one that was strictly mechanical to one that was called "clinical" because the scores represented the judgment of one of the authors on what all the available data added up to. The aim in trying different combinations was to see, first, what variations in the proportion of presumably well-adjusted and poorly-adjusted children they would produce, and, second, which combination of scores and ratings would be most satisfactory for later use in relation to various other aspects of adoption.

In all combinations, the approximate quintile scores (20 per cent ranges) described in the preceding section of the chapter were used. For the BDC, the quintiles referred to the "average" score calculated as previously described.[1] It was necessary to use this score because the BDC yielded three scores, which were found not to be closely related to each other. The California Test of Personality also resulted in three scores, but here it was possible to use only one of the scores (the "total") because its relation to the other two was fairly high. (See Table 34.) For this test, quintiles were already at hand in the "percentile scores" that the scoring system itself produces. As to the sociometric test, the scores that each quintile should cover were determined from the control-group figures, on the assumption that these most nearly represented the norm.

Combination I

In this first combination of test findings, only the three tests given by the staff psychologists were used: the BDC, the California, and the sociometric. Numerical values ranging from 1 to 5 were given to the quintile ratings on each test, and these were added to produce a total score. For example, if a child had a score in the top quintile on the Behavior Description Chart, in the second quintile on the sociometric test, and in the third on the California "total," his score for the combination was 5 plus 4 plus 3 or 12.

---

[1] See Chapter X.

Combination II

In the second combination, the same three tests were used but they were combined by counting for each case the number of quintile scores that were average or above. The top group of children consisted of those whose scores on all three tests were in the three upper quintiles, these being the "average or above" categories. The next group consisted of the children who were "average or above" on two tests; the next, "average or above" on one test; and the last, below average (that is, all scores in the lower two quintiles) on all tests.[1]

Combination III

The third combination was like the preceding one except that it took account of the social workers' ratings also, these ratings being treated as a fourth test score. For this purpose, Categories 1, 2, and 3 of the social workers' ratings were called "average or above," Category 4 was given the next lower score, and Category 5 the lowest. The few children in Category 6 (insufficient information) were grouped with the "average or above."

Combination IV

The next kind of combination was one we called clinical. It took into account not only the quintile scores on the three tests given by the study staff but also the achievement test scores as compared with the I.Q. ratings. In addition, teachers' comments and the ratings based on the parents' descriptions of the children were considered in assigning each child to a category. All these were combined according to specific rules, but personal judgment (which consisted of weighing all the elements in a somewhat clinical manner) also entered into the final result.

Combination V

The fifth combination was one that paid particular attention to what the teachers had to say in their comments about the

---

[1] The proportion of children rated as below average on two or three tests was much the same as that reported by Eli M. Bower, "The Emotionally Handicapped Child and the School," *Exceptional Children*, vol. 26, January, 1960, pp. 232–247. Since Bower's tests attempted to measure the same facets of adjustment as those we used, it is of interest to note that Bower found close agreement between clinicians' ratings of maladjustment and low scores on two of three tests.

children, the ratings based on these comments being used in place of the BDC scores when there was sharp disagreement between them. In a few cases social workers' judgments were also taken into account. This was done when these ratings differed markedly from the BDC scores, the BDC scores were markedly out of line with other test scores, and the teacher had made no comment. The children were divided into four groups based on these ratings and the quintile scores on the other two tests given by the staff psychologists.

The *best adjusted* consisted of nearly all the children who had scores that were average or above on all three tests given by the psychologists. The seven exceptions were children who were described by their teachers in such a way as to be rated 3 (somewhat maladjusted) or who, in the absence of teacher comments, were put in a low adjustment category by the social workers. Into the top category were also put some children who had slightly lower scores but whose teachers described them as either very well adjusted or as having only slight problems (Categories 1 and 2 on "teacher comments").

The characteristic combination of test scores in the second category, *somewhat less well adjusted*, was one test in one of the lower two quintiles and a teacher-comment score that was high (Categories 1 or 2). In other words, most of these were children who received a low rating on one or another test but whose teachers described them as either well adjusted or only slightly maladjusted. The only exceptions to this rule were a few children whose test scores were average or above but whose teacher-comment ratings indicated considerable maladjustment. Again, in a few cases and in the absence of comments by the teachers, the social workers' ratings of maladjustment were used.

The characteristic test scores in the third group, *rather poorly adjusted*, were combinations of scores that contained two test ratings in the lower two quintiles and a rating of 3 (somewhat maladjusted) on teachers' comments. The only exceptions to this rule were two children whose test scores were not so low but whose teacher-comment ratings were 3 or 4. Five cases in which teacher comments were lacking and social worker ratings were 4 were included in this category.

The lowest category, *seriously maladjusted*, was made up of children whose scores were very low on at least two tests and whose teachers' comments or, in the absence of those, social worker ratings were in the least favorable category. Only about a third of these children had any test score in the average group, and most of these were California test scores, which are presumably more accurate in indicating maladjustment than its opposite.

This classification, logically considered, seemed to us the best of those so far described. Nevertheless, because it contained about ten cases in which parents' descriptions were partially relied on for assignment to a category, the sixth way of combining scores was devised.

Combination VI

In this combination of scores, only cases on which the teacher entered comments on the Behavior Description Chart were used. The teacher-comment ratings were substituted for the BDC scores and were combined with the rating of one or the other of the two remaining tests. For this, the sociometric rating was chosen when its score indicated popularity and the California rating when its score indicated maladjustment.

Such use of the sociometric and California scores seemed justified by the following reasoning. As was pointed out earlier, children who received high scores on the sociometric test were, by definition, very popular, but the meaning of the test findings for those who received low scores was in doubt. In addition, there was no justification in fact for the cutting points, and no way within the test findings by which one could know the point at which the scores indicated genuine unpopularity among classmates.

In contrast, the California test is said to be more valid for maladjustment than good adjustment.[1] By knowing and checking

---

[1] On this point, Paul Bowman and colleagues, who used the California test in their Quincy study and carefully examined its relations with other data, concluded: "It appeared to us that a high maladjustment score on the California Test of Personality was truly an indication of maladjustment but also that a good many maladjusted children turned up with low scores and were not identified by this test." Bowman, Paul H., Robert F. DeHaan, John K. Kough, and Gordon P. Liddle, *Mobilizing Community Resources for Youth.* Supplementary Educational Monographs, no. 85, University of Chicago Press, Chicago, 1956.

the "right answers" a bright but emotionally disturbed child who is accustomed to tests may conceal his true feelings and achieve a high score on adjustment. If a child, however, checks the opposite sort of statements, it seems probable that he does so because he finds them truly in accord with his feelings.

OVERALL ADJUSTMENT RATINGS COMPARED

Table 36 shows the variation in the proportion of children classified in the four adjustment categories according to these six different ways of determining overall adjustment. The most striking finding is the extent of similarity among the percentages. The resemblance is particularly close between Combinations II and III and between Combinations IV and VI. Combination V is somewhat similar to Combination I.

TABLE 36. PERCENTAGE DISTRIBUTION OF ADJUSTMENT OF CHILDREN ON SIX COMBINED RATINGS

Combined ratings	Well adjusted	Fairly well adjusted	Rather poorly adjusted	Maladjusted	Total
I. Sum of scores on three tests	33	26	22	19	100
II. Number of tests with scores average or above	26	34	26	14	100
III. Number of scores average or above, including social worker ratings	24	31	25	20[a]	100
IV. Clinical assessment of scores and ratings	44	28	17	11	100
V. Teacher-comment, BDC, or social worker rating, and other scores	34	38	20	8	100
VI. Teacher-comment rating; sociometric or California test score	46	24	20	10	100

[a] According to this 5-point scale, 12 per cent were in the fourth category and 8 per cent in the lowest.

That Combinations II and III should result in much the same proportions was somewhat unexpected, since the social worker ratings had not correlated highly with the test scores. The pair, Combinations IV and VI, also consists of one combination that included social worker ratings and one that did not, and the same is true of the pair, Combination I (the most mechanical way of combining scores) and Combination V. Apparently, the inclusion of these social worker ratings based on parents' descriptions of their children's behavior only slightly altered the proportion of children in the various adjustment categories.

The percentage distributions, however, tell only one part of the story: the extent to which the combinations agreed in the proportion of children rated well or poorly adjusted. Even when they are alike, the percentages do not tell whether the same children received similar ratings in any two of the combinations under consideration. This question is answered in part by the correlation coefficients listed in Table 37.

TABLE 37. INTERCORRELATIONS AMONG THE SIX COMBINED ADJUSTMENT RATINGS

Combined ratings	I	II	III	IV	V
I. Sum of scores					
II. Number of tests average or above	.84				
III. Number average or above, including social worker ratings	.79	.93			
IV. Clinical assessment of scores and ratings	.73	.70	.80		
V. Teacher-comment or social worker ratings and test scores	.72	.71	.73	.78	
VI. Teacher-comment ratings; sociometric or California scores	.72	.72	.71	.74	.90

Table 37 shows that the various ways of combining test and other ratings correlated at least fairly well with each other. This was to be expected, since they had much in common. Also obviously, some of these combinations were highly correlated because they include the same measures. Some of the combinations correlated very highly with each other, indicating that most children were in the same category in both combinations. These were Combinations II and III and Combinations V and VI, which correlated .93 and .90, respectively. For Combinations I and II, I and III, III and IV, IV and V, the correlation coefficients were a bit smaller, ranging from .84 to .78. The most usual amount of correlation was .70 to .75, which was displayed by the other sets of combinations.

As with the percentage distributions, Combinations II and III yielded very similar results in spite of the fact that Combination III included the social workers' ratings of material based on mothers' descriptions of children's adjustment. Combinations IV and VI, however, were less alike than previously suggested, as were Combinations I and V.

As would be expected, the amount of correlation tended to vary with the extent of difference in content among the combinations being compared.[1] The question, then, was which of these ways of combining scores should be selected as the best measure of the children's overall adjustment. There is probably no single, right answer to that question but the following was our decision and the reasoning used in arriving at it.

We considered first the uses to which an overall adjustment score would be put and noted that a major use was to find out how much of a relation there was between the home ratings and the adjustment ratings. This led us to decide not to put reliance on any combinations of scores that gave considerable weight to social worker ratings. It was not that we thought those ratings inferior *per se* but that, in the comparison of home and adjustment scores, we wanted to avoid the possibility of "contamination"— the possibility, that is, that the social workers were influenced in their ratings of the children by what they knew of their homes or vice versa.

This decision eliminated Combinations III and IV from consideration, and it also cast some doubt on Combination V, since social worker ratings were used in it in a few cases. The elimination of III did not seem serious, since it correlated .93 with II and .84 with I, suggesting that any one of these could be substituted for the other. The elimination of Combination IV seemed unavoidable, even though it had the advantage of being based on the widest range of evidence. As to Combination V, its high correlation with Combination VI (.90) made the two interchangeable.

These eliminations narrowed the choice to Combinations I, II, and VI. Since I and II were rather highly correlated (.84), either one could substitute for the other. Hence, the choice was I

---

[1] For instance, Combination II (number of tests average or above) correlated most highly with Combination III, which used the same data plus an additional set of ratings, those made by the social workers. It correlated next best with Combination I (sum of test scores), which, like it, was based on only psychological tests but used a different way of combining scores. Its correlation with the three ways of measuring adjustment that put more reliance on descriptive statements was in the low 70's.

Again, Combination IV (clinical), which gave considerable weight to the social workers' ratings of home-interview material, correlated best with Combination III and V, which also included such ratings. It correlated somewhat less well (.70) with the combinations that did not include them.

or II versus VI. Of these, Combination VI seemed preferable because it put chief emphasis on the teacher-comment ratings. Those ratings, in turn, seemed best because (1) they had the highest degree of correlation with both the tests and the social workers' ratings (Table 34), and (2) they probably distinguished, more clearly than the others, between the children who were truly maladjusted and those who were merely obstreperous in the classroom. This better performance was possible because the teacher-comment ratings were based on verbal descriptions of individual children rather than on the pre-formulated statements of the BDC, which did not make much allowance for degrees and variety of deviant behavior.

Combination VI, however, had the disadvantage of providing ratings for only about two-thirds of the children tested, since teachers made pertinent comments on only that proportion of cases. In spite of this limitation, we decided to use it whenever the smaller number of cases was not a serious disadvantage. When the full number was needed (as in subgroup comparisons), Combination V was used instead, the correlation of .90 between it and Combination VI seeming to justify such a substitution.

Taking Combination VI, then, as the measure selected to show the range in the adopted children's overall social-emotional adjustment at the time of the follow-up study, we find (Table 36) that 70 per cent of the children were at least fairly well adjusted and that 30 per cent were doing rather poorly. The latter figure includes the 10 per cent who were rated as definitely maladjusted.

As was pointed out in connection with the home ratings, figures of this sort must be hedged by a statement of the extent of their statistical "error." This is because the figures refer to a sample of cases, while what is wanted is information about the whole population of adopted children from which the sample was drawn.

Calculation of the standard errors of the figures for Combination VI resulted in the following ranges in the percentages of children in each category of social-emotional adjustment:

Well adjusted	46 ± 3.1
Fairly well adjusted	24 ± 2.6
Rather poorly adjusted	20 ± 2.5
Definitely maladjusted	10 ± 1.8

With the last two percentages combined, the proportion of at least fairly maladjusted children in the total population from which the sample was drawn would be 30 ± 2.8. These figures mean that the chance was 99 out of 100 that the true proportion of children at least somewhat maladjusted (as judged by the measures we used) lay between 23 and 37 per cent.

We conclude, therefore, that from a fourth to a third of the adopted children probably had some degree of social-emotional difficulty, and that from 6 to 14 per cent were rather seriously maladjusted. These figures are much the same as those yielded by the individual tests.[1]

THE RELATION BETWEEN ADJUSTMENT AND HOME RATINGS

Having arrived at these estimates of the overall social-emotional adjustment of the adopted children, we looked next to see to what extent the combined adjustment scores and the home ratings were in agreement. The figures for Combinations V and VI are given in Table 38. The corresponding distributions for the other combinations were also worked out but are not included here.

Each of the combinations of adjustment ratings told essentially the same story as to its relation with the home ratings. The size of the percentages varied from combination to combination but in each case there was a steady decline in the proportion of best-adjusted children and a steady increase in the proportion of least well-adjusted children as the home ratings went down. Combination VI (our preferred combination) was the only one that deviated at all from this rule. It did so in only two places, as Table 37 shows, and even there the deviation was compensated for in the nearest category of adjustment ratings.

The consistency of the decline of percentages at one end of the adjustment scale and the equally consistent increase at the other suggests that the ratings of homes and adjustment had some face validity, at least at the extremes. If there were not some real

---

[1] When Combination VI ratings were calculated for the control children, it was again found that a somewhat similar proportion of them were seriously maladjusted. When the comparison was limited to the 172 pairs of children about whom the teachers had commented in both cases, the proportion of seriously maladjusted was 8 per cent for the adopted children and 4 per cent for the controls.

TABLE 38. HOME RATINGS[a] BY CHILDREN'S ADJUSTMENT ON COMBINATIONS V AND VI OF ADJUSTMENT SCORES

Combinations of scores and ratings	Home ratings											
	Number						Per cent					
	A	B	C	D	E	Total	A	B	C	D	E	Total
Combination V												
Well adjusted	39	44	42	12	3	140	48	43	39	21	5	34
Fairly well adjusted	37	43	38	19	21	158	45	42	36	33	34	38
Rather poorly adjusted	6	15	24	20	17	82	7	14	22	34	28	20
Maladjusted	..	1	3	7	20	31	..	1	3	12	33	8
Total	82	103	107	58	61	411	100	100	100	100	100	100
Combination VI												
Well adjusted	35	29	36	10	9	119	60	48	54	29	24	46
Fairly well adjusted	19	22	12	8	2	63	32	37	18	23	6	24
Rather poorly adjusted	5	8	12	13	13	51	8	13	18	38	35	20
Maladjusted	..	1	7	3	13	24	..	2	10	10	35	10
No relevant comments by teacher	23	43	40	24	24	154	..	..	..	..	..	..
Total	82	103	107	58	61	411	100	100	100	100	100	100

[a] The home ratings run from A, the homes that were regarded as affording the children maximum opportunity for good development, to E, the least advantageous homes in this respect.

difference between the quality of the A and B homes, the B and C homes, and so on (or between the 1 and 2, 2 and 3, 3 and 4 adjustment ratings) the percentages could scarcely have exhibited the regularities the tables reveal.

It is clear that at the extremes there was a definite association between degree of adjustment and quality of the home. According to Combination VI, 92 per cent of the children from A homes had an adjustment that was classified as 1 or 2, which may be interpreted to mean either good or fairly good adjustment. This was true of only 30 per cent of the children from E homes. (This difference of 62 percentage points was much too large to have been due to chance.) At the other extreme, there was the same amount of difference between homes with good and poor ratings. Eight per cent of the children in A homes were rated 3 or 4 in adjustment, as compared with 70 per cent of the children in E homes.

In the B and C homes the proportion of children rated 3 or 4 increased, being 15 and 28 per cent, respectively; in the D homes the proportion of such adjustments became 48 per cent and in the E homes, as has been noted, it was 70 per cent.

In this connection it should be noted that the average age of the children in the study was eleven years. Since this is not an age at which serious social and emotional difficulties are likely to appear, it seems especially impressive that a third of the children in E homes were rated 4 in adjustment.

Overall, the figures in Table 39 indicate that the adopted children had a better chance of making a good adjustment if they were placed in the kinds of homes we called good than in those we called poor. How great was that superior chance is indicated by the following proportions that result when home and Combination V adjustment ratings are dichotomized—that combination being chosen for comparison because it was based on the larger number of cases.

TABLE 39. PERCENTAGE DISTRIBUTION OF COM-
BINED ADJUSTMENT RATINGS BY HOME
RATINGS

	Home	
Adjustment rating	A B C	D E
1 or 2	84	46
3 or 4	16	54
Total	100	100

The figures indicate that, according to the measures used in this study, the children who were in homes rated fair to excellent had a five to one chance of making a relatively good adjustment, while for those in homes rated poor the chance was less than one out of two. If only the homes rated good to excellent (A and B) are considered, the chance of relatively good adjustment was about seven to one. In general, then, it looks as if being in a home rated good weighted the chances strongly in favor of good adjustment, while being in a poor home appeared less definitive.

Viewing the figures differently, one might say that the adopted child's chance of making a relatively good adjustment (as measured in this study) was twice as high when the home rating was fair to excellent as when it was poor; and that his chance of making a relatively poor adjustment was over three times as great in a home rated poor as in one of the others. As to serious maladjustment (Category 4), the chance of such an outcome was more than twenty times as great in a D or E home as in an A or B home.[1] Combination VI adjustment ratings yielded quite similar findings.

The relation between adjustment and home ratings was examined by correlating the two series of figures. For Combination VI, the correlation between home rating and adjustment was found to be .44; for Combination V, it was .45. For the other combinations of adjustment ratings the correlation coefficients ranged from .30 to .58,[2] increasing with considerable regularity as additional information about the children's adjustment was encompassed by the combined rating.

With the exception of Combinations I and II, all the coefficients are considerably larger than those yielded when the relation between home and adjustment was calculated for each test separately. They are, however, somewhat lower than would be expected if one postulates a close connection between the social-emotional adjustment of an individual and the quality of the attitudes and interpersonal relations prevailing in his childhood home.

It is possible that the rather low correlation between the home and adjustment ratings resulted in part from the acknowledged

---

[1] The situation was a little different for boys from that for girls. A boy's chance of making a relatively good adjustment (1 or 2) was more than twice as great in a home rated A, B, or C as in one rated D or E, but a girl's chance was increased by only 1.5. In contrast, a boy's chance of making a relatively poor adjustment was about three times as great in a D or E home as in an A, B, or C home, but a girl's chance was almost 4 to 1. A bit more than twice as many boys as girls were rated as being in the lower two adjustment categories that we have been calling "at least rather poor adjustment"—a not unusual finding, to judge by figures published by child guidance clinics. Nevertheless, the indication that good homes were slightly more influential with the boys than with the girls, and that the girls seemed more handicapped than boys by being placed in poor homes, was unexpected. As such, it merits testing in other series of cases.

[2] The correlation coefficients (Pearsonian r) were as follows:

Combination Adjust-ment Rating	r
Combination I	.35
Combination II	.30
Combination III	.41
Combination IV	.58
Combination V	.45
Combination VI	.44

limitations of the ratings themselves. It is evident from the nature of both the adjustment ratings and the home ratings that the correlation between them could not be very high. The adjustment ratings were based on information about only a few of the numerous aspects of children's social and emotional functioning. The home ratings were derived from single home interviews, usually with mothers only. Moreover, the two sets of ratings were derived from somewhat different orientations.

In addition, a number of the judgments about the homes were made with only a moderate degree of confidence: 301 of the ratings were made with the second degree of confidence, although only 19 were made with the third, or lowest, degree. As was reported in Chapter VI, the interviewers were much more likely to be confident in rating A or E homes than in rating those in between.

Apparently reliability as well as confidence was stronger at the extremes. The reliability check gives some support for this statement, and the correlation coefficients produced by cases with first degree confidence ratings give somewhat more. In Chapter XV a comparison is made between the correlation coefficients produced by cases with first degree confidence ratings and those produced with second or third degree confidence. This comparison refers to the various measures of adjustment (sociometric, BDC, and the like) considered separately. In every case the coefficient was higher when only first degree confidence ratings were used but only on one measure was the increase statistically significant.[1]

When the same computation was made using Combination V adjustment categories, the correlation of this measure with home ratings made with the first degree of confidence was found to be .65. This compares with the coefficient of .45 that resulted when all cases, regardless of confidence ratings, were used. The difference between these correlation coefficients is too large to be attributable to chance.

Limitations on the reliability and validity of both home and adjustment measures would also lower the size of the correlation

---

[1] The increase was due in part to the fact that the ratings that were made with high confidence were concentrated at the extremes.

coefficients. Since, in spite of this, statistically significant coefficients emerged, the "true" relation between home and adjustment must be a stronger one than our figures indicate.

In this connection, the experience of a recent investigator of much the same subject is instructive. This investigator used paper-and-pencil tests to measure both parental attitudes and children's adjustment, and he did not combine his measures to produce single scores for either set of traits. Analysis of the relations among the measures revealed no significant correlation between home and adjustment. The investigator attributes this finding largely to defects in his measuring instruments.[1]

Another kind of consideration must be taken into account in considering the rather low correlation between home and adjustment ratings. The figures show a closer fit between adjustment and home ratings in homes rated good than in those rated poor. Over two-fifths of the children in homes rated poor were judged to be making a good or fairly good adjustment. In other words, "good" homes were apparently more influential in producing "good" adjustments than "poor" homes were in producing "poor" adjustments.

A full search for the reasons for this finding must be postponed for later study. There are many possibilities—among them, that we were too harsh in our judgments of homes or that the tests were too lenient in their rating of adjustment.

It could be, however, that no explanation is needed. Instead, the finding may be a fairly accurate picture of what usually happens, and what needs revision may be not our figures but the popular assumption that poor homes almost inevitably produce maladjusted children. Two studies contribute bits of evidence in support of the latter point: the Cambridge-Somerville Youth Study[2] and a more recent study by Dr. Irving D. Harris, a child psychiatrist.[3]

[1] Burchinal, Lee G., "Parents' Attitudes and the Adjustment of Children," *Journal of Genetic Psychology*, vol. 92, 1958, pp. 69–79.

[2] Powers, Edwin, and Helen Witmer, *An Experiment in the Prevention of Delinquency.* Columbia University Press, New York, 1951, p. 400.

[1] Harris, Irving D., *Normal Children and Mothers.* The Free Press, Glencoe, Ill., 1959, p. 269.

The Cambridge-Somerville Youth Study was a longitudinal investigation of boys' adjustment between ten and seventeen. In it, the final rating of homes was made on a three-point scale of good to poor, while the rating of adjustment was on much the same four-point scale as the one we employed. Twenty-six per cent of the boys lived in homes rated poor, practically identical to the proportion of D and E homes in our study. Fourteen per cent of the boys were rated poor in adjustment—again much like our study's finding. The distribution of home and adjustment ratings is shown in Table 40.

TABLE 40. CHILDREN'S ADJUSTMENT RATINGS BY HOME RATINGS: CAMBRIDGE-SOMER- VILLE YOUTH STUDY

Adjustment	Good home	Fair home	Poor home	Total
Good	52	23	1	76
Fairly good	26	52	18	96
Rather poor	4	12	20	36
Poor	..	10	24	34
Total	82	97	63	242

As in our study, good homes were more closely associated with good adjustment than were poor homes with poor adjustment. Thirty per cent of the boys whose homes were rated poor were making a good or fairly good adjustment. In view of the crudity of the measures, this proportion is of much the same order as the 44 per cent of the boys in our study.

Dr. Harris' study dealt with 54 children selected by their teachers as "rather normal." These children and their parents were examined in the usual child-guidance-clinic manner. No severely disturbed children were found but some children were judged to be "mildly disturbed" and were much like many of the patients of child guidance clinics. The same was true of the mothers.

An exact equating of Harris' ratings of mothers and children and those used in our study is not possible. Nevertheless, it is interesting that he found that 2 of the 14 children of "dependable and understanding" mothers were "mildly disturbed" and that 6 of the 20 children of mothers who were "undependable and not understanding" were making a "very good" adjustment.

These two pieces of evidence lead us to suspect that, although the correlation between home quality and children's adjustment found in these studies may be minimal measures, the extent of relation between these traits is probably not as great as popular accounts of psychological theory would imply.[1] Specifically, it may be that more children than would be expected can withstand the adverse influence of a poor home. The aim of adoption law, however, is not to test how much children can endure but to maximize their chance of doing well. For all the crudity of the measures, the finding that the chance of not doing well was much greater in the kinds of homes rated D or E than in those rated A or B is significant for the evaluation of the independent adoption process.

THE OVERALL OUTCOME OF ADOPTIONS

At the end of the previous chapter we concluded that the approximate similarity between the adopted children's adjustment ratings and those of their controls did not provide sufficient evidence for saying that the outcome of the independent adoptions under study was satisfactory. The present chapter has shown that the children who got into adoptive homes of the sorts envisaged by adoption law were much more likely to adjust well than those who got into poor homes. Since a considerable proportion of the adopted children got into poor homes, we conclude that the outcome of the independent adoptions was not as good as that which the law aims to achieve.

For a count of the number of adoptions that in an overall sense turned out well and the number that turned out poorly, the figures in Table 39 on page 272 were examined and the following condensation of categories was made: Home ratings were grouped into A and B—good; C—fair; and D and E—poor. Adjustment categories 1 and 2 were combined to represent good adjustment; 3 was taken to denote fair adjustment; and 4 to denote poor.

---

[1] For a discussion of present professional opinion on the extent of this relationship, see Caplin, Gerald, editor, *Prevention of Mental Disorders in Children*, Basic Books, New York, 1961.

Table 41 shows the number of cases in the various home and adjustment categories. It will be noted that Combinations V and VI adjustment ratings give almost identical percentage distributions.

TABLE 41. PERCENTAGE DISTRIBUTION OF COMBINED HOME
        AND ADJUSTMENT OUTCOME RATINGS

Outcome by combined home and adjustment ratings	Combination V		Combination VI	
	Number	Per cent	Number	Per cent
Outcome good on both counts:				
Home A or B; adjustment 1 or 2	163 ⎫		105 ⎫	
Good in one respect; fair in the other:				
Home C; adjustment 1 or 2	80 ⎬	64	48 ⎬	64
Home A or B; adjustment 3	21 ⎭		13 ⎭	
Fair in both respects:				
Home C, adjustment 3	24	6	12	5
Good in one respect; poor in the other:				
Home AB; adjustment 4	1 ⎫		1 ⎫	
Home DE; adjustment 1 or 2	55 ⎭	14	29 ⎭	12
Fair in one respect; poor in the other:				
Home C; adjustment 4	3 ⎫		7 ⎫	
Home D or E; adjustment 3	37		26	
	⎬	16	⎬	19
Poor in both respects:				
Home D or E; adjustment 4	27 ⎭		16 ⎭	
Total	411	100	257	100

To produce a figure on the proportion of satisfactory and unsatisfactory outcome, these groupings can be combined in various ways. Probably most would agree in judging the first two categories to be a satisfactory outcome, and many would say that the last two categories represent an unsatisfactory outcome. If so, the proportions would be 64 per cent of the adoptions satisfactory (according to both Combinations V and VI) and 16 or 19 per cent unsatisfactory, depending on which measure of adjustment is used. The 6 (or 5) per cent called "fair in both respects" can be added to either the satisfactory or the unsatisfactory group, or left to itself, without affecting the final conclusions markedly. Probably, however, this group should be regarded as representing a reasonably satisfactory outcome.

The question then is what to do with that 14 (or 12) per cent in which either the home or the child's adjustment was rated poor. The answer will depend on whether one thinks the home rating or the adjustment rating is the major indicator of adoption outcome.

If the home rating is regarded as the more important, the additional percentage (the DE cases) would be added to the proportion already listed as unsatisfactory, making the total 30 (or 31) per cent. If the adjustment measure is preferred, the total for unsatisfactory outcomes would be only slightly changed from the 16 (or 19) per cent shown in the table. The total count for satisfactory outcomes including the cases rated "fair," would be either 70 (or 69) per cent or 84 (or 81) per cent, depending on whether the home rating or the child's adjustment at the time of the follow-up study was deemed the more important measure.

If one is interested in adoption outcome as an evaluation of the independent adoption system (as it operated in Florida in the years under study), the decision should probably be made in favor of the home ratings. This follows from the fact that it is only in the choice of homes that the court, in granting or refusing adoption petitions, can exercise control. Moreover, that a child should do well in spite of a poor home is nothing for which a court or an adoption agency can take credit. If, however, the study is looked on chiefly as a means of investigating the theoretical question of the influence of home factors on adopted children's adjustment, the decision on adoption outcome should probably be made in favor of the children's adjustment. The difference between the conclusions, depending on which criterion is used, amounts to only 12 to 14 percentage points. This difference may well be outbalanced by the fact that none of the ratings—and, therefore, the percentages based upon them—is established with a high degree of certitude. In view of all this, it may perhaps be best to split the difference and conclude that about three-fourths of the adoptions appeared to be working out at least fairly well, according to the measures used in this study.

CHAPTER XII

Relation of Various Factors to the Outcome of Adoption

Having looked into the extent to which the independent adoption process resulted in children getting into good homes, as well as into the children's social-emotional adjustment and its relation to home ratings, we have next to consider three subsidiary questions. First, did these findings hold equally well for all categories of children, especially for those who came into adoption with handicaps? Second, are certain attributes of the adoptive parents, in addition to those already used in rating the homes, related to the quality of care they provided and the children's adjustment? Third, was there any relation between adoption outcome and the manner in which adoption was arranged? Answers to these questions should bring greater refinement to the overall findings and may be of practical value in adoption work.

CHARACTERISTICS OF THE ADOPTED CHILDREN

Sex of the Adopted Child

As measured by Combination V adjustment rating, girls were considerably less likely than boys to be regarded as maladjusted. Six girls and 28 boys received such a rating and 85 girls and 68 boys had ratings at the other extreme. The percentage distribution of the Combination V ratings by sex is given in Table 42. This sex difference was not an unexpected finding, for it is in line with the experience of child guidance clinics and with numerous studies of children's adjustment.

TABLE 42. PERCENTAGE DISTRIBUTION OF COM-
BINED ADJUSTMENT RATINGS BY SEX

Adjustment rating (Combination V)	Boys (238)	Girls (200)
Good	29	41
Fairly good	35	41
Somewhat poor	25	15
Poor	11	3
Total	100	100

Age at Follow-up

Rather unexpectedly, adolescents did not receive adjustment ratings that were significantly lower than those of younger children. The percentage distribution of the Combination V ratings by age is given in Table 43.

TABLE 43. PERCENTAGE DISTRIBUTION OF COM-
BINED ADJUSTMENT RATINGS BY AGE

Adjustment rating (Combination V)	Children 9 to 11 years old (335)	Children 12 to 15 years old (103)
Good	36	29
Fairly good	37	40
Somewhat poor	20	20
Poor	7	11
Total	100	100

This similarity on the part of the two age groups was not attributable to the older children being in homes that had a higher rating. In fact, the opposite was the case to a slight extent. Twenty-five per cent of the children nine to eleven years old were in homes rated D or E as contrasted with 43 per cent of the older children. At the other extreme (A and B homes) the corresponding proportions were 50 and 33.

Age at Placement

It is often said that children who are adopted as infants are more likely to develop well, socially and emotionally, than those who are adopted later. If this is so, it may be because—among other reasons—the older children have become attached to their own parents or they have had unpleasant experiences at home or in foster homes. The present series of cases is not very adequate for checking on these expectations, for "early" placement was very early indeed, and "later" placement was seldom very late. About three-fourths of the children had been placed in their adoptive homes before they were a month old, and half of the others were in their adoptive homes by the age of six months. Only 20 children were more than eighteen months old at placement, only three of these being four or older. The oldest child was five and a half.

Perhaps because of this limited age range, age at adoption was found to be only slightly associated with the child's later adjustment, as measured by Combination V. The figures are given in Table 44 for the children whose parents participated in a follow-up interview.

TABLE 44. COMBINED ADJUSTMENT RATINGS BY AGE AT PLACE-
MENT

Age at placement	Good	Fairly good	Some-what poor	Poor	Total
Under 1 month	127	122	68	14	331
1 to 5 months	13	21	10	10	54
6 to 18 months	6	18	5	4	33
Over 18 months	7	4	7	2	20
Total	153	165	90	30	438

The only exception to the general rule appeared in the group of 20 children who were over eighteen months of age at placement. Forty-five per cent of these children as compared with 25 to 37 per cent of the other age groups made a poor or somewhat poor adjustment. Because of the small number of cases in the older age group, even the differences between these percentages have little statistical significance.

The lack of close association between two traits, however, does not tell the whole story about their relationship, for both traits may be associated with one or more others that are controlling. In the present case there is evidence that the children's adjustment was related to some extent to the kinds of adoptive homes they got into. Since adjustment and age at placement were somewhat related, we must ask whether age at placement and home quality were also related. The figures are given in Table 45.

TABLE 45. HOME RATINGS BY AGE AT PLACEMENT

Age at placement	Home rating					Total
	A	B	C	D	E	
Under 1 month	74	89	86	41	38	328
1 to 5 months	7	9	6	14	9	45
6 to 18 months	6	7	9	2	8	32
Over 18 months	4	5	6	5	13	33
Total	91	110	107	62	68	438

The correlation between age at placement and home rating is .22. Examination of the figures shows that this was accounted for largely by the fact that the children who were placed when less than a month old were less likely than the others to get into poor homes.

Factor analysis[1] indicated that the relation between age at placement and home ratings, although slight, was independent of the various traits, such as economic status and adoption arranger, with which age at placement was also associated.

Since this was so and since the overall adjustment rating was not included in the factor analysis, it seemed that the question of the extent to which age at placement influenced adjustment could be answered only by holding the home ratings constant. This was done by comparing children placed at less than a month old with those placed later. The children were matched with each other for home ratings and adoptive father's education (an index of socioeconomic level) and for the presence of a serious physical or intellectual handicap. Table 46 gives the figures.

The majority of children in both of these groups had good or fairly good adjustment ratings. However, the proportions of children with such adjustment was larger among those placed earlier, 75 per cent as compared with 61 per cent. The difference

[1] Factor analysis is a statistical means of determining which of a collection of interrelated traits have some element in common. See Part II, Chapter XVII. The "loading" of age at placement on the home rating factor was .20.

between these percentages (which is not great but is not likely to have been due to chance) was contributed chiefly by the children placed when older than eighteen months. It still cannot be concluded, however, that age at placement in itself affects later adjustment, since our data do not permit the separation of age from the effects of adverse pre-placement experiences.

TABLE 46. COMBINED ADJUSTMENT RATINGS AND AGE AT PLACEMENT: HOME RATING, ADOPTIVE FATHER'S EDUCATION, AND PRESENCE OR ABSENCE OF HANDICAP HELD CONSTANT

Adjustment rating (Combination V)	Age at placement	
	Under one month	One month and over
Good	36	22
Fairly good	41	40
Somewhat poor	16	23
Poor	9	17
Total	102	102

"Older" Children

Because of the current concern about the number of older children who need adoptive homes, an analysis was made of adoption outcome for the 26 children who were two years or older when they were placed for adoption. Fifteen of these children had adoptive homes rated D or E and 10 had homes rated A, B, or C. (A home interview was not possible in one case.) These children also differed from the total in the ways their adoptions were arranged. The adoptive homes of two-thirds of the older children were selected directly by the natural parents or their close relatives, as compared with one-fourth of the cases in the total sample. None of these placements was arranged by a doctor or lawyer, as contrasted with two-fifths of the placements in the sample as a whole.

Another difference between early and late placements lay in the striking proportion of "older" children who were born in wedlock—over two-thirds, as compared with one-fifth of the total sample. This difference is perhaps to be expected, since the decision to place babies born out of wedlock is likely to be made at or before their birth, while children born in wedlock are more likely to be placed because of death or family breakdown that occurs some time after the child's birth.

Another difference was found in the reasons parents decided to adopt an older child. The answer seems to be that, for the most part, those who adopted older children made no such decision but took a child who happened to be available. Many of them were moved to adopt by the plight of the child, and the descriptions leave no doubt that the plight of many of them was pitiable. Several who had decided to adopt an infant were captivated or moved to pity by an older child.

> One couple had gone to the home of the natural parents in order to take a newborn baby for adoption. As they entered, they saw a beautiful little girl of four who looked at them "so appealingly" with large violet eyes full of tears. They asked why she was unhappy and she replied that she was going to get a whipping because she had spilled the milk. Both husband and wife decided on the spot that she was the child they wanted and they took her instead of the baby.

A majority of the older children had pre-placement histories of the kind described in the following section. Given these circumstances, the fortunate results of some older-child placements, even though in the minority, are impressive.

> An emaciated little boy, placed at two, was covered with sores, had been in several foster homes, and was so afraid of losing his adoptive mother that he shrieked if she left the house and went into spasms of fear if he was taken out in the car. Today his mother describes him as a conscientious, dependable, outgoing boy, a "very sociable leader." His teacher says he is "a fine student, liked by all." The school record and psychological tests show him to be above average in leadership, popularity, and school achievement, and rate him above average in general adjustment.

The adoptive home situation apparently helps to explain why some of these older children adjusted well. The boy cited was one of the six children two years of age or older whose homes were rated A or B. Four of these six children were rated as being well or fairly well adjusted when the follow-up study was made, and only one as rather poorly adjusted. Of the 15 children of this age in homes rated D or E, only one was rated well adjusted at follow-up and 14 were considered at least rather poorly adjusted. Apparently, then, the older children's adjustment was more influenced than the younger children's adjustment by the kind of home adoption provided.

Adverse Pre-placement Conditions

Closely related to age at placement was another characteristic whose predictive possibilities seemed worth investigating: the presence or absence of possibly traumatizing conditions or events in the lives of children before they were placed for adoption. Information in the pre-adoption records may not account for all the children who had had such experiences but, according to the coders, there were 56 such cases among the 296 children who were placed for adoption when they were more than one week old.

These children were suffering in obvious physical ways from the effects of the conditions under which they had been living. "Terrible," said one mother succinctly, when asked about her child's physical condition at placement. Several were undernourished, poorly cared for, dirty. One had lice; some had body sores. One or two were half-starved.

Psychologically the children were even more pathetic. Of the 26 children who were at least two years old when placed for adoption, 22 had been in boarding homes, institutions, or both. In addition, a few had been rejected by a first set of adoptive parents. Some had undergone several changes in boarding homes, while others alternated living with natural parents or relatives and homes of strangers. Some had lived through much marital strife between their parents. The example below could be multiplied many times.

> Billy was four and a half when he was placed in his present adoptive home. Before this, he had been in a succession of boarding homes and had twice been taken back by his own father, only to be returned after a period of weeks. Still earlier, he had been subjected to severe punishment, such as being locked in a room for several days, had witnessed violent conflict between his parents, had seen his father drunk most of the time, and was finally deserted by his mother.

The majority of the children who had had such unhappy experiences before placement were apparently in good physical health by the time the adoption was completed, according to the medical certificates signed by the examining physicians. At the time of the follow-up study, no physical or intellectual problem was reported for 47 of the 56 children. Of the remaining eight for whom there is information, three had asthma to a mild degree, four were considered "slow learners" by their teachers, and one had a disability that his parents considered a handicap.

The percentage distribution of the adjustment ratings (Combination V) of the 56 children who had had adverse experiences as compared with those who did not is given in Table 47.

TABLE 47. PERCENTAGE DISTRIBUTION OF COM-
BINED ADJUSTMENT RATINGS BY POS-
SIBLE PRE-PLACEMENT TRAUMA

Adjustment rating (Combination V)	Possibly trauma-tized children (56)	Other children (392)
Good	20	36
Fairly good	44	37
Rather poor	18	21
Poor	18	6
Total	100	100

The proportion of "possibly traumatized" children who appeared to be making a good or fairly good adjustment at the time of follow-up was a bit less than usual. Because of the small number of cases, these differences are not statistically significant. A matched-control analysis of the effects of age at placement on adjustment and home quality differences between the possibly traumatized and other children was made. Even the slight differences disappear when these factors are controlled. Nevertheless, it seemed worth looking into some possibly associated factors— specifically age at adoption and the quality of the adoptive home—to see whether these accounted for the somewhat poorer showing. When the "possibly traumatized" children were matched, case by case, with children who were placed at about the same age and who got into homes of similar quality, the differences in adjustment ratings disappeared. This seemed to suggest that adverse experiences *per se* did not account for the differences in question.

However that may be, within the "possibly traumatized" group, home quality was a factor definitely associated with later adjustment.

TABLE 48. COMBINED ADJUSTMENT RATINGS BY HOME RATINGS: CHILDREN WITH UNFAVORABLE PRE-PLACEMENT EXPERIENCES ONLY

Adjustment rating	Home rating			Total
	A, B, or C	D or E	Not known	
Good	8	1	1	10
Fairly good	15	6	1	22
Somewhat poor	5	4	1	10
Poor	..	9	..	9
Not known	1	2	2	5
Total	29	22	5	56

According to Table 48, the chance of good adjustment decreased as the home rating went down. Twenty-three of the 29 children who got into good homes made a good or fairly good adjustment as compared with only 7 of the 22 children residing in poor homes. While the number of children concerned is far too small for firm conclusions, it appears that the quality of home is especially important for children who have been neglected, abused, or otherwise mistreated.

Health Status; Physical and Intellectual Handicaps

Health is another factor that might be expected to have a bearing on a child's adjustment. The health condition of the children at the time they were placed in their adoptive homes and the physical and intellectual handicaps that they had then or acquired later have been described in Chapters IV and V. As shown there, 50 children were classified as having had one or another physical disability or disorder before the adoption process was completed. At the time of follow-up, 12 of these 50 still had a handicapping disability, though not necessarily the one they had at placement. In addition, one child had died of the disorder he had at the time of adoption, and the health status of one child was unknown. The remaining 36 children were said to be in good health.

In addition to the 12 children who continued to be disabled, 26 others were found at follow-up to have chronic ailments or other handicapping physical or intellectual conditions, or to have had such difficulties at some time after they were adopted. In Table 49, on which the following analysis of findings is based, figures are presented for the three subgroups of children separately.

Group I. Children who had recovered from health problems recognized before adoption (36)

Group II. Children with health problems before adoption and at follow-up (not necessarily the same problem) (12)

Group III. Children who acquired health problems after adoption (problem usually still present at follow-up) (26)

In Table 49 these three groups of children are compared with the rest of the children in the study with respect to their adjustment at follow-up (Combination V rating), the kind of home they acquired (home ratings), and the age at which they were placed for adoption.

As shown in this table, over half of the children who had health difficulties at one time or another received good or fairly good adjustment ratings at the time of follow-up. The proportion of children with such ratings did not differ greatly among the three subgroups into which the children were divided.

The situation was much the same with respect to their homes, about half of these too being of high quality (A or B) according to our ratings. (The only exception was in the group of children once somewhat disabled but now in good health.) As to age at placement, two-thirds of all these children went into their adoptive homes when they were less than a month old. In this respect, there was some difference among the subgroups. All but one of the children whose disabilities developed later were in their adoptive homes by six months of age. In contrast, a fifth of the other children were placed for adoption when they were older.

The proportion of rather poor adjustment ratings among these children (46 per cent) was higher, however, than among the children who had always had good health (25 per cent)—prob-

TABLE 49. HOME AND ADJUSTMENT RATINGS AND AGE AT PLACEMENT: CHILDREN WITH PHYSICAL OR INTELLECTUAL DISABILITIES COMPARED WITH OTHERS

Adjustment rating (Combination V)	Poor health at adoption				Physical or intellectual disability at follow-up		Total		No physical or intellectual disability
	Good health now		Still disabled						
	Number	Per cent	Number	Per cent	Number	Per cent	Number	Per cent	Per cent
Good	7	20	4	33	1	4	12	16	37
Fairly good	13	37	2	17	13	50	28	38	38
Rather poor	9	26	1	8	8	31	18	25	19
Poor	6	17	5	42	4	15	15	21	6
Not known	1	..	..	..	..	..	1	..	..
Total	36	100	12	100	26	100	74	100	100

Home rating

	Number	Per cent	Number	Per cent	Number	Per cent	Number	Per cent	Per cent
A	4	11	2	17	8	31	14	19	21
B	7	20	4	33	6	23	17	23	24
C	8	23	1	8	4	15	13	18	27
D	8	23	..	..	7	27	15	21	12
E	8	23	5	42	1	4	14	19	16
Not known	1	..	..	..	..	..	1	..	..
Total	36	100	12	100	26	100	74	100	100

Age at placement

	Number	Per cent	Number	Per cent	Number	Per cent	Number	Per cent	Per cent
Under 1 month	23	64	6	50	20	77	49	66	75
1 to 5 months	7	20	3	25	5	19	15	21	11
6 to 18 months	3	8	1	9	..	..	4	5	8
Over 18 months	3	8	2	16	1	4	6	8	6
Total	36	100	12	100	26	100	74	100	100

ably not an unexpected finding. This difference of 21 percentage points was too large to have been due to chance.

As to age at placement, Table 49 makes it clear that, *in toto*, these children were no more disadvantaged than the others, although in one of the subgroups, as previously mentioned, almost all the children had the advantage of being placed at a very early age.

In home ratings, the children who, at one time or another, were in poor health were a bit more likely than the others to be at a disadvantage. Forty per cent of them as compared with 28 per cent of the children who had always had good health lived in homes rated D or E. This difference, however, is not statistically significant.

Because of the small number of disadvantaged children, the picture is not quite clear. The children in question were not adjusting as well, on the average, as the rest of the children in the study. On the one hand, the homes in which they were placed turned out to be less good on the whole than those the other children received, while, on the other hand, the age at which they were placed presumably favored one subgroup of the disabled children.

Inasmuch as this was so indefinite a finding on an important question, another method of testing the relation between physical and intellectual disabilities and adjustment was tried. Each of these children was matched with one whose health had always

TABLE 50. COMBINED ADJUSTMENT RATINGS OF CHILDREN WITH AND WITHOUT HEALTH PROBLEMS: MATCHED FOR HOME RATING, AGE AT PLACEMENT, ADOPTIVE FATHER'S EDUCATION, PRE-PLACEMENT ENVIRONMENT

| Adjustment rating (Combination V) | Health problem at adoption | | | | Physical or intellectual disability later | | Total | |
| | Good health later | | Health still poor | | | | | |
	Handi- capped	Matched control	Handi- capped	Matched control	Handi- capped	Matched control	Handi- capped	Matched control
Good	8	6	4	5	1	8	13	19
Fairly good	11	12	2	4	13	15	26	31
Rather good	11	6	1	1	8	2	20	9
Poor	5	11	5	2	4	1	14	14
Total[a]	35	35	12	12	26	26	73	73

[a] Total is one less than in Table 49 because one child's home had not been visited.

been good in order to secure pairs of cases that were substantially alike in age at placement and home rating, as well as in adoptive father's education (a fairly good index of socioeconomic status) and in presence or absence of poor environmental conditions before placement. The adjustment ratings (Combination V) of the three groups of matched children were then compared, as is shown in Table 50.

Again the total column shows that, even with these possibly influential factors controlled, the children who had had health problems at one time or another were less likely to be adjusting well than those whose health had always been good. Although the differences are not statistically significant, it is noteworthy that the relatively poor adjustment scores were mainly those of children whose disabilities either persisted from infancy or were acquired later. Eighteen of these 28 children were classified as making a poor or rather poor adjustment at the time of follow-up as contrasted with six out of 28 of their controls.

In contrast, the children who were in good health by (and, usually, long before) follow-up had adjustment ratings that practically paralleled those of their matched controls. These were the children who were in poor physical condition at the time of placement or who had a remediable illness or congenital malformation. Insofar as 35 cases can justify a generalization, the conclusion would seem to be warranted that such sorts of handicaps have no bearing on later outcome and that, accordingly, adoption of such children carries few hazards for parents.

With the question of the relative adjustment of the various groups of children who had physical or intellectual difficulties answered as well as could be done with the data at hand, we next asked which of several conditions favored the good adjustment of children with physical or intellectual difficulties. For this analysis the children were divided into two overlapping groups. Into the first were put all the children who were disabled at the time of follow-up or whose disabilities had persisted for a considerable length of time—the so-called "handicapped children" (those listed as "health still poor" and "disability later" in Table 50). Into the second were put the children who were in poor physical condition or otherwise handicapped before adoption (those listed as "good health later" and "health still poor"). The reason for making this distinction was to permit conclusions to be drawn both about children whose disabilities persisted and about those whose health was not up to par at adoption, regardless of what happened later. Information about the latter group might be useful to adoption practitioners in selecting homes for infants whose health is not good.

We consider first the children who were physically or intellectually disabled at or near the time of the follow-up study— that is, the children whose condition had persisted for a long time. In this group, neither age at placement nor the severity of the disabling condition was found to be associated with degree of adjustment. Age could not be a factor because all except two of these children had been placed in adoptive homes when they were less than six months old, three-fourths of them at less than a month. The figures with respect to severity are given in Table 51.

TABLE 51. COMBINED ADJUSTMENT RATINGS BY SEVERITY OF HANDICAP: CHILDREN IN POOR HEALTH OR MENTALLY RETARDED AT TIME OF FOLLOW-UP

Adjustment rating (Combination V)	Degree of disability at follow-up (intellectual or physical handicap)			Asthma and allergies	Total
	Severe	Substantial	Moderate		
Good	1	2	..	2	5
Fairly good	5	2	3	5	15
Somewhat poor	2	2	..	5	9
Poor	4	2	..	3	9
Total	12	8	3	15	38

This table shows that, with the exception of the small number of children with a handicap classified as "moderate," good or fairly good adjustments were just as frequent in one category as another. Apparently, then, these children's degree of social-emotional adjustment did not depend on how severely disabled they were.

A substantial explanation of the differences in adjustment within this group of children was found in the ratings given to their adoptive homes. The correlation between these children's adjustment and home ratings was .71, a marked increase over the .45 obtained for the study as a whole. The difference between these two correlation coefficients is statistically significant.

This finding suggests that, if they are to develop well, socially and emotionally, "handicapped children" even more than other children are in need of homes of the kind rated good.

We turn next to the 48 children who had congenital defects or were ill or in poor condition at the time of adoption, in order to see to what extent the factors discussed above influenced their adjustment.

These children varied more than the others in the age at which they were placed for adoption. Nine of them were over six months old (some of them much older) at placement, and only three-fifths were placed at less than a month of age. Even so, age at adoption showed practically no relation to the children's ratings on later adjustment.

Severity of the handicap was also not a factor of importance. Only three of these children had handicaps that were classified as substantial or severe, and two of the three had adjustment ratings in the highest category.

With these children who were in poor health during the adoption process, as with those in Table 52, it was the home rating that largely differentiated the children who made a good or a fairly good adjustment from those who did not. For the 26 children in homes rated A, B, or C, the chance of this sort of an adjustment was five out of six, while for the 21 children in homes

TABLE 52. COMBINED ADJUSTMENT RATINGS BY HOME RATINGS: CHILDREN IN POOR HEALTH OR MENTALLY RETARDED AT TIME OF FOLLOW-UP

Adjustment rating (Combination V)	Home rating					Total
	A	B	C	D	E	
Good	2	3	. .	. .	. .	5
Fairly good	6	4	3	2	. .	15
Somewhat poor	2	1	1	4	1	9
Poor	. .	2	1	1	5	9
Total	10	10	5	7	6	38

rated D or E the chance was about one out of five. In short, the findings about the factors affecting later adjustment were the same for these children as for those previously discussed.

We conclude, then, that the adjustment outlook for the children who were ill or in poor health or who had congenital malformations at the time of adoption was different from that of the children who were severely handicapped, in the popular sense of the word, at the time of follow-up.

The former children's adjustment depended largely on the quality of the home they got into; not upon the conditions of their health. In contrast, the children who were "handicapped" by severe physical or intellectual disabilities, including chronic diseases, were not likely to do as well, on the average, as the children who were in good health even if they got into the same sorts of homes as the others did. Within this handicapped group, however, the child's chance of making a good adjustment depended much more on the character of his adoptive home than on the severity of his disability.

Summary

Summarizing the findings about differences between various groups of adopted children, we conclude that certain categories of children made a somewhat poorer than average adjustment on the whole and that this was accounted for, to a considerable extent, by the kinds of homes they got into. This conclusion, however, did not hold in every case. The proportion of boys who received low adjustment ratings was higher than that of girls.

For children who were placed for adoption after they were eighteen months old, for those who had had adverse home experiences before being placed, and for those who had health problems or who were in poor physical condition when they were placed—for all these children (who were to some extent the same children) the quality of the adoptive home was an especially significant factor in adjustment. Not only were these children unusually likely to get into poor homes but the quality of the home was itself unusually closely related to the degree of adjustment they made.

CHARACTERISTICS OF THE ADOPTIVE PARENTS

The next question to be discussed is whether certain characteristics of the parents were significantly associated with the home and adjustment ratings. These characteristics include: (1) psychological traits on which the home ratings were so largely based, and (2) more overt traits such as the parents' age at the time of placement, their socioeconomic status, their marital history, and whether they had children of their own, either before or after adopting a child.

Personality and Interpersonal Relations

With regard to psychological characteristics, a point to be considered is their relation to the children's adjustment. The coefficients of correlation between the field director's ratings of these parental traits and the combined adjustment ratings were as follows:

Marital relations	.42
Mother's personality	.38
Mother-child relations	.43
Father's functioning as family member	.29
Overall home rating	.44

The relative size of the coefficients suggests that the adopted children's adjustment was most strongly related to the quality of the marital relations and of the mother-child relations. These were apparently a bit more influential than the mother's personal adjustment and definitely more influential than the degree of adequacy with which the father was judged to perform his family role.

The finding with respect to the correlation with father's functioning might be discounted on the basis of inadequate information were it not that the information about the marital relation was also inadequate. It suggests that in subsequent studies more attention should be paid to the father's relations with the child, especially since our finding is out of line with much of current theory on the subject. The correlation between marital relations and adjustment ratings may indicate that a careful study of marital relations at the time of placement would provide a promising clue to the probable outcome of adoption.

Age of Adoptive Parents at Time of Placement

A much-discussed question is whether the age of the parents at the time they seek to adopt a child is prognostic of the adoption outcome. On the one hand, some maintain that it is undesirable for an infant to be adopted by a mother who is over forty (or perhaps even over thirty-five) or by a father who is over forty-five, while others say that couples who want to adopt children should not be denied that privilege because of their age.

As was reported in Chapter IV, nearly two-thirds of the adoptive mothers and a bit over half of the adoptive fathers in our sample were in their thirties when the children were placed with them. On the other hand, 13 per cent of the adoptive mothers

TABLE 53. HOME RATINGS BY AGE OF PARENTS AT PLACEMENT OF CHILD

Mother's age	Home rating					Total
	A	B	C	D	E	
20 to 34	61	62	64	31	34	252
35 to 39	25	32	28	20	15	120
40 to 44	5	12	11	6	12	46
45 to 49	..	2	4	2	4	12
50 and over	..	2	..	3	3	8
Total	91	110	107	62	68	438

Father's age	Home rating					Total
	A	B	C	D	E	
20 to 34	38	43	30	20	16	147
35 to 39	30	27	30	17	22	126
40 to 44	14	26	33	12	13	98
45 to 49	9	7	10	6	9	41
50 to 54	..	4	3	4	4	15
55 and over	..	3	1	3	1	8
Total	91	110	107	62	65	435[a]

[a] In three adoptive homes there were no fathers.

were forty or older at that time, and about the same proportion of adoptive fathers were forty-five or more. Among those for whom we have follow-up information, 19 adoptive mothers were forty-five or older, and 23 fathers were fifty or over. Only 4 per cent of the children were over two years old at placement, and there was no significant relation between their age and that of the adoptive parents. Accordingly, most of the adoptive parents who were over forty at the time of placement were in their fifties or sixties by the time the adoptive child was ten.

There was a slight negative correlation between the adoptive parents' age at placement and the rating of the home in the study, the older parents tending to have somewhat lower home ratings. For the father's age, the correlation was $-.16$; for the mother's, $-.19$. These correlations are statistically significant but very low.[1] In fact, the major importance of the finding is not that there was a correlation between the age of the parents at adoption and the home ratings but that the correlation was so low. The figures are given in Table 53.

[1] This low correlation suggests that age of parents was not an important criterion used by our staff in rating the homes. This point is made because the raters, being social workers, might be thought to have had a bias against "older" parents.

Reduced to percentages, the amount of difference between older and younger parents shows up clearly. Half of the mothers under forty when the child was placed, as compared with a third of those forty or over, had homes rated A or B ten or so years later. For homes rated D or E, the comparable figures were 27 per cent for the younger mothers and 45 per cent for the older. The difference between the fathers under 45 and those who were older was a bit less than for the mothers.

The finding that age of parents was less important for adoption outcome than is often assumed was strengthened by the results of the factor analysis. Contrary to Table 53 and the "zero-order" correlation based upon it, the factor analysis[1] showed that the age of the adoptive parents had almost nothing in common with the home rating, the "loading" of age on the "home rating factor" being below the cutting point of .20. Apparently, then, the parents' age was not directly related to the home ratings, that is, to the quality of family life and relationships provided the adopted children.

As for the overall adjustment of the children at the time our follow-up study was made, there was no association between it and the age of the adoptive parents at the time of placement. The percentages are indicated in Table 54.

The individual tests, with one exception, also showed no relation between the two traits. The one exception was the teacher ratings of "aggressive" and "withdrawn" maladjustment on the BDC test. There was some tendency for children of younger fathers to be more frequently rated high in aggressive maladjustment and for children of older fathers to be rated high in withdrawn maladjustment than was true of the adopted children as a whole. The correlation between the measure of aggressive maladjustment and the age of the adoptive father at the time of placement was −.13. When only the ratings of the 66 children whose fathers were 45 or more were correlated with these adjustment scores, the coefficient was .37. The corresponding correlation for the 63 mothers forty and over was only .06, suggesting that the father's age was a stronger factor than the mother's in this respect.

---

[1] The factor analysis and its findings are described in Chapter XVII.

TABLE 54. PERCENTAGE DISTRIBUTION OF COMBINED ADJUST-
MENT RATINGS, BY AGE OF ADOPTIVE PARENTS AT
TIME OF PLACEMENT

Age of adoptive parents	Good or fairly good adjustment	Somewhat poor	Poor	Total
Father's age				
20 to 34 (151)	73	20	7	100
35 to 39 (137)	68	22	10	100
40 to 44 (101)	68	28	4	100
45 to 49 (45)	76	13	11	100
50 to 54 (16)	69	31	..	100
55 and up (7)	57	43	..	100
Mother's age				
20 to 34 (261)	70	22	8	100
35 to 39 (122)	76	17	7	100
40 to 44 (44)	68	23	9	100
45 to 49 (12)	59	32	9	100
50 and up (7)	71	29	..	100

A small but statistically significant association between the
home ratings and the amount of age difference between the
adoptive parents was found. In the whole sample of cases studied,
there were 27 adoptive mothers who were four or more years
older than their husbands. In addition, 42 adoptive fathers were
twelve or more years older than their wives. These homes with
marked age differences between the adoptive parents tended to
have lower average home ratings than those in which the age
difference fell within conventional norms.

No significant associations were found between age differences
and the various measures of child adjustment. Test scores averaged somewhat lower in cases in which the mother was four or
more years older than her husband, but the number of such
couples was too small for the difference to be statistically
significant.

Except for the association between age differences and home
ratings, the data gave no evidence that the age of the adoptive
parents was a factor of practical significance in determining the
outcome of the adoptions.

Socioeconomic Status

A frequent requirement of adoption laws is that petitioners
have sufficient income to provide suitably for an adopted child.

This requirement was met by nearly all the adoptive parents in our series of cases, apparent exceptions being five families whose income was under $1,800 at the time of petitioning for adoption. (Forty-one others had an income of less than $2,400 at that time.) Exact information about income was not obtained in the follow-up interviews.

In overall socioeconomic status, the parents were predominantly middle class or lower-middle class, as indicated by their education, income, and husband's occupation at the time of petitioning for adoption. Ten or so years later the occupational distribution of the families had not shifted markedly, although some fathers had changed their type of job. At that time, four out of five of the adoptive fathers were engaged in occupations usually classified as middle class or lower-middle class, while about one in five was engaged in a relatively high-status occupation.

In addition to occupation, the variables used as indicators of the adoptive families' socioeconomic status were income at time of petition, education of adoptive father and mother, and the social-economic level of the neighborhood in which the family lived at the time of follow-up, as judged by the interviewers.

All these traits showed small but statistically significant associations with both the home ratings and some of the individual measurements of the children's performance in school. The differences that were found slightly favored the children from homes of higher social status (as indicated by the adoptive father's education and occupation), the correlations ranging from .12 to .16.

Factor analysis confirmed the finding that the relation between home rating and socioeconomic status of the adoptive family was perceptible but slight. Only the neighborhood variable "loaded on" Factor I (the Home Rating Factor) and that loading was only a bit above the cutting point of .20. Apparently, then, even though the presence of very poor living conditions was one of the factors the interviewers were instructed to consider in rating homes, the raters were little influenced by socioeconomic considerations in making their ratings.

Factor analysis indicated that socioeconomic status was a factor in its own right. Associated with it (Factor IV) were certain attitudinal and behavioral characteristics of the adoptive parents that were on the checklist or were noted in the questionnaire given to the parents at the end of the follow-up interview. These traits and their loadings on the Socioeconomic Status Factor were:

Parental reservations about adoption outcome	.31
Frequency of discipline	.29
Difficulty in supervising adopted child	.24
Freedom from anxiety about child rearing	−.22
Age at which the child was told he was adopted	−.21

The loading of these traits on this factor suggests that claiming to be firm in disciplining a child, frankly admitting anxiety about child rearing, having difficulty in supervision, and telling the child about his adoptive status when he was very young were characteristics of the higher socioeconomic status parents. (In these days of overpermissiveness and parental anxiety such findings are not too surprising.) That "parental reservations about adoption outcome" also was related to this factor is more difficult to explain, especially since so very few parents expressed reservations of any kind. (See Chapter V.)

The relation of socioeconomic characteristics to the kind of home the child found was also slightly suggested in Factor III, the Rejection-Aggression Syndrome.[1] The socioeconomic traits were far below the cutting point in their loading on this factor, but the "arranger" variables, which themselves were somewhat related to socioeconomic traits, did "load on" it. This strengthens our impression that socioeconomic status is important for its by-products rather than in itself as an influence in adoption outcome. Poor education, low-status occupation, poor neighborhood do not in themselves determine how a couple arranges an adoption placement or rears a child. But this study suggests that people with little education may be more likely than others to use certain child-rearing practices. These relations indicated in Factor III are suggestive of the extent to which socioeconomic differences involve cultural differences.

Turning next to the question of the relation of socioeconomic characteristics at adoption (adoptive father's education and

[1] Discussed in Part II, Chapter XVII.

occupation) to adjustment, we find that they bore no statistically significant relation to the Combination V rating of the children's adjustment at the time of the follow-up study. In the various categories of these traits, the proportions of children making a good or fairly good adjustment are indicated in Table 55.

TABLE 55. PERCENTAGE OF CHILDREN HAVING FAVORABLE COMBINED ADJUSTMENT RATINGS BY EDUCATION AND OCCUPATION OF ADOPTIVE FATHER

Adoptive father's education and occupation	Per cent of children having good or fairly good adjustment (Combination V)
Education	
Did not finish eighth grade (38 cases)	71
Completed eight grades of elementary school (58)	67
Some or all of high school (190)	75
Some or all of college (198)	67
Postgraduate work (30)	77
Occupation	
Primary professions and top managerial (35)	71
Large proprietors or top sales (60)	72
Secondary profession (22)	73
Small business or salesmen (116)	70
Skilled (132)	73
Semi-skilled (72)	72
Unskilled (5)	40
Not employed (5)	80

The adoptive father's education and his occupation at the time of adoption were, however, slightly related to the child's performance in school. The correlation coefficients showing the relation of these traits to I.Q., achievement, and "leadership," in terms of BDC ratings, ranged from .12 to .16. The adoptive mother's education was also slightly predictive of the adopted child's achievement in school.

These traits of the adoptive parents, however, were slightly related to the natural mother's education. (The latter trait, for instance, "loaded on" the socioeconomic factor to the extent of .20.) Hence this finding may mean only that the better-educated parents were somewhat likely to secure brighter children by adoption, or that—as is often reported—their children are better equipped for, and more highly motivated to, good school performance.

In all, then, the adoption petitioners' socioeconomic characteristics at the time of adoption gave little, if any, indication of how the adoption turned out.

Marital History Before Adoption

It was noted in Chapter IV that 80 per cent of the adoptive couples had been married at least five years when the child was placed with them, that in 30 per cent of the cases at least one of the marital partners had previously been divorced, and that a pre-adoption history of divorce was most frequent among those who had been married least long.

No significant relation was found between the duration of the marriage and the rating given to the home. There was, however, a low but statistically significant correlation ($-.14$) between the home rating and a history of previous divorce for the adoptive parents.[1]

TABLE 56. HOME RATINGS BY PRE-PLACEMENT MARITAL HISTORY OF ADOPTIVE PARENTS

Marital history	Home rating					Total
	A	B	C	D	E	
No divorce before adoption	73	75	76	43	40	307
Father divorced once	6	17	12	7	5	47
Mother divorced once	9	11	9	6	8	43
Both divorced once	3	7	7	4	10	31
Multiple divorces[a]	..	..	3	2	2	7
Not ever married	..	..	..	..	3	3
Total	91	110	107	62	68	438

[a] At least one divorce for each spouse and more than one divorce for at least one spouse.

The figures in Table 56 show that this slight correlation was attributable largely to the few couples with a history of "double divorce." A or B ratings were given at follow-up to about half of the homes in which neither parent, or only one, had been divorced before adopting the children. If both had been divorced,

[1] "Marital history" and all but one of the other traits discussed below were excluded in the factor analysis.

the proportion of A or B homes fell to 32 per cent; if one or both had been divorced twice (only seven cases) none of the homes was rated A or B.

If both husband and wife had been divorced at least once before the adoption, they were more likely to separate later than if neither had been divorced. Of these "double-divorce" couples, over one-fourth were again divorced after the child had been placed with them. This percentage compares with 6 per cent for the marriages in which neither partner had ever been divorced and a nearly similar proportion (9 per cent) for those in which one of the partners had previously been divorced.

As has been said, pre-adoption divorce on the part of one of the petitioners was not predictive of poor outcome in terms of the kind of home provided for the child. Previous divorce on the part of both applicants, however, increased the probability of later divorce and its usual accompaniment of a poor home rating, the correlation between home rating and post-adoption divorce being $-.35$.

As to the adopted children's adjustment, as judged by Combination V, divorce before adoption on the part of one or both adoptive parents was not predictive unless one or both marital partners had been twice divorced. The proportions of good or fairly good adjustments in cases in which adjustment ratings were available are shown in Table 57.

We have evidence, then, that pre-adoptive marital disruption was associated with later poor home ratings if both parents had been divorced or if one or both had been divorced twice. An association with the adopted children's adjustment appeared only in the latter case, and the number of such marriages was too small to put much dependence on this finding.

The chief predictive clue relating to marital history appears to be the fact that if both partners were previously divorced, a subsequent divorce was more likely than if neither or only one of them had been divorced before the adoption. Even so, about three-fourths of these couples' marriages were still intact at the time of our study, nearly half of their homes were rated C rather than D or E, and a third of their adopted children were making a good or fairly good adjustment. These proportions are lower

TABLE 57. PERCENTAGE DISTRIBUTION OF FAVORABLE COMBINED ADJUSTMENT RATINGS BY PRE-PLACEMENT MARITAL HISTORY OF ADOPTIVE PARENTS

Marital history	Number of cases	Per cent favorably adjusted
No divorce before adoption	285	70
Only the father divorced	47	70
Only the mother divorced	38	67
Both divorced once	32	83
Multiple divorces[a]	9	36

[a] At least one divorce for each spouse and more than one divorce for at least one spouse.

than those of the study group as a whole but they are mentioned to avoid the possible implication that all such couples' adoptions turn out poorly.

Health at Time of Adoption

At the time of the initial investigation, some health problem was noted for 49 of the adoptive couples, five of whom reported a health defect for both members. Information given at the time of follow-up added 17 couples to the list of those somewhat disabled when the adoption took place. Fourteen of the first group had health problems that would raise definite question about medical suitability for parenthood, while the diagnoses of 16 others would make an investigator wish for a thorough medical exploration. (See Chapter IV for explanation of these categories). Our incomplete information, then, leaves no doubt that at the time of placement a minimum of 6 per cent of the adoptive couples presented health problems that might raise a question about the desirability of the adoption.

The possible early death of an adoptive parent is one reason for the concern about the health of adoptive applicants. By the time of the home interview, however, only two of the adoptive parents (fathers) had died as a result of the health problems indicated in the early record. In contrast, 30 other adoptive parents, for whom no health problem had been reported at placement, had died by the time of our study. Figuring in terms of adoptive parents rather than adoptive couples, 4 per cent of those for whom no health problem was indicated and 4 per cent of those for whom one was noted had died by the time of the study. Inconclusive as they are, the figures do not suggest greater mortality among those for whom a health problem was reported at the time of adoption.

The interview records were reviewed to discover whether the deaths of the 30 parents resulted from conditions that might have been revealed by an adequate examination at the time the child was placed. Here too the information was incomplete; frequently the cause of death was not specified or full details were not given. For five parents, however, it seemed likely that careful medical examination at placement would have raised some question concerning their health. On the other hand, three parents had died in accidents; a number of others apparently became ill some time after the adoption had been completed; and the cause of death of seven parents was not known.

The available data suggest that careful physical examination before adoption became final might have revealed reason for concern about some of the parents who later died, but whether the proportion would have been significant could not be determined.

An equally weighty reason for concern about the health of adoptive applicants is the possibility that illness or physical handicap might interfere with their performance as parents. Thirty-eight of the 54 parents for whom a health problem was reported before adoption made no mention of current health difficulties during the home interview. Four reported a problem different from, and apparently not related to, the one noted in the early record. Ten reported the same problem mentioned earlier. For the most part these problems were not severe, nor were they of a kind that would necessarily interfere with "parenting." They included such ailments as mild arthritis, asthma, a "bad back," a "lame leg" resulting from poliomyelitis. Some were more serious. One father was suffering grave effects from a condition described as "nervous hypertension" at the time of placement. A mother who originally said she "never felt good" was still not feeling well. Two fathers, as noted above, had died of conditions at least related to the health problem they had reported earlier.

The pertinent question about health problems that were not fatal is, how much did they affect the quality of the home? On the whole, the existence of a physical health defect in the adoptive parent either at the time of placement or at the time of the follow-up study appeared to have no relation to the rating given to the home in the study. No significant correlation was found between home rating and the parent's current health status. A spot check of records showed that unless the adoptive parent's health problem involved his or her mental health, the home rating was made on wholly different grounds.

Although the numbers are too small to be of more than passing interest, certain types of health disabilities did appear to be reflected in the home ratings. For example, none of the eight homes in which a parent was reported to have a venereal disease or a nervous disorder at placement had a rating higher than C at follow-up, and four of these homes were rated D or E. In contrast, of the five in which the father reported a service-connected injury, four were rated A, B, or C.

All in all, the findings tell little about the relation between the physical health of the adoptive parents and adoption outcome. There was little evidence, however, that the parents' physical health was the main or even an important reason for low home ratings, except in the few cases in which physical illness was directly associated with mental ill health. It is difficult to know whether these findings spring chiefly from the inadequacy of the medical information or from the fact that, in the judgment of our interviewers, physical illness as such did not interfere substantially with "parenting." The lack of correlation between home ratings and the current health of the adoptive parents gives some support to the second speculation.

Difference in Religious Affiliations of Adoptive Parents

"Mixed marriage" is often cited as a possible cause of home difficulties and, possibly, of poor social-emotional adjustment on the part of the children concerned. Our study does not substantiate this suspicion.

In the whole series of cases there were only 31 families in which the adoptive husband and wife had different religious affiliations. There were 17 cases in which the mother was Catholic and the father Protestant, and 8 in which the mother was

Protestant and the father was Catholic. There were 2 cases in which the mother was Catholic and the father Jewish, and 6 in which the reverse situation obtained.

Fifty-nine per cent of the homes in these "mixed marriage" cases were rated A, B, or C at the time of the follow-up study, as compared with 70 per cent in the total series. Sixty-three per cent of the "mixed marriage" parents had children who were rated as making a good or fairly good adjustment, according to Combination V. The corresponding figure for all the adopted children was 75 per cent. The differences between these percentages were not large enough to rule out the possibility that they occurred by chance.

Among the various combinations of religious affiliations, no differences in the proportion of children making a good or fairly good adjustment appeared. The home ratings for the 17 families in which the mother was Catholic and the father was Protestant were a bit lower than those in the other groups. Again, however, the differences were too small to be of any significance.

Reasons for, and Attitudes toward, Adoption

Rough classifications were made of the reasons the adoptive parents gave for wanting to adopt a child and of the extent of agreement between the parents in their desire to adopt a child. For the most part, these points were not greatly emphasized in the Welfare Department's social investigations, since the aim was not to select the best parents for a particular child but rather to eliminate the petitions of those who seemed too ill equipped for parenthood to justify leaving the child in their home.

1. **Reasons for Adoption.** Four categories of reasons for adopting were distinguished. These were broad and superficial categories, based on brief comments the adoptive parents made in the course of the Welfare Department's social investigation rather than on specific efforts to determine what the parents' real reasons were. The first and by far the most frequent category was that of inability to have children of their own and a general desire to have children. Information as to whether parents who gave this reason had medically established causes for infertility was not obtained systematically.

The second category related to family composition: wanting a companion for another child in the family or a child of a specific sex. The third covered the adoptions that had been undertaken because the adoptive parents were sorry for the child. A number of couples in this group had thought vaguely about adoption before seeing or hearing about the child's plight but had made no move toward adoption until that time. The fourth category of reasons was one we termed "self-oriented." It included such reasons as a desire to compensate for the death of an "own" child, a fear of pregnancy or childbirth, and a desire to have a child as a companion. As would be expected, some petitioners gave more than one reason for adoption, but in the following analysis only the one that seemed primary was used.

As Table 58 shows, there was a relationship between the type of reason given for wanting to adopt at the time of the petition and the home rating assigned at follow-up.

TABLE 58. HOME RATINGS BY ADOPTIVE PARENTS' REASONS FOR WANTING TO ADOPT

Reasons for adoption	Home rating					Total
	A	B	C	D	E	
Inability to have a child, love of children	84	104	96	54	51	389
Improve family composition	4	3	4	5	6	22
Rescue child from plight	2	1	5	1	9	18
Self-oriented reasons	1	2	2	2	2	9
Total	91	110	107	62	68	438

Combining all reasons except those in the first category, and changing the numbers to percentages, one sees that the chance of the home being rated D or E almost doubled when the reasons were other than inability of the adoptive parents to have a child of their own or "love of children."

Reasons for adoption	Home rating		
	A, B, or C	D or E	Total per cent
Inability to have child	73	27	100
Other reasons	49	51	100

The direction of the relationship held for the various categories of reasons separately, even though the number in each was small.

TABLE 59. COMBINED ADJUSTMENT RATINGS BY ADOPTIVE PARENTS' REASONS FOR WANTING TO ADOPT

	Adjustment rating (Combination V)				
Reasons for adoption	Good	Fairly good	Somewhat poor	Poor	Total
Inability to have a child, love of children	142	141	88	28	399
Improve family composition	8	10	2	2	22
Rescue child from plight	2	12	..	4	18
Self-oriented reasons	2	5	2	..	9
Total	154	168	92	34	448

This seems to suggest that reasons given for adoption may have some prognostic significance.

No relation between the reasons given for adoption and the children's overall adjustment ten years or so later was found. Table 59 gives the figures.

With the largest category of reasons (inability to have a child or love of children) again contrasted with the others, very little difference in percentages appears. Seventy-two per cent of the children adopted for the first set of reasons were found to be making a good or fairly good adjustment at follow-up, as contrasted with 79 per cent of those adopted for other reasons.

2. Extent of Agreement About Adopting. Over two-thirds (298) of the adoptive couples said they were in agreement about wanting to adopt a child. Concerning 59, the extent of agreement could not be determined. In 75 cases, one parent (usually the father) was not enthusiastic or was reluctant; in six cases, both parents were reluctant but were finally persuaded by others to adopt the child. The correlation between agreement about the adoption and home rating was .20. This characteristic "loaded on" Factor I, the Home Rating Cluster, to the extent of .21.

Reluctance to adopt was associated with greater age of the father, which, in turn, had a slight negative correlation with the home rating. The association between father's age and lack of enthusiasm about the adoption was confirmed by the factor analysis. Age of father had a "loading" of .66 on Factor VI (which was named Age of Adoptive Parents after that and other considerations). Disagreement between the parents about adopting had a loading of −.23 on the same factor.

Extent of agreement to adopt did not correlate significantly with any of the various measures of child adjustment.

Other Children in the Home

In their adoptive homes 60 per cent of the children had brothers or sisters who were either "own" children of the adoptive parents or other children adopted by them. Even so, the number of "only" children among the adopted was almost four times as numerous as in the nonadopted control group.

For two-thirds of the couples, the adopted child was their first. Nineteen per cent had children of their own before they adopted the children who were the subject of our study, and 16 per cent had previously adopted one or more children. (Seven of these couples had both adopted and "own" children.)

Subsequent to the adoption of the children we were studying, children were born to 13 per cent of the adoptive parents, and 25 per cent of the parents adopted other children. (Twelve of the couples both adopted other children and had children of their own.) Two-thirds of the parents had no children subsequent to the adoptions our study deals with.

How these various sorts of pre-adoption and post-adoption situations were distributed with respect to home ratings is shown in Table 60.

TABLE 60. HOME RATINGS BY PRE-PLACEMENT AND POST-PLACE-MENT COMPOSITION OF ADOPTIVE FAMILY

Children in home before adoption	Home rating					Total
	A	B	C	D	E	
None	62	85	72	39	37	295
"Own" only	12	12	20	14	16	74
Adopted only	16	12	14	7	13	62
"Own" and adopted	1	1	1	2	2	7
Total	91	110	107	62	68	438

Children entering home after adoption	Home rating					Total
	A	B	C	D	E	
None	53	72	77	44	50	296
"Own" only	10	10	11	5	7	43
Adopted only	22	26	18	11	10	87
"Own" and adopted	6	2	1	2	1	12
Total	91	110	107	62	68	438

The homes in which there were children before the study children were adopted contained a higher proportion of D and E homes than those that had no children—a difference that was statistically significant. The percentages of D and E homes in the following groups shown in Table 60 were:

No children prior to present adoption	26
Own children prior to present adoption	42
Adopted children prior to present adoption	35

In contrast, the homes of couples who either adopted other children or had children of their own subsequent to the adoptions here under consideration were slightly less likely than the rest of the homes to be rated D and E. The percentages of D and E homes in the various groups were:

No children subsequent to adoption	32
Children of own subsequent to adoption	27
Adopted children subsequent to adoption	24

When figures for "own" or adopted children, or both, were combined, the proportion of D and E homes was found to be 38 per cent if these children were in the home when the child in our sample was adopted and 26 per cent if they entered the home later.

These findings suggest, on the one hand, that the presence of children in the family before adoption was a somewhat unfavorable sign. On the other hand, the fact that the parents subsequently had children of their own or that they adopted other children was not related to the kind of home they provided for the children in our series of cases. These findings seem noteworthy because it is sometimes said that the birth of a natural child after adoption might be a hardship for the adopted child. Our data offer no support for such misgivings.

The lower average ratings (and the higher proportion of D and E ratings) in the homes in which natural children preceded adoption does not mean, of course, that all such homes received poor ratings or that children should not be placed for adoption in any such homes. On the contrary, over half of these homes were rated A, B, or C. A case-by-case analysis suggested that the lower average ratings of these homes were not the direct result of mixing "own" and adopted children. (Such a mixture appeared to work out as well as or better than usual when the "own" children came later.)

One factor involved in this apparent relationship was the age of the adoptive parents. The parents who had had children of their own before they petitioned to adopt the children we studied were likely to be older than those whose "own" children were born after the placement. More than one-fourth of them were forty or older, as compared with 14 per cent in the total sample. A good many of them had children who were grown and had left the home by the time the sample child was adopted. It was homes of this sort that, for the most part, received the D and E ratings. In contrast, the homes with younger mothers were the ones that were more likely to receive A, B, or C ratings.

Another factor involved was that having to do with the reason for adoption. This factor was also closely associated with the age factor. A considerable number of the older mothers who adopted children after their children were adults seemed to be seeking companionship and the gratification of again caring for a baby. This kind of motivation, with its implications for lack of emotional maturity on the part of the mother, has been shown above to be associated with a lower-than-average home rating.

In contrast, the mothers who were young enough to bear children after placement appeared to have a different kind of motivation for adoption, being less often of the type we have termed "self-oriented." Some of them expressed the belief that adoption had made it possible for them to bear their own children, and this apparently endeared the adoptive children to them. Most of them said that their feelings toward the adoptive children were the same as toward their own, and that rearing adopted and natural children in the same home presented no problems. A few, however, thought it did pose problems, although some of the mothers said that the advantage lay with the adopted rather than with the natural children. One mother, for instance, reported that her own child felt left out because of not being "chosen" and was only satisfied when the parents "adopted" her also.

Apparently, then, if the adoptive mother is fairly young (say, forty or younger) and if the reason for wanting to adopt a child does not suggest an unfavorable prognosis, the fact that the adoptive parents already have children of their own does not prejudice the adoption outcome.

The percentages cited above suggest, however, that the most favorable situation for an adopted child is probably that in which there are no natural children in the family when he enters it but to which either natural or adopted children come later. The interviewers described the adoptive parents of such children as more relaxed and adequate in the maternal role. They tended to regard the presence of additional children as benefiting the adopted child. The impressive fact here to us was that it appeared to matter little whether the child who came later was adopted or was born to the parents. Equally impressive was the lack of evidence that the children's adjustment was adversely affected by the presence of natural children in the home.

Summary

The foregoing analyses suggest that, in addition to the parental traits that were used in rating homes, a few others distinguished the homes that were rated good or fair from those rated poor. Those traits, however, were not sharply differentiating, and they characterized so few couples that they would not be very helpful as prognostic criteria for selecting adoptive homes.

The differentiating traits were: residence in a poor neighborhood, marked difference in the ages of husband and wife, both adoptive parents previously divorced, wanting to adopt for reasons other than love of children and inability to have them, lack of agreement between husband and wife about adopting, and already having children of their own. Only the first of these traits "loaded" on the Home Rating Factor.

The rest of the traits that were examined proved to be even less helpful as criteria to be used in predicting home quality. These were: adoptive parents' age at the time the child was placed with them; social-economic characteristics other than neighborhood at time of follow-up; health, religious differences, and the presence of children born after or adopted after the adoption in question took place.

The only trait in either of these two lists that was significantly related to the children's overall adjustment ratings was that referring to the adoptive parents' marital history. If one or both parents had previously been twice divorced, the outlook for a good adjustment on the part of the adopted child was poor. None of the other traits that were examined proved to be of predictive value when the relevant factors were controlled.

This being so, we concluded that, in spite of the fact that some of the traits somewhat differentiated poor homes from good, they were not essential parts of the definition of home quality, so far as its influence on children's adjustment is concerned. In contrast, the four traits referring to personality or interpersonal relations, on which the home ratings were largely based, were fairly closely related to the adjustment ratings. Of the four traits, the quality of the marital relationship and of the mother-child relationship were the most closely related to the children's adjustment.

HOW THE ADOPTION WAS ARRANGED

Among the numerous variables to be considered for their relation to adoption outcome, the set that we named the "arrangement syndrome" had an especially complicated involvement with other factors. The syndrome consisted of the following items: who arranged the adoption; whether there was contact between natural and adoptive parents; whether the natural parents created difficulties before the adoption was granted.

We have seen that when a professional person (most often a physician) arranged the placement, the natural and adoptive parents were unlikely to have contact with each other, while contact occurred in a considerable proportion of cases when the natural parents or close relatives did the arranging. We have seen too that problems with natural parents were unlikely to occur if a professional person made the arrangements and if there was no contact between the two sets of parents; and that, although such problems were not frequent, when they did occur it was likely to be in placements that were arranged by natural parents or close relatives and included contact between the natural and adoptive families.

These arrangement traits had a slight but statistically significant association with the home ratings. The correlation between "nonprofessional adoption arranger" and home rating was —.14; between contact with natural parents and home rating it was —.17. The correlations appeared to be a product of selectivity. On the surface it would appear that the kind of people who obtained children for adoption through a professional source were apparently somewhat more likely than others to be the kind that provided "good" homes for the children. However, this conclusion must be modified by the fact of a near zero loading of this variable on the Home Rating Factor.[1]

Table 61, expressed in percentages, shows that differences between the various sorts of arrangers in the proportion of homes given particular ratings were indeed slight, although the use of professional arrangers was a bit more likely to be associated with favorable home ratings.

TABLE 61. PERCENTAGE DISTRIBUTION OF HOME RATINGS BY ADOPTION ARRANGER

Home rating	Professional person[a]	Natural parent, relative, or friend	Other person
A	23	19	20
B	29	20	25
C	23	27	21
D	13	14	19
E	12	20	15
Total	100	100	100

[a] Includes doctor, lawyer, Juvenile Court.

The variables that made up the arrangement syndrome have also been shown to be related to certain characteristics of both natural and adoptive parents, and these characteristics in turn were related to each other. The better-educated parents (natural and adoptive) were more likely than those with less education to use professional persons as adoption arrangers. (See Chapter IV.) This meant that the better-educated adoptive parents were likely to receive children whose natural mothers had a somewhat similar education, since it was such mothers that physicians tended to serve. Similarly, adoptive parents with less education were more likely than others to receive children whose own parents had attended school for fewer years. In short, a partial

[1] See Part II, Table 70.

matching of educational background was effected because the better-educated adoptive and natural parents were likely to turn to a doctor for help in adoptive placement, while the less educated tended to arrange placements directly. The amount of correlation between the education of the natural mother and the adoptive father (.40) reflected this tendency.

Since, in the United States, education, occupation, and income are strongly related to each other and to social status, the better-educated adoptive fathers usually had higher incomes and "better" occupations than did the others. This meant that the children placed by physicians tended to find their way into homes of higher socioeconomic status than did those placed by their own parents or relatives.

The pervasiveness of the arrangement syndrome went beyond these relations with characteristics of adoptive and natural parents. The syndrome was also related to certain characteristics of the adopted children, including that of their later adjustment.

Some of these relations were to be expected. For example, two of the three variables (arranger and contact with natural parents) were related to the child's age at placement. This association was hardly surprising, since physicians nearly always placed children for adoption directly from the hospital while parents and relatives placed children when they were a bit older, and since almost all contacts occurred in relation to children placed by close relatives.

From this difference in age at placement, it followed that the arrangement syndrome was also related to the children's pre-placement history and to their physical condition at the time of placement. A few children placed directly from the hospital were ill or had some health defect, but they did not suffer from neglect or undergo possible psychological trauma through shuttling back and forth between caretakers or through witnessing marital strife. The children who did undergo such experiences and later showed what may have been adverse effects were, for the most part, those placed by relatives, friends, or acquaintances of the natural mothers; hence, the association between the arrangement syndrome and the children's pre-placement histories and physical condition at the time of placement.

To a considerable extent the mothers who placed their babies for adoption through a physician were his patients. Perhaps their prenatal care was better than that received by mothers who placed their children themselves. Since the adoptive parents who received a child from a doctor were likely to be his patients, it is also possible that these children received more thorough physical examinations before placement than did the others. If this is true, it would be expected that a larger proportion of children placed by their close relatives than of those placed by physicians would have physical defects. To some extent the figures supported that assumption (see Chapter V), although the difference is slight, and any causal inferences are blocked by selective factors in the arrangement syndrome.

The arrangement syndrome factors also correlated to a slight extent with the information about the children secured through the schools. This was perhaps to be attributed to the difference in educational level (and presumably lower intelligence) of the natural mothers who used one or the other sort of placement arranger, or to the difference in educational level of the parents who secured the children through different sorts of "arrangers." However that may be, in achievement tests and I.Q. the children whose natural and adoptive parents had contact with each other during the adoption arrangements averaged significantly lower than those whose natural and adoptive parents never met. Those whose natural parents or relatives arranged the placement also averaged somewhat lower on achievement tests, although on I.Q. the difference was not statistically significant.

Similar associations were found between the presence or absence of contact and the results of the psychological tests administered in the classroom. On two of the three parts of the teacher ratings, all three parts of the California test, and on the sociometric test the children whose adoptive parents had contact with their natural parents averaged lower than those placed by professional people. Correlations with the kind of person who arranged the adoption were similar but less marked, falling below statistical significance in three instances.

Because the sociometric test showed significant correlation with the presence or absence of contact, shall we say that direct contact between the two sets of parents results in lower school and test performance? Or shall we conclude again that the kind of people who use adoption arrangements in which there is no contact are the kind likely to beget and to rear children able to do reasonably well in school and in relations with their schoolmates? Remembering the correlations between parents' education and the arrangement syndrome, as well as between other socioeconomic factors and education, it is easy to favor this latter explanation.

This assumption seems the more plausible when another set of correlations is added. The child's age at placement correlated significantly with each trait in the arrangement syndrome, on the one hand, and with the test findings, on the other. Children placed before they were over a month old did significantly better in school performance, teacher ratings, California, and sociometric tests than the children who were more than a month old at placement. Without deciding definitely for or against an interpretation, it may merely be noted at this point that the arrangement syndrome showed correlations with characteristics of both parents and children.

With such an interrelatedness among factors, we could not answer from the "zero-order" correlations the question of the extent to which the quality of the adoptive home secured for a child depended on the type of person who arranged the adoption. Factor analysis indicated, however, that home ratings and the "arrangement syndrome" were independent.

To put the conclusion this way (as has been done with respect to certain other characteristics also) is not to say, for instance, that the doctors in our study did not select somewhat better homes for the children they placed or that these children did not tend to make a somewhat better adjustment. One reasonable interpretation is that such results were not necessary consequences of the fact that physicians did the placing—in the sense that if all placement of children for adoption were left to physicians the results would be as good as these. Rather, the seemingly good results could be attributable to one or another of the factors we have found to be related to outcome, which, in turn, were themselves related to the type of person who made the adoption arrangements.

CHAPTER XIII

Clues to How Adoptive Homes Will Work Out

THE FINDINGS about the relation between home and adjustment ratings (that is, about how important it is that an adopted child gets into a home of the kind we have called good) cast no light on an important question: Could the homes later rated good have been distinguished at the outset from those later rated poor? Were there signs by which the social investigators could have determined fairly well which petitioners would and which would not have the resources—physical, intellectual, emotional, financial—for rearing children well?

If the standards used in this study for judging homes and the ratings given to the homes are accepted as reasonably satisfactory, the possibility of answering that question depends on (1) the extent to which personality and attitudes toward children and family life are set by the time people reach the age at which most couples adopt children, (2) the extent to which changing circumstances can change the child-rearing capacities of parents, and (3) the evaluators' ability to discern and interpret relevant clues.

In addition to these unknowns, the possibility of answering the question is also limited by the amount and nature of the information contained in the Welfare Department's records and in those of our own interviewers.

Aside from these limitations, the independent adoption situation in Florida, in the years to which the present study refers, provided a fair—although not ideal—opportunity for exploring the extent to which favorable or unfavorable adoption homes can be recognized when, or before, children are placed. The proportion of agency adoptions in the state was rather small and the adoption agencies were probably not so well known or so outstanding that the picture of independent adoption petitioners was much affected by factors determining who used such agencies. In addition, the Court's policy of rejecting a petition only in the most extreme cases left a wide range in many of the characteristics thought to be important elements in outcome. During the period studied, the Court accepted about half of the Welfare Department's infrequent recommendations to reject petitions, and the Department persuaded some couples to withdraw their petitions. The numbers involved were small, however, and, as far as can be judged, these withdrawals and rejections did not materially restrict the range of characteristics to be studied.

The kinds of information available about the adoptive homes at the time of placement are far less satisfactory than the situation itself. Comparison is made especially difficult by the fact that the follow-up interviews put chief stress on attitudinal factors and on the emotional tone of interpersonal relations, while the early investigation records paid chief attention to more objective "common sense" criteria, such as income, marital history, and criminal record.

Nevertheless, three kinds of check were attempted on the extent to which information available at the time of placement might have indicated the adoption outcome. These employed judgments made by (1) the Welfare Department's investigators, (2) outside raters who were unfamiliar with the study, and (3) the field director.

CASES THE DEPARTMENT OF PUBLIC WELFARE CONSIDERED DUBIOUS

A few of the records of social investigations made by the Department contained statements that could be regarded, in a sense, as prognoses of outcome. The most definite statement of this kind was a recommendation to the Court to reject the petition. Such a recommendation was made in six of the cases in our series but was not accepted by the Court.

These cases represent the kinds of home situations that the Department thought would be unsuitable within the Court's conception of that term. Most of them revealed more than one reason for concern by the Department. For example, as reported earlier three applicants did not have husbands—one being single, one divorced, and one widowed. In addition, two of these applicants were well beyond fifty, one being a widow of sixty-five with a meagre and uncertain income and "a very neurotic personality"—unstable, easily enraged, and often incoherent.

Other grounds for advising against granting a petition included inadequate education, early history of excessive drinking, presumed low intelligence (as evidenced by an I.Q. of 75), ill health, and common-law marriage.

In addition to these six cases, there were 33 about which the Department's investigators at some point in the record expressed definite doubt. These doubts centered chiefly on the physical capacity of a petitioner to rear a child (16 cases), on the couple's financial competence (3 cases), on psychological handicaps (10 cases), and on a combination of these reasons (4 cases).

Some of the reasons for doubt seemed relatively slight—for example, the fact that a couple was in the middle or late forties or differed from the child in ethnic background. Others seemed much more serious. Three of these records, in fact, contained early recommendations to reject the petition, which were changed after home conditions had been improved. Two involved homes that were broken shortly after the child was placed but reestablished before the final hearing. Among other reasons for misgiving on the part of the investigators were questionable reputation of the applicants, extreme nervousness of the adoptive mother, gambling proclivities of the husband, lack of regular income, and very bad living conditions, such as a two-room house with no "conveniences" or a tavern frequented by "shady characters."

The outcome of these "dubious" adoptions is shown in Table 62. As the table indicates, the cases in which the Department had recommended dismissal of the petition at one time or another had rather low home ratings in the follow-up study. None of the eight cases in which interviews were secured had home ratings higher than C, and five homes were rated D or E.

Analogous home ratings turned up in a majority of the cases that moved the investigators to voice doubts. The ten A and B homes in Table 62 were largely those in which only the petitioner's physical capacity to rear a child had been questioned.[1]

So far as home ratings are concerned, then, it would seem that the Department's adverse recommendation and the investigators' explicit misgivings were definitely associated with lower than average home ratings ten years later. Of course, this recommendation, and even the expressed doubts, were reserved for the most extreme cases.

TABLE 62. HOME RATINGS OF PETITIONS QUESTIONED BY DEPARTMENT OF WELFARE

Home rating	Group I[a]	Group II[a]	Group III[a]
A	2	..	..
B	8	..	..
C	8	1	2
D	2	1	..
E	8	1	3
Not interviewed	2	..	1

[a] Group I. Doubt expressed but favorable recommendation made.
Group II. Recommendation against adoption made but withdrawn later.
Group III. Recommendation against adoption made.

PREDICTIONS BY OTHER ADOPTION WORKERS

Whether the information available to the investigators afforded a basis for predicting how the homes would work out was also tested by securing the judgments of experienced adoption workers from the staffs of seven well-known adoption agencies.[2]

The feasibility of the plan turned primarily on whether the records were adequate for the purpose. There was reason for considerable doubt on this score. The evidence furnished by the records was limited both by lack of training on the part of the investigators and by Department policy. The investigators were

[1] Seven of the total 16 petitions of this sort had home ratings of A or B at follow-up; four were rated C and four E; and one family was not interviewed. In the other categories of reasons for doubt, there were only 3 A or B homes; 5 were C, and 8 were D or E.

[2] Family and Child Services, Washington, D. C.
District of Columbia Department of Public Welfare, Washington.
Children's Aid Society of Pennsylvania, Philadelphia.
Department of Public Welfare, Baltimore.
Children's Bureau of Delaware, Wilmington.
The Spence-Chapin Adoption Service, New York City.
Chicago Child Care Society, Chicago.

expected to report only such overt and highly visible psychological problems—personal or interpersonal—as are recognized
by the man-in-the-street, and to give very concrete evidence of
any they did report. As a result, they tended to confine their
reports to factual findings and not to include impressions that
might have been difficult to substantiate. Moreover, because the
adoption law was a new one and the investigative procedure
itself not wholly acceptable to some judges, it was the Department's deliberate policy to recommend against adoption only in
extreme cases. Consequently, the records were unlikely to contain
a full account of the investigators' observations and opinions,
except in the few cases in which an adverse recommendation was
made. This approach probably helped the Department maintain
maximum effectiveness in relation to the Court, but it kept to a
minimum the kind of information on which our prognosticators
were accustomed to rely.

Senior staff members of the invited agencies, after reading a
few of the pre-adoption records and discussing the proposed rating scheme, were interested enough in the experiment to advise
proceeding with it. A random sample of 150 records was selected
for review, 25 being sent to each of the seven cooperating agencies. A simple five-point scale for judgments on the points in
question was devised. One of the research staff "trained" the
social workers who were to make the ratings by discussing with
them, through case examples, our conception of the meanings of
the various points on the scale.[1] As a check on the reliability of
the ratings, 60 of the 150 cases were rated by social workers in
two different agencies.

Perhaps because so much needed information was lacking in
the records of the Department's social investigation, the agency
workers made rather few definitely unfavorable prognoses. In
only 18 of the 150 cases was their prognosis mildly unfavorable;
in 11 it was strongly unfavorable. Moreover, in 21 of these 29
cases, the prognosis was made with only third degree confidence.[2]

---

[1] See Appendix A for rating form.

[2] The records sent to the agencies included a few cases in which a home interview
could not be secured. If only cases with home ratings are considered, the above
numbers would be: mildly unfavorable, 11; strongly unfavorable, 6.

It is significant for practice, if not for prediction, that the raters seldom recommended removing children from homes with a mildly unfavorable prognosis, chiefly because by the time of the investigation strong ties had formed between the children and their adoptive parents, and removal might have done more harm than good. In only four of the 18 homes with mildly unfavorable prognoses did the rater say she would have removed the child from the home. In all but one of the 11 strongly unfavorable prognoses, removal from the home was recommended.

The test showed little correspondence between the prognoses made by the social workers and the outcome of adoptions, as judged by either the home ratings or the various tests of the children's adjustment. The correlation between the social workers' prognoses and the children's adjustment did not exceed that which could have occurred by chance, although all the coefficients were in the expected direction. The correlation between their prognoses and the home ratings was .19, indicating a slight but statistically significant ability to predict the judgments made about the homes some ten years later.

With such low correlation coefficients, one certainly cannot hold that the prediction of adoption outcome was demonstrated as being practicable. On the other hand, the test cannot be held to demonstrate the opposite conclusion.

One immediate question about the results involves the reliability of the social workers' judgments. The re-rating of 60 cases resulted in correlation coefficients of .50 for ratings on the husband's psychological suitability, .67 for the mother's suitability, and .57 for the prognosis of outcome. The highest of these coefficients referred to the topic about which there was the most information in the records.

The percentage distribution of the two sets of ratings showed that in 45 per cent of the cases the two sets of judges agreed completely both about the mother's suitability and about the prognosis for outcome. In almost all other cases they agreed within one step on the five-point scale. In only one out of 60 cases was there a two-step difference in their judgments about a mother's suitability for adoptive parenthood, while on prognosis they disagreed seven times by two or more steps.

These well-qualified social workers, then, were in rather close agreement with each other in judging the prospective adoptive homes. Yet most of their judgments did not agree with the ratings made at the time of the follow-up study by equally well-qualified social workers who shared the same orientation. Does this mean the adoption outcome cannot be foreseen? That social workers are not good prophets? That the ratings made at follow-up were incorrect? Or that the records did not give the needed information?

Unfortunately, the first three questions cannot be answered satisfactorily because of the obvious answer to the fourth. The character of the investigation records has been explained. A few additional points about them are relevant here, however. First is the fact that the social investigations were conducted for the purpose of ruling out poor homes rather than for choosing good ones. Accordingly, the records went into detail chiefly to document unfavorable conditions of the kind the Court would be likely to consider. They omitted the material required for making fine distinctions about the petitioners' adequacy as adoptive parents and about the general outlook for the homes.

Second, the agency raters probably accepted the investigators' descriptions and judgments more or less at face value, especially when the supporting information was slight. For one thing, they could hardly do otherwise. For another, they were probably inclined to accept other social workers' statements about clients as given.

Third, the ratings with which their predictions were compared referred to personality traits and interpersonal relations revealed in intensive interviews directed toward securing such information. In other words, the material from which they were predicting seldom jibed with the material to which their predictions were directed.

All three points suggest that one source of failure in prediction lay in the nature of the records on which the predictions were based. They are presented here, not to defend a low predictive score but to indicate how important it is that, in future studies, predictions and outcome ratings are based on full and comparable records.

REVIEW OF INFORMATION ABOUT D AND E HOMES

As a third check on the possibility of determining at the outset which homes would later prove to be unsuitable, the field director undertook to re-evaluate the information about the D and E homes in both the original records and those written by our interviewers. Her purpose was to find clues that might warrant more careful attention in social investigations for courts and in follow-up studies. The only information she secured was inferential. She could not "predict" because she already knew the outcomes and because, in addition, she paid chief attention to the D and E cases. Her review of the information was essentially a retrospective, clinical evaluation (in the medical tradition of case review of failures[1]) made in the hope of discovering what, if anything, was lacking in the social investigations that might have been supplied.

The limitations of the records of the social investigations for such a purpose have already been described. The records of the follow-up interviews also had limitations. In addition to those noted in previous chapters, two others should be mentioned.

First, no systematic attempt had been made in those interviews to discover how stable the marriages were at the time the petition for adoption was under consideration, or when family difficulties that were discovered began. The same was true of the parents' mental and physical health at the time of adoption. Occasionally the interviewers learned of significant facts that had not emerged in the Department's social investigation, but they made no systematic effort to reconstruct the situation at the time the adoption petition was filed.

Second, information on some topics that were covered regularly in the follow-up interview (for instance, why the couple wanted to adopt a child, how they obtained a child, and how they felt about him at first) may have been biased by the passage of time and the influence of subsequent events. To some extent, such information could be checked against the record of the

---

[1] As an example of this kind of study, see Kris, Marianne, "The Use of Prediction in a Longitudinal Study," *Psychoanalytic Study of the Child*, International Universities Press, New York, 1957, vol. 12, pp. 175–189.

original investigation and could be regarded either as an elaboration or a check on it.

How much can be told in advance about an adoptive home is a question especially important in connection with the D and E homes. As a check against the findings regarding these cases, a brief review of the pre-adoption situation in a random sample of 66 A homes was undertaken. In this review, attention was focused chiefly on the marital situation, since at follow-up this factor correlated as well with adjustment as did the overall home rating.[1]

Without going into detail about the findings in this sample of A homes, we can summarize by saying that all evidence—both in the records of the social investigations and in the retrospective material from the follow-up records—pointed to the deep satisfaction of these couples in marriage and to their happiness in each other's company.

As to the homes rated D or E at follow-up, a good deal of evidence in the records suggested that home conditions at adoption were at best dubious in many of these cases, and that in other cases important clues that might have revealed future home difficulties were either not recognized or not pursued.

We are not presuming to say that the Welfare Department should have advised against these adoptions or that the Court would or should have denied the petitions if the evidence of their unsuitability had been presented. Even though it disapproved an adoption, the Court at that time did not have the power to remove the child from the home. Moreover, public sentiment might not have supported the Court in denying adoption petitions on other than the most flagrant grounds. In suggesting that, in many of these homes, clues to later difficulties probably existed and could have been detected, we are indicating how such judgments might be arrived at and not what use should be made of them under the present law.

Gross Social Pathology

Among the various reasons given for rating homes D or E were several that might have existed at the time the child was

---

[1] See Chapter XII.

placed. These include alcoholism, extreme poverty or very poor living conditions, severe physical illness, marital friction, and emotional disorder.

As usual, the overt characteristics are the easiest to determine. The records of the follow-up interviews showed that 12 of the 14 homes in which living conditions were very poor were similarly handicapped at the time the child was placed. Of 16 adoptive parents found at follow-up to be alcoholic, 13 drank to excess at the time of placement; of 12 adoptive parents who died before the study was made, 4 were already ill at the time of adoption and 4 others died of illness so soon after adoption as to suggest that their ill health could have been detected when the petition was investigated.

Nineteen homes were classified D or E partly because the adopted children were seriously neglected or abused. Nine of these were among those in which one parent was alcoholic and four others were among those in which outright poverty or very bad living conditions were found at the time of the original investigation.

Marriage Disrupted, Discordant, Distorted, or Nonexistent

Less tangible elements of trouble also seem to have been present at the time of placement in at least some of the homes later classified D or E. One of these is a marriage disrupted, discordant, distorted, or nonexistent—a description that covers all but three of the D and E homes at the time of the follow-up study. Eliminating the three homes in which there had never been a father, the 12—mentioned above—in which the marriage was broken by death, and 19 in which information was rather scanty, we shall concentrate on the 35 cases of divorce and the 22 cases of severe marital discord, and consider whether these couples were having marital difficulties at the time the children were adopted.

Divorce. The records suggest that marital difficulties probably existed in a considerable proportion of the 35 cases in which divorce later occurred. At least 15 couples were having marital problems at the time the adoption petition was investigated, though frequently this fact did not come to light until the follow-up interview. In 13 cases both husband and wife had been divorced previously, and in five others one spouse had been divorced twice before the current marriage. We have seen that the fact that one or both marital partners had previously been divorced did not in itself show a significant relation to the overall home rating, but that a history of "double divorce" was associated with a greater likelihood of subsequent divorce. Accordingly, such evidence is a signal that the marital relationship should be studied with special care.

Of the 23 couples who had some history of divorce, over half had been married so short a time when they took the children for adoption that it would have been difficult to assess the stability of the marriage. At the extreme were a couple who had been married only six months and one whose marriage took place during the course of the social investigation.

In most of the 35 homes disrupted by divorce, other problems existed. Eighteen of them are among those referred to earlier, where there were problems of alcoholism, poverty, or seriously deprived living conditions. In five other cases either the original investigation or the follow-up interview revealed serious personality difficulties dating back at least to the time of the adoption, or else very peculiar reasons for wanting to adopt a child.

> One couple suddenly decided to take a child when they were well along in middle age. The investigator thought the mother seemed very ill at ease in handling the baby and overprecise in planning for his future. The mother said she would not tell the child he was adopted until he was ten years old and that she would then send him to a military school. She added that since she was not on friendly terms with any of her neighbors, she was not worried that the boy would discover his adoptive status.

> Another couple had had the child in their home from the time they were married. During the follow-up interview the mother said she had married the adoptive father out of anger at her first husband's leaving her. She disliked the second husband at the time they adopted the child. She divorced him before the child was a year old.

Severe Marital Discord or Dissatisfaction. The follow-up investigation showed 22 homes in which there was much marital discord or dissatisfaction. Review of the records suggested that in some instances this condition existed at the time of adoption and might have been suspected if the interviewer had been free to explore certain clues and trained to do so.

A husband and wife had both been divorced twice before the current marriage. During the investigation they explained that they could not have children of their own and loved children. This was accepted as sufficient reason for wanting to adopt one. Their statements about their own compatibility and their explanations of why the four previous marriages had failed were also accepted at face value. In the follow-up interview, however, it was learned that the wife had thought adopting a child would solve her marital problems. She said it had helped, but it seemed to the interviewer that she belittled her husband and disliked the child.

In nine such cases in this group, the husband, wife, or both had been divorced previously. Explorations of the previous marital experiences, the reasons for the divorce, the new marriage as compared with the other, and the reasons for wanting to adopt a child might have led to information that would have permitted better assessment of the current situation and of the adoption prospect.

Such study seemed especially needed when, as was the case with several of these couples, the current marriage was very recent.

One couple were still in their twenties and had been married only a year when they petitioned for adoption. The husband was in military service when the wife took the child into their home, and they had lived together only briefly when the adoption decree was granted. In the follow-up interview the wife said that she and her husband had been quarreling ever since he left the Navy. He drinks heavily, she added, and dislikes and mistreats the child.

Another couple, both previously divorced, had been married only six months when they applied to adopt a child they had happened upon while traveling. In the follow-up interview this wife complained bitterly of her lack of gratification in marriage and her dissatisfaction with the adopted child. When she was asked for suggestions for prospective adoptive parents, she said she would advise against adopting a child too soon after marriage.

Another clue was given in four cases by the fact that the couple's reasons for wanting to adopt a child were unusual and held implications for the state of their marriage.

One wife told the investigator that she needed a child because her son was grown up and was no longer a companion to her. She added that she would see that the adopted child did not develop so many outside interests and grow away from her as her own child had done. This was an adoption that was considered dubious by the Department of Welfare, partly because of the mother's dominating character, as shown in the marriage and toward her children. The follow-up study showed the child greatly rejected by his adoptive parents and the marriage clearly one without satisfaction to the couple.

In another case, the wife, married thirteen years, took a child for adoption because she thought her husband, shortly returned from military service, needed something to take him out of himself. This woman told the follow-up worker that she had never been interested in children and had little to do with her husband.

Another clue was evidenced in several cases by the investigator's observation that the wife was "nervous" or "peculiar" and that the baby had been taken on a doctor's advice in order to restore the wife's emotional balance. The investigators apparently did not learn of marital disharmony in these families, but on follow-up the wives reported that things had never gone well between them and their husbands.

Of the total 22 D and E homes in which severe marital discord or dissatisfaction was found when the follow-up study was made, there were only six in which the original records provided no clues of these sorts. In the other 16 it was learned that marital conflict and unhappiness dated back at least to the time of the adoption. Apparently in these cases marital disharmony was not something that developed after the adoption took place but, rather, was present and perhaps could have been discovered when the petition was investigated.

Marriage Distorted to Meet Parents' Emotional Needs.   Thirty-two additional couples in D or E homes were found on follow-up to have marriages that have been described as "skewed" to fit the personality needs of one or both of the marital partners. In these cases the major clue to the existence of marital peculiarities lay in the personality makeup of the individuals. Previous divorces were much less frequent than in the preceding groups, only 9 out of the 32 couples having had that experience. Motives for adoption were frequently said to be the mother's nervousness or her grief over the loss of a child.

In view of the mandate behind the original investigations it was not surprising to find that these skews in marriage were seldom detected. What was noted, however, in some case records was that the wife (or sometimes the husband) was nervous, had had a nervous breakdown, was very emotional, or was somewhat peculiar. Perhaps this observation could have led into discussion of domestic arrangements, and this, in turn, might have revealed the distortion of the marriage that was learned about at the time of the follow-up study. Then, too, in the nine instances of divorce, discussion of the previous marriage and the reasons for dissatisfaction with it might have brought to light what was hoped for in marriage and to what extent the present marital relations were meeting those hopes.

> The most striking among these nine cases was one in which the mother had left her own child with her husband's relatives when she married a second time. She and her new husband then took three children from an institution, largely, it appeared, in an effort to relieve the wife's nervousness and restless feelings. This husband was an emotionally disturbed individual, as indicated by his rejection by the Army on the basis of neurosis.

As the example just given suggests, personality rather than the marital situation probably afforded the clearest evidence of the home's possible unsuitability at the time the social investigation was made.

Mother's Mental Health Impaired

In all the homes rated D or E the mental health of the mother was judged to be impaired at the time of the follow-up study. The reported impairment ranged from that classified "capacity for adult functioning limited but some ability to give and receive affection" to "very disturbed, psychotic-like behavior or extreme eccentricity" (Category 5). Forty-one mothers were classified as belonging in the first category and 11 in the last. The remaining were classified as "severely impaired capacity for personal relationships."[1]

Neither the early record of the social investigation nor the follow-up study shed much light on the state of the adoptive mother's mental health at the time of placement. It seems a fairly safe assumption, however, that extreme personality trends do not develop suddenly, and that ten years earlier many of these women were much the same in personality as they were when interviewed for the study. Information supporting this assumption was found in some of the records of the original investigation, especially in those involving the eleven most disturbed mothers. Even here, however, the clues to the mothers' mental state were likely to be ambiguous or slight. Whether this resulted from the character of the investigation or whether it indicated that the emotional disturbances were less severe at that time cannot be determined.

Several women classified at follow-up as severely disturbed made remarks in the course of the original social investigation, that in retrospect—and with the advantage of hindsight— seemed to suggest serious emotional disorders. One of them, it was later learned, was under psychiatric treatment at the time and was finally committed to a mental hospital. Three others had a nervous breakdown or some sort of hysterical disorder before or very shortly after the adoption became final. For the most part, however, evidence in the early records was more elusive or nonexistent. One woman who later seemed close to psychotic was described as unusually quiet. But, on the whole, such comments as were made did not point directly to impaired mental health.

Some pertinent information about the mother's mental health at the time of the adoption was noted in the original investigation or learned at follow-up in a fourth of the cases classified as "severely impaired capacity for personal relationships." Some of these women were described by the Department's investigators as highly nervous, very tense, or wanting a child for reasons suggestive of possible emotional problems, such as "loneliness" or "something to live for." In other cases emotional instability was evidenced by excessive drinking on the mother's part—usually learned about only in the follow-up visit. Another fact, more

---

[1] See pp. 206–211 for explanation of categories.

often learned at that time than before the adoption was completed, was that in a few cases adoption was sought in order to improve the mother's mental health.

For the least disturbed mothers, the evidence from the original records was even less impressive.[1] A few were described in terms that suggested a nervous personality or immaturity and dependency. For the most part, however, there was nothing in the records to indicate that these women were different from most.

Prognostic Clues

To come back, then, to the overall question under scrutiny: In how many of these D and E homes were conditions detectably unfavorable or detectably inauspicious at the time the petition was filed? From the details just given, it is clear that this question cannot be answered with precision. Yet a review of the evidence just described indicates a considerable number of cases in which information suggestive of poor home conditions came to light.

To estimate the proportion, a count was made in which no attention was paid to such inconclusive clues as previous divorces or very brief marriages. Nor was weight given to the psychiatric generalization that most individuals who exhibit emotional or character disorders in middle age probably had such disabilities earlier in their lives. All that counted were statements in the records of the original investigations or the follow-up interviews that at least one of the following conditions existed at the time the adoption was granted: poverty or very poor living conditions, alcoholism, severe physical illness, marital friction, or emotional disorder.

Such a count yielded evidence of at least one of these conditions in 60 per cent of the homes later classified D or E. In 12 homes the income was very low or the living conditions quite unfavorable. In 13 either father or mother was said to have drunk to excess. The marriages of 31 couples were said to have been highly unsatisfactory, resulting in many cases in divorce later. Thirty-three mothers were emotionally maladjusted, as evidenced by extreme nervousness, nervous breakdowns, being under the care

[1] Since the original classification of mothers according to these mental health categories had been based on the follow-up interviews, without reference to the early investigation records, it was reassuring to find a consistent decrease in each successive category in the proportion of mothers evoking comment related to possible personality impairment.

of a psychiatrist, or the like. Some homes had more than one of these adverse characteristics but 76 out of the total 126 were reported to have had at least one of them.[1]

Whether the other D and E homes were similarly handicapped at the time of adoption could not be determined. It seems quite certain, however, that poverty and poor living conditions were not a factor in them, for on this point the original records were quite explicit. On the other hand, it is fairly likely that some of the personality disorders that interfered with later parent-child relations were present, in incipient form at least, at the time the social investigation for the court was made. There were some homes, of course (though they appeared to be few in number), in which the unfavorable home condition found at follow-up was attributable to later events. This was particularly true of the five, noted in Chapter IX, in which the adoptive mother died. It is also possible that in a few cases the conditions that led to alcoholism, divorce, or marital discord developed after the adoption became final. For the most part, however, it seems unlikely that ten years earlier the adoptive parents were very different in personality makeup and capacity for mature interpersonal relations from what they appeared to be when the follow-up study was made.

A great deal of the information reported here was not learned by the original investigators and became known only at the time of the follow-up study. It is reasonable to assume that a great deal of pertinent information eludes any investigation, however thorough and prolonged. Nevertheless, it is very difficult—at least for a social caseworker—to doubt that a moderately intensive investigation by well-trained professional workers could have revealed a good deal of what became known only later.

---

[1] In Chapter II it was reported that a professionally trained social worker with recent experience in a private adoption agency had estimated that from 80 to 90 per cent of the petitions she investigated for the Florida Department of Public Welfare were acceptable by social-agency standards. The investigation was made by one Department staff member, in one section of the state, and for the most part involved families not in the present study; nor was any effort made to systematize and record the criteria used in the earlier assessment. Nevertheless, it is interesting to compare these two estimates. To say that 10 to 20 per cent of the total caseload would have been rejected by a social agency is not radically different from saying that 60 per cent of the D and E homes might have been recognized at the time of adoption as inauspicious for a child—even though it may be assumed that a certain proportion of future D and E homes would have gone unrecognized and a certain proportion of future A and B homes would have been ruled out by error.

CHAPTER XIV

In Conclusion

Adoption laws assume that it is important for children to get into good adoptive homes—homes that will maximize their chance to develop their full potential. To secure such homes for children is, in fact, the purpose of adoption in the United States, as testified to by numerous judicial decisions. As one judge put it in his decision relating to a disputed adoption case: "The ultimate purpose of adoption statutes is the welfare of the child, and the wishes and wants of the natural parents and also the proposed adoptive parents can be considered only as secondary to that purpose."[1]

The general purpose of this study has been to discover the extent to which the purpose of the adoption law was realized in independent adoptions in which the suitability of the petitioners' home was determined by the Court after a social investigation had been conducted by the State Welfare Department, and after the child had been in the home for some time. The inquiry was made in one state, and with respect to a time when the provisions for social investigation of the adoptive home, the natural parents, and the child—provisions designed to provide protections for all three—were carried out minimally. This very fact permitted us to find out what happens when most adoption petitions are granted, and thus suggests a basis for deciding whether more control would be needed in order to reduce the proportion of unfavorable outcomes—and if so, what kind.

---

[1] McKensie *et al.*, App. 275, s.w. 2d, 365.

In carrying out the general purpose, this study sought to answer a number of specific questions. The first was: What proportion of these independent adoption placements seemed to be working out well, and what proportion not well, in terms of the primary objective of adoption laws? Part of the answer lies in the extent to which the adoptive homes offered the children a chance to fulfill their capacities for development and well-being. This, in turn, was judged by looking both at the homes and at the children. What proportion of the homes showed the characteristics currently believed to support and enhance a child's capacity for happy development? How well were the children doing? Did being in "good" homes significantly favor the children's development and well-being?

THE HOMES

It is necessary to give special attention to the adoptive home, not only because of the weight ascribed to it by theories of child development but also because when an infant is placed—and most of the adoptive children were infant placements—a good deal more can be learned about the home than about the child.

According to the measures used, almost half of the homes studied (46 per cent) appeared to offer the child a "favorable"[1] setting, about one-third (30 per cent) appeared definitely unfavorable, and about one-fourth (24 per cent) lay in between, with something approaching a balance between favorable and unfavorable. Putting it differently, the study found that over two-thirds of the homes (70 per cent) were rated as ranging from fair to excellent. Generalized to the population represented by the sample, this means that between 25 per cent and 35 per cent of the homes would be rated poor and between 41 per cent and 50 per cent good to excellent.

Whether this result is cheering or distressing depends on whether one emphasizes the fact that more than two out of three of the homes appear at least passable, and nearly one out of two definitely good; or the fact that almost one out of three appears definitely unsatisfactory.

---

[1] As defined in this study. See Chapters VI and VII.

Probably few if any citizens would be willing to settle for an unsatisfactory home for one out of three children placed, without efforts to reduce that proportion. On the other hand, this proportion is perhaps lower than would be expected by those most troubled about the outcomes of independent placements. It would appear, then, that the overall picture of the homes is not as bad as some had feared, but not as good as those concerned about children think it could and should be.[1]

It should be added that the "worst" homes in our sample were doubtless not the worst homes in the state. While a few of the homes studied showed extreme examples of characteristics that almost everyone would view as likely to harm a child, for the most part the range from poor to excellent begins well above the very lowest level of homes for children. In this respect, our findings show considerable improvement over the studies that were made when the agitation for social investigation was at its height.[2] The change is probably due more to the general rise in individual incomes and to changes in the reasons for, and assumptions about, adoption than to social investigation *per se*.

THE CHILDREN

Did being in the homes we rated poor affect the children adversely? To answer this question we had to assess that elusive, sprawling cluster of elements known as "adjustment." Fallible as our measures may be, they are at least the same for the adopted children in the sample and the control group of "own" children. And they indicate that the adopted children were getting along nearly as well as their controls.

Taken as a whole, the adopted children showed no significant difference from the control group with regard to I.Q. or school achievement. According to these measures, they were equally

---

[1] The proportion of homes with definitely favorable ratings (A or B) is lower than that prevailing among follow-up studies conducted by or for adoption agencies. Typically, such studies use a smaller sample and methods not strictly comparable. Accordingly, figures derived from them furnish hints rather than solid facts about the comparative results of agency and independent placements. Our hope is that larger studies, using comparable methods and extra-agency staff, will be conducted in order to provide a more dependable base for comparison. Our immediate purpose, however, is not comparison but a picture of the outcomes of these independent adoption placements.

[2] See Chapter I.

bright. On the measures of adjustment, however, they were slightly below the control group—and the differences, though small, were statistically significant. When the adjustment measures were combined to produce overall adjustment ratings, the same slight difference in favor of the control group appeared.

The picture changed, however, when the children placed at later than one month of age (25 per cent of the sample) were removed from the group, along with their nonadoptive controls. When this was done, only one of the differences between the adopted and the control children remained statistically significant. The one exception was a slight indication that the adopted children may have been more "aggressive" than the natural children.

It may be argued—and sometimes is—that adoption should improve upon nature in the chance it gives a child for development. If this is true, and feasible, then the comparison just reported leaves much to be desired. On the other hand, there are at least suspicions that the fact of being adopted—a fact known to 90 per cent of our children—imposes problems that may tend to interfere with emotional adjustment. True, these problems are currently believed to become apparent when the children are a little older than most of our sample.[1] Yet, pending other evidence, it is necessary to recognize the possibility that adoptive status in itself may be a disadvantage.

Regardless of these points, however, the study indicated that the kinds of homes rated good were more likely than those rated poor to produce "well-adjusted" children. Children placed in homes rated A or B had a seven to one chance of a favorable adjustment rating, while children placed in homes rated D or E had less than an even chance. As to seriously maladjusted children, only four children out of the 292 in A, B, or C homes were given such an overall rating according to Combination V, as compared with 27 of the 119 children in D or E homes; that is, about one per cent as compared with 23 per cent.

Since such evidence as we have indicates that one kind of home gives a child a much better chance of being well adjusted, it

---

[1] The majority of the children were under twelve years of age when the study was made. This means that most of them still had to meet the hazards of adolescence and (according to current assumptions) the full impact of adoption.

would seem worth a good deal of effort to give him the better chance. Since another kind of home gives him a much smaller chance of being well adjusted, it seems well worth trying to avoid that kind.

An unexpected corollary of these findings was that the quality of the home seemed to be especially important for children who were or had been disadvantaged. Children who were adopted when they were two or older, those who had had adverse experiences before being adopted, those who were or had been ill or who had a serious injury or defect were even more likely than usual to be well adjusted in an A or B home and poorly adjusted in a D or E one.

The correlation between home and adjustment ratings was not as high as might have been expected, however, being .45 for the children as a whole. It may be that the range of homes in each of the rating categories somewhat depressed the correlation coefficient. Possible defects in the measures used is another explanation. Even so, the small size of the correlation suggests that the development of adopted children has considerable independence of the home situation. Whatever independence there is, however, is more marked when the home is poor than when it is good.

THE ADOPTION OUTCOME

An estimate of the proportions of favorable and unfavorable adoption outcomes should include both the home environment and the way the child seems to be faring in it. Accordingly, the information obtained about each child through the home and through the school was pooled in order to classify the "outcome" to date as reasonably satisfactory or definitely unsatisfactory. By this rough estimate, almost two-thirds of the outcomes could be called reasonably satisfactory, and an additional 10 per cent could not be classified as definitely unsatisfactory. According to the measures used in the study, between one-fifth and one-fourth were definitely unsatisfactory. Thus, whether one views the homes alone, the children's adjustment alone, or a combination of the two, in this sample at least two out of three were judged fair to excellent, and at least one out of four definitely unsatisfactory, according to current ideas of what a child should have in his home environment and what evidence of adequate development he should show. These figures are, of course, approximate. Viewing the different estimates separately and together, however, we can say that a considerable majority were working out well and a substantial minority were not.

The adoptive parents' assessment of the adoption outcome was far more positive than the ratings made by uninvolved outsiders. The overwhelming majority of the parents (85 per cent) expressed unqualified satisfaction, even when allowance is made for those who expressed satisfaction but were rated by the interviewers as having mixed feelings. Relatively few indicated, through the advice they offered to prospective parents, that if they had it to do over again they would want to proceed differently.

The opinion of the parents, then, would certainly not reduce our estimate of the proportion of satisfactory outcomes. Probably it should not raise the estimate either, since some of the best-pleased parents had children who were not doing well and provided homes that clearly failed to offer the children a favorable setting for fulfilling their potential. In such cases, the blindness of the parents to existing deficiencies or problems was one of the difficulties. For practical purposes, then, the assessment of outside observers seems more reliable than the verdict of the parents, even though parents' attitudes are so overwhelming a part of adoption outcome.

The results reported here were obtained under a system in which the investigator was not given responsibility for finding the best possible homes—as placement agencies attempt to do—but only for keeping children out of definitely unfavorable homes; and in which the Court's decision was often made after the child had been in the home long enough for strong bonds to form between him and the adoptive parents. Under such circumstances it may often seem that the effects of removing a child from a questionable home to which he had become accustomed and attached could prove more destructive than the defects of the home itself. This kind of concern was often expressed by the agency caseworkers who rated some of the follow-up records. Many who would not have placed a child in a particular home if they could have prevented it still said that, since he had been there for a substantial period, they would hesitate to remove him.

If the proportion of unfavorable homes seems high, then, and if steps are to be taken to reduce it, early investigation of homes must be one objective of those steps. This point can be considered more fruitfully after some comments on another main aspect of our study.

FACTORS RELATED TO FAVORABLE OR UNFAVORABLE OUTCOMES

As we have seen, the chief aim of adoption law in the United States, as of the professional people concerned with adoption and of the public at large, is the welfare of the child who is to be adopted. But this concern can become effective only if guides are available for making decisions that will promote the child's welfare. Many opinions and assumptions are current regarding what those guides should be, but so far they have been little tested by systematic investigation.

Accordingly, in addition to inquiring how these independent adoption placements were working out, the study attempted to discover: (a) what factors are related to favorable or unfavorable adoption outcomes, and (b) to what extent such factors can be known at the time of placement.

Some information relating to these two questions has been reviewed in the previous chapters. At this point we will merely comment on some implications of those findings as we interpret them—comments with which the reader will agree or disagree according to his own interpretation of the data that have been presented.

Characteristics of the Child

Age at Placement. Other things being equal, adoption outcomes appeared slightly more favorable for children who were placed early than for the others. Even when allowance was made for such secondary factors as could be controlled, a slight but statistically significant relationship remained between the age at which the child was placed and the way his adoption seemed to be working out approximately ten years later.

There is some question whether the relation would survive effective control of all relevant factors. Moreover, there is a vast difference between a statistically significant relationship and an invariable or overriding relationship. This simple and obvious fact is worth repeating because it is so often slighted when study findings are interpreted. The slight and still uncertain association between age at placement and adoption outcome, for example, may mean that—other things being equal—the outcome prospects are slightly more promising if the child is placed before he is a month old. The fact that the association is relatively low, however, also means that other more important factors, favorable or unfavorable, are operating simultaneously and could either reinforce or nullify the effect of this one.

It is desirable, and necessary, to know where the probabilities lie in connection with the many factors that influence adoption outcome. It is, moreover, incumbent upon those responsible for, or personally involved in, the granting of adoption petitions to take cognizance of these probabilities. But it is equally necessary to recognize the multiplicity of factors involved and the need to be both flexible and realistic in appraising the chances for successful outcome in a particular placement.

The qualified nature of our conclusions is only in part the result of ambiguities or defects in our measures. It is partly the result of qualities in human beings that defy absolute assessment, for example, the constitutional factors in an infant that may interact with his environment to produce a happy outcome from a home situation that looks discouraging, or an unhappy one from a situation that seems highly promising. We are equally obligated to recognize the existence of unpredictables, on the one hand, and on the other hand to maximize for each child whatever safeguards are indicated by more or less predictable relationships.

In connection with the child's age at placement, these comments add up to the conclusion that the present trend toward earlier placements is desirable. At the same time, our findings by no means demonstrate that placements of "older" children are likely to lead to unfavorable outcome. On the contrary, to the extent that we can generalize from our very limited data on older placements, the "older" children who found favorable homes had a good chance for successful adoption outcomes.

The tentativeness of this statement arises from the fact that most of the children who were at least two years old when they were placed found homes that were unfavorable, according to the study criteria. Only six of the 26 children placed at two or older were in homes rated A or B, and four of these were well adjusted, according to the study measures—which were independent of the home ratings. On the other hand, all but one of the 16 children in homes rated D or E were below average according to these adjustment measures. Clearly we need more information about the extent to which a favorable home can counteract unfavorable pre-placement factors.

Pre-placement History. In our findings, the effects of age at placement could not be separated entirely from the effects of physical or psychological misfortunes before placement, since many of the children placed after the age of two had lived under physically or psychologically hazardous conditions before they were placed. They represented about two-fifths of the children with this sort of pre-placement history. Moreover, the painful experiences of the older children were, almost by definition, of longer duration and greater intensity than those of the younger, and were likely to include a larger psychological component. It is especially striking, therefore, to find that a traumatic pre-placement history did not in itself appear to impair the future adjustment of the children. Nevertheless, as a group, the children with unfortunate pre-placement histories were less likely than the others to be well adjusted, largely because they were more likely to get into unfavorable homes. Although the figures are small, they suggest that the quality of the home may have a stronger effect on the ultimate adjustment of traumatized children than on the others.

The implications are both cheering and challenging. It appears that an unfortunate history, in itself, need not jeopardize a child's later adjustment—*if* he finds a particularly good home. This is cheering because, as already indicated, probably the majority of children two or older who are placed in adoption have had painful experiences to cope with. The study findings on age at placement and on pre-placement trauma, taken together, hold out hope for these children. They also hold out a challenge to those responsible for placing them, for while a "good" home is important for every child it may be even more important for these children. Further investigation of this point will be needed before it is more than a challenging possibility.

Our data imply, then, that study of child and home *before* placement is especially desirable with children beyond the age of twenty-three months. By this time it is possible to learn a good deal more about a child and his probable needs than one can about an infant. Adoptive parents can be informed about the child's current development and can have an opportunity to discuss what his developmental prospects are and how best to help him achieve his potential. Even though no absolute prediction can be made, the probabilities can be assessed. Perhaps even more important, parent and child can be given help toward achieving the best possible adoption outcome for them. Part of this help may be in alerting the parents to the child's difficulties in adjusting to a new home. Some of the parents of older children seemed not to realize that the child needed special support in this; rather, they assumed that for him the change spelled merely a sudden, wonderful chance to live happily ever after. This kind of assumption was associated with the general lack of sensitivity, awareness, and readiness to see the child as an individual in his own right that accounted for many of the unfavorable home ratings.

Health Status. Our data do not suggest that the risk of receiving a handicapped child is, in itself, a major argument against independent adoptions. For the most part, the adoptive parents who received a child with some health disability or disorder knew about it if it could be known. And if it could not be known at placement, it was likely to become apparent only after the age at which most adopted children are placed.[1]

It is true that, when handicaps did develop, they were somewhat more likely to appear in children who had been ill or in poor physical condition at placement than in the others. Nevertheless, the great majority of these children did not have handicaps at the time of the study.

---

[1] In 1960, 79 per cent of all children adopted by nonrelatives were less than a year old when placed, and 71 per cent were less than six months old. Children's Bureau, *Statistical Series 66, Child Welfare Statistics—1961*. Washington, 1962.

The quality of the home may be especially important for a disadvantaged child. Thus, the advantage of early and expert investigation lies, not in the probability of earlier detection of handicaps, but rather in the possibility that more adequate social investigation will ensure better homes and will help the adoptive parents recognize and cope with the special needs of children who have physical or intellectual difficulties.

Family Background. Little systematic information was available about the natural families of the adopted children. The one item that proved feasible for analysis was the education of the natural mother. The meaning of the relationships found was ambiguous, however. The better-educated natural mothers were likely to place their children through a professional person rather than directly. The better-educated (and more prosperous) adoptive parents were also likely to use a professional intermediary rather than to obtain a child directly from the natural parents. Accordingly, by a process of natural selection, the children of better-educated mothers were somewhat more likely than children of poorly educated mothers to be placed in homes of higher socio-economic status.

This leaves a question about the meaning of the fact that children of better-educated mothers were likely to do a little better at school than those whose mothers were less well educated. It is a familiar finding that children of privileged homes are likely to do better in school work than children of intellectually and socially deprived homes. At the same time, there is some evidence that children of better-educated natural parents may be brighter than children whose parents have little education.[1] Our data do show a slight but definite advantage for children of better-educated natural mothers; but they do not tell whether this advantage derives from their intellectual inheritance or from the selective factors that helped them find more favorable homes.

Future Unknown. All in all, a child adopted in early infancy is pretty much an unknown quantity in the present state of our knowledge. Except for obvious handicaps, his future physical and intellectual development are largely unpredictable and may be influenced greatly by the kind of home he finds. Few infants are

---

[1] Honzik, Marjorie P., "Developmental Studies of Parent-Child Resemblance in Intelligence," *Child Development*, vol. 28, June, 1957, pp. 215–228.

likely to develop severe physical or intellectual handicaps, and the majority of the handicaps that will develop probably cannot be detected until the child is past the optimum age for adoption. On the other hand, the majority of infants who are ill or in pitiable condition at the time of placement apparently have the capacity to respond to a favorable home environment and attain full health and gratifying development.

The advantages associated with, if not caused by, early placement have been noted. It has also been noted, however, that even for children past infancy our limited data suggest a hopeful outlook—provided they find the kind of home that will give them an opportunity to develop their full potential. The limitations that qualify this statement are of two kinds. First, very few children in our sample were over two and none was over six at placement. Second, the children who were two years old were likely to find unfavorable homes and to enter them only after prolonged painful experiences. There is a clear and present need for systematic investigation of adoption outcomes for older children, in studies not subject to the limitations of this one. At the same time, this study—like a number of others—does hold out hope that a good adoptive home can often counteract the effects of painful deprivation and trauma in early childhood.[1]

In another way also it underwrites a widespread conviction that a child need not be deprived of a home because he is over two, because he has had painful experiences, or even because he suffers some physical or intellectual handicap. Many of the parents who received a handicapped child were able to give him full acceptance and were ready to make great efforts in his behalf.

Characteristics of the Adoptive Parents and Homes

Since the majority of adopted children are placed in infancy, much less can be learned about them than about their adoptive parents at the time of placement. Accordingly, efforts to improve

---

[1] See, for example: Bowlby, John, Mary Ainsworth, Mary Boston, and Dina Rosenbluth, "The Effects of Mother-Child Separation: A Follow-up Study," *British Journal of Medical Psychology*, vol. 29, parts 3 and 4, 1956, pp. 211–244; Lewis, Hilda, *Deprived Children*, Oxford University Press, London, 1954; Rheingold, Harriet L., and Nancy Bayley, "The Later Effects of an Experimental Modification of Mothering," *Child Development*, vol. 30, 1959, pp. 363–372.

adoption outcomes must depend more on assessments of adoptive applicants than those of the children they wish to adopt.

Unfortunately, most of the overt characteristics of the adoptive applicants (which are the easiest to determine and on which independent observers are most likely to agree) gave little indication of the kind of home afforded the children in later years. While a number of these overt indicators showed statistically significant associations with adoption outcome, their influence was usually either indirect or else too slight to counteract the force of other, less tangible factors.

Marital History. Take, for example, the divorce history of the would-be adoptive couple. The study found that if both wife and husband had been divorced previously, they were more likely to separate again than if neither, or only one, had been divorced. However, if they did not separate, the prospects for the adoption outcome were not different from those for families in which there had been no divorce. And three-quarters of the "double-divorce" couples did remain together. If only one of the adoptive applicants had been divorced before the present marriage, the probability of later separation was approximately the same as for the "no-divorce" couples.

For practical purposes, this means that if both members have been divorced previously, one should have confidence in the present marriage before recommending that the adoption petition be granted. If there is confidence in the stability of this marriage there is scant basis for ruling out adoptive applicants solely because both husband and wife have been divorced. The divorce of one member would not in itself be a reason for special misgivings about the adoption outcome.

Parents' Age at Placement. Our data, on the whole, suggest only indirect relations between the parents' age and various measures of adoption outcome. Home ratings were likely to be a bit lower than average when the parents were above the average in age, and analysis indicates that this was not because age was used as a criterion in rating the homes. Analysis also indicates, however, that the age-related difference in home ratings probably springs from age-related characteristics of the older parents in this sample rather than from the age *per se*. Moreover, we found no relation between the child's overall adjustment and the parents' age. Our evidence, then, suggests no basis for concluding that the prognosis is necessarily poor if the adoptive mother is in her forties or the adoptive father in his early fifties.

Socioeconomic Status. The general social and economic status of adoptive applicants can be determined at the time they file an adoption petition. The future income of the family cannot be known, but other studies have found that the most significant index of socioeconomic status is education, which is not likely to change substantially after a couple have come to the point in their life cycle where they are ready to file an adoption petition.[1]

In our study, the socioeconomic factors show a slight but significant relation to home ratings, partly because extreme poverty was used as a criterion in rating the homes. The majority of the sample families were in a relatively modest income bracket, so that this relationship merely reflects the generally accepted view that to live in severely deprived economic circumstances is a detriment to a child's well-being. It does not imply that a child is necessarily better off in a wealthy home than in one that is economically stable but far from prosperous. On the contrary, some of the A and B homes were headed by fathers in working-class occupations.

There is no evidence in the findings that a child's overall adjustment is conditioned by his adoptive father's education, occupation or income, or by the fact that his mother continued working after he was placed.

The school performance of these children, like that of others who have been studied, does seem to be affected by the educational attainments of their parents. This relationship has become familiar to those acquainted with the literature on the subject. Children in homes where parents are highly educated bring to school an academic equipment superior to that of children whose parents have little education. They are familiar with books and ideas. More important, they are more likely than other children to have assimilated values that would motivate them to greater interest in school work and a higher evaluation of books and

---

[1] For our indicators of socioeconomic factors, we have used education, father's occupation, and neighborhood of residence.

ideas. Some believe that their parents are more likely to stimu-late—or even push—them toward high achievement in school.[1]

Some also believe that, on the whole, children from educa-tionally privileged families are brighter children. Such a belief may receive some support from the slightly but significantly higher I.Q.'s of children from educationally privileged homes. In our sample, this relation is coupled with a relation between the education of the adoptive father and the education of the natural mother. That is, children of better-educated natural mothers tended to be placed in homes of better-educated fathers.

The correlations that support these statements are low but statistically significant. If school performance is a significant objective in child placement, then better-educated parents should have some preference—although a slight one, subject to other con-siderations, since the relationship itself is slight. However, most of those responsible for placing children put greater emphasis on psychological and emotional well-being. Excellent school perfor-mance is no guarantee of excellent adjustment, and very poor school performance may, or may not, reflect poor adjustment.

Provided the home is economically stable, then, and the in-come is enough to guard against severe deprivation, the socio-economic status of the adoptive applicants does not in itself appear to be a significant clue to the desirability of a home for an adoptive placement.

Religion. Another easily determined characteristic that has often caused concern is religious affiliation. There has been fear that children whose adoptive parents belong to different religious faiths may fare less well than others. The number of such "mixed marriages" in our sample was too small to yield reliable evidence. However, for the 33 families involved, neither home ratings nor the child's overall adjustment showed significant differences from those for families in which both parents were of the same faith. On this point, then, we can say merely that our evidence

---

[1] See, for example: Hollingshead, August B., *Elmtown's Youth*, John Wiley and Sons, New York, 1945; Toby, Jackson, "Orientation to Education as a Factor in the School Maladjustment of Low-Class Children," *Social Forces*, vol. 35, no. 3, 1957, pp. 259–266; Masland, Richard L., Seymour B. Sarason, and Thomas Gladwin, *Mental Subnormality: Biological, Psychological and Cultural Factors*, Basic Books, New York, 1958.

offers no basis for concern about the future well-being of an adoptive child whose parents are of different religious faiths, but that this evidence is too slight to be more than suggestive.

Other Children in the Home. Because some people feel that it may be a disadvantage to have both natural and adoptive children in the same family, the findings on this point are reassuring. Home ratings tended to be at least average and possibly higher than average when "own" children were born after the adopted child was placed or when other children were adopted later. This was not true when the parents had children of their own *before* adopting, probably for reasons relating to the motivation of the adoptive mothers—many of whom wanted a baby to fill the void caused when a child had grown up and left the family home. No differences in overall adjustment were associated with mixing natural and adoptive children.

Since adopted children apparently are at least as well off if siblings are later born into the family as if they are adopted, the child's welfare is not a reason for being concerned about the infertility of adoptive applicants. There may, of course, be psychological reasons for such concern, in connection with assessing the personality makeup and the marital relations of the adoptive applicants. There may also be reasons for concern about motivation if parents who already have grown children want to adopt an infant or a young child.

Psychological Characteristics. The overt traits just reviewed were less strongly related to the child's overall adjustment than were the psychological aspects of homes and parents that were rated in the study interview. The general climate of the home, the quality of the adoptive parents' marriage, the personality makeup of the mother, the quality of her and the father's relations with the adopted child are intangible and elusive. Each of the categories under which these characteristics were rated covered a considerable range. Nevertheless, the relations between these elusive variables and the children's overall adjustment, assessed independently, were stronger than the relations between overall adjustment and any of the overt characteristics that can be determined with greater accuracy. These relations have been referred to in preceding sections of this chapter.

The implication seems to be that the overt, easily recognized characteristics of would-be adoptive parents and their homes cannot be relied on heavily for determining whether these people could offer a child a good opportunity to develop to his full potential.[1] If the less tangible and more elusive characteristics could be determined with some certainty at the time of placement, they would form a better basis for decision. The question is, then, to what extent is this possible?

The quality of parent-child relations would have to be ruled out as a criterion except for those adoptive applicants who are already parents—and even here it would not necessarily predict the applicants' future relations with the child they want to adopt although it would certainly suggest something about their philosophy and practice with regard to child-rearing. The other aspects—home climate, marital relations, parents' personality— at least exist when the placement is considered and offer the possibility for study. How much reliance can one place on such study?

The answer depends partly on what is demanded. Within the independent adoption system the mandate to social investigators is not to differentiate between degrees of goodness in homes but rather to identify those homes that would be definitely unfavorable. The evidence on which definitely unfavorable home ratings were made, about ten years after placement, has been reviewed. In many instances it was evidence clearly manifest within one interview. Is it a reasonable speculation, then, that competent staff, empowered to assess the less overt home characteristics, could probably detect in two or three interviews, at or before placement, a considerable proportion of the homes that would be rated D and E about ten years later?

To this question our study gives answers that are uncertain and not wholly consistent. The few homes the Department wholly disapproved were rated C to E at follow-up. The homes about which the investigators expressed doubt or definite disapproval had mixed ratings ten years later. The prognoses made by case-workers in child-placing agencies, on the basis of those early

---

[1] For a divergent view of some of the methodological issues involved in this discussion, see Part II, Chapter XVI.

records, showed agreement with each other but were only slightly predictive of the later home ratings.

A review of the early records with an eye to determining clues to what the homes would be like ten years later, and made with knowledge of what the follow-up ratings were, pointed out that a large proportion of the "poor to rather poor" ratings were given on the basis of evidence that probably existed at the time of the early investigation; for example, marital discord, alcoholism, severe personality disturbance. In the kind of investigation made, this evidence either was not brought out or else was not considered likely to impress the Court. If the courts had been more responsive to the kind of evidence used in the later home ratings, would the investigators have secured more of it and presented it more emphatically? If the investigators had been trained social workers, would they have been more skillful at eliciting evidence (such as alcoholism or overt marital discord) that would have impressed even an "anti-psychological court"? Was it the lack of evidence, the lack of predictability, or a reluctance to seem biased against independent placements that made the highly trained raters in the seven adoption agencies give favorable prognoses for homes that later were rated as poor?

These are not precisely the questions that will be answered by follow-up studies of agency adoption, for in agency placements the focus is on ruling in the best homes rather than on ruling out the worst homes. Nevertheless, the outcome of agency placements should throw some light on the extent to which the adequacy of parental performance can be predicted. It is to be hoped that future studies that are undertaken will use methods that afford a base for comparison with our findings.

The Placement Process

The Risks of Independent Adoptions. A special aspect of the adoption outcome relates to the much publicized risks of independent placements: the risk of receiving a handicapped child and the risk of encountering problems with the natural parents. There were such outcomes but only in a small proportion of the cases.

Four per cent received children with some degree of physical or intellectual defect. The danger of receiving such a child is emphasized less than formerly in warnings against independent adoptions. The arguments for agency placements in recent years have emphasized the kind of parents the child receives, and the maximizing of their potentiality for "parenting," rather than the kind of child the parent receives. Our findings suggest that this trend is realistic.

Another much discussed risk of independent adoptions is the possibility of difficulties with the natural parents. Such difficulties did occur in 7 per cent of the sample and for the most part involved placements made directly by natural parents or grandparents. Some of the problems were acute and may have had lasting effects. On the other hand, almost none of them continued after the adoption became final, and most of the adoptive parents said they regarded them as problems of the past. It should be noted, moreover, that although most of the problems with natural parents arose when there had been contact between the natural and adoptive families, no such problems were reported for 84 per cent of the adoptions in which such contact occurred.

These are the findings. Whether the one-in-fourteen chance of such problems is large or small must be decided by prospective adoptive parents and also by the community. Trouble with the natural parents is one kind of problem very unlikely to occur in agency adoptions, or in independent adoptions where the identity of each set of parents is unknown to the other. Apparently it could be avoided, to a large extent, by eliminating contact or mutual knowledge of identity. The fact that such a problem occurs in a relatively small proportion of cases does not necessarily imply that taking steps to render that proportion negligible is not worth while.

In support of preventing contact between the two sets of parents, one is tempted to add that—despite a few rare exceptions—such contact on the whole was obviously no advantage either to children or to parents, and at times caused acute—if temporary—anxiety and distress. Since absence of contact is so strongly associated with absence of one kind of problem, and since contact almost never proved an advantage, the case for avoiding it seems fairly clear.

In this connection it is interesting that, in answer to a direct question, 80 per cent of the adoptive parents said they preferred to know nothing about the child's natural family, or else to have only limited and impersonal information, such as health background or education.

The "Arrangement Syndrome." For convenience, we have used the term "arrangement syndrome" to include (1) the kind of person who arranged the placement (that is, a professional intermediary—doctor, clergyman, lawyer—or natural parents, close relatives, or friends); (2) the presence or absence of contact between the two sets of parents; (3) the presence or absence of problems in the adoption process caused by the natural parents—chiefly through threats to revoke consent, efforts to reclaim the child, or insistence on visiting the child. The second and third components depend upon the first, since contact rarely occurred when children were placed by a nonrelated professional person but usually did occur when they were placed directly by relatives; and problems with natural parents almost never arose in the absence of direct contact.

Small but strikingly consistent relations were found between the components of the arrangement syndrome and various measures of adoption outcome. These relations favored the children who were not placed by natural relatives or their friends, and whose adoptive parents did not have contact with, or problems caused by, the child's natural parents. However, these relations were slight as well as indirect. The correlation coefficients were less than .20, and factor analysis showed that home ratings and the arrangement syndrome were independent of each other.

Nevertheless, we cannot rule out the possibility that parent-child relations may have been affected by an adoptive parent's acquaintance with the child's natural parents. There may have been a tendency to ascribe to the child attributes of the natural parents, or to have a more vivid conception of the natural parents as potential rivals for the child's affection because they had been seen in the flesh. Such influences could not be determined in this study, however, and remain in the field of conjecture.

The findings do indicate, however, differences in the kind of people who make different kinds of placement arrangements.

These differences, and the tendencies associated with them, have already been discussed. On the basis of this study, then, we can conclude that indirect placement may have a slight advantage over direct placement, but that in itself the type of arrangement exerts only a slight, if any, influence on overall adoption outcome.

OVERALL COMMENT ON THE FINDINGS

What does all this imply for the extent to which the independent adoption process achieves the aim of the adoption law, and for the part that social investigations play in promoting the law's objectives?

In considering the answers provided by this investigation it must, of course, be remembered that their general application may be limited by certain conditions in Florida at the time the adoptions under study were legalized. These conditions were: (1) the relative scarcity of adoption agencies and of adoptions arranged by such agencies; (2) the newness of the adoption act and its unacceptability to much of the public, including many judges; (3) the necessity of entrusting the social investigations to workers who were not professionally trained, and the Welfare Department's policy of making adverse recommendations only in the most extreme cases. In addition, the findings must, of course, be viewed in the light of the methodological limitations which we have attempted to point out and assess as the methods were discussed.

Under these conditions and limitations, the independent adoption process resulted in about 30 per cent of the children being placed in homes that, ten or so years later, appeared to be seriously inadequate. On the other hand, it produced eminently satisfactory homes for almost half of the children, and fairly adequate homes for about one-fourth.

The findings support the law's reliance on seeking good homes for adopted children as a means of achieving its objective of promoting their welfare. Almost none of the children in A or B adoptive homes was found to be seriously maladjusted while about a fourth of those in the D or E homes were so characterized. At the other extreme, the chance of a child's making at least a fairly good adjustment was seven to one when his adoptive home was one that was rated A or B and less than fifty-fifty when it was D or E.

With the value of a good home thus indicated, is the fact that 30 per cent of the adoptive homes were rated poor to be regarded as satisfactory or unsatisfactory? Here several points are relevant.

First, it is not to be expected that any process will be successful in every case.

Second, in a certain proportion of cases the adverse conditions that underlay the rating of "poor" may have developed after the petition was granted, or, at least, were not recognizable at that time. Even with the benefit of hindsight, our field director, in reviewing the original records, saw clues to poor outcome in only about 60 per cent of the D and E homes—and in none of a sample of A homes. On the extreme assumption that the B's and C's were like the A's, this means that adverse recommendations should have been made to the Court in about 15 per cent of the cases.

Third, the fact that the Department's investigators were not professionally trained doubtless increased the likelihood that subtle clues to petitioners' qualifications as parents would be overlooked. When, as an experiment, the Department had an unselected series of social investigations made by a professionally trained adoption worker, she estimated that 10 to 20 per cent of the petitioners would have been rejected by an adoption agency. This proportion comes close to the estimate of our field director, based on her review of the A, D, and E homes.

Fourth, though not strictly comparable with the present investigation (or with each other), most of the follow-up studies[1] of agency adoptions show a failure rate of 10 to 25 per cent.

It is interesting that, despite gross differences in criteria and in research precautions, these various findings point to about the same range of figures for "success probability." In view of the range of reported agency failures (10 to 25 per cent for the majority), and the estimated proportion of detectably unsuitable Florida applicants (15 per cent) reported separately by two trained caseworkers, it seems that a "success" rate in the neighborhood of 85 per cent might reasonably be hoped for in the

[1] See footnote, p. 145.

process of selecting adoptive homes. By this reasoning, it d
seem that the 70 per cent "success rate" in the study reporteu
here falls considerably short of what is feasible.

Can the independent adoption system be improved or should
it be replaced by a better system? To answer this question adequately would take us far beyond the data at hand. Our interpretation of the findings of this study leads us to suggest, however,
that certain improvements in the independent adoption process
could be made.

First, since we interpret our findings to mean that the major
criteria of "good" homes are the more elusive rather than the
overt, easily determined characteristics of the petitioners, the
social investigations should be made by people of professional
competence in adoption work. Probably even such persons could
not predict with great accuracy just what *degree* of goodness a
promising home would show in later years. Nevertheless, they
should be better equipped than untrained workers to recognize
the symptoms of severe defects in a marital relationship or severe
disturbance or inadequacy in adoptive applicants—that is, to
recognize at least some of the kinds of individuals who were the
parents in the D and E homes. Thus, the need for competent
staff seems clear—not to ensure that every child will find the best
of all possible homes for him but, rather, to reduce the number of
children who are placed in definitely unfavorable homes.

Second, for this first improvement to be effective, it would be
necessary that judges accept the Welfare Department's recommendations in a larger proportion of cases. In the 1944 to 1947
period only half of the Department's very rare (2 per cent)
adverse recommendations were accepted, and this situation has
not changed greatly. The social investigations were more useful
to the children than that slight figure would imply, for some
unsuitable would-be parents withdrew their petitions for adoption after discussion with the Department's workers. Nevertheless, a considerable change in the attitude of judges would be
needed if the expected 15 per cent of petitions were to be refused.

Third, and most important, if at all possible the home investigations should be made before the children are placed in their
prospective adoptive homes. Once a child has formed strong ties

with potential adoptive parents, it may do more harm than good to remove him, even if the home is far from ideal—and especially if he has already experienced painful separation. This conviction was strong enough in the agency caseworkers who rated our placement records that they would have left a number of children in homes they considered undesirable rather than subject them to another uprooting. It is strong also in the public that responds to some cases much publicized in the newspapers, cases in which foster parents are threatened with the loss of a child they have come to feel is their very own. An indispensable safeguard, then, is to have the investigation made before the child is in the home, if possible, or at least immediately after he enters it.

A great advantage of agency placements is that the investigation is made before the child enters the home. Some states have attempted to ensure, through their placement laws, that this is done in independent adoptions also, with varying degrees of success or failure.[1] Whether it is possible to achieve adequate investigation of independent placements, and investigations made soon enough to permit adequate screening of homes, remains to be seen.

A legal provision requiring such prompt investigations would be prerequisite but would not necessarily ensure that they were carried out in the way here envisaged. Equally important would be sufficient staff, sufficiently trained. So far, few states seem willing or able to provide the funds and staff needed to make such a provision effective.

Aside from these suggested improvements, the question of whether to retain or dispense with the independent adoption system can be answered only after strictly comparable studies are made of agency adoptions and of independent placements in other states. Even such studies would not answer these questions, for basically they involve public values. The studies, however, are indispensable prerequisites to answering them. Once we are clear about the outcomes of independent adoptions, the extent to which they can be improved by feasible measures, the extent to which agency placements produce more satisfactory results—

---

[1] "Moppets on the Market: The Problem of Unregulated Adoptions," *Yale Law Journal*, vol. 59, March, 1950, pp. 715–736.

then we have one segment of the facts on which enlightened value decisions can be based.

Also important to consider are the conditions and alternatives involved in our decisions. The proportion of independent adoptions in this country is decreasing, but such placements accounted for an estimated 39 per cent of the nonrelative adoptions in the latest year for which we have figures.[1] Two states have legislation that, in effect, permits only close relatives to adopt without prior agency placement. Probably the net result of such legislation is to increase both the number and the proportion of adoption placements that are made through agencies. We do not know, however, how many placements are made in evasion of such laws, for example, by going out of state, claiming a nonexistent relationship to the child, or other ruses. Thus, there is some uncertainty about the extent to which such legislation is improving the quality of placements.

Other facts to be considered in making the decision are: the shortage of trained staff for making placements, the cost of agency placements (estimated at $2,000 per child by one study);[2] the length of time they require, with the corollary stimulus to shorten the waiting period through by-passing the law; and the unmistakable evidence that some people will find ways to adopt even if the approved avenues are too narrow to accommodate the desired number of adoptions. These facts, in turn, must be weighed against a perceptible trend toward training and recruiting more staff, and toward speeding up the process of agency placement, partly through shifting the focus from achieving the one clearly best placement for each child to screening out the clearly undesirable possibilities.

Shall we, then, devote our efforts to improving independent adoption placements on the assumption that they are not likely to be eliminated soon, to legislating against them, or to simultaneously improving independent placements and increasing agency resources with a view to gradually making agency place-

---

[1] Children's Bureau, *Statistical Series 60, Child Welfare Statistics, 1959*. Washington, 1960.

[2] Schwartz, Edward E., "Adoption and Foster Home Costs" in *Cost Analysis in Child Welfare Services*. Department of Health, Education, and Welfare, Social Security Administration, Children's Bureau, Washington, 1958.

ments the sole means of adopting a child? The decision will depend on the estimate of the satisfactoriness—actual and potential—of independent placements, the extent to which they can be improved, the relative merits of agency placements, and the realistic probabilities of supplanting independent placements by agency placements. Such a decision is ultimately a value judgment, but a value judgment that is worthless unless it is supported by evidence.

Obviously a single study cannot supply all the requisite facts, nor has this one aspired to do that. A single study can, however, furnish a fraction of the needed information, stimulate other related investigations that will supply other needed fractions, and contribute to the readiness for evidence-oriented decisions on a subject that calls equally for evidence and for the values represented by professional standards and the public conscience.

Part II

SOME METHODOLOGICAL PROBLEMS
AND THEIR IMPLICATIONS

By Eugene A. Weinstein

Introductory Note

THE QUESTION OF HOW TO EVALUATE ADOPTION OUTCOMES is not an easy one. The preceding chapters certainly indicate that there are no easy or pat answers. Given the present state of research knowledge in human development, not only do issues arise as to the kinds of tools to be used in the evaluation procedure but in the very logic used in approaching the problem. The following chapters give testimony to that fact. While they are based on the same data, the approach differs considerably from that in Part I. The differences are both in analytic technique and in basic conceptions of how the study could be designed and executed.

As shown in Chapter VI, there are two possible starting points for evaluating adoption outcome, the development of the adoptive child or the adequacy of his home environment. In previous chapters the latter approach has been given primary emphasis. In Chapter VI and again in Chapter XI, a good home is described as one that is likely to favor the social and emotional development of the child. The datum of interest in evaluating Florida's system of independent adoptions was the proportion of children who failed to get into "good homes" under this system.

But to use this proportion for the evaluation of an adoption system makes two assumptions: (1) that the characteristics of homes conducive to healthy development in the child are known; and (2) that our rating procedures reliably and validly assess these characteristics.

The correctness of both assumptions is open to question. The rapidity with which theories of child rearing come to the fore, gain wide acceptance, and then fade away, and the paucity of consistent substantial relationships between measures of home characteristics and child adjustment give one pause. It is not likely that many researchers in the area of child development would argue that we have "truth by the tail" concerning what constitutes a good home. Moreover, there are serious logical and empirical problems with the techniques we have used to measure home quality.

If the validity of the home ratings is limited, a direct assessment of the adjustment of the adopted child becomes critical in evaluating outcome.[1] From this point of view, the optimum strategy would be to begin with assessments of the adjustment of the children and attempt to discover the factors that are associated with variations in adjustment. Of course, characteristics of the adoptive home would be centrally involved in the analysis of underlying factors. However, the child, rather than the home, would be the starting point for answering the evaluative question.

To some extent, this approach has also been taken. In Chapter X it may be seen that the approach to assessing adjustment was comparative. Test results of adopted children were compared with nonadopted peers in the same classroom matched on the basis of school grade, race, sex, and socioeconomic status. If we knew more clearly what the results meant, the answer to the question of how these adoptions were turning out would be more clear. However, the absence of data on the homes of these control children creates difficulty in interpreting the findings.

The failure of the study to provide data on the homes of the control children is a serious weakness in its overall design. Had such data been available, they could have served three important purposes.

First, they could have served as a benchmark for interpreting the results of the ratings of adoptive homes. For example, one might regard differently the fact that 30 per cent of the adoptive homes were rated D or E if, let us say, 60 or 70 per cent of the control families fell into the same categories. Moreover, it would be important to know how similar were the distributions of more specific aspects of the home environment.

Second, the data could have served as a check on possible bias in the home ratings. It is possible that social workers might tend

---

[1] The validity of the measures of adjustment is also open to serious question. Most of the instruments we used have some evidence available concerning their validity and not much of it is very encouraging. However, the absence of evidence concerning the validity of a measuring instrument does not make it *ipso facto* better than one with limited validity.

to be more stringent in their evaluation of homes of independently adopted children than they would be of homes in general. Data on the overall assessments of both sets of homes and/or more specific parental attitudes and child-rearing practices could have been used to test for this kind of bias. It would involve comparing the relationships between specific home factors and overall evaluation for each group.

Third, the data could have been used to explore the effects of adoption *per se* on the adopted child. These effects could come about in two ways. First, adoption could have a direct detrimental effect on adjustment. Second, because of his status, the adopted child might be more responsive in his adjustment to the kind of home environment he has. A comparison of the relations between home environment variables and measures of adjustment in the adopted and control groups could begin to provide clues concerning the likelihood of these possibilities.

The primary issue to which this study is addressed is how independent adoptions are turning out. The answers that data from a control group of homes could have provided do not directly answer that question. However, their absence places limitations on the meaningfulness of the answers we did get.

Because of these limitations, it is even more necessary to evaluate critically the assessment procedures that were used. It is to this end that the following three chapters are directed. The first discusses the logical and empirical problems with the overall home rating as a measure of adoption outcome. The relationships between the home ratings and more specific child-rearing attitudes and practices are then presented in order to give a more systematic picture of the major influences on these ratings and the influences of such factors on the adjustment of the child are explored. In the last chapter an attempt is made to sort out some of the complex interrelationships among the variables and establish empirically based dimensions of outcome by means of factor analysis.

The approach in these chapters tends to be more technical than in Part I. As a result, perhaps some of the sensitivity to nuances of a more clinical approach is lost. The gain is the availability of tools that can detect, describe, and summarize relationships using uniform criteria based on a body of theory rather than on impressions, arbitrary weighting and combining, and classifications of dependent variables when values of the independent variables have been seen.

CHAPTER XV

Analysis of the Overall Home Rating
as a Measure of Adoption Outcome

THIS BOOK represents an attempt to bring together the approaches of social science and social work within the same research framework. The diagnostic judgments of social workers were used as a measuring instrument for the evaluation of adoption outcomes, in the form of global ratings of the quality of adoptive homes. As a research tool, these ratings must have certain properties in order to satisfy certain basic rules of inference. Two of the chief properties are reliability and validity. If the home ratings are to be made the foundation of the evaluation process, it is essential that their reliability and validity be demonstrated.

Some Logical Problems

Validity has reference to the extent an instrument accurately measures the characteristic it is purported to measure. When speaking of the quality of homes this ultimate criterion is the probability that a child in the home will develop to the upper limits of his physical, social, and psychological potentials, all non-home related factors being equal. Homes are poor or good to the extent that this probability is minimized or maximized.

Underlying the overall home ratings is a rather imprecisely articulated causal theory. From this theory are deduced the characteristics of home environments presumed to affect the child's development and statements of the direction in which these effects should occur. Thus the overall home rating can be regarded as an estimate of a child's probability to have developed maximally within the given home environment, which was based on a theoretically oriented subjective combination of the presumed effects of certain characteristics of the home environment. The assessment of these in turn was based on comments and reactions of the adoptive parents (usually only the mother) in a two or three-hour interview with a social worker. As such, this estimate is four levels removed from "true" home quality. On each level there are potential sources of error.

The raw data for the home rating come from the parent's interaction with the worker in the interview situation. The parent's words, gestures, reactions are a source of cues for the assessment of dimensions held to be important aspects of home quality. At this level error could occur in several ways. The parent's comments might not accurately reflect her behavior in the home, which could be due to particular conditions in the interview situation, such as arousal of motivation to cover up as a defense against negative evaluation. Distortion could also occur through the selective perception of the worker. He may "hear" comments or remember them in ways that differ from their original intent or even occurrence.

A second level at which error could occur is the interpretation of cues. The causal model underlying the overall home ratings posits the importance of certain general attitudes, modes of perceiving the child, and feelings toward him, as well as more specific attitudes and ways of handling. Even if the mother's comments accurately reflect her behavior and specific attitudes in the areas covered by the interview, inferences to more general characteristics may be in error. Error could come from an insufficient sample of relevant cues. The absence of the adoptive father serves as an example. It could also come from drawing incorrect inferences from available cues. For example, the manner in which the parent related to the worker in the interview situation was used as a basis for assessing her general capacity for interpersonal relationships. If this is not a general, but situationally specific capacity, invalid assessments could occur.

Even if the cues elicited in the interview accurately reflected the parent's behavior and specific attitudes, and the relationship of these to more general dimensions was accurately perceived, error could creep in at a third level. The home rating involves a combination of dimensions into an overall estimate. The process of combining involves a subjective weighing and balancing of a number of factors. The relative weight given any dimension or combination of dimensions could fluctuate from worker to worker or from case to case for the same worker. Overweighing of irrelevant factors could also lower the validity of the estimate. Inordinate weight may be given to cues or characteristics that have relatively little association with the criterion in question.

Finally, the psychodynamic theory underlying the ratings may itself be in error. One must take into account the possibility that the theory omits some important factors, overstates the importance of others, or misstates the direction of the relationship of some to the child's development.

Reliability

Reliability, when discussed in reference to measuring instruments, has a variety of meanings and a number of techniques are used to evaluate it. Reliability can refer to the internal consistency of a measuring instrument, to its consistency over time, or to consistency between independent observers of the same phenomenon. Only the last approach has been used in this study.

In Chapter VI two reliability coefficients are reported. The first, .42, was based on independent re-evaluations of the case records by workers who were on the study staff. It was pointed out that this coefficient might be an underestimate of true reliability. The workers were aware of the purpose of the reratings and tended to make fewer judgments at the extremes.[1] A second check on reliability was made by trained workers at a Chicago agency. This time, a coefficient of .74 was found. This latter value comes closer to those found in the literature for global ratings of the type we have used. To this extent, the second attempt came closer to producing a satisfactory picture. However, such a judgment must be tempered by the fact that the correlation of .74

---

[1] It was proposed that the field director serve as a reliability check by having the worker and the field director rate each case independently prior to their conference. This was objected to on the grounds that it might prove threatening to the workers. It is unfortunate that such data are unavailable inasmuch as they would have been valuable in analyzing the rating process and the effects of the conference.

indicates that over one-fourth of what was being measured by the ratings was random error rather than consistent differences in home quality.

It should be pointed out that the procedure used to estimate interrater reliability is only an approximation since it is based upon interview records rather than an independent evaluation of the home itself. This factor could work in two ways. On one hand, since the interview records do not present the worker with the information in depth that direct experience with the home would provide, it could be argued that interrater agreement might be lowered by our procedure. On the other hand, the records are not always straightforward verbatim accounts of what went on in the interview. Such terms as "tense," "friendly," "upset," "pleasant" abound. They could serve as signposts to prior evaluation and heighten the correlation.

Finally, it must be pointed out that interrater agreement is not the only form of reliability of concern to the study. Of special importance is ignorance concerning the reliability of the ratings over time. Would the evaluations of the homes be the same if they were independently interviewed and rerated two weeks or two months later? Interviews lasted from two to three hours, which is fairly long as interviews go. Yet one wonders about the adequacy of a three-hour sample to generalize about such broad characteristics as the mother's capacity for human relationships or the father's role in the family (especially when he has not been seen). People may seem to be almost totally different under different conditions of personal or social pressures. We might ask whether a home might not have appeared differently to the worker if the interview happened to be conducted during a particularly trying time in the mother's relationship to the child.

Interworker Differences

Examining interworker variation affords opportunity for another approach to assessing the reliability of the overall home ratings. The home interviews were conducted by five different workers (with a sixth interviewing five cases in the Miami area). The field director participated in the evaluation of every case. This method had two purposes. First, the field director was the most experienced of the field staff. Her additional experience was allowed to enter into all of the ratings in the hope of improving validity. Second, the field director, by being involved in all ratings, might serve to minimize the effects of differences in interpretation, importance assigned to various factors, and so on from worker to worker. This was done to improve internal consistency.

There are several reasons why these procedures do not guarantee high reliability. First, there may be some case-to-case fluctuation for the field director. Second, her raw data were the case records and any other additional information brought out in the evaluation conference. Both of these data sources may be affected by selective perception on the part of the worker. Thus the field director may ensure comparability in interpretation and in the importance assigned various factors, but to the extent that different workers may evoke different kinds of responses from the adoptive parent in the interview situation or tend to develop different kinds of "sets" about homes and perceive and describe the interview in terms of those sets, interworker variation may exist and reduce reliability.

To test this possibility, average home ratings were computed for each worker and compared by means of the analysis of variance. Variation among workers for the total sample (less five cases rated by a sixth worker) is greater than one would expect by chance alone.

TABLE 63. MEAN HOME RATINGS BY WORKER

Cases	N^1	Mean	N^2	Mean	N^3	Mean	N^4	Mean	N^5	Mean
					Worker					
Total sample	108	2.74	74	2.96	102	3.61	45	3.29	104	3.47
Dade and Duval Counties only	26	2.85	36	2.78	44	3.48	37	3.43	27	3.52

The results in the first line of Table 63 are open to question because cases were not randomly assigned to workers for interviewing but were assigned largely on the basis of geographical area. To compensate for this difficulty, geographical area was held constant by taking only cases in the Miami and Jacksonville areas, where all workers had some interviews. As a further check for possible bias due to nonrandom assignment, interworker differences in the socioeconomic distributions of adoptive families were examined. Analysis indicated that differences from worker to worker in the education, occupation, and neighborhood level distributions of Miami and Jacksonville families whom the workers interviewed could have occurred on the basis of chance alone. Yet the pattern of differences in average home ratings observed for the total sample persists. Even with the smaller number of cases, the differences are larger than one would expect by chance alone.

In a further investigation of interworker differences, the correlations between certain socioeconomic variables and the overall home rating were computed for each worker. These correlations appear in Table 64.

TABLE 64. CORRELATIONS BETWEEN SOCIOECONOMIC VARIABLES AND HOME RATINGS BY WORKER

Variable	Worker				
	1	2	3	4	5
Education of adoptive father[a]	.104	.188	−.072	.560	.279
Occupation of adoptive father[a]	.056	.169	−.056	.453	.321
Socioeconomic level of neighborhood	.139	.174	.186	.484	.404
Number of cases	108	74	102	45	104

[a] Differences are statistically significant.

While most of the correlations are small, for the first two socioeconomic indicators, the differences among the correlations are larger than would be expected by chance. This stems mainly from the higher correlations for workers 4 and 5. Thus the influence, whether direct or indirect, of socioeconomic status on the perception of home quality varies significantly among workers.

Finally, there were differences among workers in the confidence assigned to the ratings. Proportions made with the first degree of confidence ranged from 14 to 56 per cent. The differences were significant.

Even if there were no significant differences among workers in the average level at which they rated homes, high reliability would not have been guaranteed. If the ratings were simply made at random rather than on the basis of deliberation, one would not expect to find significant differences. However, the presence of significant interworker variation has definite negative implications for the internal consistency of the home rating distribution. These implications are supported by the findings of significant interworker variation in the correlations between two socio-economic variables and the home ratings and in the level of confidence assigned the ratings. In part, they may account for the relatively low interrater agreement.

Validity

What is the criterion against which the validity of the home ratings can be evaluated? If a good home is one that favors the child's social and emotional development, it would be predicted that, on the average, the higher the home quality, the higher the child's adjustment. This is not to say that a perfect correlation is to be expected between the two. Constitutional factors, physical handicaps, the influence of school and peer groups, perhaps adoptive status itself, all could tend to depress adjustment even though home quality was high. However, in the long run, over a relatively large number of cases, one would expect a substantial relationship.

The tests and ratings of the adoptive child provide several estimates of his adjustment made independently of the home ratings. They give us a means of testing empirically the validity of the home ratings, through their correlation (or lack of correlation) with them. Of course, to the extent that the adjustment measures themselves have limited validity, their use as a validating criterion is equivocal.

Table 65 represents the correlations between the overall home rating and the separate adjustment measures. The correlations, while all statistically significant, are quite low.

When combined adjustment measures are used, the picture is somewhat better. Table 66, based on Chapter XI, reviews the correlations between the home ratings and various combinations of adjustment measures. With the exception of Combinations I and II, it should be noted that these measures contain ratings that were not made independent of knowledge of the home ratings and tend to select parts of distributions that would maximize association with the home ratings. This is especially true of Combination IV; to a lesser extent it is true of Combinations III, V, and VI.

TABLE 65. CORRELATIONS BETWEEN CHILD AS-
SESSMENT VARIABLES AND THE OVER-
ALL HOME RATING[a]

Variable	Correlation
Achievement tests	.16
BDC Withdrawn Maladjustment	.15
BDC Aggressive Maladjustment	.16
BDC Leadership	.22
Sociometric Rating	.20
CTP Social Adjustment	.21
CTP Personal Adjustment	.24
CTP Total Adjustment	.24

[a] Based on 410 cases.

TABLE 66. CORRELATIONS BETWEEN THE OVER-
ALL HOME RATING AND COMBINED
ADJUSTMENT MEASURES

Combination I	.35
Combination II	.30
Combination III	.41
Combination IV	.58
Combination V	.45
Combination VI	.44

Then, at best, the home ratings account for no more than 20 per cent of the variation in the measures of children's adjustment. If this study were primarily one in child development, such a finding would be encouraging. It is rare to find even this much association in a study with as extensive a battery of measurement procedures and a sample as large as the present one.

However, if the findings are to be used to judge the adequacy of our procedures for assessing adoption outcome, they are much less encouraging. As stated previously, many factors outside the home could influence the child's development. However, when one considers the totality of experiences a large group of children are likely to encounter, one would expect the relative influence of home factors to be more than 20 per cent.

A series of further analyses of the home rating-test correlations were undertaken in an attempt to explore some of the conditions that might have a depressing effect. One such condition is the confidence with which the home ratings were made. In the evaluation conference an indication was given of the level of confidence in the home rating. Of the 438 ratings, 118 were made with the first degree of confidence, 301 with the second, and 19 with the third. The relationship between levels of confidence and the home ratings can be seen in the accompanying figure.

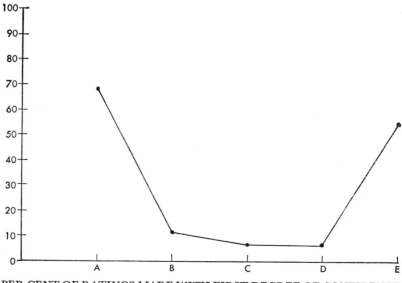

PER CENT OF RATINGS MADE WITH FIRST DEGREE OF CONFIDENCE
BY LEVEL OF RATING

This figure reveals a familiar U-shaped distribution in which confidence is higher for extreme judgments. If confidence is related to validity, one would expect a closer association between the home ratings and test results for those ratings made with higher confidence. Accordingly, the home ratings were divided into two groups, those made with the first degree of confidence and those made with the second or third. Home rating-test correlations were computed for each group separately. The results appear in Table 67.

Correlations in the high level of confidence group are uniformly somewhat higher. However, only in the case of the sociometric ratings was the improvement greater than might have occurred by chance alone. When one considers that the high group was heavily loaded with judgments at both extremes, where the association would be expected to be greatest, these are not very encouraging results. It would seem there is relatively little association between the confidence with which ratings were made and their validity, as estimated by the test correlations.

TABLE 67. CORRELATIONS BETWEEN CHILD ASSESSMENT VARIABLES AND THE OVERALL HOME RATING BY LEVEL OF CONFIDENCE

Variable	First degree of confidence	Second or third degree of confidence
Achievement tests[a]	.29	.12
BDC Withdrawn Maladjustment	−.18	−.10
BDC Aggressive Maladjustment	−.22	−.13
BDC Leadership	.30	.17
Sociometric Rating	.36	.11
CTP Social Adjustment	.26	.21
CTP Personal Adjustment	.26	.25
CTP Total Adjustment	.26	.25
Number of cases	113	297

[a] For Achievement tests, N for the high confidence group is 90; for the low, 253.

The presence of a time lag between inadequate parenting and maladjustment might serve to depress correlations between measures of home quality and child adjustment. For example, emotional damage to the child might not show up in the "latency" period when psychological pressures are low, but in adolescence when there may be great stress, or in later life when the roles of spouse, parent, and breadwinner would be assumed. It is possible to test the first of these possibilities with data from the study by comparing the test-home rating correlations for pre-adolescent children in the sample (9 to 11 years) with those for the children entering or in adolescence (12 to 15 years).

There is nothing in the findings that would support the hypothesis. In some instances the differences are opposite to what would be expected. In no case did the differences exceed what might have occurred by random fluctuation.

TABLE 68. CORRELATIONS BETWEEN CHILD ASSESSMENT VARI-
ABLES AND THE OVERALL HOME RATING BY AGE OF
CHILD

Variable	9 to 11 years	12 to 15 years
Achievement tests[a]	.23	−.01
BDC Withdrawn Maladjustment	−.13	−.16
BDC Aggressive Maladjustment	−.18	−.11
BDC Leadership	.21	.21
Sociometric Rating	.22	.12
CTP Social Adjustment	.21	.16
CTP Personal Adjustment	.21	.30
CTP Total Adjustment	.22	.27
Number of cases	311	99

[a] For Achievement tests, N for the younger group is 261; for the older, 82.

As a further check on the possibility of a greater impact of
adolescence on the adopted child, the differences in adjustment
between adopted and control children were analyzed for their
possible interaction with age. It might be hypothesized that the
discrepancies in adjustment between the groups would be greater
in adolescence. Statistical analysis revealed this was not the case.

There may be differences from worker to worker in the validity
of perceptions of the home he brought to the evaluation conference. If so, the overall correlation may be lowered by ratings
involving workers whose perceptions of the home tended to be
inaccurate. Table 69 presents correlations between tests and
home ratings, computed separately for each worker. While there
are some differences, in no case do they exceed those that can be
expected by chance. Also, in only one case are the correlations
for a worker consistently higher or lower than the average.

TABLE 69. CORRELATIONS BETWEEN CHILD ASSESSMENT VARI-
ABLES AND OVERALL HOME RATING BY WORKER

	Worker				
Variable	1	2	3	4	5
Achievement tests[a]	.13	.23	−.02	.25	.26
BDC Withdrawn Maladjustment	−.13	−.21	−.01	−.08	−.17
BDC Aggressive Maladjustment	−.16	−.12	−.24	−.05	−.20
BDC Leadership	.21	.28	.16	−.00	.30
Sociometric Rating	.20	.28	.13	.12	.25
CTP Social Adjustment	.25	.15	.31	.28	.15
CTP Personal Adjustment	.28	.07	.25	.28	.33
CTP Total Adjustment	.28	.13	.28	.32	.26
Number of cases	105	68	94	43	95

[a] N's for Achievement tests are 91, 54, 73, 38, and 82 respectively.

On the basis of current mental health theory, it could be argued that it is difficult for outside factors to compensate for the inadequacies of a home environment in facilitating the child's healthy social and psychological development. On the other hand, a number of factors outside the home could serve to depress adjustment, even though home quality was high. Following this line of reasoning, an adequate home environment would generally be a necessary but not sufficient condition for good adjustment. If this is the case, one would expect more variability in adjustment among children from favorable home environments, while adjustment should be uniformly low among children from less favorable homes. That is, even though average test scores tend to become higher as the home ratings increase, if there is greater dispersion around those averages in homes rated high as compared with those rated low, the overall correlation would be lowered. In order to test this possibility, variances were computed by home rating level for each test. The results appear in Table 70.

TABLE 70. VARIANCES BY HOME RATING LEVEL FOR CHILD ASSESSMENT VARIABLES

| Variable | Home rating level | | | | |
	A	B	C	D	E
Achievement tests	17.42	14.78	12.35	14.58	12.08
BDC Withdrawn Maladjustment	12.40	10.92	13.48	12.12	12.80
BDC Aggressive Maladjustment[a]	12.96	14.04	13.96	15.04	18.08
BDC Leadership	18.64	22.32	19.76	20.28	19.48
Sociometric Rating[a]	40.35	25.20	29.36	24.64	12.68
CTP Social Adjustment	15.96	20.61	20.79	21.48	19.41
CTP Personal Adjustment	14.34	18.72	19.38	15.99	18.12
CTP Total Adjustment[a]	12.51	18.48	21.51	16.44	17.70

[a] Differences are statistically significant.

There does not appear to be a consistent pattern in the results. In three cases there are significant differences among the home rating levels in the dispersion around test scores. In one case, aggressive maladjustment, the direction is opposite to that hypothesized with variability highest in the low home ratings. In a second instance, CTP Total Adjustment, variability in D and E homes is slightly lower than average, but the chief source of significance appears to come from the low variability in the A cases. Only for the sociometric ratings do the results indicate a significant tendency for there to be more uniform agreement between home ratings and test scores in the low rated homes.

Some Implications

The use of psychological test scores as validating criteria for the home ratings is not free from methodological shortcomings. Errors in either or both instruments would tend to depress the association between them. Unfortunately, it is not possible statistically to evaluate and disentangle the effects of each source of error on the home rating-test correlations. Any judgments concerning relative deficiencies will have to be made on inferential rather than empirical grounds.

The methodological findings concerning the home ratings merit special attention. The proportion of poor homes that an adoption system fails to eliminate has been proposed as the primary factor in evaluating its adequacy. In Table 39 in Chapter XI, and again in this chapter, we have evidence that low home ratings are less valid than the high ratings, which leads to the possibility that the proportion of poor homes may be overstated. Measurement errors, instead of falling equally in both directions, may have tended to cluster in the lower categories. This would be consonant with the recognized tendency of clinical judgment to be heavily oriented to the perception of pathology.

However, the accusing finger should not be pointed exclusively at either set of assessment procedures. It seems more reasonable to conclude that the low correlations are due to limited validity in both. Because of these limitations, it is unfortunate that the findings concerning the adequacy of independent adoptions are not more clear-cut, and, with respect to the home ratings, that a comparative benchmark was not provided.

CHAPTER XVI

What Did the Home Ratings Rate?

THE OVERALL HOME RATINGS, when regarded as an indication of adoption outcome, represent an approach to evaluation through comparison with a set of standards. They are composite judgments in the sense that a number of different factors were taken into account, weighed, and balanced one against the other in the process of formulating a single global rating for each home. However, the factors to be taken into account in the composite were not exhaustively specified beforehand nor were any rules for weighing, balancing, or combining set forth. The complexity of the concept of home quality, the elusiveness of some of the characteristics held to be important, and the generally imprecise nature of current mental health theory militated against developing a highly specific set of criteria in the beginning. However, in their absence, we are left with the problem of discovering, on a *post hoc* basis, just what the standards were.

In Chapters VII to IX this problem was approached clinically. From a level-by-level examination of the case materials, a clinical picture of families at each level of evaluation was drawn. In Chapter XII a selective review was made of some of the systematic relationships between characteristics of the home and the home ratings drawing upon the findings of this and the succeeding chapter. In this chapter the statistical findings between the home ratings and more specific home characteristics are examined in detail.

There is one major difficulty in this procedure that is probably inherent in the *post hoc* analysis of any judgment data. It is not always possible to tell why a correlation is found. There are three ways in which a variable might be related to the home ratings: (1) as a *criterion*, a factor which the workers were to take specifically into account in making the ratings; (2) as an *indirect criterion*, a factor which was not taken into account directly but influenced the interpretation of other material in ways that would affect the ratings; and (3) as a *correlate*, a factor whose association with the ratings was independent of the judgment process. Thus correlations cannot be regarded as a statistical model of the judgment process. However, whether criteria or correlates, they do allow one to estimate the extent to which the judgment could have been predicted on the basis of each characteristic. In discussing these relationships, an attempt is made to point out whether a variable served as a criterion, an indirect criterion, or a correlate. These judgments are based upon discussion with the field director and examination of the evaluation summaries.

Five subratings, in addition to the overall home rating, were made in the evaluation conference. These were of rather broad aspects of the home situation, including the quality of the marital relationship, the mother's degree of manifest anxiety in the maternal role, the quality of her emotional response to the child, the degree to which she exercises control over the child's everyday activities, and her regard for the child as an individual in his own right. The intercorrelations among these ratings appear in Table 71.

In examining the table, one is immediately struck with the large size of the correlations among the additional ratings, not only with the overall home rating but with one another. Except in relation to the overall rating, the ratings are not interdependent by definition. For example, just because a parent was highly controlling, her rating on emotional response would not necessarily be lowered. It could be argued, of course, that the correlations reflect the actual levels of interrelationships among these general characteristics. Close inspection of the pattern of correlations in the table suggests a more plausible explanation. It may be noted that the hierarchy of correlations of the overall home rating with the other variables is duplicated by the ratings of emotional response, control, and regard for the child as an

TABLE 71. INTERCORRELATIONS AMONG HOME RATINGS[a]

	1	2	3	4	5	6
1. Overall home rating						
2. Marital relations	.83					
3. Manifest anxiety in maternal role	.32	.31				
4. Emotional response to child	.83	.74	.29			
5. Adequacy of control	.64	.49	.29	.61		
6. Regard for child as an individual	.86	.76	.34	.84	.68	..

[a] Based on 438 cases.

The control ratings were scored for quality rather than degree of control. The two ends of the control continuum were defined negatively, that is, overcontrolling and overpermissive, with the midpoint regarded as the ideal level. In two ratings allowance was made for situations that seemed qualitatively different from that which would be indicated by the usual rating system. In the first case, emotional response, a category was added called narcissistic warmth, in which the mother's display of affection for the child seemed designed to serve her own needs. There were 48 such cases. In the second case, the control rating, a special category was added because the midpoint, defined as a balance between control and permissiveness, did not seem adequate to describe situations in which the mother was highly overcontrolling in some areas and highly overpermissive in others. There were 34 of these cases. In 36 cases in which there was divorce or death of a parent, marital relations were not rated. In all of these exceptions, cases were given the numerical equivalent of a "D" rating for the purpose of analysis.

individual. There are minor deviations in their correlations with anxiety and marital relations. While the control correlations are lower, the pattern is essentially the same. The difference is probably due to lower reliability. It would appear that there is a strong "halo effect" in the emotional response, control, and regard ratings, so that they are not perceived differentially from the general perception of the home. The marital relations rating is also involved in the halo effect although to a slightly lesser extent. Only for the anxiety ratings does there appear to be the possibility of any appreciable amount of independent information.

There are methodological implications from these findings that seem worthwhile to discuss at this point. As initially conceived, the control rating was to have focused on the pattern of the mother's overt behavior. During the course of the study, the notion of the child's being controlled through emotional "strings" became incorporated into the ratings. Considerations of the extent to which the mother's neurotic needs were served entered into the rating of her emotional response to the child. The same considerations entered into the rating of regard for the child as an individual. Initially it was hoped that this would reveal the extent to which the parents' handling of the child was oriented toward fostering independence or dependence in him. In anxiety, the main instance in which the focus was on the *manifest* actions of the mother, some independent information was obtained.[1]

These empirical findings confirm what would be expected on logical grounds. As interpretations at increasing levels of generality enter into the ratings, the possibility of overlapping interpretations with a consequent "halo effect" is increased. Thus the finding of a high correlation between global ratings of marital relations and home quality is ambiguous. Is the home rated poor because of substantial evidence that the marriage is poor? Or is the marriage seen as poor because the mother is interpreted as neurotic and constricted in her capacity for human relationships in general? Examination of the interview records and evaluation summaries indicated that this type of "reasoning backwards" occurred but not frequently on an explicit basis. There is a strong possibility that it did occur frequently on an implicit level.

Because of these tendencies for overlapping interpretations, we must turn to more specific attitudes and behavior to get some systematic idea of the cues on which the home ratings were based. The main source of information concerning specific characteristics is the checklist, filled out by the worker shortly after completion of the interview. It contained both objective information, such as the current occupation of the adoptive father, and more subjective categorization of relatively specific attitudes, such as the adoptive parents' attitudes toward the natural parents. In addition, there were seven items that came from a content analysis of the interview records. Current home information has been grouped into five main areas: characteristics of the adoptive child, general characteristics of the adoptive family, child-rearing attitudes and practices, characteristics specific to adoptive families, and characteristics of the interview situation.

The first area, characteristics of the child, contains six items: age, sex, current physical handicaps, general health level as de-

---

[1] The correlation between anxiety and the overall rating was depressed because of two types of cases. Some "E" mothers were given ratings indicating low manifest anxiety because they appeared to the workers to be near psychotic, with very little outward display of any kind of affect. The second group contained homes rated at the "C" level in which some of the upper and upper-middle socioeconomic status mothers were given ratings indicating high manifest anxiety.

scribed by the adoptive parent, the parent's description of the child's temperament, and her description of his pattern of social relations.

There were only random differences in home ratings between homes in which the child had some handicap or general poor health, and those in which he did not. Sex differences were also nonsignificant. Significant relationships were found for the other three variables.[1] The parent's description of the child's temperament correlated $-.30$ with the ratings. The negative correlation indicates lower home ratings in cases where the child was described as moody or irritable. On the average, home ratings were significantly lower when the child was described as preferring to be with adults or by himself, as compared with preferring to be with children of his own age.[2] If this variable is dichotomized, there is a correlation of .27 between the ratings and the child's preferring to be with peers. The current age of the child correlates $-.22$ with the ratings.

It should first be noted that these, as is the case for most, correlations in the study are quite low although they meet our criterion of statistical significance. Unreliability in both measures is one major factor in reducing them. A second is the lack of normality in the distributions. Furthermore, since the home ratings are a summary judgment presumably encompassing many factors, very high correlations with any single variable would not be expected.

In attempting to account for these relationships we encounter the criterion-correlate problem. The question at issue is whether the observed correlations are due to actual relationships between true home quality and the personality of the child or are an artifact of the rating process. The home ratings were supposed to be based on the evaluation of the *home* and not the *child*. The implication that a home was *ipso facto* bad because the child did not seem to be making a good adjustment was to be avoided. Such implications would be contrary to the logic of the study design, in which a major problem to be investigated was the

---

[1] N = 438 rated cases. In all relationships, cases in which the particular checklist information was missing were routinely combined with the modal category.

[2] The means are 2.00, 2.35, and 3.34, respectively.

relationship of evaluations of home quality to the child's adjustment.

One could take either side of this debate, possibly with equal effectiveness. One would expect that rejecting mothers would tend to perceive their children more negatively. On the other hand, it would not be fair to assume that the mother was rejecting her child merely because she perceived him in this way. Children who do not prefer to be with their peers may develop this characteristic because of the parent's overprotection or discouragement of normal relationships. However, when such an interpretation is present, it is difficult to tell to what extent it is based on an inference from the child's behavior.

The problem is equally complicated when the correlation with the child's current age is considered. The negative correlation could be due to normal difficulties between parents of adolescents and their children that were not allowed for in the ratings. Perhaps if the homes had been seen several years earlier the evaluations might have been different. On the other hand, because of the nature of the sampling design, there is a high correlation between the child's current age and his age at placement ($r = .59$). If selective factors are operating with respect to the kinds of adoptive parents who obtain their children after the first month of life, these same selective factors could be producing the relationship with current age. The partial correlations between age at placement and current age with the home ratings are both .115, which is low but still statistically significant. Obviously it is not possible to demonstrate that the child's adjustment did or did not serve as an unconscious or indirect criterion of home quality. What can be said is that a conscious attempt was made when formulating the ratings to avoid having it do so.[1]

Included under the heading general characteristics of the home are the following variables: the adoptive parents' health, marital history since adoption, current occupation of the adoptive father,

---

[1] There is another possibility that should be taken into account. The checklist was filled out on the basis of the worker's recollections of the home interview. Judgments about attitudinal items sometimes required some interpretation as well as recollection of what was said. In such cases there is the possibility of some "halo effect" with the worker's general impressions of the home. It is unlikely, however, that this effect would be as great as was the case for the more general ratings.

socioeconomic level of the neighborhood, and whether the adoptive mother was currently in the labor force. With the exception of this last factor, these findings are discussed in detail in Chapter XII.

In 159 families the adoptive mother was currently in the labor force. In 107 of these cases she was working full time; in 52, part time. On the average, home rating scores were significantly lower in both cases as compared with the homes in which the mother was not working. However, the level of association is low; $r = .14$. The adoptive mother's working was occasionally used as an indirect criterion. Along with other evidence it was sometimes interpreted as raising questions about her satisfaction in the maternal role, which in turn was a major criterion.

The area of general child-rearing attitudes and practices consists of items having to do with patterns of discipline and control, including frequency of discipline, the types of acts disciplined, methods used, the mother's feelings about administering discipline, the extent of agreement between the parents about discipline, and the extent to which the child "gets away with" disapproved behavior. Also included under this heading are the mother's attitudes toward the child and his friends' using the home as a place to play, her attitudes toward the child's school performance, her feelings about the child's future, her reaction to his health, and the frequency of pleasurable activity of each parent with the child.

Three variables in the area of discipline show significant relationships to the home ratings. Frequency of discipline is correlated $-.14$ with the ratings. Cases in which the child is disciplined for his attitude toward his parents (being "sassy," "disrespectful") or for undesirable personality traits ("sissy," "bully") are, on the average, rated lower than those in which the parent had to keep after the child for routine matters such as schoolwork, table manners, and the like, or not at all. A correlation of $-.36$ was found between the ratings and extent of disagreement between the parents about matters of discipline.

Frequency of discipline and the types of acts disciplined may have served indirectly as criteria in that they, along with other confirmatory evidence, could lead to the conclusion that there was some rejection in the mother's feelings about the child. Parental disagreement about discipline served as an indirect criterion in two ways. First, it served as a clue to the quality of the marital relations. Second, it was negatively evaluated as providing the possibility that the child might be "caught in the middle," which was assumed to be unfavorable for his development.

Being inappropriately concerned about the child's health was given some negative evaluation in the ratings. In 43 such cases the average home rating was 2.81, significantly less than 3.26, the average for cases in which the mother's reactions appeared appropriate. The presence of such reactions was seen as indicating excessive anxiety and possible overinvolvement with the child. The same kind of interpretation is involved in the relationship of the home rating to the parent's concern about the child's future. Some concern about what the child's future career was seen as desirable by the raters. However, being overly concerned, having one's heart set on the child's having the "right" kind of future, was regarded as possibly more negative than being indifferent because of its implications of overinvolvement.

The parent's attitudes toward the child and his friends' using the home as a place to play and her attitude toward the way the child is getting along in school are both associated with the home ratings, the correlations being .27 and .31, respectively. Both variables served indirectly as criteria for the home ratings. Unfavorable attitudes in these areas were regarded as clues to possible feelings of ambivalence or rejection on the part of the parent.

The frequency with which the parents and the adoptive child engaged in shared pleasurable activities was a major direct criterion for the evaluation of homes. This is reflected in the correlation of .35 between the ratings and frequency of shared pleasurable activity with the adoptive mother, .38 with the adoptive father, and .40 for an arithmetic combination of both called joint family activity.

A fourth cluster of items contains characteristics in which the fact that these are adoptive homes is involved. Included in this group are the following variables: family structure (number of children, whether in the home before or after the sample child, and "own" or adoptive status), initial parental agreement in deciding to adopt the child, post-adoptive contact between natural and adoptive parents, the child's initial reaction to placement in the adoptive home, the adoptive parent's attitude toward the natural parents, her preference for knowing as much as possible about the natural family, how the child was told he was adopted (themes used, person who told him, age at telling, description of natural parents, child's reaction to telling, child's interest in knowing about natural parents), the parents' degree of satisfaction with the way the adoption is turning out, conceptions of the child's similarity to the adoptive family, problems seen as special to adoptive parents, and advice to prospective adoptive parents.

In the interview, questions were asked that dealt with the parent's recollection of certain conditions around the time the child was first placed in the adoptive home. Among the areas covered was the reaction of the family and child to his placement. Cases in which the child showed some difficulty were, on the average, rated lower than those in which there was no reported problem. The relationship is difficult to interpret since the 61 cases in which the child had some problems were all "post one-month placements." Thus it is probably a reflection of whatever underlies the association between age at placement and the ratings. Also associated with the home ratings is the parent's recollection of the family's process of arriving at a decision to adopt the child. The lack of clear-cut consensus between the parents in wanting an adoptive child was negatively related to evaluation of the home ($r = -.28$). The lack of such enthusiasm raised questions about the quality of the marital relationship and about possible later rejection of the child, which, presumably, were confirmed or disconfirmed on the basis of other interview evidence.

The adoptive parents' relations with, and feelings about, the natural parents are associated with the home ratings. In the 63 cases in which there was contact between the two families after the adoption had been completed, the average home rating is significantly lower. Post-adoptive contact is highly related to preadoptive contact. In all 63 cases there had been some contact between the families prior to the completion of the adoption. It is likely that whatever factors are at work in producing the relationship between pre-adoptive contact and the home ratings are at work in this instance as well.

The parent was asked about her preferences for knowing about the natural parents, their backgrounds, personalities, and so forth. There are significant differences in average home ratings among various categories of answers. Those parents who are interested only in certain characteristics of the natural parents had the highest average home ratings. The checklist revealed that the characteristics they were interested in almost exclusively were health, intelligence, and occasionally social background. Other types of preference served indirectly in the judgment process by raising questions of two kinds. In the case of adoptive parents who wished to know nothing about the natural parents, the possibility of their desiring subconsciously to deny the fact of the child's adoption was taken into account along with its implications of possible overinvolvement. Parents who wished to know everything possible about the child's natural parents were sometimes regarded as tending to ascribe all of the child's development to hereditary factors, thus denying any personal responsibility for the way the adoption was turning out.

The adoptive parent's attitudes toward the natural parent served as a criterion for the home ratings. A correlation of $-.28$ was found between the ratings and negative feelings toward the natural parents. This attitude was taken as a clue to the parent's warmth and acceptance of both people in general and the child in particular.

The quality of sibling relations in the family served as an indirect criterion for the home ratings. Cases in which the mother described problems in sibling relations were, on the average, rated significantly lower than those in which there were no problems or no sibs. The presence of difficulties frequently raised questions about the mother's capacity to handle the situation. In part, this may account for the relationship.

The way the child learned he was adopted is related to the evaluation of his adoptive home. Of importance are: who told the child, when he was told, his reaction to being told, certain themes used in telling, and the way his natural parents were described.

Table 72 summarizes the results, with the exception of the age at which the child was told he was adopted. This is negatively correlated, r = −.24, with the home ratings, indicating the earlier the better as far as evaluation of the home is concerned.[1]

TABLE 72. HOW THE CHILD LEARNED OF HIS ADOPTION BY OVER-ALL HOME RATINGS[a]

	Number of cases	Average rating
Persons who told[b]		
Child not told	40	2.75
Adoptive parents	377	3.31
Others	21	2.38
Themes used in telling[b]		
Reassuring statements included	159	3.55
Reassuring statements omitted	279	3.02
Description of natural parents[b]		
Described positively	24	3.04
Not described or only acknowledged	395	3.27
Described negatively	19	2.21
Child's reaction[b]		
No evidence of unfavorable reaction	402	3.27
Mildly upset	20	3.10
Severely upset	16	2.00

[a] Except persons who told the child he was adopted, "not told" cases were combined with the modal category. In all relationships this tended to reduce the contrast. However, it allows the conclusion that differences are due to groups other than the "not told" cases.

[b] Differences are statistically significant.

The relationship is probably not a direct one. Rather, questions are raised in cases of later telling about the kinds of parents who would put off this duty and the possible consequences for the child.

Who told the child of his adoption is probably a more direct criterion of the home ratings than any of the remaining variables. The most appropriate persons are obviously the child's adoptive parents. Note that not telling the child is not evaluated as negatively on the average when the detrimental consequences have not occurred as when they have, that is, when the child accidentally learned of his adoption from someone other than his parents.

[1] "Not told" cases were assigned the average age at telling.

A wide variety of themes and combinations of themes were used in telling the child of his adoption. They range from elaborately constructed fairy tale analogies to the concept of the chosen baby to a simple statement in which the word "adopted" was used. Sometimes included were statements of the motives of the adoptive parents for taking the child, statements about how they got him, and statements reassuring him that he is no different from, or less loved than, natural children. The last-named include indications that the child was picked out because of his special qualities ("We knew it was you from the moment we saw you"), indications that the child was wanted equally or even more than natural children, because his adoptive parents chose to have him ("We didn't just have any baby, we picked you out"), and assurance to the child that the adoptive parents were his real parents even though he didn't "grow inside of mother." Such statements often suggested to the raters that the mother was sensitive to the child and to the possible effects of adoptive status on him. This, along with other evidence, provided a clue to the general quality of the mother's handling of the child.

The chief source of significance in the relation between the home ratings and how the natural parents were described to the child comes from the extremely low average rating in cases where the parents were described negatively. ("Your mother was bad. She didn't deserve to keep you.") Implications of lack of sensitivity, or possibly rejection of the child in such cases, probably account for the relationship.

Being told he was adopted infrequently evoked perceptible negative reaction on the part of the child. In the few cases in which this was true, the child was not told until after pre-school age. Thus the relationship between the child's reaction and the home ratings may have elements in common with the relationship between age at telling and the ratings. Also possibly involved are indirect implications about the inadequacy of the parent's handling drawn from the child's reaction *per se*.

Among the questions routinely asked in the interview was whether the parent felt the child resembled anyone in the family. The answers, scored for degree of dissimilarity, are correlated at a level of −.27 with the home ratings. Seeing the child as completely dissimilar to the adoptive family gave rise to interpretations of possible feelings of rejection on the part of the mother. Thus it served as an indirect criterion.

The great majority of adoptive parents expressed complete satisfaction with the way the adoption was working out. In 67 cases (15 per cent) there was an indication by the mother of something less than complete satisfaction for either her or her husband. These cases are, on the average, rated significantly lower than the remainder.[1] Parent satisfaction is one of the major criteria of adoption outcome. A correlation of .38 with the composite home ratings was found. A high correlation would be expected because of its direct inclusion in the ratings. In addition, there is strong evidence that rejection of the child is more frequent among dissatisfied parents. Use of disciplinary measures is more frequent. Pleasurable activity with the child is less frequent. Parental disagreement about discipline occurs more often, and attitudes toward the child and his friends' using the home as a place to meet or play tend to be more negative. It is also interesting to note that there is a significant correlation ($r = .21$) between dissatisfaction on the part of the parents and the age at which the child was placed in the adoptive home.

Two variables characterizing conditions of the interview situation show low but statistically significant relationships to the home ratings. The first is the degree of resistance on the part of the mother when she was initially approached by telephone to request her cooperation in the study. This variable, obtained from a content analysis of the interview records, is correlated $-.18$ with the ratings. There may be an association between willingness to cooperate and more general aspects of the mother's manner of relating to others which underlies the observed correlation. Also to be taken into account is the possibility that an initial "set" about the home may have developed in some instances which could have influenced the conduct of the actual interview or subconsciously affected interpretations. However, if this were the case, the influence was not very great, as indicated by the size of the correlation.

---

[1] The mean is 2.03 as compared with 3.44 for the completely satisfied cases.

A second characteristic of the interview that is associated with the ratings is the presence of the adoptive father. In about 35 per cent of the interviews (152 cases) the adoptive father was present all or part of the time. Average home ratings are significantly higher in these cases, the mean being 3.46 as compared with 3.08 for those where the father was not present. (Expressed as a correlation, r = .13.) While this is not very high, it should be pointed out that the proportion of "D" and "E" rated homes in the group in which the father was present is 22 per cent as compared with 34 per cent of the others.

Because of limited time and money resources, it was decided when designing the study that no systematic attempt would be made to interview both adoptive parents. There was some hope that through discussion with the mother, an adequate picture of the father's role in the family, his relations with the mother, and his influence on the child could be obtained. With the presence of a systematic difference in home evaluations when the fathers happened to participate in the interview, a serious problem is raised. Perhaps fathers who made arrangements to be present during the interview were more interested and participated more fully in the life of the family in general. However, to infer this on the basis of his presence alone hardly would seem justified. Moreover, there is little in the data about other characteristics of the home that would support it. The adoptive father's presence is uncorrelated with any of the other variables describing him or his role in the family, including socioeconomic status, parental agreement about use of disciplinary measures, or his frequency of pleasurable activity with the adoptive child. Perhaps there were differences in the way the mother represented herself and her husband or the way she related to the interviewer when her husband was not present. In a number of "D" and "E" homes the father was described as a "cipher," indicating that he had little or no influence in the life of the family other than bringing home a pay check. Perhaps if he had been seen in the flesh this would not have been the case. In either event, the systematic differences as observed cannot be regarded as comforting when one considers the validity of the home evaluations in cases where the father was not seen. Their presence emphasizes the possibility that the distribution of home ratings might have been different if it had been possible to see both parents in all cases.

The preceding paragraphs have been devoted to a detailed consideration of the relationships between certain characteristics of adoptive homes and the way they were evaluated. The purpose of this exploration was to estimate how well the home ratings might have been predicted on the basis of knowledge of each characteristic. As an extension of this approach one may ask how well the home ratings might have been predicted on the basis of knowledge of a number of characteristics taken jointly. Since some of the characteristics are related to one another as well as to the ratings, the procedure used should allow for only the independent contribution of each variable to affect the results. This may be done through multiple correlations.

Nine independent variables were used in computing the multiple correlation.[1] By inspection it was determined that additional variables would not raise the correlation more than two or three points in the hundredths place. The variables selected were post-adoptive marital disruption, socioeconomic level of the neighborhood, attitudes toward natural parents, age at which the child was told of his adoption, parent's conception of child's similarity to family, parental agreement about discipline, attitude toward the child and his friends' using the home, mother's frequency of pleasurable activity with the child, and parent's satisfaction with the way the adoption was turning out. These yield a multiple correlation of .66 with the home ratings. It should be noted that this is only an estimate. Since the variables were selected on a *post hoc* basis, the results would have to be validated against a new sample.

The multiple correlation of .66, while high, accounts for only 44 per cent of the variation in the home ratings. Inclusion of additional checklist characteristics would not raise this percentage very much. What is left over includes among its components associations with variables not covered by the checklist and instrument error.

---

[1] Because they were summary judgments and because of the evidence that their relationship with the home ratings might be a result of halo effect, the five sub-ratings were not included.

Specific Home Characteristics and Adjustment

We may ask whether those *specific* aspects of the current adoptive situation involved in (or at least correlated with) the home ratings have any relationship to the adjustment of the child. For example, would there have been a closer agreement between the home and adjustment measures if certain factors had been given greater weight in the overall home rating, others less? Correlations between such specific characteristics and the adjustment measures may provide some clues concerning the answer to this question.

Certain cautions must be emphasized before interpreting such correlations. Both sets of variables are subject to error. The checklist data are crude and probably have rather limited reliability. The test and rating data fare reasonably well as far as reliability is concerned but cannot be assumed to have equally high validity. The net effect is an increased likelihood that relationships will be reduced. The possibility of incorrect causal inferences should also be pointed out. In the logic of this research design, the child assessment measures are dependent variables, the "effect" we are trying to explain. However, since both sets of measures in the following relationships are current, this may not always be the case. In some of the relationships, the child's adjustment may be prior to the parent's attitudes. For example, the child's maladjustment may lead to feelings of rejection on the part of the parent rather than the reverse. Or there could be a reciprocal effect such that each builds on the other.

Table 73 presents correlations between characteristics of the adoptive child and the psychological tests. As is the case throughout this volume, even the significant correlations are quite low. Lack of reliability and validity in both sets of measures would lower the correlations. Furthermore, the underlying relationships may be quite weak.

The pattern of correlations observed here tends to support the notion that the sex differences are due to higher aggressiveness in boys. The correlation with aggressive maladjustment and the difference in correlations between the two scales of the California Test of Personality lead to this inference.

TABLE 73. CORRELATIONS BETWEEN ADJUSTMENT MEASURES AND CHARACTERISTICS OF THE CHILD

	Achievement tests	BDC Withdrawn Maladjustment	BDC Aggressive Maladjustment	BDC Leadership	Sociometric	CTP Social Adjustment	CTP Personal Adjustment
Current age	-[a]	.10	-	-	-	-	-
Male sex	-	-	.21	−.18	−.12	−.28	−.10
Handicaps	-	-	-	−.10	−.13	-	−.12
General health	-	-	-	-	.10	-	-
Description of temperament	-	-	.26	−.22	−.10	-	−.10
Description of social relations	-	-	-	.13	-	.15	.17

NOTE: N = 410 tested and interviewed cases. All reported values are significant at the .05 level.

[a] Blanks indicate that the relationship was not significantly greater than zero.

Current age is associated only with withdrawn maladjustment. The level of association is quite low. This is interesting to note in the light of the high relationship between current age and age at placement ($r = .59$), which in turn is associated with most of the tests except withdrawn maladjustment.

Average test scores for handicapped children are lower on the average than those of the nonhandicapped in three tests. The level of association is low, partly because of the small number of the adopted children having handicaps. While the number is too small to permit statistical analysis by type of handicap, inspection of the pattern of averages shows the group with chronic diseases (mainly asthma and allergies) to fare worse than the physically handicapped on most tests exclusive of the sociometric ratings. It will be noted that children described as in poor health by their parents are also preferred less frequently by their peers, as indicated by the correlation between general health and the sociometric ratings. The relationship is depressed by the infrequency of cases in the poor health group.

The correlations between the mother's description of the child's temperament and the tests present a problem in interpretation. Being described as moody and irritable is positively associated with aggressive maladjustment, and negatively associated with leadership, sociometric rating, and CTP Personal Adjustment. On the one hand, this relationship might be due to the common association of the tests and the mother's description with the child's actual behavior. On the other, there may be a causal relationship involved in which the mother's negative perception of the child is associated with her rejection of him, which in turn has a negative effect on adjustment. For example, there is a correlation of $-.32$, between perceiving the child negatively and the social worker's rating of the mother's warmth toward the child. However, it is not necessary to conclude that lack of warmth comes before negative perception.

The child's preferring to be with his peers is associated with higher average scores on leadership and the California Test of Personality than is his preferring to be with adults or by himself. To the extent that the child's actual preference is reflected in the mother's description, the correlation may be due to negative weight given to nonpeer preferences in the mental health criteria underlying the test. Withdrawn maladjustment is also significantly associated with the mother's description of the child's social relations. The most withdrawn children were in the group who prefer to be with adults. There is relatively little difference in the average scores of those who prefer to be by themselves and those who prefer to be with their peers.

Included in the area of general characteristics of the home are the health of the adoptive parents, the adoptive father's current occupation, the socioeconomic level of the neighborhood in which the adoptive family lives, whether the adoptive mother is currently working, and marital history since adoption. With the exception of health of the adoptive parents, all of these variables are significantly associated with one or more of the tests. However, the correlations appearing in Table 74, though significant, are quite low.

The correlations between socioeconomic variables and the test results are similar to our earlier findings. The association between occupation of the adoptive father and Achievements tests, while not statistically significant, is in the expected direction. The correlation of Achievement tests with the neighborhood ratings is the highest for any of the socioeconomic variables examined. The positive correlations with CTP Personal Adjustment may reflect some socioeconomic bias in the test itself as well as differences in

TABLE 74. CORRELATIONS BETWEEN ADJUSTMENT MEASURES AND GEN-
ERAL CHARACTERISTICS OF THE CURRENT HOME SITUATION

	Achieve-ment tests	With-drawn Malad-justment	Aggressive Malad-justment	Leader-ship	Socio-metric	CTP Social	CTP Personal
Occupation of adoptive father	_b	-	-	-	.11	-	.12
Socioeconomic level[a] of neighborhood	.21	-	-	-	-	-	.13
Marital disruption since adoption	-	-	-	-	-	−.11	−.17
Adoptive mother working	-	-	.16°	.13°	-	-	-

[a] Signs reversed because of direction of coding (High = 0).

[b] Blanks indicate that the relationship was not significantly greater than zero.

° Eta, a measure of nonlinear association. The corresponding F ratios are significant.

personality of the adoptive parents, child-rearing patterns, and so on.

A relationship between post-adoptive marital disruption and the CTP scales is certainly to be expected on the basis of current mental health theory. If anything, the absence of significant associations with the other tests and the very low correlations with the CTP variables is somewhat surprising. In part this may be due to the unbalanced distribution with only a small proportion of post-adoptive deaths, divorces, and separations (about 15 per cent).

It should be noted that the correlations are based on a dichotomization in which death of a parent is grouped with divorce and separation. While average scores are lower for children of divorced or separated adoptive parents than for the group in which one parent died, the difference is not statistically significant. The major contrast is between no marital disruption and some, whether by death or divorce.

The correlations reported for the adoptive mother's current participation in the labor force are measures of nonlinear association. It may be recalled that the mother's working was associated with the overall home ratings, the average ratings being highest in cases in which she did not work, lowest in cases in which she worked full time, and intermediate in cases in which she worked part time. The pattern for aggressive maladjustment and leadership is different. Aggressive maladjustment is highest and leadership lowest in the group in which the mother is working full time. However, the main contrast is between the group where the mother worked part time and the other two groups. Aggressive maladjustment is significantly lower and leadership significantly higher in this group. These findings are in line with some current views on the working mother. It has been maintained that it may actually be conducive to parent-child relations for the mother to find interests outside the home, such as a part-time job after her children have reached school age. One might speculate about this being particularly true in the case of adoptive mothers where there may be greater danger of overinvolvement with the child. On the other hand, the relationships are quite small and could easily come from the joint association of other variables to the tests and the mother's working.

A number of variables characterizing child-rearing attitudes or practices are significantly correlated with the tests. The results are summarized in Table 75. Among the variables of this type not showing significant relationships with the tests are the parents' feelings about the child's future career, the types of acts for which the child is disciplined, the mother's feelings about administering discipline, and the use of physical punishment as a method of discipline.

There appears to be a pattern in the correlations in Table 75, which indicates an association between rejection of the child and aggressive maladjustment, perhaps coupled with feelings of anxiety or insecurity. Negative attitudes toward the child's school performance, frequent use of disciplinary measures, opposition to the child and his friends' using the home, and infrequent pleasurable activity of mother and child, all have implications of possible feelings of rejection toward the child and all are significantly associated with aggressive maladjustment. All but one are also associated with the California Test of Personality. While the correlations are not very high, their consistency is striking. Their similarity to the findings of Wittenborn's follow-up study of adoptive children (in this case, agency adoptions) is noteworthy.[1] For his older sample (post-first grade but not yet

---

[1] Wittenborn, John R., and others, "A Study of Adoptive Children," *Psychological Monographs*, vol. 70, 1956, pp. 93–115. See Table 4, p. 101.

pre-adolescent), Wittenborn reports correlations of .31 between a cluster of items, indicating rejection of the child and the child's aggressiveness as described by the mother. Similar results are found for his unsympathetic cluster and his punishment for aggression cluster, the correlations with the child's aggression being .25 and .26 respectively. He also has a combined anxious aggressive cluster, which could be regarded as analogous to a combination of our aggressive maladjustment and California Test of Personality measures. The correlation of this cluster with rejection of the child is .36; with unsympathetic child rearing, .27, and .33 with punishment for aggression. Sears, Maccoby, and Levin show a similar relationship in their study of patterns of child rearing.[1] Among the correlates of the child's aggression in the home they report the following which, on theoretical grounds, may be tied in with rejection of the child: dissatisfaction with the current situation ($r = .19$); low value for the mother role ($r = .12$); warmth toward child ($r = -.20$); punishment for aggression toward parents ($r = .16$) and physical punishment ($r = .22$).[2]

For many of the correlations reported in Table 75, the chicken-egg problem can be raised. For example, is the relationship between difficulty in supervising the child and the child's adjustment a reflection of the effects of maternal inadequacy or a reflection of the fact that maladjusted children are likely to be more difficult to supervise, or both? Similarly, rejection of the child could both breed and be bred by the child's maladjustment. The problem is perhaps most acute in the case of the relationship between frequency of discipline and aggressive maladjustment. We would certainly expect overly aggressive children to evoke disciplinary responses from their parents more frequently. There are also theoretical grounds for expecting the frequent use of disciplinary measures to produce a sense of frustration in the child which has aggression as its customary reaction. Or both may be operating in a kind of cumulative fashion. In any event, we may safely conclude, as Sears, Maccoby, and Levin do, re-

---

[1] Sears, Robert R., Eleanor E. Maccoby, and Harry Levin, *Patterns of Child Rearing*. Row, Peterson and Co., Evanston, Ill., 1957.

[2] *Op. cit.*, pp. 257 and 527.

TABLE 75. CORRELATIONS BETWEEN ADJUSTMENT MEASURES AND CURRENT CHILD-REARING ATTITUDES AND PRACTICES

	Achievement tests	Withdrawn Maladjustment	Aggressive Maladjustment	Leadership	Sociometric	CTP Social Adjustment	CTP Personal Adjustment
Attitude toward child's school performance[b]	.38	−.22	−.32	.43	.30	.25	.22
Frequency of discipline	−.13	-	.28	−.16	-	−.17	−.18
Frequency with which child "gets away with" disapproved behavior	-[a]	-	-	-	-	−.11	−.13
Parental agreement about discipline[b]	-	-	−.12	-	.11	.13	.12
Attitude toward child and friends using home[b]	-	-	−.13	-	-	-	-
Frequency of pleasurable activity with child-adoptive mother[b]	.12	-	−.22	.16	-	.18	.13
Degree of difficulty in supervising child	-	-	.16	−.18	−.11	−.14	-

[a] Blanks indicate that the relationship was not significantly greater than zero.

[b] Signs reversed because of direction of coding which ran from positive to negative or high to low.

garding the effectiveness of punishment, that frequent discipline does not seem to curb the types of behavior toward which it is directed.

The relatively high correlations found for the parent's attitudes toward the child's school performance are somewhat unexpected. The correlation with achievement tests is understandable since achievement tests are associated with the child's school grades, which in turn would be expected to be related to how satisfied the parent was with the child's school performance. There may be some circularity involved in the other relationships as well. On the average, children who are maladjusted in other areas are not likely to do well in their academic work. There is also a possibility that the reliability and validity of this particular item tends to be higher than some of the other attitudinal items which would tend to increase the correlations.

Included in the area of characteristics specific to adoptive families are variables describing how the child was told about his adoption, the structure of the adoptive family, attitudes toward the post-adoptive relations with the natural parents, conceptions of the child's similarity to the adoptive family, the family's reac-

TABLE 76. CORRELATIONS BETWEEN ADJUSTMENT MEASURES AND CHARACTERISTICS SPECIFIC TO ADOPTIVE FAMILIES

	Achievement tests	Withdrawn Maladjustment	Aggressive Maladjustment	Leadership	Sociometric	CTP Social Adjustment	CTP Personal Adjustment
Post-adoptive contact with natural parents	—.13	—ᵃ	-	-	—.13	-	—.12
Child's reaction to placement	-	-	.13	—.18	—.15	-	-
Age child told of adoption	-	.12	-	-	-	-	-
Child's reaction to being told of adoption	—.17	-	.12	-	-	-	-
Parent's conception of child as dissimilar to family	-	-	-	-	—.10	-	—.10
Parent's attitudes toward adoption outcome (Neg.)	—.13	-	.21	—.18	—.17	—.19	—.19

ᵃ Blanks indicate that the relationship was not significantly greater than zero.

tion to the child's placement, the process of deciding to adopt a child, and the parents' satisfaction with the way the adoption was turning out.

Results in this area are rather scattered, as can be seen from Table 76, which contains all variables showing a significant relationship with one or more of the test results. Only two of the five variables describing how the child was told of his adoption show significant correlations with any of the tests and these are quite low. Average scores of the children not told they were adopted were about the same as those of children who were, except on the California Test of Personality. They were lower in that instance but the difference was not statistically significant. While our categorization of the themes used in telling the child he was adopted and the way in which the natural parents were described to him are very crude, no systematic differences in adjustment among the categories could be observed.

One might ask how much improvement over the home rating-test correlations could be gained if combinations of these home characteristics empirically weighted rather than subjectively weighted were used. The multiple correlations in Table 77 give a rough estimate. In comparing them with the test-home rating correlations, it must be remembered that the combinations are based on *post hoc* analysis and would require cross-validation on a new sample.

From the table it can be seen that the multiple correlations average nearly double the comparable correlations with the home ratings. Thus nearly four times as much variation in the tests is accounted for by these combinations of specific characteristics as by the home ratings. This is substantial improvement.

TABLE 77. CORRELATIONS BETWEEN ADJUSTMENT MEASURES, COMBINATIONS OF HOME CHARACTERISTICS, AND THE OVERALL HOME RATINGS

Child assessment variables	Independent variables	Multiple correlation	Home-rating correlation
Achievement tests	1,3,8	.41	.16
BDC Withdrawn Maladjustment	1,7	.24	−.15
BDC Aggressive Maladjustment	1,3,6	.39	−.16
BDC Leadership	1,4,6	.45	.22
Sociometric Rating	1,2,4	.31	.20
CTP Social Adjustment	1,2,5	.30	.21
CTP Personal Adjustment	1,2,3	.28	.24

Independent variables:

    1. Attitude toward child's school performance
    2. Satisfaction with adoption outcome
    3. Frequency of discipline
    4. Degree of difficulty in supervising child
    5. Frequency of pleasurable activity
    6. Parent's conception of child's temperament
    7. Age at which child told of adoption
    8. Socioeconomic level of neighborhood

The improvement is not as great if one used the test combinations of Chapter XI as a basis for comparison, with the exception of Combinations I and II. It is estimated that multiple correlations between home variables and test combinations would be in the .50–.60 range. However, it must be remembered that Combinations III–VI probably are overestimates of the test-home rating correlation. Combinations III, IV, and V are partly based on the social work evaluation of the child's adjustment, made from the case records and in full knowledge of the home rating for the case. That this is not an independent assessment of adjustment can be clearly seen in the next chapter. Combinations IV, V, and VI are partly based on the categorized teacher's comments. These comments were available only for an unrepresentative sample of the total, and their utilization was not completely independent of the home ratings.

In conclusion, then, focused detailed description rather than professional assumption may be a more effective approach to the problem of evaluation. Future studies of adoption outcome would be well advised to make adequate provision for obtaining reliable data on specific aspects of parental attitudes and child-rearing practices as well as more general "psychodynamic" characterizations.

CHAPTER XVII

Patterns of Outcome

IN THE PRECEDING CHAPTERS we have been concerned with the relationships between many characteristics of the adoptive situation, and two sets of assessments that represent attempts to measure the current outcome of adoptions. We have also examined in detail some of the interrelations among the outcome measures themselves. Frequently it appeared that some of the characteristics of the adoptive situation were related to one another as well as to the measures of outcome. Thus interpretation of any single relationship was made even more hazardous.

Our initial results, along with those of other studies in the field of child development, strongly suggest the presence of patterns in which certain characteristics of the home cluster together, possibly along with certain clusters of adjustment measures. By isolating such clusters and attempting to identify the elements the characteristics have in common, we may be able to clarify some of the issues raised in conjunction with the interpretation of single relationships. Perhaps we may discover a general outcome pattern in which certain child-rearing attitudes and practices, measures of child's adjustment, and the social work evaluation of the home cluster together. Perhaps each of these sets of variables constitutes one or more independent clusters. Or there may be some combination of these two extremes.

The Factor Analysis

The method used in this attempt to isolate patterns is factor analysis, which is a statistical procedure for reducing a number of variables to a smaller number of more general traits or factors. This procedure has the advantage of avoiding arbitrary cutting points or *a priori* combinations of measures. It begins with the intercorrelations among all the variables. Table 78 on page 419 contains the matrix of these intercorrelations.[1] Each of the variables has two classes of elements involved in its distribution. First, it has elements in common with other variables in the matrix. These elements in common are called its communality. Second, it has elements not in common with any of the other variables in the matrix. These may be elements specific to itself, or the product of error in measurement, that is, unreliability. The combination is called uniqueness. Factor analysis is primarily concerned with communality. It statistically partitions communality into clusters or factors, and measures the strength of the relationship of each variable to the cluster. The end product of the statistical analysis is sets of these measures of association for each factor, which are called factor loadings. Table 79 on page 421 contains the matrix of rotated factor loadings.[2]

The rotated factor loadings, while mathematical end products, are but starting points for the major task of factor analysis— identification of common elements. They provide an empirical answer to the question of what clusters together. But the analysis does not answer the question of what the clusters mean, that is, what is the element common to all variables having substantial associations with a given factor. This second step is the process of defining (or "naming") the factors. It is a conceptual process. As such it is arbitrary, subject to the theoretical biases and

---

[1] Based on 410 cases for which both test and home interview data were available. In all cases, missing information was included in modal category. Home characteristics were selected on the basis of previously having shown significant relationships with one or more of the outcome measures. One variable, parent's attitude toward the child's school performance, was omitted from the matrix through clerical error. Its principal factor loadings are estimated to be .250 on Factor I and .450 on Factor V.

Some of the correlations are based on distributions that are highly skewed. If it had previously shown significant correlations with outcome measures, a variable was included as long as the proportion of cases in the modal class interval did not exceed about 80 per cent. This is a considerable stretch of the assumption of normal distribution underlying correlation analysis. However, it was felt that since the objective was a search for patterns of co-variance rather than a precise identification of underlying factorial structure, their inclusion was justified.

[2] Centroid factors. Rotation was machine programmed, employing a quartimax solution. Twenty-two rotation cycles were used. Inspection of the two-dimensional plots indicated that further rotation using graphic methods was not necessary.

assumptions of the interpreter. The factor loadings in no sense "prove" the interpretations based upon them. When dealing with data that are crude and come from a variety of sources, as in the present study, it is especially important to keep the logical distinction between data and interpretation clearly in mind.

FACTOR I: HOME RATING CLUSTER

Positive Loadings

Overall Home Rating .895
Marital Relations Rating .844
Emotional Response to Child Rating .798
Freedom from Anxiety Rating .385
Parental agreement in deciding to adopt .213

Negative Loadings

Social work rating of child's degree of maladjustment —.583
Parental dissatisfaction with adoption outcome —.481
Parental disagreement about discipline —.426
Parent's conception of child's disposition as moody and irritable —.395
Infrequent pleasurable activity of mother with child —.392
Post-adoptive marital disruption —.349
Opposition to child and his friends' using home —.349
Negative attitudes toward natural parents —.328
Parent's conception of child as dissimilar to adoptive family —.286
Age child told of adoption —.276
Current age of child —.236
Low socioeconomic level of neighborhood —.225
Age of child at placement —.204

Principal loadings on this factor come from the ratings of broad aspects of home quality as seen by social workers, with the overall home rating being the highest. Along with the home ratings, their major direct and indirect criteria have substantial loadings.[1] Common to all of these variables is their relationship to the worker's general perception of home quality as expressed in the overall home rating. Thus the factor is named the home rating cluster.

The social work rating of the child's degree of maladjustment also loads very high on this factor. Our earlier indication that this variable is not highly differentiated from the general perception

---

[1] The cutting point for interpretive significance selected here, .200, is low compared to usual practice. Its selection is justified on two grounds. First, error due to the crudeness of some of our measures and highly skewed distributions has acted to depress correlations and consequently factor loadings as well. Second, both the number of cases and the number of variables are rather large, which would tend to minimize the likelihood of loadings as high as these being due to chance.

of home quality tends to be confirmed, especially when one also notes the relatively minimal loadings of the other adjustment measures.

Age at placement and the child's current age both have moderate negative loadings. Since the two are not independent, it is not possible to tell which, if either, is basic. For example, later placement may impair the development of identification with the child, leading to difficulties in the parent's relations with him. Or the loadings may reflect a somewhat typical pattern of parental exasperation with adolescent children. In either event, what is common to the interpretations is their association with something less than amicable parent-child relations, an important component of the worker's perception of home quality.

FACTOR II: CHILD'S PERCEPTION OF APPROPRIATE RESPONSES

Positive Loadings		Negative Loadings	
CTP Personal Adjustment	.829	Frequency of discipline	−.202
CTP Social Adjustment	.738		
Achievement tests	.302		
I.Q.	.256		

The two major scales of the California Test of Personality are highly saturated on this factor. It accounts for about 95 per cent of the communality of each. As a global measure of adjustment, the California Test of Personality attempts to tap the child's feelings about himself, his relationships with others, and his standards of conduct. As with most self-reporting instruments, the most serious criticisms leveled at the California Test of Personality challenge the assumption that what the child reports is necessarily what he thinks or feels. The fact that the test pulls out as a separate factor in this analysis does nothing to dispel such arguments. Consequently, in interpreting this factor we are loath to make the assumption that the test is measuring the child's true feelings of security, sense of belonging, adequacy of social relations, and so forth. Instead, items on the test are viewed as indicating what generally are regarded as desirable ways to think, feel, and act. Whether or not his responses stem from, and correspond to, what is actually the case, the child who scores high on this test at least is aware of the appropriate or "right" ways to respond. Hence this factor is called the child's perception of appropriate responses.

The secondary loadings of the two measures of intellectual functioning are easy to understand from this point of view. A certain amount of intellectual ability is required for one to know just what are the right answers. The negative association of frequency of discipline with this factor can be similarly interpreted, rather than having to assume some kind of causal relationship. Bright children who are also aware of what is "correct" are less likely to get into situations in which they would be disciplined by their parents.

FACTOR III: REJECTION–AGGRESSION SYNDROME

Positive Loadings

BDC Aggressive Maladjustment .484
Contact between natural and adoptive parents .421
Nonprofessional adoption arranger .419
Parent's conception of child's disposition as moody and irritable .344
Frequency of discipline .319
Negative attitudes toward natural parents .249
Infrequent pleasurable activity of mother with child .208

Negative Loadings

BDC Withdrawn Maladjustment −.404

Perceiving the child as moody and irritable, disciplining him frequently, having negative feelings about his natural parents, and rarely engaging in shared pleasurable activities with him are interpreted as stemming from the same general feeling, rejection of the child. As indicated by the BDC items, the characteristic pattern of the child's behavior associated with parental rejection is excitability, attention demanding, and the acting out of hostile impulses. From this association, Factor III gets its name, rejection-aggression syndrome.

The negative relationship of withdrawn maladjustment to the factor should be noted. In part, this may be expected because of the negative zero-order correlation between aggressive and withdrawn maladjustment. However, the correlation is not extremely high, $r = -.265$. With a correlation of this size, withdrawn maladjustment could possibly have had a zero loading. Instead, its loading exceeds the correlation. Evidently, withdrawing tendencies are disproportionately infrequent in homes characterized by parental rejection. One might conceive of a continuum ranging from parental rejection to parental overinvolvement. Associated with the first extreme is aggressive maladjustment. It is interesting to speculate whether withdrawn maladjustment would be the characteristic pattern at the opposite pole. If we had reliable independent measures of parental overinvolvement, we might expect them to load negatively as well, producing a clearly defined bipolar factor.

The high loadings of two variables characterizing the pattern of placement arrangements are among the most striking findings of the study. Obtaining the baby through nonprofessional channels (other than a doctor, lawyer, minister, or social worker) and having contact with the natural parents prior to adoption are highly correlated, since in many cases where nonprofessional channels were used the arrangements were made directly with the natural parents. The loadings strongly suggest the operation of a selective factor in the kinds of parents whose adoptive children come to them in different ways. The method of obtaining a baby directly from the natural parents or from their family or friends, under circumstances in which contact is made directly with the natural parents, tends to select parents who are likely later to have feelings of rejection for the child.[1] Our data are not very illuminating as to why such a selective factor may be operating. Perhaps it is related to the motives or personalities of couples who would adopt children who came to their attention through newspaper advertisements, children whom they were asked to adopt after a brief acquaintance, or children of families they knew before they considered adopting a child. These three types make up the bulk of cases where there was contact between the natural and adoptive parents during the course of the placement arrangements.

In Chapter X it was noted that differences in adjustment between the adopted sample and a matched group of "own" children tended to disappear when age at placement was held

---

[1] As an alternative hypothesis, one might suggest that this method of placement arrangements causes parental rejection. However, this does not seem as likely as the interpretation offered above.

constant, except for aggressive maladjustment. The loadings on Factor III would lead one to expect that the principal source of the differences in aggressive maladjustment lies in those cases where contacts between the natural and adoptive parents and a nonprofessional arranger were involved. The most favorable circumstances seem to be those in which placement was arranged by a physician, the child was taken in his first month of life, and there was no contact between the natural and adoptive families.

FACTOR IV: SOCIOECONOMIC STATUS

Positive Loadings	*Negative Loadings*
Education of adoptive father .644	Low socioeconomic level of neighborhood −.508
Current occupation of adoptive father .577	Contact between natural and adoptive parents −.404
Parental dissatisfaction with adoption outcome .310	Nonprofessional adoption arranger −.366
Education of natural mother .294	Freedom from Anxiety Rating −.217
Frequency of discipline .292	Age child told of adoption −.206
Degree of difficulty in supervising child .242	

Factor IV gets its name from the three components of socioeconomic status that load highest on it—occupation, education, and neighborhood level. The negative loadings of nonprofessional placement arranger, contact between adoptive and natural parents, and the positive loading of education of natural mother are reflections of socioeconomic selectivity in methods of arranging for the placement of the child. Telling the child about his adoption as early as possible is a pattern one might expect to be associated with higher socioeconomic status. It is strongly recommended as "correct" in many books and magazine articles which parents at higher socioeconomic levels are likely to see and be influenced by.

The positive loadings of parental dissatisfaction with adoption outcome, frequency of discipline, and difficulty in supervising the child, and the negative loading of Freedom from Anxiety Rating are more difficult to account for. The interaction of two processes is suggested, the socioeconomic components of which are reflected in these factor loadings. The first is a tendency in higher socioeconomic groups toward greater self-consciousness about the process of child rearing; more concern about whether one is "doing the right thing." The second is a similar tendency toward higher expectations for the child and greater demands upon him. Within this pattern, more frequent discipline is used in an attempt to narrow the gap between what the child does and what the parent expects of him. However, the use of discipline is not without accompanying anxiety, nor is it likely to be very effective under such conditions. This tends to breed a feeling of frustration about getting the child to conform to the parent's expectations and some dissatisfaction with the way the adoption is turning out.

FACTOR V: SCHOOL ADJUSTMENT

Positive Loadings

BDC Leadership .840
Sociometric Rating .463
Achievement tests .353
I.Q. .299

Negative Loadings

BDC Withdrawn Maladjustment −.488
BDC Aggressive Maladjustment −.395
Degree of difficulty in supervising child −.219
Social work rating of child's degree of maladjustment −.213

This factor is seen as representing the reciprocal relationships between the teacher's perception of the child, his academic and intellectual achievement, and popularity with his classmates. Brighter children are likely to be perceived positively by their teachers, which in turn may influence their popularity in the classroom. Similarly, the teacher's notion of the child's adjustment is probably influenced by what she believes his popularity to be. Furthermore, bright children are likely to be preferred by their classmates. The locus of these reciprocal relationships is the child's adjustment in one of the major areas of daily activity— school. Hence the factor is named school adjustment.

The negative loadings of the social work rating of maladjustment and the parent's degree of difficulty in supervising the child are seen as representing the overlap between the child's adjustment outside the home and in the other major area of his activities—his adjustment in the family. The parent's feelings about how difficult it is to supervise the child fit directly into this interpretation. The social work rating of the child's maladjustment and its relationship to the worker's conception of parent-child relationships was mentioned in conjunction with Factor I. The same interpretation is being offered here.

FACTOR VI: AGE OF ADOPTIVE PARENTS

Positive Loadings

Age of adoptive father at time of placement .662
Age of adoptive mother at time of placement .652

Negative Loadings

Parental agreement in deciding to
adopt −.234
Parent's conception of child's disposition
as moody and irritable −.219

Factor VI derives its name from its two principal loadings, the age of each adoptive parent at the time of placement. It should be pointed out that for correlational purposes, these are practically equivalent to their current ages. The negative loading of parental agreement in deciding to adopt a child comes chiefly from the greater frequency of reluctance in this respect on the part of older fathers. Hesitancy or opposition on the part of older fathers constitutes the bulk of cases in which there was not a clear-cut consensus. This is understandable. They are likely to have fears about the radical shifts in time-tested family routines that may be occasioned by adoption. Seeing the child as moody and irritable tends to be more characteristic of younger parents, as indicated by the direction of the loading. This may reflect a somewhat more quiet and possibly passive environment in the older homes, or perhaps a tendency for more "mellowness" and tolerance toward the child's irritability, should it be present.

FACTOR VII: AGE AT PLACEMENT SELECTIVITY IN PLACEMENT PATTERN

Positive Loadings: Age of child at placement .738
Current age of child .690
Nonprofessional adoption arranger .374
Contact between natural and adoptive parents .339

The chief loadings on Factor VII come from the child's age at placement and his current age. These two variables are highly associated because of the nature of our sampling design in which there is a six-year age range in a sample drawn from a four-year study period. The selectivity of certain patterns of placement arrangements with respect to the age at which the child is placed has been discussed previously. Placements arranged by doctors almost exclusively result in the adoptive family's taking the child directly from the hospital. As indicated earlier, the great majority of post one-month placements occurs when the placements are arranged directly with the natural parents or by nonprofessional intermediaries. These are also the cases in which contact between the natural and adoptive families is most likely to occur.

The loadings on Factor VIII are somewhat too scattered to permit any but the most speculative kind of interpretation.

Interrelations Among the Factors

It is possible for a variable to have elements in common with, and consequently load on, more than one factor. When this occurs, the variable defines an area of overlap or linkage between factors. An examination of such areas of overlap (or the lack of overlap) may shed further light on the operation of the variables and the meaning of the factors. However, it should be noted that any inferences drawn from this kind of analysis are even more tentative than those concerning the individual factors.

One of the important patterns to be observed in examining Table 79 is the existence of four separate adjustment factors, three of which are quite clearly defined. The first, Factor II, is defined primarily by the two major scales of the California Test of Personality. The connection of this factor with other adjustment measures, such as the child's popularity and the teacher's description of his behavior, appears to come chiefly through their common association with the child's level of intellectual functioning. This pattern raises some questions about the function of the California Test of Personality as a general measure of adjustment. As a general measure, one would have expected stronger bonds between Factor II and the other adjustment factors. Of course, one could raise similar questions about the other adjustment measures.

Characteristics of the home environment contribute to the variance of all four adjustment factors. The contributions are relatively minor on Factors II and V. Factor III, Rejection-Aggression Syndrome, represents the most pronounced of the patterns of association. It is similar to the findings of recent studies on both adopted and "own" children. Two major questions arise in the interpretation of this factor. The first is the question of bipolarity in both terms of the syndrome. The second is that of temporal primacy between the terms.

The pervasiveness of intellectual functioning in the areas of adjustment tapped by this study is worthy of note. Our two measures of intellectual functioning load on, and provide the major links between, three of the four adjustment factors. To some extent this may be an artifact of a research design in which teacher judgments, I.Q., and Achievement tests account for five of the eight adjustment variables. On the other hand, there are strong theoretical grounds for expecting such results. We may think of adjustment as involving the ability to perform various classes of interpersonal tasks. Among the prerequisites to successful performance on many of these tasks are the ability to perceive correctly the expectations of others, the ability to draw appropriate inferences from generalized conceptions of the expectations of others to the context of the situation at hand, and the ability to anticipate the consequences of various sources of action through deduction from these antecedent conditions. These abilities involve logical facility and skill at symbolic manipulation, major elements of measured intelligence.

A great deal of overlap was previously noticed between the following variables: who arranged for the placement, age of child at placement, contact between the natural and adoptive parents, and the socioeconomic status of both natural and adoptive parents. All of these variables showed significant relationships with one or more of the test results and with the home ratings. The problem of primacy was thus an issue.

From the initial results, we might have expected a general placement pattern factor on which the characteristics of the placement arrangements loaded, possibly along with some of the test results and home ratings. Instead, three distinct patterns emerged, linked together by their common association with nonprofessionality of the adoption arranger and the presence of contact between the adoptive and natural families. In all three cases it has been suggested that these two variables indicate the presence of a selective factor. Thus interpreted, we are dealing with not one but three kinds of selectivity. First, on Factor III, we are dealing with selectivity with respect to parents who tend to reject their adoptive children. Second, on Factor IV, there appears to be socioeconomic selectivity with respect to both the natural and adoptive parents. Third, on Factor VII, there is selectivity with respect to the age at which the child enters the adoptive home and, consequently, his current age.

Especially interesting is the behavior of age at placement in the factor analysis. Previous analysis tended to support the idea that age at placement might be the primary factor in the relationship between several characteristics of the placement arrangements and the child's adjustment. The factor analysis suggests that the relationship, at least with the child's adjustment outside the home, is less direct than had been thought originally. Age at placement loads on Factor I, and with the other placement variables on Factor VII, but not directly on any of the adjustment factors. On the other hand, nonprofessional arranger and contact with natural parents load directly on Factor III, one of the adjustment factors but not on Factor I, the home rating cluster.

Because of these patterns we regard it unlikely that the zero-order relationships between age at placement and adjustment stem primarily from a direct effect on the child. Rather, we interpret later age at placement as being associated with a generalized disturbance of parent-child relations and poorer adjustment in the home. Contact and nonprofessional arranger are seen as selective factors with respect to one type of disturbed parent-child relationship, a kind of hostile and punitive rejection of the child. The relationship between this more specific type and the worker's general perception of parent-child relationships is seen in the overlap between Factors I and III. This overlap is in the negative direction and consists primarily of three variables— negative attitudes toward the natural parents, parent's conception of the child as moody and irritable, and infrequent pleasurable activity of mother with child.

The built-in association between age at placement and current age of the child and the similarity of their loadings on Factor I make it difficult to disentangle their respective roles in parent-child relations as perceived by the worker. If we are dealing simply with the normal *Sturm und Drang* between the adolescent and his parents, implications of these findings for adoption policy are limited. If we are dealing with a situation in which the development of parental identification with the child is impeded by not getting the child immediately, there are important research and policy questions to be raised about the practice of retaining children in foster homes for several months prior to placing them for adoption.

Finally, the fact that the home ratings pull out as a separate factor which is not directly linked with any of the adjustment factors should be noted. While the loadings of the psychological tests on Factor I are consistently in the expected direction, in no case do they exceed our .200 arbitrary limit. Moreover, in no case do the ratings of home quality load on an adjustment factor. The only connections between the ratings and adjustment are in their common association with a handful of variables indicating rejection of the child (Factors III and VIII) and the social work rating of the child's degree of maladjustment (Factor V). From this pattern, there is little to indicate a direct connection between the worker's general conception of home quality and the child's adjustment.

Such a conclusion may be too harsh. Adjustment would be regarded as being situationally specific. While there may be a central core common to all situations (akin to Spearman's g factor in intelligence), from this point of view there is much variance that is specific to classes of situations. Our adjustment measures tend to be heavily weighted with one kind of situation, the school environment, while having little direct bearing on another, the home environment. From the pattern of loadings on Factor I and the variables that load jointly on Factor I and one or another of the adjustment factors, it seems reasonable to suggest that the home ratings are related to the child's adjustment in the home.

One could argue that the amount and kinds of overlap between Factor I and the adjustment factors fall far below what one would expect to be the relationships of the child's adjustment in the home to his adjustment in the areas tapped by the tests. Attendant to such an argument would be usual considerations of the reliability and validity of each set of measures and their depressing effects on the observed levels of association. It is also possible to take a less conservative stand about these variables, accepting the results of the factor analysis more nearly at face value. From this latter point of view, one would be led to conclude that expectations concerning the amount of variance in children's adjustment outside the home that is attributable to patterns of interrelations in the family may be seriously overstated.

TABLE 79. ROTATED FACTOR MATRIX

	I[a]	II	III	IV[a]	V[a]	VI[a]	VII[a]	VIII	h²
1. Achievement tests	106	302	033	108	353	-024	-065	338	.359
2. BDC Withdrawn Maladjustment	-115	081	-404	-055	-488	124	151	066	.467
3. BDC Aggressive Maladjustment	-136	-195	484	033	-395	-169	-058	-024	.480
4. BDC Leadership	159	095	-109	-005	840	061	-028	003	.756
5. Sociometric rating	182	135	093	050	463	-032	-034	023	.280
6. CTP Social Adjustment	138	738	-085	013	094	032	-027	-020	.582
7. CTP Personal Adjustment	167	829	-020	074	064	-012	-032	010	.726
8. Social work rating of child's degree of maladjustment	-583	-087	029	116	-213	-072	159	-063	.442
9. I.Q.	057	256	095	101	299	019	-082	278	.262
10. Education of adoptive father	131	059	-010	644	-025	017	-063	-017	.441
11. Post-adoptive marital disruption	-349	-103	-063	-086	150	089	108	256	.251
12. Current occupation of adoptive father	132	070	053	578	-041	121	-027	-011	.375
13. Adoptive mother currently working	-131	-014	004	-141	-018	056	086	064	.035
14. Low socioeconomic level of neighborhood	-225	-118	061	-508	-016	028	040	-094	.338
15. Negative attitudes toward natural parents	-328	060	249	-080	044	-105	135	-154	.234
16. Age child told of adoption	-276	-051	039	-206	-075	-056	049	067	.138
17. Parent's conception of child as dissimilar to family	-286	-083	044	073	-015	075	124	-099	.128
18. Parent's conception of child's disposition as moody and irritable	-395	-004	344	107	-159	-219	090	-014	.367
19. Frequency of discipline	-176	-202	319	292	-135	-013	046	077	.285
20. Extent to which child "gets away with" disapproved behavior	-051	-139	-037	037	-045	073	-016	227	.084
21. Parental disagreement about discipline	-426	-120	065	011	-016	165	-008	298	.317
22. Opposition to child and his friends using home	-349	042	176	-066	-042	-025	-033	-276	.239
23. Infrequent pleasurable activity of mother with child	-392	-031	208	-049	-044	011	113	-234	.270
24. Parental dissatisfaction with adoption outcome	-481	-191	131	310	-110	-063	156	113	.434
25. Adoptive father present during interview	136	101	011	083	-009	061	180	-093	.081
26. Overall Home Rating	895	049	030	114	047	-072	-027	046	.828
27. Marital Relations Rating	844	071	023	115	007	-055	-019	-113	.747
28. Freedom from Anxiety Rating	385	-068	-139	-217	112	075	131	-097	.264
29. Emotional Response to Child Rating	798	050	005	-043	066	-068	-113	077	.669
30. Degree of difficulty in supervising child	-148	-139	174	242	-219	027	019	182	.212
31. Parental agreement in deciding to adopt	213	-073	-057	-034	127	-234	073	070	.136
32. Current age of child	-236	006	-041	-012	000	019	690	012	.534
33. Age of child at placement	-204	-062	049	-070	-074	-089	738	-028	.612
34. Education of natural mother	041	069	-107	294	191	-098	-096	033	.161
35. Age of adoptive father	-188	052	-087	037	037	662	-004	-022	.487
36. Age of adoptive mother	-175	-033	040	-021	063	652	-056	043	.468
37. Contact between natural and adoptive parents	-034	-113	421	-404	-119	156	339	025	.508
38. Nonprofessional adoption arranger	-025	-126	419	-366	-092	130	374	071	.496

[a] Factor multiplied by -1 so that defining variables are positive.

Appendices

APPENDIX A

Parental Characteristics—
Rating Categories

Marital Relations

1. Happy with each other, mutually supportive; both husband and wife have status in family roles and respect each other's performance; many interests in common.

2. Good marriage but characteristics of Category 1 not as strikingly demonstrated; such as, not much sharing in child rearing, one or the other parent overdominant; not much "fun" together; not quite as much ability to have a life separate from the children.

3. Stable marriage but less "togetherness" and mutuality; on negative side, there may be some actual complaints made by mother about father and considerable conflict over particular topics but evidently no widespread or overt dissatisfaction; on positive side, there may be interests in common, pleasure in children or other single traits characteristic of good marriages.

4. Poor marriages but not the worst.
   a. Marriages that meet parents' needs in a neurotic way but not to the degree of those in Category 5.
   b. Affectless, insensitive couples; or considerable discord and dissatisfaction, but not totally so.
   c. Insufficient information to classify accurately but no evidence that marriage was a good one.

5. Chronic and severe discord or dissatisfaction (a) with divorce or (b) without divorce; included also are some extreme cases of skewed marriages with one or both parents apparently psychopathic.

Mother's Personality

1. Emotionally healthy; happy and competent in roles of wife and mother.

2. Slightly insecure and anxious, especially about child rearing; but warm and outgoing in interpersonal relations.

3. Lacking in personal security and in sense of adequacy but able to derive some satisfaction from personal relations within immediate family. Either overly dependent, anxious, and fearful (much like 4c except for being protected by favorable emotional circumstances) or rigid and self-sufficient.

4. Not much capacity for adult functioning but some ability to give and receive affection and to be aware of others' feelings and desires.
   a. Much like 5b, but not so severely handicapped.
   b. Psychoneurotic.
   c. Very immature and dependent; anxious, self-centered, uncertain of self, "nervous."

5. Seriously impaired capacity for interpersonal relations.
   a. Psychotic or very eccentric.
   b. Markedly self-centered; very insensitive to desires and feelings of other people; unable to express real affection; lives by maxims and "textbook-like" rules. Either no overt anxiety, friendly and outgoing, shallow relations with husband and child; or guarded and suspicious, unwilling or unable to admit difficulties, everything about self and family perfect.

Mother–Child Relations

1. Affectionate, proud of child, puts no excessive demands on him for affection, companionship, and so forth. Pleased with his ability to have close relations with others. Able to set limits and handle discipline without anxiety. Pleased to see child develop uniquely and supportive of him in his growth.

2. Affection for child, proud of him and interested in him. Some minor difficulties: such as somewhat overindulgent or overprotective; some difficulty in letting child develop own individuality or have a life of his own; a bit anxious on certain points, such as adoption; presses child for achievement; worries about discipline.

3. Fond of child but rather insensitive; inclined (a) to demand considerable affection and emotional support from child and to have difficulty in setting limits; or (b) to dominate child but not so much as to interfere seriously with his relations with father and others.

4. Insensitive and inconsistent or overpermissive and ineffectual.
   a. Inconsistent; much like 5c below, but some warmth for children and not such completely harsh attitudes.
   b. Overpermissive; weak and indulgent out of inability to make decisions; makes emotional demands on the children; may treat children as more mature than their age or may "spoil" them greatly.
   c. Although qualitatively very different, a few mothers who were "lower-lower" class, ignorant, and probably of low intelligence were included in Group 4 because of their poor handling of children, although accepting and fond of them.

5. Overinvolved with child, or very rejecting, or highly ambivalent.
   a. Overinvolved: mothers regard children as extension of selves; isolate them from other adults and from children; very demanding and controlling of children; and seriously overidentify with them. (Category includes some very protective and indulgent mothers who are slightly less extreme in their overinvolvement.)
   b. Rejecting: mothers are highly critical of children; anything they see right about the children redounds to mothers' own credit; cold and insensitive.
   c. Ambivalent: mothers insensitive and unloving, even though some qualities or actions of children may please them and elicit favorable comments.

Father's Functioning as a Family Member

1. Warm, affectionate, very secure; happy at home and work; successful on job; supports wife and children both emotionally and financially; shares in discipline of children and in family pleasures, yet has own separate interests and status in own group.

2. Has some but not all of the above traits; not quite so emotionally secure; less adequate in relations with child than fathers in Category 1; either somewhat too dominating or too easily "bossed."

3. Either (a) a passive, ineffectual person but one who has considerable warmth of feeling for the child; or (b) one who participates more adequately in family life but with little enjoyment, though giving some emotional support to wife and child; or, the overdominating sort of man. All are interested in and fond of the children but usually do not show it much.

4. Either (a) a solitary, withdrawn person who takes no part in family life beyond (usually) providing financial support; or (b) one who is greatly overinvolved with child, alone or with his wife.

5. Resentful or highly critical or abusive of child and/or very irresponsible about family duties; does not meet minimum standards in husband or father role.

APPENDIX B

Forms, Schedules, and Instructions

GUIDE TO HOME INTERVIEW

A. HISTORY OF ADOPTION

1. Reasons for wanting to adopt: extent to which shared by both parents.

    (a) Was it because mother couldn't have children of her own?

2. How the adoption was arranged.

3. Contacts with natural parents since adoption.

    (a) Frequency and nature.

    (b) Problems arising from contact with or interference from natural parents.

4. What did parents know about the natural parents; do they wish they knew more or less; what kind of information do they wish they had?

5. Have parents ever seen the natural parents? Do they wish they could see them?

6. Child's knowledge, if any, about being adopted; parents' intentions and opinions about telling.

    (a) If child knows, who told him and how; at what age; his and the parents' reactions when he did learn.

7. Child's knowledge, if any, about natural parents; attitudes toward them.

428

8. If there were other children in the home at the time of placement, or since then, how are things working out? For example:

> Reactions of children to the adoptive situation and to each other.
> Any problems arising from presence of other children.
> How they get along together.
> Whether adoptive parent now feels advantage or disadvantage in having the sibling situation as it is.

9. Child's initial reaction to placement, especially if beyond infancy.

10. Parent's feeling when he first saw child.

B. THE CHILD

1. *Physical and psychological characteristics*
   (a) Appearance (perhaps ask to see picture if parent does not offer it unasked).
   (b) "Is (child's name) like anybody in your family?" (Question always asked.)
   (c) Disposition:
   > Whether an active child or on the quiet side.
   > General temperament—happy, moody, irritable, placid, etc.
   (d) Parents' views about child's strong and weak points.

2. *Interests, activities, and ideas about the future*
   (a) Things child is especially interested in and likes to do.
   (b) What he wants to be (including educational plans).
   > (1) Parents' ideas about what he will be good at, his chief aptitudes and talents.
   > (2) What parents would like him to be.
   (c) Friends.
   (d) Clubs, Scouts, or other organized activities.
   (e) Parents' interests: "What do *you* do for fun?" (Some variation may be used.)

3. *School*
   (a) Name of school child attends; grade.
   (b) If not in school, reason for substitute arrangements.
   (c) Does child seem to like school?
   (d) Parents' view of how child gets along in school; feelings about this.

4. *Health*
   - (a) General picture of child's health: usually well versus specific health problems.
   - (b) Chronic or recurrent ailments; defects; handicaps; age at which first noticed.
   - (c) Parents' general attitude toward child's health.
   - (d) What doctor do you use for the child; how long have you had him; is your doctor a pediatrician?
   - (e) (If the child has chronic illnesses or defects, ask for permission to talk with his doctor about it.)

C. PARENTS AS INDIVIDUALS AND AS A COUPLE (THE HOME)

1. *Economic situation*
   - (a) Current occupation of the father.
   - (b) Current occupation, if any, of the mother; full or part time.

2. *Discipline*
   - (a) Who takes chief responsibility for disciplining the child?
   - (b) Kinds of things for which discipline is needed; what is done when it is needed?

3. *Rough spots in child rearing*
   - (a) Problems parents have had to work on most with the child.
   - (b) Parents' ideas about causes of the problems—e.g. inheritance.

D. QUESTIONS ASCRIBED TO THE DEPARTMENT OF PUBLIC WELFARE

1. Do you think there are special problems in being an adoptive parent?

2. What advice would you give to people who are planning to adopt a baby?
   - (a) About getting a baby?
   - (b) About other aspects of adoption?

INSTRUCTIONS FOR CHECKLIST

Some general interpretive comments have been prepared for certain of the checklist items to ensure clarity of meaning. Since many of the checklist items are sufficiently clear, the comments will be directed by number to the items in question.

The checklist should be prepared following the dictation of the home interview. The material of the interview forms the basis on which the evaluator prepared the checklist. It is not our plan to attempt to secure specific answers or use the checklist as a guide to the interview. The only checklist item that is based on a specific routine question is No. 34 and, of course, the face sheet information included in items 1 through 5. It was also agreed in the planning meeting to routinely secure permission to contact physicians in the event of mental or physical handicaps under item 6.

No. 7: The condition of the home refers to those aspects of the home that the adoptive parent is able to control. For example, if parents live in an apartment building in which the condition of the exterior is poor but the apartment is well kept, this would be considered the appropriate part of the home on which to rate the parent.

No. 8: This refers to any type of contact—letters, telephone, as well as face to face contact.

In this item secure the age of the child at the time of contact. A rather transitory contact that did not continue should be checked once or twice. If contact continued over a period of time, it may be checked "regular basis."

No. 12: For the purpose of this study, miscarriages will not be counted as children prior to placement. Stillbirths, however, will be counted.

If mother had a child or children a number of years prior to adoptive placement, but according to her statement was desirous but unable to conceive during a long intervening period, it may be checked as "functional sterility." In such instances, cross out *if no children.*

No. 13: The middle category in this item is reserved for the child who according to the parents probably knows he is adopted, but has not been told by them.

The second part of this item refers to the person who first tells him of adoption; that is, where "he first gets the word."

No. 14: Try to get the main theme used by the parents in their explanation—may include highlights of way parents told him.

No. 15: This does not refer specifically to the first moments following knowledge, but includes the child's reaction during the first month or so.

No. 16: Column 1 regarding the child will usually be less significant when the child has been placed in infancy and it may be necessary to routinely check insufficient evidence if child was placed in infancy.

Column 2 will be based on mother's description and worker's judgment of the same.

Column 3 is naturally only pertinent if there are other children in the home. This is to secure instances of regressive or other symptomatic behavior that occurs in reaction to the placement of the adoptive child.

No. 17: In the second part of this item try to find out from mother if the fact that the child is adopted enters into the cause of the difficulty or is used in any way in the quarreling. If a child's adopted status comes out even in a minimal way, this should be noted.

No. 19: This is somewhat of a projective question. The way mother says it should help us decide the appropriate item to check.

No. 25: This is also a judgment question.

No. 26: Worker's judgment is based on mother's general material and affect, as well as what she says about this particular subject.

No. 28: This item is an attempt to get at how free the child is in having friends at his home. There will probably need to be some judgment exercised by the scorer based on general material as well as any specific statements by the mother.

No. 29: This item is not meant to be restricted to recreational activities. It may include any activities in which parent and child are involved together that appear to be gratifying or pleasurable from mother's point of view; for example, if father and son build something together or if mother and daughter enjoy sewing together.

If the activity includes both parents and child, both columns may be checked.

No. 34: This item is based on a specific and standard question that is asked routinely in the interview. However, the evaluator's judgment should be based on feeling-tone, and other material in the history, as well as the parent's answers to the question.

CHECKLIST FOR HOME INTERVIEW

NAME_____   Petition No._____

WORKER_____   Date_____

1. Current marital status:

             _____ married

             _____ widowed

             _____ divorced

             _____ separated

             _____ single

             _____ married or remarried since adoption. If home broken, age of child when this occurred_____

2. Current occupation of adoptive father:

    Specify:_____

3. Adoptive mother working:

             _____ full time

             _____ part time

             _____ not working

    Occupation (specify): _____

4. Other children of adoptive parents:

Age	Sex	Status (own, adopted, other)	In home before or after placement

5. School attended by child: _____

           Location: _____

           Grade: _____

6. Marked physical or mental handicaps:

             _____ no evidence of handicaps

             _____ evidence of handicap

    Specify:_____

    Age at which first known_____

    Permission to see doctor:

             _____ granted

             _____ not granted

7. Rating of home and neighborhood:

Adequacy of living space	*Condition*	*Neighborhood*
_____spacious	_____well kept	_____good
_____adequate	_____fairly kept	_____medium
_____cramped	_____run down	_____poor

8. Contacts with natural parents since adoption:

    _____none

    _____once or twice

    _____frequent or regular

    If contacts occurred:

        _____problems resulting from such contacts

        _____no problems resulting from such contacts

9. Adoptive parent's attitude toward natural parent(s):

    _____comments indicate generally positive feelings (warm, friendly, sympathetic, etc.)

    _____comments indicate mixed feelings (ambivalence, positive in some respects, negative in others)

    _____comments indicate indifference (lack of interest in natural parents)

    _____comments indicate generally negative feelings (hostility, resentment, blame or criticism, etc.)

10. Preference for knowing about natural parents:

    _____prefers to know as much as possible about natural parents

    _____ambivalent or prefers to know only certain kinds of things (e.g. background but not personality, etc.)

    _____prefers not to know anything about natural parents.

11. Placement arrangements:

Placement arranged through (specify): _____

12. Prior fertility experience:

    _____had children of own prior to placement

    _____no children prior to placement

If no children:

    _____no mention of medical basis

    _____mention of medical basis

    (Specify diagnosis if given):_____

13. Child's being told of adoptive status:

_____has been told he is adopted

_____not told but parent thinks he suspects

_____was not told he is adopted

If he knows, told by (specify):_____

at what age:_____

14. Main points used in telling the child he was adopted (specify):

_____

_____

_____

15. Child's reaction to being told he was adopted:

_____considerably upset

_____mildly disturbed

_____no perceptible unfavorable reaction

16. Familial reaction to placement:

	Child	Parents	Other Children
Immediate fitting in, no difficulties	_____	_____	_____
Brief period of adjustment	_____	_____	_____
Prolonged or serious adjustment period	_____	_____	_____
Insufficient evidence	_____	_____	_____

17. If other children, parent's picture of sibling relationships:

_____no difficulties in situation

_____some problems with situation

_____serious problems with situation

If problems:

_____difference of children's statuses involved (i.e. own vs. adopted)

18. Child's interest in natural parents:

_____interested in knowing about natural parents

_____little interest in knowing about natural parents

19. Parent's conception of child's similarity to family:

_____very similar to member or members of family

_____somewhat similar or similar in some ways, different in others

_____little or no similarity

20. Parent's conception of child's general temperament and disposition:

_____predominantly positive (lovable, easy to get on with, appealing)

_____mixed (gets along in some situations, not in others, etc.)

_____predominantly negative (irritable, moody, mean)

21. Child's social relations:

Generally tends

_____to be with friends of about his own age

_____to be with grownups

_____to be by himself

22. Parent's aspiration for child's career:

(Specify)_____

_____check here if none (e.g. "whatever he wants to be," etc.)

23. Parent's feeling about child's future:

_____parent has heart set on child having "right kind" of future career

_____parent has definite preference but would not be upset if child made another choice

_____parent completely indifferent

24. Types of acts for which parents have to "keep after" child:

(Specify):_____

_____

Discipline required:

_____often

_____occasionally

_____seldom

25. Parent's feelings about administering discipline:

_____seems to be fairly comfortable

_____seems to be somewhat upset (e.g. guilt, anxiety)

_____seems to get abnormal satisfaction

_____hard to tell on the basis of the evidence

26. Extent to which child "gets away with" disapproved behavior:
_____nearly always disciplined
_____occasionally disciplined
_____often "gets away" with disapproved behavior
_____insufficient evidence

27. Parental agreement about administering discipline:
_____parents nearly always agree
_____parents occasionally disagree
_____parents often disagree

28. Parent's attitude toward the child and his friends using the home:
_____very accepting
_____somewhat accepting
_____generally opposed

29. Frequency of pleasurable activity with the child:

	Mother	Father
Often............	_____	_____
Occasionally.......	_____	_____
Seldom...........	_____	_____

30. Parent's feelings about child's school performance:
_____very pleased
_____satisfied
_____indifferent
_____negative

31. Picture of child's general health:
_____generally healthy (no more than the usual run of colds, childhood diseases, etc.)
_____not healthy (frequently ill, run down, delicate, needs special diet or treatment, etc.)

32. Parent's reaction to child's health:
_____seems to react appropriately
_____seems somewhat overconcerned
_____seems highly overconcerned

33. Parent's statement about the way the adoption is turning out:

    _____says she is satisfied, pleased, wouldn't have it any other way, etc.

    _____says she is pleased or happy about some things, but wishes some were different

    _____says it is not working out well, expresses dissatisfaction with situation.

34. Parent's statement about spouse's feelings about the way the adoption is turning out:

    _____positive

    _____mixed feelings

    _____negative

35. Father present during all or part of interview:_____

Father not present. . . . . ._____

36. Evidence of obvious abuse or neglect of child:

    _____evidence

    _____no evidence

PROCEDURE IN PREPARING EVALUATION OF HOME AND CHILD

1. Review record of interview and make notes on Topics 1 through 5 in "Evaluation of the Home." Also on "Summary Description of Child."

2. Make tentative rating of home as A (very good) or E (very poor), or somewhere between (B, C, or D).

3. Confer with Miss Sullivan on evaluation and ratings of home and description of child. Make joint rating and fill out rating sheet (2 copies).*

4. Prepare evaluative statement on home and description of child for inclusion in record (3 copies/minimum).

5. Add to the record any important nonrecorded facts brought out in the conference.

---

* In making these ratings (especially in the early days of the study before norms are fully worked out), do not be overconcerned about just where to put the mark. Use your best judgment. At a later date A's, B's, C's, etc. will be compared and perhaps revised. Out of this process it may be that definitions of the various categories can be evolved that will simplify the rating of later cases.

EVALUATION OF THE HOME

1. *Mother as a person:*
   Comment on such points as:
   > Maturity
   > Security in herself; self-confidence
   > Acceptance of self as wife and mother
   > Ability to relate to people, to be interested
   > in things outside herself

2. *Father as a person:*
   (as described or implied by mother)
   > His adequacy as an individual
   > His place in the home

3. *Husband-wife relations:*

4. *Mother's (and father's, if possible) feelings, attitudes, and relations with child,* such as:
   > Warmth of feeling
   > Consistency of response
   > Ability to view child as an individual
   > Ability to set limits to permitted behavior
   > Protection—indulgence—rejection

5. *Other significant facts about home:*
   (Note here, if present, poor physical environment and care, poor moral standards or training, neglect, abuse, as well as other emotional factors not listed above)

   Home rating: Enter the rating and degree of confidence in rating on the evaluation sheet and explain briefly why you rated as you did.

SUMMARY DESCRIPTION OF CHILD

Note main points in mother's description of what child is like and interviewer's impression of correctness or realism of this description. (This is the child as seen by the mother; it may tell more about the mother than the child.)

DEFINITIONS FOR USE IN HOME RATINGS

These definitions are applicable to the extreme positions and central point of each scale. The rater has an opportunity to indicate gradations by using the total range of each scale ("B" and "D").

HOME RATINGS

A. Considering all information secured in the home interview, this seems to be the kind of home situation one would want a child to have; the kind in which a child would have the best opportunity for healthy development.

C. This relates to the kind of home situation in which some factors are not as one would like them to be, but not the kind that seem likely to be seriously harmful to the child.

E. Considering all information secured in the home interview, this seems to be the kind of home situation from which one would like to protect a child; the kind likely to interfere with his happiness and healthy development.

RATINGS ON SPECIFIC ASPECTS

1. Marital relations
   A. Apparently a good marital relationship; may be disagreement about concrete matters, but not the kind of conflict that would have threatening implications for the child or for the parents' relationship to each other.
   C. A relatively stable marital relationship. May be evidence of some friction, competitiveness, or hostility which could have moderate or temporary adverse effect on the child.
   E. Hostility, conflict, mutual disrespect. The kind of situation in which the child is likely to be a casualty in the war between the parents.

2. Manifest anxiety in maternal role
   A. Fairly comfortable in most aspects of relationship with child. Secure in ideas about handling, evidence of little or no overt anxiety.
   C. Somewhat overanxious.
   E. Clear, open, high degree of concern. Overwhelmed by responsibilities regarding child.

3. Emotional response to child

   A. Evidences high degree of warmth and affection for child.

   C. Somewhat excessive ambivalence; indication of some reservation in mother's feelings about or emotional response to child.

   E. Clearly rejects by attitudes or open admission. May claim to love child but obviously doesn't. For example, says almost nothing good about child, avoids contact, obviously does not regard child as "own."

4. Control of child's behavior

   A. Lets child do anything he pleases. Almost never says "no." Sets up almost no rules. Makes few demands for obedience or seeking of permission. Requests no fulfillment of duties by the child. (Include neglectful, indifferent mother, as well as the one who is unable to set any limits.)

   C. Moderate freedom, moderate restriction.

   E. Hems the child's life in with rules and limitations. Places many restrictions on his freedom and activities. Burdens him with duties and obligations. Supervises most facets of his daily life.

5. Regard for child as an individual

   A. Child responded to as a person and personality in his own right, with needs of his own and a right to his own life, both present and future.

   C. Moderate overinvolvement in child's life.

   E. Child responded to as a source of gratification of parents' needs, as an extension of parent, or as an instrument for the fulfillment of parents' ambitions. Overemotional participation in child's experiences. "Mother-love."

NOTE TO RATERS:

Since all ratings can be made with a first, second, or third degree of confidence, make every effort to avoid pushing people to the middle points in the rating scale. The degree of confidence factor permits us to indicate any uncertainties which we have based on lack of conclusive material.

NAME_____   PETITION No. _____

INTERVIEWER_____

HOME RATINGS

Overall Rating:

A	B	C	D	E

Degree of confidence: 1_____ 2_____ 3_____

RATINGS ON SPECIFIC ASPECTS

1. Marital relations

Very good   Very poor

Degree of confidence: 1_____ 2_____ 3_____

2. Manifest anxiety in maternal role

Little   Very much

Degree of confidence: 1_____ 2_____ 3_____

3. Emotional response to child

Very warm   Very cold

Degree of confidence: 1_____ 2_____ 3_____

4. Control of child's behavior

Very little   Much too much

Degree of confidence: 1_____ 2_____ 3_____

5. Regard for child as an individual

Much   Extremely little

Degree of confidence: 1_____ 2_____ 3_____

INSTRUCTIONS
ABOUT
PARENTS' PRACTICES QUESTIONNAIRE

1. Present questionnaire at end of interview.

2. Explain that United States Children's Bureau is requesting that the people we are interviewing be asked to check this questionnaire. The Bureau publishes bulletins on child care (for instance, *Infant Care*) and, recently, one on adolescents, so it is interested in keeping in touch with what parents find are useful ways of handling children.

3. Assure parent, if necessary, that there are no "right" answers to these questions.

4. Suggest that she check answers quickly, not ponder over them. Check them for her (that is, with her) if you wish. If it seems suitable, say that you know that she's already told you what she thinks about some of these matters but you want to be sure you have gotten her ideas correctly.

5. If parent says she does different things with different children, say that all we've taken responsibility for getting is what she does with the adopted child we've been talking about. If she wants to fill out more than one questionnaire, the Children's Bureau will be glad to get her replies for any or all of her children.

6. Put petition number and your name in upper right hand corner of questionnaire after leaving the home.

PARENTS' PRACTICES
IN SUPERVISING AND DISCIPLINING CHILDREN

As you know, many parents nowadays are concerned about how much they should supervise their children and how they should discipline them. Information about what parents do about these matters may therefore be helpful to many people.

Your answers to the following questions will be greatly appreciated. All answers will be anonymous, of course. No names will be attached to any reply.

* * * * * * * *

1. How much do you supervise your child in the following? (Please check)

	Supervise closely	Supervise somewhat	Mostly leave to child
Choice of friends.........	————	————	————
What he does with his friends..............	————	————	————
Dating (if old enough)....	————	————	————
Schoolwork............	————	————	————
Responsibilities around home..............	————	————	————
Hours the child keeps (including bedtime)....	————	————	————
Manners..............	————	————	————

Other matters (Please specify.)

———————————— ———— ———— ————

———————————— ———— ———— ————

———————————— ———— ———— ————

2. How much trouble do you have with your child about the following?

	Good deal of difficulty	Some difficulty	Little or no difficulty
Choice of friends........	————	————	————
What they do together....	————	————	————
Dating (if old enough)....	————	————	————
Schoolwork.............	————	————	————
Responsibilities around home...............	————	————	————
Hours the child keeps (including bedtime)....	————	————	————
Manners...............	————	————	————

Other matters (Please specify.)

——————————— ———— ———— ————

——————————— ———— ———— ————

——————————— ———— ———— ————

3. If you find it necessary to discipline your child, which of the following methods do you usually use? (Check more than one if necessary.)

Physical punishment such as spanking........... ————

Taking away some privilege.................... ————

Financial penalty like reducing allowance......... ————

Confining to room or keeping home after school, etc. ————

Giving extra work or chores around the house...... ————

Just a good scolding......................... ————

Other (Please specify.)

——————————————————— ————

——————————————————— ————

——————————————————— ————

SCHEDULE FOR RATING SOCIAL INVESTIGATION RECORDS [1]

EXPLANATORY NOTES

Terms Used

"Psychological Suitability of Adoptive Parents." Despite the obvious inadequacies of these records, they do provide a number of significant—and at times very convincing—clues concerning the capacity for parenthood of the adoptive parents. Accordingly, we would like for each parent a rating of general capacity for parenthood, based on whatever evidence the record affords concerning relevant factors, such as emotional stability, maturity, warmth, motivation for adoption, etc.

"Prognosis." In asking about prognosis, we are asking for a judgment about what kind of opportunity the adoption placement is likely to provide for the child's development. We assume that if features are present which would incline an adoption agency to reject the application of the adoptive parents, the prognosis is unfavorable. How unfavorable, would depend on the nature, force and definiteness of the specific elements involved.

We assume also that an unfavorable prognosis does not always mean an unfavorable outcome. In adoption, as in medicine, signs and symptoms are not absolute; a patient may recover in spite of a bad prognosis and an adoption may turn out well in spite of one. At the same time, if the prognostic indices are sound, one would expect a larger proportion of unfavorable outcomes from placements including definitely unfavorable indices than from those including only favorable ones.

We are asking our agency raters to specify which cases seem likely to turn out badly, according to the current criteria for adoption placements. Because the available records are crude and sketchy, the judgments made will often be tentative. In a number of cases, however, the evidence will be striking enough to permit considerable confidence.

"Recommendations." An unfavorable prognosis may or may not mean that at this point it would be advisable to remove the child from the home of the adoptive parents. Accordingly, we are asking as a separate question whether, given the circumstances presented in the record, it would have been better at the time of the court hearing to recommend a course that would involve removing the child or one that meant continuing in the same home.

---

[1] This schedule was used by outside agency workers who rated a sample of the Welfare Department's records of the original social investigations.

"Degree of Confidence." Because of the difficulties posed by the nature of the records, space is provided for noting the degree of confidence with which the ratings are made. These ratings will, of course, draw on the information and clues available in any part of the record.

"Recommendation." The recommendation should *not* take into account problems of the Public Welfare Department's relations with court or public, or of persuading the court to accept the recommendation. What we are asking is the judgment of a trained worker as to what is likely to be best for the child. That is, taking into account the total situation as presented in the record, is the child's welfare so threatened that she would recommend removing the child from the home?

Items to Be Coded

Items I through IV should be coded for all cases—circling only one number under each heading.

If the prognosis is favorable and no clear reasons appear for concern about the outcome of the adoption, no further entry should be made. If the prognosis is favorable on the whole, but nevertheless there are elements that raise questions or concern, appropriate entries should be made under V and VI.

If the prognosis is unfavorable, entries should be made under V and VI, marking one or more categories under V, as appropriate. Each category marked under V should have a corresponding entry under VI, numbered to match and indicating very briefly the evidence on which it is based.

VII is entirely optional, and is intended to catch relevant comments not covered by the first four items.

Under VI and VII full sentences are not necessary; a catchword or telegraphic indication will suffice.

If the prognosis is favorable, do not answer VIII and IX. If it is unfavorable—either mildly or strongly—please circle the appropriate numbers under VIII and IX.

CODE

I. *Psychological Suitability for Parenthood* (circle one for each parent)

Adoptive Mother   *Adoptive Father*

5	Very good	5
4	Adequate	4
3	Barely adequate	3
2	Inadequate	2
1	Very inadequate	1

II. *Degree of Confidence with Which Rating re Psychological Suitability Is Made* (circle one for each parent)

Adoptive Mother   *Adoptive Father*

3	Reasonably strong confidence	3
2	Moderate confidence	2
1	Mainly hunch	1

III. *Prognosis for the Adoption* (circle one)

5	Highly favorable
4	Favorable
3	Mixed, or unable to decide
2	Mildly unfavorable
1	Strongly unfavorable

IV. *Degree of Confidence with Which Prognosis Is Made* (circle one)

3	Reasonably strong confidence
2	Moderate confidence
1	Mainly hunch

V. *Reasons for Concern about Success of Adoption** (circle one or more as appropriate)

1	Marital history of adoptive parents
2	Marital relations of adoptive parents

* Please check appropriate category or categories and also specify briefly, on next page, basis for coding. Number each statement to indicate the category to which it refers.

3   Incomplete adoptive family (e.g. adoptive parent single, widowed, divorced, separated)

4   Doubt concerning psychological suitability for parenthood of adoptive father

5   Doubt concerning psychological suitability for parenthood of adoptive mother

6   Age of one or both adoptive parents

7   Other children in the home. Specify: ＿＿ own, ＿＿ adopted or ＿＿ other.

8   Possibility that adoptive parents will have other children

9   Illness or physical defect of one or both adoptive parents

1A   Matching factors

2A   Socioeconomic level of adoptive parents

3A   Motivation for adoption

4A   Attitudes toward adoption (e.g. one or both parents not fully wanting it; not planning to tell child, etc.)

5A   Child-rearing attitudes or practices

6A   Adoptive mother working

7A   Acquaintance of adoptive and natural parent(s)

8A   Suitability of child (e.g. medical history, mental or physical handicap, emotional factors, hereditary disorders in family, etc.)

9A   Other

VI.   *Specify* (Evidence indicating basis for concern about outcome. Please number each item to correspond with the category it explains on the preceding page.)

＿＿＿＿＿＿＿＿＿＿＿＿＿＿＿＿＿＿＿＿＿＿＿＿＿

＿＿＿＿＿＿＿＿＿＿＿＿＿＿＿＿＿＿＿＿＿＿＿＿＿

＿＿＿＿＿＿＿＿＿＿＿＿＿＿＿＿＿＿＿＿＿＿＿＿＿

＿＿＿＿＿＿＿＿＿＿＿＿＿＿＿＿＿＿＿＿＿＿＿＿＿

＿＿＿＿＿＿＿＿＿＿＿＿＿＿＿＿＿＿＿＿＿＿＿＿＿

VII. *Additional Comments re Prognosis* (optional)
           (e.g. clearly favorable indications, balance of plus and minus, further considerations, etc.)

_____

_____

_____

_____

_____

_____

_____

VIII. *Recommendation* (Answer this question only if the prognosis is unfavorable—either mildly or strongly.) (circle one) What do you think would have been the best recommendation for the worker to make to the court at the time of the hearing?

    1   That the child remain in the home of the adoptive parents. (That is, that the adoption petition be granted.)

    2   That the child be removed from the home and placed in the custody of a licensed child-placing agency which would then make plans for him. (That is, that the adoption petition be dismissed.)

    Comments (optional) _____

_____

_____

IX. *Degree of Confidence with Which Plan Is Recommended* (circle one)

    3   Reasonably strong confidence

    2   Moderate confidence

    1   Slight confidence

SOCIOMETRIC TEST

Boy?_____ or Girl?_____

You are asked to choose three classmates in answering each of the three questions below. When you have read the question, write the names of the three classmates that you choose. Write both the first and last names of your choices. List names in order of your choice for each question. You may use the same or different names for the three questions, depending on how you feel about it. Any classmate named on Question 1 or 2 may be named again on Question 3. Be sure you make three choices of classmates for each question.

1. Which classmates do you like to play with or talk to at recess, or in the halls before class starts?

    First choice:

    Second choice:

    Third choice:

2. Which classmates would you like to work with on a class project or a class play?

    First choice:

    Second choice:

    Third choice:

3. Which classmates would you like to invite to a party at your home?

    First choice:

    Second choice:

    Third choice:

Index

Index